The Simpsons' Beloved Springfield

DELPHI PUBLIC LIBRARY

222 East Main Street
Delphi, Indiana 46923
765-564-2929

D1258324

Also by Karma Waltonen and
Denise Du Vernay

The Simpsons *in the Classroom: Embiggening the Learning
Experience with the Wisdom of Springfield* (McFarland, 2010)

Edited by Melissa Bender and
Karma Waltonen

*Twenty Writing Assignments in Context: An Instructor's Resource
for the Composition Classroom* (McFarland, 2017)

The Simpsons' Beloved Springfield

*Essays on the TV Series
and Town That Are Part of Us All*

Edited by KARMA WALTONEN *and*
DENISE DU VERNAY

McFarland & Company, Inc., Publishers
Jefferson, North Carolina

ISBN (print) 978-1-4766-7455-1
ISBN (ebook) 978-1-4766-3612-2

LIBRARY OF CONGRESS AND BRITISH LIBRARY
CATALOGUING DATA ARE AVAILABLE

Library of Congress Control Number: 2019942437

© 2019 Karma Waltonen and Denise Du Vernay. All rights reserved

*No part of this book may be reproduced or transmitted in any form
or by any means, electronic or mechanical, including photocopying
or recording, or by any information storage and retrieval system,
without permission in writing from the publisher.*

Front cover illustration by dwellephant (www.dwellephant.com)

Printed in the United States of America

*McFarland & Company, Inc., Publishers
Box 611, Jefferson, North Carolina 28640
www.mcfarlandpub.com*

Karma dedicates this book to her brother, Adrian,
who is gonna help her get that lemon tree back,
or we'll choke their rivers with our dead.

Denise dedicates this book to her dude.

Acknowledgments

The coeditors would like to thank our friends and family, including our friends from Springfield, especially Chris Ledesma, Alf Clausen, Josh Weinstein, David Silverman, and Marc Wilmore, who have been very generous with their stories and swag. We would also like to thank dwellephant, the contributors, all the folks at McFarland, especially our editors, Layla Milholen and Gary Mitchem. Finally, thanks to Paul Takushi, Roberto Delgadillo, and Scott Shaw!

Karma would like to thank her book group (The Margaret Atwood Book Group), The Out of Fucks Writing Group, Luis Samayoa, and Denise.

Denise thanks the Schade-Schillers, K.B. and Justin Shady, T.J. Young, Karma, and her husband. You are all fantastic. I love you.

Table of Contents

Introduction

Putting the Spring in Springfield

KARMA WALTONEN *and*
DENISE DU VERNAY

This town is a part of us all.

When we published our first book, *The Simpsons in the Classroom: Embiggening the Learning Experience with the Wisdom of Springfield* (McFarland, 2010), *The Simpsons* had only been on the air for twenty-one years.

Now, as we complete this book, we anticipate Season 31.

The first book's introduction made a case for studying the show and for its relevance in the classroom.

The Simpsons is amazing—are we agreed? It changed television—right? Good.

Now let's talk about some other stuff.

Here's what else we've been thinking about since the first book came out.[1]

1. When you love something, when you are the biggest geek about something, no one cares—oh, you're the kind of person who goes to the bi-mon-sci-fi-con, they say, shaking their heads in pity for you. Even if you teach a college course on the thing, no one really cares. But when you write a book, people care. A couple of wonderful people from *The Simpsons* reached out to us after publication, inviting us down to the studio. With McFarland hitting "print," we went from crazy superfans to people who could be trusted with tours and secrets (and no, we're not telling you what they are) and getting close enough to our heroes to lick them. And we didn't lick them—even though the temptation was there. But there were hugs, drawings, meals, Christmas cards, and laughter.

So, write about what you love.

2. We have introduced more students and more people to the show.

And we astound them by answering that yes, we have seen every episode. What do they think we are, amateurs?

3. *The Simpsons'* writers are not psychic, but we are constantly asked how they make all of these predictions. They aren't making predictions. When you have more than 600 episodes, you are going to have some things work out, coincidentally. But most of the time, people don't understand how time works. *The Simpsons* drew Trump on the escalator *after* the real life thing happened, not before. The fact that Lisa talking about President 45 ruining the economy was certainly never supposed to be a prediction. The writers chose the most absurd person—to get a laugh. The fact that America elected a literal joke is anything but funny.

Take one of the other supposed predictions, when people "discovered" that *The Simpsons* made an Ebola joke in 1997. This was evidence, apparently, that *The Simpsons* knew there would be an Ebola outbreak in 2014, rather than being evidence that *The Simpsons* made a joke about an earlier outbreak (which is why we all *got* the joke in 1997).[2]

It's tempting to see things and to try to create a pattern. Karma did it years ago when she noticed that three *Simpsons'* episodes about spiritual quests feature the song "Short Shorts" ("The Mysterious Voyage of Homer," "She of Little Faith," and "Homer the Heretic").

Thus, she did what any *Simpsons'* scholar would—she asked someone on the show. Chris Ledesma, music editor extraordinaire, took her question to the writers/producers. They were floored by the coincidence. They were also floored that geeks like us are paying that much attention.

She would still like to believe that the show has a subtle message: to achieve enlightenment, wear skimpier clothes. All that said, we're surprised we haven't been bombarded by articles about something *The Simpsons* may *actually* have anticipated.

Remember back to a few years ago, when bacon with chocolate was new? When it seemed odd, but you decided to try it? In 2003, Homer Simpson commands God (through prayer) to come up with a new taste sensation—a new snack. Homer's prayer then inadvertently (or advertently—God works in mysterious ways) causes an accident between a bacon truck and a fudge truck.

Homer thinks it's awesome.

So do we.

Coincidence?

While the writers aren't psychic, they are great at capturing trends—mean-spirited voters who will vote to punish and expel immigrants; a Republican party full of rich, evil people; and Democrats too weak to fight back hard enough.

It's not their fault they show us a fun house mirror of ourselves—

our worst selves taken to extremes—and that we then become the reflection.

For example, 16 years ago, they showed an idiot celebrity decide to go into politics: "Entertainers are always winning elections."

He runs as a Republican.

He asks the party leaders, "Are you guys any good at covering up youthful and middle-aged 'indiscretions?'"

They ask, "Are these indiscretions romantic, financial, or treasonous?"

"Russian hooker. You tell me."

"Oh, no problem. We'll say you were on a fact-finding mission."

The candidate goes on to sexually harass women and to offend Latinx people and other nations.

Since he is rich, he doesn't connect with people at first. But then he says he's going to fight for the little guy. And "johnny six tooth" believes him.

Fox News gets behind him.

He wins.

And he helps one family—a loyal family. He screws over poor people to do it.

"Mr. Spritz Goes to Washington" was Episode 14 in Season 14.

Krusty was an unqualified joke—a literal clown—with no care for actual people—with no sense of respect for other people—with a Russian hooker scandal.

The Simpsons warned us.

We didn't listen.

4. All those articles saying the show is beloved, but not good anymore, or that simply postulate the show needs to go off the air and no self-awareness make Denise and Karma something something.

In truth, the show itself hasn't changed all that much since its "heyday"; rather, it changed the world of television, bringing us animation for adults, sitcoms without laugh tracks (and thus faster pacing in the comedy), imperfect lower class families, TV families who actually watch TV, postmodern pastiches that mix high and low comedy, and satire for the masses. It took a while, but then a lot of other shows started imitating the innovations. And then, over the years, new shows with new innovations (like cartoons not just for adults but *sick* adults) came along.

The Simpsons should certainly not attempt to mimic these shows, to keep pushing the television envelope. It ushered in a revolution; it should not attempt to one-up *Archer*. (Something will, though. *Archer* will become quaint. Whatever makes it so will shock us for a while, until something comes out to make it seem tame.)

The Simpsons is basically the same. It's we, the audience, who are different. We expect a lot now—because the show has taught us to. Because the show opened the door for so many other shows to experiment. And we watched those experiments, and we keep expecting more.

And then the audience gets cranky and says *The Simpsons* is not funny or relevant anymore. Hey, you don't have to like it now—you're a different audience than you were. But so are we. And we still think it's funny. True, there are not as many episodes that catch us the way our old favorites do (it should be noted, of course, that not all fans agreed that what we now consider the best episodes were good—"Deep Space Homer," one of our all-time favorites, was often lambasted by viewers at the time. Check out on *The Simpsons Archive* [snpp.com] how many now-classic episodes received grades of B- at the time).

However, there are still newer episodes that do catch us. "Coming to Homerica" was an instant classic. There are still jokes that make us laugh way too much (such as Maggie's "first" word—in Norwegian—and her mother's reaction to it, in the above episode). And there are still episodes that move us. "Lisa Simpson, This Isn't Your Life" features Lisa going to a private school, as she has often wanted. Lisa hurts Marge deeply in this episode, insulting her mother, her mother's intellect, her mother's choice to be a stay-at-home mom. However, Lisa then finds out that Marge has taken on some demeaning and grueling work to allow her to go to this school. It's hard to watch that moment.

We care about the series and its characters. One of the things that makes *The Simpsons* special is that the characters are imperfect, but lovable. The show's imitators (with the exception of *Bob's Burgers*, which is excellent) have often neglected this part of the equation. You can kill Kenny hundreds of times, and not just because he's coming back. And we would cheer if they killed Peter Griffin—who can keep watching him physically and mentally abuse his daughter? And Stewie can insult and try to hurt Lois until the end of time. There may be moments of humor, but we don't feel for Lois, who cannot apparently be emotionally hurt (and is thus unrelatable), nor does she have a reason to understand Stewie's vendetta against her.

Lisa's tension with her mother and her mother's ultimately loving response takes us back to what we loved about all those old episodes people apparently long for—the moment when Bart writes "Hero" on his father's bald head, when Homer tries to win his daughter back after her crush on a teacher exposes a problem in the father-daughter relationship, when Marge takes Homer back, despite his tattered rags being caught on the coffee table.

The other reason for our annoyance at the naysayers is a selfish one. We now have friends who work on the show. We have no doubt that we could continue teaching and scholarship on the show once it's off the air (in the same way we still read that damn Shakespeare guy, whom Karma also teaches), but we want our friends, who are writing jokes, animating scenes, composing music, and putting everything together, to keep doing what they love. Especially since what they love is something we still love.

(And, c'mon, *The Simpsons* is still better, even in a not great episode, than 95 percent of the crap on TV; 40 percent of all people know that!)

5. *The Simpsons* continues to change the way we watch TV.

We used to feel an obligation to watch all of the cartoon children and grandchildren *The Simpsons* spawned, mostly because whenever people learn about us being Simpsonologists, they ask us about *South Park*, *Family Guy*, etc. But we just can't watch Seth MacFarlane's[3] works any more. They have their moments, and they constantly reference the seminal works of our childhood, but we've never loved the characters or the shows. And then one day, Karma's teenage son exclaimed, "Why are we watching *American Dad*? It's so sexist!" When a teenage boy can't take the sexism in a show anymore, it's time to turn it off.

Karma is also unable to watch shows with laughtracks now. *The Simpsons* gave us something amazing in 1989—remember, even *Scooby Doo* and *The Flintstones* had laughtracks. It wasn't until *Malcolm in the Middle* in 2000 that another great family sitcom followed *The Simpsons'* lead. Laughtrack shows (multiple camera shows) are limited in their settings, have more predictable jokes, don't trust the audience to know when something's funny, and have a much slower pace.

6. On a personal note, since the publication of the first book, we've been interviewed about the show several times on public radio, local Fox affiliates, and on podcasts; Denise presented various *Simpson*-y topics to such revered audiences as the Wisconsin Historical Society; Karma got to give a sermon on the "Sacrilicious Spirituality of *The Simpsons*" at a UU Church (and yes, she did note Grampa's belief that if the one true religion is UU, he'll eat his hat); we have published several articles on *The Simpsons*, including a couple of articles in which Denise interviewed the lovely people who work on the show, after the publication of the book and the joy of Twitter connected us[4]; Denise got married to a fantastic guy; Karma turned down some proposals. Her plan: "Well, I'm going to be a famous Simpsonologist. I've got it all figured out. I'll be unappreciated in my own country, but my gutsy obscure references will electrify the Finns. I'll avoid the horrors of drug abuse, but I do plan to have several torrid love affairs, and I may or may not die young. I haven't decided."

7. Finally, we want to acknowledge that although there's a groin-grabbingly good number of books and essays and podcasts on *The Simpsons* out there,[5] we were still missing some vital pieces of scholarship. We have put together a collection of scholarly (and fun!) essays on *The Simpsons* written by the two of us, some friends, and some friends we've never met.

"This Town Is a Part of Them (and Us) All," by Denise Du Vernay, discusses the importance of civic engagement in the town of Springfield, for better or worse.

"*The Simpsons*, Gender Roles and Witchcraft: The Witch in Modern Popular Culture," by Sarah Antinora, explores the ways that *The Simpsons* works with and builds upon the idea of the witch in popular culture to make statements about gender and sexual politics.

"'Owning Your Okayness': The Simpsons as 'Good Enough' Parents," by Summer Block, examines the parenting styles of Marge and Homer and how their "good enough" approach is more indicative of the 1970s than the helicopter style of parenting that has become more the norm during the show's tenure.

"Be Sharp: *The Simpsons* and Music," by Durrell Bowman, gives an extensive overview of the significance of music on the show, using "Homer's Barbershop Quartert" including the importance of Alf Clausen's compositions, the regular references to music on the show, and the numerous and influential musical guest stars.

"RIP in Springfield: Rhetorics of Death," by Jennifer Richardson Burg, explores the unique (as far as sitcoms go) ways that *The Simpsons* handles death and dying, combining reverence and humor, as appropriate.

"The Grotesque and the Beautiful: The Bodies of Springfield," by Brent Walter Cline and Matthew Nelson Hill, examines the oftentimes repulsive appearance of the characters and discursiveness of beauty among *Simpsons*' characters.

"'Will you take us to Mt. Splashmore?': Commercials and Consumerism," by Brian N. Duchaney, explores the complicated relationship the Simpson family has with its TV, and ultimately, the viewers' relationship with the show and our own TVs.

"'I'll repress the rage I'm feeling!': Food Politics," by Timothy L. Glenn, implores the audience to consider how food choices are political actions and demonstrates how the people of Springfield engage in food politics, whether they (and we) know it or not.

"This Is Not a Library! This Is Not a Kwik-E-Mart!: The Satire of Libraries, Librarians and Reference Desk Air-Hockey Tables," by Casey D. Hoeve, examines the show's satire of libraries through the concept of the library as place, attitudes toward the library, and librarian demographics.

"Just a Little Kick in the Bum: *The Simpsons* vs. the Nations of the World," by Travis Holland, shares the ways that *The Simpsons* uses stereotypes to examine Americans' perceptions of the world beyond (and within) the borders.

"'So you're calling God a liar!': An Unbiased Comparison of Science and Religion," by Wm. Curtis Holtzen, analyzes the show's use of satire in its depiction of the science vs. religion debate.

"'Animation is built on plagiarism': *The Simpsons* and Hitchcock, Parody and Pastiche," by Zachary Ingle, examines how Hitchcock's images and themes are replicated in *The Simpsons* and how the intertextuality enlightens a reading of *The Simpsons* and demonstrates how Hitchcock maintains his cultural cache through reappropriation.

"Is Yellow the New Green? The Banal Environmentalism of *The Simpsons*," by David Krantz, offers an analysis of *The Simpsons*' and its peers' places in nudge theory—the idea that small inputs (like the frequent, subtle environmental messages on the show) can help shape viewers' attitudes about the environment.

"Fear of a Yellow Planet: The Eight-Fingered Cartoon Version of Anxiety," by Seth Madej, discusses how the show's depictions of anxiety mirror the universal nature of anxiety itself and gives this comforting message: Those who suffer from anxiety (even severe, debilitating anxiety) are not alone.

"In Search of Another Story: Satire and *The Simpsons*," by Duncan Reyburn, offers a reading of *The Simpsons* and its satire through the lens of mimetic realism—a perspective developed by literary theorist, philosopher, and anthropologist René Girard.

"'It's not selling out; it's co-branding!': Watching and Consuming *The Simpsons* in a Digital Age," by Tyler Shores, argues that the changes in media have changed the way fans engage with *The Simpsons*, enabling us to enjoy it as more than just a television show, but rather a multimedia, intertextual phenomenon.

"Aristotle in Springfield: On Friendship," by Zachary Tavlin, explores the deep and abiding friendship of Lenny and Carl through the lens of Aristotle and his idea of the "the perfect friendship." It's more than just a bromance.

"Homer as Homework: *The Simpsons* in the College Classroom," by Lisa Whalen, uses her experience as a college literature teacher to discuss how familiarity with *The Simpsons* can help students learn how to analyze and evaluate texts. She focuses on using "Bart vs. Thanksgiving" to teach satire, especially "A Modest Proposal."

"What We All Came Here to See—Sex," by Karma Waltonen, explores how *The Simpsons* has tackled feminism, sex, and sexuality, including issues like kink and consent, over the past three decades.

Please note, in the works cited pages, when episodes are available on DVD, they are cited as DVD instead of broadcast episodes regardless of how the contributors accessed the episode for the readers' reference. Readers (especially Karma's students) should note that the publisher uses Chicago Manual of Style guidelines for possessive apostrophes.

These summaries are brief, but we hope they give you an idea of where you might want to begin engaging further with this new collection of discussions about our favorite family and our favorite town. We look forward to hearing your opinions on these essays on social media.

Thus, for your pleasure, we present The Simpsons' *Beloved Springfield: Essays on the Town and TV Series That Are Part of Us All.*

NOTES

1. Some parts of this section were first published on Karma's blog: dr-karma.com. Many people come for entries on *The Simpsons*, but stay for the sadly hilarious chronicles of her unsuccessful online dating adventures.

2. "Weird Al" Yankovic also made an Ebola reference on his 1999 album, *Running with Scissors*.

3. Even though Seth McFarlane is officially dreamy.

4. This can still be found at the time of this writing at https://www.ocweekly.com/best-simpsons-moments-castmembers-share-their-favorite-contributions-to-celebrate-the-500th-episode-6578292/.

5. Dr. Roberto Delgadillo has compiled an excellent list of *Simpsons'* sources here: https://www.pinterest.com/rcdelgadillo/the-whole-thing-smacks-of-effort-man-the-emergence/.

The *Simpsons* Timeline (Forever Incomplete)

Karma Waltonen *and*
Denise Du Vernay

In our first book, we included a *Simpsons'* timeline. We are pleased to present you with an updated one.[1]

April 5, 1987—*Married with Children* premieres. It is the first primetime series to air on Fox. *The Tracey Ullman Show* airs immediately thereafter.

April 19, 1987—The Simpson family appears in an animated short on *The Tracey Ullman Show*.

[January 20, 1989—George H.W. Bush takes office.]

[November 9, 1989—The Berlin Wall is dismantled by crowds.]

December 17, 1989—"Simpsons Roasting on an Open Fire"—first full-length episode premieres.

January 14, 1990—"Bart the Genius" premieres with the classic opening credits, including the first couch gag and the first chalkboard gag ("I will not waste chalk").

[February 1990—Nelson Mandela released from jail.]

October 11, 1990—The first episode in Season 2, "Bart Gets an F," pits *The Simpsons* against the most popular sitcom of the time, *The Cosby Show*.

October 25, 1990—The first "Treehouse of Horror" airs.

November 8, 1990—In "Dancin' Homer," Tony Bennett appears as himself, the first guest star on the show to do so (other stars did characters).

November 20, 1990—"Do the Bartman" video premieres around the

9

world. The single was #1 in many countries. Michael Jackson was a co-writer, although contractually he could not receive credit.

[August 6, 1991—The World Wide Web is publically available, but not widely used.]

January 27, 1992—President George H.W. Bush, campaigning for re-election, says: "We're going to strengthen the American family to make them more like the Waltons and less like the Simpsons." (Note that this line recurred in slightly different wording in several of his speeches at around this time)

January 30, 1992—a rerun of "Stark Raving Dad" has a short new opening, in which Bush's comments about the Simpsons is aired. Bart, who is watching him on television, retorts, "We're just like the Waltons—we're praying for an end to the Depression, too."

March 26, 1992—"Colonel Homer" airs. This is the last episode to be played opposite *The Cosby Show*. This is (still) the only episode with Matt Groening listed as principal writer.

April 30, 1992—*The Cosby Show*, which had been up against *The Simpsons* on Thursday night for years, goes off the air.

June 25, 1992—The blackboard gag in a rerun is changed so Bart writes "It's potato, not potatoe," mocking Vice President Dan Quayle's inability to spell the word during an elementary school visit. Episode: "Two Cars in Every Garage and Three Eyes on Every Fish."

October 1992—Tracey Ullman sues for some *Simpsons*' money. She loses her suit.

October 1, 1992—"A Streetcar Named Marge" offends some people in New Orleans.

October 8, 1992—The chalkboard in "Homer the Heretic" reads, "I will not defame New Orleans."

[January 20, 1993—Bill Clinton takes office.]

April 29, 1994—The 100th episode airs. "Sweet Seymour Skinner's Baadasssss Song" has Bart write, "I will not celebrate meaningless milestones" on the chalkboard.

March 5, 1995—Matt Groening takes his name off the credits for "A Star Is Burns," as he feels the episode is an ad for another Fox show, *The Critic*.

April 30, 1995—Willie calls the French "cheese-eating surrender monkeys" in "'Round Springfield."

May 21, 1995—"Who Shot Mr. Burns?" airs, marking the end of the sixth season, the beginning of a contest to solve the mystery, and the only two-part *Simpsons* episode (to date).

January 14, 1996—"Two Bad Neighbors" allows Homer a fistfight with

George H.W. Bush (not playing himself). The DVD feature shows an exchange of letters between Barbara Bush and the staff, after she had said the show was dumb. The letters make their way around the internet after Barbara Bush's death on April 17, 2018.

February 18, 1996—"cromulent" is invented in "Lisa the Iconoclast"; it is now found in *Webster's New Millennium Dictionary of English.* ("Embiggen" also appears in the episode.)

February 9, 1997—"The Itchy & Scratchy & Poochie Show" episode marks *The Simpsons* overtaking *The Flintstones* as the longest-running prime-time animated series. (Krusty refers to television history within the episode.) The Comic Book Guy declares the Itchy and Scratchy episode the "worst. episode. ever.," sparking a much-coined catchphrase.

April 26, 1998—The 200th episode, "Trash of the Titans," airs.

May 28, 1998—Phil Hartman dies; Troy McClure, Lionel Hutz, and many other characters silenced.

December 31, 1999—*Time* declares *The Simpsons* the best television show of the 20th Century.

January 14, 2000—Awarded a star on the Hollywood Walk of Fame.

February 13, 2000—Maude Flanders dies in "Alone Again, Natura-Diddily."[2]

[January 20, 2001—George W. Bush takes office.]

June 14, 2001—"Doh"/"D'oh" added to *Oxford English Dictionary.* (It appears in scripts and titles as "annoyed grunt.")

September 11, 2001—Terrorist attack in New York, Washington. "The City of New York vs. Homer Simpson" not aired by some stations for a while, due to its depiction of the World Trade Center towers. One of many so-called *Simpsons* predictions is born, as a sign advertising $9 train fares to New York appears next to the Twin Towers, which look like an eleven.

March 31, 2002—"Blame It on Lisa," the episode in which the family goes to Brazil, airs. Brazil complains about the portrayal.

June 26, 2002—*South Park* airs "Simpsons Already Did It."

February 2, 2003—300th episode, "Strong Arms of the Ma," appears.

November 23, 2003—Prime Minister Tony Blair appears as himself in "The Regina Monologues."

2005—*Al Shamshoon*, an Arab version of *The Simpsons*, appears on Middle Eastern networks.

February 28, 2006—The Associated Press reports on a study that confirms that Americans know more about *The Simpsons* than the First Amendment.

May 20, 2007—400th episode: "You Kent Always Say What You Want."

July 27, 2007—*The Simpsons Movie* opens. (Karma flies to Milwaukee to see it with Denise on Denise's birthday.)

April 28, 2008—*The Simpsons Ride* opens, replacing *Back to the Future* at Universal Studios Florida.

April 2008—Venezuelan TV replaces *The Simpsons* with *Baywatch*, after the former is criticized as inappropriate for children.

May 19, 2008—*The Simpsons Ride* opens, replacing *Back to the Future* at Universal Studios Hollywood.

[January 20, 2009—Barack Obama takes office.]

February 2009—Denise and Karma join Twitter as @Simpsonology. Shortly thereafter, they connect with other *Simpsons* enthusiasts and people who work on the show. This makes them love Twitter, despite its faults.

February 15, 2009—*The Simpsons* is broadcast in HD and features a new opening sequence "Take My Life, Please."

March 17, 2009—"In the Name of the Grandfather" premieres in the UK before being broadcast in the U.S.

January and August 2011—Karma and Denise first visit the set!

February 19, 2012—500th episode: "At Long Last Leave," airs.

May 2012—*Mr. Burns, a Post-Electric Play* by Anne Washburn premieres in Washington, D.C. The play opens with a group of survivors of a large-scale catastrophe attempting to find normalcy and comfort in recreating the episode "Cape Feare." The play quickly becomes a hit, with productions in theaters across the country. Karma and Denise are invited to give talks at their local theatres.

October 25, 2013—Marcia Wallace, the voice of Edna Krabappel, dies.

August 2014—(1st) Every. *Simpsons*. Ever. marathon on FXX.

October 2014—FXX launches the *Simpsons World* app.

December 17, 2014—*The Simpsons* 25th anniversary!

March 8, 2015—Sam Simon, co-developer of *The Simpsons*, dies of cancer at 59.

October 16, 2016—600th episode: "Treehouse of Horror XXVII."

January 20, 2017—45 takes office, seventeen years after *The Simpsons* joked about how he would be the most absurd choice in "Bart to the Future" (2000).

April 19, 2017—the family's 30th anniversary on Fox.

August 30, 2017—After 27 years, composer Alf Clausen is replaced by Hanz Zimmer's custom scoring company, Bleeding Fingers Music. Clausen won two Emmys for his work on *The Simpsons*.

2018: "Embiggen" is added to the dictionary. It's a perfectly cromulent word.

April 8, 2018—*The Simpsons* briefly references racial stereotypes in old media in "No Good Read Goes Unpunished" as a pointed response to criticism about the show's depiction of Apu.

April 29, 2018—*The Simpsons* becomes the longest running scripted primetime show (surpassing *Gunsmoke*), with episode 636, "Forgive and Regret."

March 7, 2019—Show runner Al Jean is so affected by the HBO documentary *Leaving Neverland* that he decides to pull the third season episode "Stark Raving Dad" (in which Michael Jackson guest stars) from streaming services and syndication. It is unknown how Disney will handle the issue going forward.

March 20, 2019—One year after Disney announced its merger with Fox, it becomes official. The futures of *The Simpsons* and *Simpsons World* are uncertain. The show may stop being syndicated when the streaming service, Disney+, launches.

July 26, 2019—Russi Taylor dies at 75. Taylor provided the voices for several Springfield Elementary School children, including Üter, Wendell, Lewis, and most notably, Martin Prince and twins Sherri & Terri. History suggests her characters will continue to be drawn into scenes but will probably no longer have speaking roles.

August 5, 2019—Alf Clausen files a wrongful termination suit against Fox, Disney, and Gracie Films alleging that he was fired as music composer for *The Simpsons* because of his age.

Awards (so far)—31 Emmy Awards, 30 Annie Awards, Peabody Award
- named by *Time* as the best television show of the 20th century
- record holder for "Most Guest Stars Featured in a Television Series"
- longest running sitcom in history
- longest running scripted American primetime show

NOTES

1. We post *Simpsons* news daily here: Twitter: @Simpsonology; Facebook: facebook.com/Simpsonology. We do longer posts here: www.dr-karma/category/simpsonology.

2. The word "diddily" often appears as "diddly," and both are acceptable, but we believe "diddily" to be canon.

This Town Is a Part of Them (and Us) All

DENISE DU VERNAY

> **Marge:** Well, I'm just shocked by this whole family. Whatever happened to good old-fashioned town pride?
> **Lisa:** It's been going downhill ever since the lake caught fire.
> **Marge:** Now just a darn minute. This town is a part of who you are. This is a Springfield Isotopes cap. When you wear it, you're wearing Springfield. When you eat a fish from our river, you're eating Springfield. When you make lemonade from our tree, you're drinking Springfield.
> **Bart:** Mom, when you give that lecture, you're boring Springfield.
> **Marge:** Bart, you have roots in this town, and you ought to show respect for it. This town is a part of us all. A part of us all. A part of us all! Sorry to repeat myself, but it'll help you remember ["Lemon of Troy" 6.24].

Of the criticisms of the Simpson family and the town of Springfield (and, boy, have there been some humdingers), no one has been able to contend that the residents of Springfield are indifferent to the goings-on in the town. In fact, Spingfieldians, regardless of age, occupation, or social status, are some of the most civically-minded and active fictional townspeople you'll find on your screen. And I'm including the residents of Stars Hollow and Walnut Grove.

Since the beginning of the series, Springfieldians have exemplified model civic engagement. They go to PTA and town meetings. They go to block sales and restaurant openings. They don't miss elementary school band concerts and wonderful evenings of theater and picking up after themselves—even, curiously, Springfieldians without elementary school-aged children. They vote. They attend parades, minor-league baseball games, and movie premieres. The show up in hoards for anything remotely interesting, including archaeological digs. And when they show up to these events, mayhem often ensues. There are many possible reasons that the show chooses to show this

15

extensive town involvement. For one, it makes for great opportunities to satirize politics, elections, and local government, but it also means the show can play with the "good old days" myth—was everything actually better in the idealized 1950s when everyone was supposedly very community minded? In Springfield, people are involved, but it doesn't necessarily make everything better. The town is susceptible to mob rule and destruction based on some boneheaded thing that Homer says or, perhaps, by a rather convincing musical number. This, sadly, mirrors American society (Springfield, after all, is a microcosm): the downfall of the U.S. is due to the fact that typical Americans are uninformed, easily swayed by logical fallacies and entertaining memes, and, sadly, quick to add their opinion to the comments section. And many of these people vote.

Demonstrating the positive side of community engagement and town pride is "Lemon of Troy" (6.24), the quintessential episode that displays the townspeople's love of Springfield so much so that it inspired the titles of this essay and even this book. In the episode, some Shelbyville hoodlums steal Springfield's beloved lemon tree, the same tree that the children of Springfield had all taken for granted until they learned its history and importance to the town. The lemon tree was planted upon Jebediah Springfield's founding of the town, where, legend has it, he explained, "we can worship freely, govern justly, and grow vast fields of hemp for making rope and blankets." Bart, Milhouse, Nelson, Martin, Database, and Todd go into Shelbyville to reclaim the town's prized tree with no luck at first, so Bart goes undercover, pretending to be from Shelbyville. Bart discovers the tree in an impound lot, which, as Martin points out, is the "impenetrable fortress of suburbia." The tree is ultimately recaptured because Bart cleverly instructs Homer to park Flanders' RV in a hospital zone so that it is towed to the same impound lot as the lemon tree. The escape from the impound lot damages the tree a bit and the RV quite a bit, but "with that, a mighty cheer went up from the heroes of Springfield."

Not only does "Lemon of Troy" show the people of Springfield displaying enormous town pride, it also shows a community respectful of its elders and traditions. "Whacking Day" (4.20), on the other hand, also depicts a town full of traditions, but this time includes a tradition, unlike pride in fresh squozen lemonade, that deserves to be questioned. And ultimately, the townspeople, led by Lisa, care enough about the town to stop embarrassing it (and wreak havoc on the environment) by killing snakes through some silly old tradition based on myth. In "Lisa the Iconoclast" (7.16), Lisa, excited for a homework assignment, does some research on Jebediah Springfield, only to learn that he was a murderous pirate and not actually the upstanding, anti-incest, virtuous leader we learned about in "Lemon of Troy." Lisa's teacher and classmates are not pleased to hear Lisa's report, but she persists in spreading the truth, with Homer's support. In the end, though, Lisa decides not to share her proof about Jebediah at the bicentennial parade although she has the perfect opportunity when Homer gets everyone's attention in his role as town crier. Again, Lisa saves the town from embarrassment, but this time by preserving a town myth instead of debunking one. Ultimately, seeing the happy, prideful faces at the parade made her realize that, in this case, the myth of Jebediah was valuable.

In "Bart After Dark" (8.5), we learn that the men of Springfield have been keeping a secret from the children and many of the women: Springfield has a burlesque house. When Marge finds out, she is particularly upset and is determined to shut the Maison Derrière down. The town is largely on her side, but a particularly rousing (and Emmy-award winning!) song changes their minds. The Maison Derrière puts the spring in Springfield and spreads some joy, too. If only there had been a song to save the town from Sanitation Commissioner Simpson ("Trash of the Titans" 9.22). In the episode, Homer loses his pride in a standoff with garbage collectors, and to regain it, he rather capriciously runs for sanitation commissioner against trusted public servant Ray Patterson. In this situation, the mob rule that is overcome with excitement about Homer's campaign based on a simple catchphrase—Can't someone else do it?—has detrimental effects on the town after Homer takes outside garbage to make up for an enormous budget deficit. In the end, the town is forced to follow Plan B and moves five miles down the road. Yes, it is Homer's fault for destroying the town, but the townspeople really should have known better than to believe that the garbage man can do all the nasty chores Homer promised. For that matter, the townspeople should have known not to elect Homer Simpson to any public office.

A personal favorite episode of mine, "Coming to Homerica" (20.21), has it all: mob rule, town pride, aquavit, and Minnesota Vikings attire.[1] When Ogdenville's tainted barley crop poisons Krusty Burger patrons, the entire economy of the town of Ogdenville is crippled, forcing its residents to move in droves to Springfield where they pick up odd jobs mainly consisting of day labor and tasks that the people of Springfield simply don't want to do. At first, things move along swimmingly. Home improvement is rampant, and Homer discovers the Scandinavian herbaceous spirit, aquavit. The first sign of trouble occurs when the wait is too long for Bart to see a doctor after he separates his shoulder showing off his mad skateboarding skills, not to mention that the intake form Marge is given is in Norwegian. The townspeople of Springfield begin border patrol to keep the Ogdenvillians out. At first, Marge is against the proposed border fence, stating, "Haven't we always taught the children to make friends with those who are a little different?" However, in an uncharacteristic sign of irrationality, Marge jumps on the bandwagon against the immigrants when Maggie's first word (that Marge knows of) is a strong, Norwegian-Minnesotan "yah" (influenced, no doubt, by the Simpsons' new nanny, Inga). "Build it, Homie," Marge exclaims, "make it as tall as the sky and deeper than hell!" Thus, even the otherwise rational can be swept up in nationalistic, anti-immigrant sentiment when they're pushed from their comfort zones or feel their ways of life are challenged. (Plus, it's easier to be bad when so many people around are behaving poorly.)

In the end, Springfield hires the Ogdenvillian workers to help the Springfield men build the wall, mainly because no one from Springfield actually knows how. The Ogdenvillians build it with doors, a move that actually makes both sides happy. It turns out, after the wall is completed, the two sides miss each other. In the process, they've realized how similar they are, whether it's through shared issues with women (what with those darn throw pillows and wanting the cat to sleep in bed with you), or having trouble finding a four-button cardigan, the men of Springfield, and Marge, finally come around.

What makes this episode so poignant is that not only are the Ogdenvillians pleasant, kind, and forgiving throughout the entire episode (even through all the rudeness and name calling, such as "barleyjacks" and "norwads"), but the point is made in not-so-subtle terms that walls don't work and borders are senseless. Not only do the two sides grow fond of each other, it's clear that the two towns' economies rely on each other from the start, from Krusty's initial decision to capitalize on potential health-conscious consumers and buys Ogdenville's barley. Because of its interaction with Springfield, the economy of Ogdenville is damaged; if the tainted barley crop had never been publicized, the people of Ogdenville would never have needed to seek employment elsewhere. Homer's annoyance at seeing Sven and the others in the medical waiting room is clearly unfounded, particularly when Sven remarks that he's there because of the work he did on Homer's septic system. In a rare, satisfying ending, Homer and the other townspeople actually learn something and don't make a colossal mess out of everything.

A similar episode, thematically, is "Much Apu About Nothing" (7.23), which also tackles the issue of immigration (namely, scapegoating immigrants) but with much worse outcomes. I hope our readers are more than familiar with the plot of this episode, but I'll quickly recap anyway. When a bear wanders into Springfield, the people of the town freak out, prompting Mayor Quimby to implement a new Bear Patrol tax. (The bear patrol, of course, is a completely unnecessary waste of taxpayer money.) When taxpayers freak out about the tax to pay for services they want, Mayor Quimby blames the tax hike on undocumented immigrants. Quimby uses immigration to take the heat off himself, his poor leadership, and his mishandling of money. This jerk move causes people to mistreat the immigrants of Springfield and begin a push to expel all immigrants from Springfield. (When I see all of the so-called predictions from *The Simpsons* on social media, I keep wondering when people are going to tweet about this connection.) Unfortunately, one of the kindest and smartest Springfieldians, Apu Nahasapeemapetilon, gets pulled into the mess. However, with Lisa and the other Simpsons on his side, he is able to pass the citizenship test and stay in Springfield legally, but not before undergoing a whole lot of undue stress and financial burden stemming from an unnecessary Americanized renovation of the Kwik-E-Mart and the purchase of fraudulent documents from Fat Tony. Unfortunately, "Much Apu About Nothing" shows the cruelty Springfieldians are capable of, and as a microcosm of the United States, it also shows the cruelty (and alarming lack of critical thinking skills) Americans often display as well. From turning on those whose function and participation had always been appreciated in the town, to churning out anti-immigrant talking points, the townspeople verbalize many of the same, nonsensical anti-immigrant sentiments resurfacing under the Trump administration, such as the mistaken idea perpetuated by Moe that English is the official language of the United States. (In actuality, the United States has no official language, which has given rise to some organizations trying to change that, such as U.S. English, whose website touts itself as an action group "dedicated to preserving the unifying role of the English language in the United States," namedrops several immigrant legislators who've supported the movement, and states that its goal is to "help immigrants.") Moe complains, "You know what really aggravazes me? It's them immigrants. They wants all the benefits of living in Springfield, but they ain't even bother to learn themselves the language." This is, of course, a brilliant moment that shows that Moe's English is awful, much worse than, say, Apu's, and it is interesting to note that English actually is one of the officially recognized languages of Apu's country of origin, India, and is one of two official languages of the Indian government.

In "Marge vs. the Monorail" (4.12), the town is faced with another destructive force, an outsider this time: a huckster named Lyle Lanley crashes the town meeting, which is being held to decide how to spend the $3 million payout from the Springfield Nuclear Power Plant. Lyle Lanley convinces the town it needs a monorail (against Marge's protestations), once again due to a very catchy song.

Fast forward to Season 29's "The Old Blue Mayor Ain't What She Used to Be" (29.6). Kent Brockman covers the opening of Skyline Park, "a reclamation project built on top of the ruins of the Springfield Monorail." Brockman is announcing from a plastic box, and various townspeople are gathered around him. When he mentions the monorail, the townspeople begin to chant, "Monorail! Monorail!" as they did in "Marge vs. the Monorail." Unfortunately, no one had thought to make sure the old monorail train was disabled, and it causes terrible destruction. A town meeting is quickly held to discuss the disaster, which, in true Springfield town-meeting style, has an excellent turnout. At the meeting, Mayor Quimby dismisses Marge with sexist comments. Interestingly, this moment offers a bit of foreshadowing for anyone familiar with "Marge vs. the Monorail" that this episode may feature Marge, as she was the only townsperson who was not brainwashed by Lyle Lanley and had been against the monorail the entire time. After the meeting, the family encourages her to run against sexist old Mayor Quimby; if anyone in Springfield deserves his own #MeToo moment, it's him. The townspeople all show up for the mayoral debate, including adults we don't see often, like Disco Stu, and children, like Martin Prince. Marge wins the election and becomes mayor, and the townspeople attend her events, some exciting, some not so much, even showing up for Marge's ribbon cutting for the new manhole cover on 4th Street (though, admittedly, the turnout for this event is probably invigorated by Marge's mean remarks about Homer).

Season 29 featured some throwback moments to older episodes in a hat-tipping, rather than derivative, fashion. With "The Old Blue Mayor Ain't What She Used To Be," the monorail was reanimated, and in "Gone Boy" (29.9), Bart goes missing and the townspeople all show up (including a prison work detail featuring Sideshow Bob) to find him in a forest after he falls into a 1960s military bunker—more than slightly reminiscent of how the town (plus Sting!) took turns keeping him company after he had fallen down a well ("Radio Bart" 3.13).

Indeed, in "Gone Boy," the town is searching for him so ardently that Lisa exclaims, "Come on, Bart! You've made your point; the whole town is looking for you, even that scary old man from the house with the broken windows." Unfortunately for Bart, Sideshow Bob is also looking for him, and with the help of Milhouse, he finds him. (But you know Bart'll be all right. Sideshow Bob, like the coyote, will never catch the roadrunner. I mean, Bart.)

In "A Star is Burns" (6.18), there is, once again, a town meeting, this time suggested by Marge, who is concerned about losing tourism dollars after Kent Brockman reports on a survey ranking Springfield the least popular city in America. Marge's idea, a film festival, is unanimously approved because the townspeople are enchanted with the idea of making their own films, particularly Chief Wiggum, who had been apparently dying for an excuse to wear makeup. The film festival idea is a good one, as film festivals have put many small or otherwise inconsequential towns on the map, and it brings film critic Jay Sherman to town. The film festival itself enjoys a great turnout, even grabbing the attention of *Entertainment Weekly*, which has already put Barney on the cover for his autobiographical film. The film festival is a success; it's really too bad Springfield didn't make it an annual thing.

When I taught a writing course on the show at Florida State, I included "mob rule" on the list of potential paper topics, and students overwhelmingly discussed how a few loudmouthed individuals were successful in effecting a large amount of damage by sweeping others up into the madness. However, it is possible to take a more positive outlook on their gatherings: the residents of Springfield care about their town and they care about each other, even if their concern sometimes makes a mess.

NOTE

1. I am from Minnesota and have a bit of Minnesota Vikings apparel myself. And no, I don't want to talk about the 1998 NFC Championship game. Too soon.

WORKS CITED

"Bart After Dark." *The Simpsons: The Complete Eighth Season.* Written by Richard Appel, directed by Dominic Polcino, 20th Century–Fox, 1996.
"Coming to Homerica." *The Simpsons: The Complete Twentieth Season.* Written by Brendan Hay, directed by Steven Dean Moore, 20th Century–Fox, 2010.
"Gone Boy." *The Simpsons,* Season 29, Episode 9. Written by John Frink, directed by Rob Oliver. 20th Century–Fox, 10 Dec. 2017. Hulu.
"Lemon of Troy." *The Simpsons: The Complete Sixth Season.* Written by Jim Reardon, directed by Brent Forrester. 20th Century–Fox, 1995.
"Lisa the Iconoclast." *The Simpsons: The Complete Seventh Season.* Written by Jonathan Collier, directed by Mike B. Anderson, 20th Century–Fox, 1996.
"Marge vs. the Monorail." *The Simpsons: The Complete Fourth Season.* Written by Conan O'Brien, directed by Rich Moore, 20th Century–Fox, 14 Jan. 1993.
"Much Apu About Nothing." *The Simpsons: The Complete Seventh Season.* Written by David S. Cohen, directed by Susie Dietter, 20th Century–Fox, 1996.
"The Old Blue Mayor She Ain't What She Used to Be." *The Simpsons,* Season 29, Episode 6. Written by Tom Gammill and Max Pross, directed by Matthew Nastuk. 20th Century–Fox, 12 Nov. 2017. Hulu.
"Radio Bart." *The Simpsons: The Complete Third Season.* Written by Jon Vitti, directed by Carlos Baeza, 20th Century–Fox, 1992.
"A Star Is Burns." *The Simpsons: The Complete Sixth Season.* Written by Ken Keeler, directed by Susie Dietter, 20th Century–Fox, 1995.
"Trash of the Titans." *The Simpsons: The Complete Ninth Season.* Written by Ian Maxtone-Graham, directed by Jim Reardon, 20th Century–Fox, 2006.
U.S. English, Incorporated. "About U.S. English." *U.S. English: Making English the Official Language.* U.S. English, Inc. www.usenglish.org/history. Accessed 22 May 2018.
"Whacking Day." *The Simpsons: The Complete Fourth Season.* Written by John Swartzwelder, directed by Jeffrey Lynch. 20th Century–Fox, 1993.

The Simpsons, Gender Roles and Witchcraft

The Witch in Modern Popular Culture[1]

SARAH ANTINORA

A young girl, of approximately the age of eight, enters her living room completely decked out in her well-constructed Halloween costume. As she is wearing her black pointy hat, buckle shoes, black dress, striped socks, and a cape, while carrying the prerequisite wand, both the audience and her friend immediately recognize her as being dressed as a witch. Her friend has always had a crush on her, and he attempts to impress her by complimenting her outfit: "I like your witch costume, Lisa." A look of indignation immediately transforms her face, as she retorts, "I'm not a witch; I'm a Wiccan. Why is it that when a woman is confident and powerful, they call her a witch?" ("Treehouse of Horror XIX" 20.4).

By now, most readers would recognize the little girl questioning the construction of the witch as none other than Lisa Simpson, from the long-running animated sitcom *The Simpsons*.[2] This particular scene stems from the series' annual Halloween episodes, a collection of three vignettes entitled "Treehouse of Horror," and while the recurring characters of *The Simpsons* are allowed to engage in both fantastic and phantasmal scenarios in these episodes, they ultimately do not stray from their traditional roles. Hence, while Lisa takes on the characteristics of Lucy from *Peanuts* in this wonderful parody entitled "It's the Grand Pumpkin Milhouse" (20.4), her question is very much in keeping with the values normally attributed to her in the series—that of the outspoken feminist with a thirst for knowledge.

As both the longest-running sitcom and animated series on American television, *The Simpsons* serves as one of the primary representations of modern American culture, especially as it has functioned as a satirical look at the

22

American middle-class family. As an animated series, the series has always been allowed to take liberties and play with the conventions of a sitcom to make its pointed comments concerning modern culture. Yet it is in the series' incorporation of the fantastic, and the witch in particular, that has allowed it to make its more significant statements regarding sexual politics and gender expectations. The female characters accused of witchcraft or presented as witches not only comment on how the witch is constructed in modern popular culture but also how issues of gender roles and expectations complicate that construction. For example, casting The Crazy Cat Lady as a witch allows the audience to transpose the characteristics normally associated with this character to the idea of "witch." This proves true with the many presentations of the witch throughout the series, whether it is with Marge Simpson, Patty and Selma Bouvier (Marge's sisters), Lisa, or even baby Maggie. *The Simpsons* reflects and reinforces the construction of the witch, drawing on the characteristics first associated with her during the early modern period in conjunction with more recent popular culture references such as *The Wizard of Oz* (1939) and *Bewitched* (1964–1972). Yet the series also comments on the gender implications of that image. This essay examines the ways in which *The Simpsons* has attempted to answer Lisa's question concerning the role of gender in witchcraft and witch accusations, and proposes that the various "answers" posed by the series not only mirror current theoretical work on the witch but also reflect the ambivalence about the role of women in modern American society.

"I've grown a costume on your face" from "Treehouse of Horror XVI" (17.4)

The third vignette in the 2005 Halloween episode offers perhaps the most conventional representation of the witch in *The Simpsons'* history. For that very reason, it is a good place to begin this analysis, as it portrays the witch according to her most popular construction and presents a theory of the gender question that is also widely held. The segment opens with Springfield holding a Halloween costume contest. In the crowd, Lisa can be seen dressed as Albert Einstein, Dr. Hibbert as Dracula, Ned Flanders as a flower, and, most importantly, little Maggie as a witch. Notably, her costume is only clear from her pointy black hat; otherwise, she is dressed in her traditional blue nightgown. On the steps of the town hall, Mayor Quimby announces a woman, who strongly resembles the recurring character widely known as The Crazy Cat Lady dressed in a witch's costume, as the winner. However, when asked her identity, she is forced to admit that she is not wearing a costume, saying, "I'm a real witch." The townspeople, who by the way are in no way shocked by the existence of a witch, are outraged that she has cheated and they rescind her "prize"—a $25 gift certificate to Kwik-E-Mart, which its owner Apu readily admits is not enough to purchase anything in the store.[3] In her anger, she casts a spell on everyone who lives in Springfield, forcing them to "become the guise [they] don." Instantaneously, Marge becomes a skeleton, Bart a wolf man, and Grandpa Abe a gorilla. As most in the town are distressed by this turn of events, Lisa as Einstein sets out to find a solution. When Maggie, now dressed in a full witch's costume, is able to move objects with a spell, Lisa realizes that Maggie has the power to conduct counter-magic and undo the hex. Unfortunately, Maggie has no interest, or understanding, of the real issue at hand, and instead turns everyone into a pacifier—her true desire. The episode ends as she flies off on her broom, witch "dust" surrounding her, and the *Bewitched* theme music playing in the background.

The Crazy Cat Lady reveals a great deal about the figure of the witch.[4] She lives alone and is always depicted with at least one cat attached to her body. I use the word "attached" because she does not hold the cat; instead, it appears to hang from various parts of her person. However, it is also a misnomer to use the word "cat," for in nearly every appearance of this character a multitude of cats are attached to her. A freeze-frame of the 2009–2010 opening credits shows at least nine cats hanging from The Crazy Cat Lady. While the representation of this character plays with the modern stereotype of a "cat lady," or a spinster woman who only has cats to give her love, the image in this episode suggests the "familiar."

As James Sharpe notes in his *Instruments of Darkness: Witchcraft in Early Modern England* (1996), the notion of the familiar is perhaps one of the most identifiable characteristics associated with the witch. This familiar, usually in the form of a toad, cat, or dog, was assumed to be a demonic spirit, capable of performing *maleficium* on behalf of the witch (71). However, it was believed that the familiar was only willing to conduct the *maleficium* in exchange for human food—sometimes in the form of animals such as chickens but more often in the form of human blood. As Deborah Willis explains in *Malevolent Nurture: Witch-hunting and Maternal Power in Early Modern England* (1995), the familiar "would suck greedily from the witch's mark or teat—sometimes described in great detail as a nipplelike protuberance" (52). Therefore, to return to The Crazy Cat Lady, the cats' attachment to her body can be read as familiars merely feeding upon her blood.[5] This idea is further supported in her representation in "I've Grown a Costume on Your Face," as the warts on her face, often used as evidence for a witch's mark, are much more clearly visible in this episode. As Barbara Rosen explains in *Witchcraft in England, 1558–1618* (1991), "This mark … gradually becomes the outstanding 'proof'" of not only the existence of a pact with the devil but that the accused woman is in fact a witch (17). Hence, *The Simpsons* clearly portrays "the real witch," as portrayed by The Crazy Cat Lady, as one that is not only easily identifiable as a witch to the modern audience but grounded in two of the most important aspects of the Early Modern construction of her: the familiar and the mark.

However, the representation of The Crazy Cat Lady also supports one of the common explanations posited to account for witch accusations and why women in particular were the main targets. One analysis of the surviving early modern pamphlets depicting the witch trials notes that the accused was most often an "economically marginalized" elderly woman, without the influence of a husband and with a reputation for "doing ill" (Sharpe 63). Her age becomes a factor as she has probably outlived her husband, if she had ever married to begin with, and is now unable to support herself financially. She, hence, becomes a burden on her neighbors, as she requires their charity to survive. Sharpe also states that the accused does not attend church regularly and is often heard scolding or cursing her neighbors (63). The woman described here is one living outside of normative gender expectations and, as such, is a threat.

There is perhaps no greater threat in the town of Springfield as The Crazy Cat Lady. With a given age of seventy-eight and having lived as a single woman for her entire adult life, it is interesting that the series depicts her as not only a "cat lady," but as a "crazy" one. She is discussed as being mentally ill in numerous episodes, but the audience learns in "Springfield Up" (18.13) that this is due to stress. It is explained that this stress is caused from having entered into the male-dominated public spheres of law and medicine. By the age of thirty-two, she had bonded with her first cat in a downward spiral of mental illness to never find a male companion. Most of what she says is unintelligible, and, yet, the few words that are clear are always curses.[6] As Merry E. Wiesner-Hanks explains, women living without male figures—whether they be husbands or fathers—were "more suspect in the eyes of their neighbors" (268). While Wiesner-Hanks refers here to the women accused of witchcraft during the early modern era, it is interesting that *The Simpsons*, a reflection of modern views regarding gender roles, chooses to portray this woman as "crazy"—crazy for being unattached to a man and attempting to enter into male-dominated fields of work. And while the series' focus on gender expectations will be discussed more in depth in relation to Patty and Selma, the show often aligns single, elderly women with witchcraft in the same manner described by Wiesner-Hanks.

"Easy Bake Coven" from "Treehouse of Horror VIII" (9.4)

This segment of the eighth Halloween episode serves to explain the beginnings of Halloween traditions. While the episode's faithfulness to the origins of the holiday is slim at best, it does prove very faithful to the context of the witch trials of the 1600s, especially in the American colonies. The vignette parodies the Salem witch trials; however, the motivations for the accusations and the construction of the witches themselves overlap with their early modern English counterparts. "Easy Bake Coven" (1997) takes place in the town of "Sprynge-Fielde" in 1649 A.D. It begins with three women tied to stakes, surrounded by townspeople holding torches. Those being condemned as witches, referred to as "hags," represent the various types of women accused in the early modern period. Luann Van Houten, Milhouse's mother, has recently left her husband. Miss Hoover, Lisa's second grade teacher, although being far from elderly, is viewed as a spinster. Agnes Skinner, the town principal's mother, is portrayed as overtly sexual and oversexed, even dressing in Jennifer Lopez's famous Grammy Awards dress in "Gump Roast" (13.17). Again, while the three women here are dressed in American Colonial attire, their conventional characteristics speak to how the image of the witch is constructed, both in the early modern and modern popular culture.[7] While the spinsterhood evidenced in Hoover has already been explained as a threat, Van Houten's and Skinner's association with insatiable sexuality is depicted as equally problematic. As Wiesner explains, sexual intercourse was viewed as a means to produce children, not as a source of pleasure in early modern England (273). In the series, Van Houten has left her husband to pursue sexual pleasure outside of marriage, while Skinner would be an example of a sex drive that has increased due to her age, a trait associated with witches, according to Wiesner. It then becomes clear that these particular female characters are chosen to portray witches to highlight the witch's association with female sexuality.

While most of the townsfolk are eager for the burning of the witches to begin, two female characters question the events: Lisa and her mother Marge. When Lisa is accused of "witch talk," she immediately retreats, but Marge does not back down. Although the first accusation comes from Moe, the most convincing evidence of Marge being a witch comes from a woman in the crowded town hall who yells, "How come your laundry is much whiter than mine?" It is notable here that this voice is female, as the myth of the witch trials, or what Mary Daly called "The Burning Times," is that of the male persecutor and the female victim. Yet *The Simpsons* presents women as having a more active role in the accusations, mirroring more closely the argument put forth by Diane Purkiss in *The Witch in History: Early Modern and Twentieth-Century Representations* (1996). As she states, "The theory that witch-hunting equals misogyny is embarrassed by the predominance of women witnesses against the accused" (92).

"Easy Bake Coven" does not portray a conventional witch trial, one of which will be discussed in "Rednecks and Broomsticks" (21.7). Instead, the townspeople take the law into their own hands, mirroring the tactics taken in later witch-hunting eras that reflect the belief that the law is "skeptical" (Rosen 29). While the most common test would be the water-ordeal, this episode takes the test to an even further extreme. To give her "due process," they hand Marge a broom and push her off a high cliff. If she flies, she will be confirmed as a "bride of Satan"; if she falls, she "dies a Christian death." While the episode demonstrates the absurdity of this test, it also alludes to witch-hunting's link with Christianity. This is even more provocative as Ned earlier indicated that seventy-five witches had already been processed to "show God whose side we're on." While the religious issues regarding what constituted "Christianity"—whether the true religion was Protestant or Catholic, and how that controversy influenced witch-hunting—is an important one, it is ultimately too large to tackle in a project of this scale. However, the idea of witch-hunting as a Christian cause, alongside the witch's link with the devil, is intrinsically tied to the construction of the witch's image. These references allow viewers to understand the witch as not only demonic but as engaging in sexual intercourse with the devil, harkening back to the early modern notion that "the witch-cult entailed sexual relations with the Devil himself " (Rosen 17).

At first, it appears that Marge has fallen to her death, but then she flies out of the canyon, her skin having turned green and her hair having turned black to simulate the witch's hat. To complete this image of her as a witch, she also is seen with familiars, although hers are the bats that inhabit her hair. She admits that she has been practicing witchcraft, naming various examples of *maleficium* such as killing livestock, souring sheep's milk, and making shirts "itchy." Two of these examples can be directly seen in pamphlets documenting the witch trials of the early modern period. For example, in *Witches at Chelmsford* from July of 1566, Mother Waterhouse confesses to having cows drowned and spoiling butter (Rosen 76). Yet even the "itchy" shirts demonstrate that the type of *maleficium* employed by Marge is of the domestic sphere, highlighting Purkiss' argument that accusations of witchcraft may have more to do with "[negotiating] the fears and anxieties of housekeeping and motherhood" (93).

Marge joins her sisters Selma and Patty in the forest, and it is clear that black magic runs in the family. As Marge nears the two others in the midst of creating a potion in a boiling cauldron, the sisters engage in a heated debate about how much "eye of newt" should be used. This reference to *Macbeth* permanently links the three Bouvier sisters with the Weird Sisters, or witches, of Shakespeare.[8] While the link between *Macbeth* and *The Simpsons* will be further explored below, the placement of Selma and Patty as witches is vital to this discussion. Marge's sisters have been linked with the image of the witch in three of the four episodes discussed here, and again it is the series' portrayal of them throughout its run that complicates the idea of the witch.

Selma and Patty are Marge's twin sisters; though it may be difficult to distinguish them, Selma has her hair parted in the middle and "S" earrings. With their hyper-masculine voices, refusal to shave their legs, and manly features, the sisters on physicality alone fit the stereotype of the witch as outside gender expectations. They are also perceived as a neighborly nuisance, especially by Homer. However, Patty and Selma are economically and socially independent—although maybe not from each other—and it is that very independence that enhances the construction of the witch in *The Simpsons*. Patty, for example, comes out as a lesbian in "There's Something about Marrying" (16.10). Although clues about her sexual orientation have been dropped since the series' inception, she becomes the only recurring openly gay character on the show up until Mr. Smithers comes out in 2016 ("The Burns Cage" 27.17). She even plans to marry a "woman" she has fallen in love with, but rejects "her" when she learns that he is only pretending to be female to play in the LPGA. While this episode comments extensively and with complexity on both same-sex marriage and homosexuality, for this discussion it is important that Patty has chosen to live a life without a man. She is a logical representation of the witch in the series, for she is truly, as Wiesner-Hanks states, a woman "unattached to a man" (268).

Selma, on the other hand, has been divorced five times (not counting the annulment from Disco Stu). While living without a man also links her to the image of the witch, it is her desire for motherhood that complicates the image. In "Selma's Choice" (4.13), Selma discusses her lack of children as an "emptiness" in her life. Matthew Henry, in his "Don't Ask Me, I'm Just a Girl," views this episode, which follows Selma's decision to not be artificially inseminated, as one that challenges "nuclear family 'norms,'" and champions a "woman's right to choose" (282). However, Selma's lack of a child to nurture, accompanied by her association with the witch, supports Willis' argument of "malevolent nurture." Willis points out that the accused witch is usually postmenopausal, and therefore unable to have a human child of her own. This anxiety, existing within her own body, causes her to "misdirect" her need to nurture towards the devilish imps, or familiars, that she feeds (33). In contrast, the victims of a witch's *maleficium* are often children, thereby allowing for a distortion of motherhood to be seen in the witch. As Willis explains, "She is a nurturing mother to her brood of demonic imps but a malevolent anti-mother to her neighbors and their children" (34).

As the remainder of "Easy Bake Coven" explains not only the origins of trick or treating but also the association of child-eating with the witch, it can be seen that *The Simpsons* offers a complex notion of the witch as "mother." After viewing in the cauldron a discussion between Ned Flanders and his wife Maude, the three sisters devise a plan to eat the children of the town, since that is what the couple most feared. Although they later decide that scaring neighbors into giving them treats is not only more fun but tastier than eating human children, it is revealed that the Flanders' home is not their first stop and that many children in the town have already perished at the hands of the witches. While theories regarding the gender implications of witch-hunting have sometimes revolved around the number of deaths of children during this time period and the finding of scapegoats in midwives, famously posited by Mary Daly and discounted by Diane Purkiss, the episode is referencing the image of the "night-flying cannibalistic female witch" (Sharpe 15). And by repeatedly placing Selma in the role of the witch, the series must also thereby be complicating this debate with the idea of the "anti-mother."

"Rednecks and Broomsticks" (21.7)

A more recent *The Simpsons* episode depicting witchcraft, "Rednecks and Broomsticks" (2009), presents a complex figure of the witch. It debunks many of the myths and stereotypes often associated with witches (most of which the series has reinforced in previous episodes), establishes witchcraft's association with nature, and centers on the phenomenon of women who embrace the identity of the witch. As this is a full-length episode, as opposed to the vignettes seen in the Halloween episodes, there is a subplot, which at times seems tangential to the witchcraft theme, but in typical *The Simpsons* fashion, neatly converges with the main plot in the end.

After getting into a car accident and being rescued from a frozen lake, the Simpson clan spends time with the town "rednecks." While Homer becomes involved in a moonshine enterprise, Lisa plays hide and seek with two of the Spuckler children. Unfortunately, the two children cannot count to one hundred, and Lisa is left hiding in the forest well into the night. She happens upon three cloaked young women conducting a chant over a boiling cauldron, and, while at first frightened, eventually becomes intrigued by their Wiccan beliefs.[9] Once their cloaks are removed, the women are revealed to be average-looking teenagers, although with lots of black eyeliner and pink-dyed hair. When Lisa expresses relief that they are not "witches," one responds that "technically" she is one, but they do not fly around on broomsticks "and things like that." This episode, therefore, becomes the first in which the physical image of the witch is challenged. Lisa learns of the esbat ritual, the influence of Lilith, and the communion of nature emphasized in Wicca, some of which she learns from *Wiccapedia*. While some of these elements define the differences between witchcraft and Wicca, the episode highlights the overlap, mirroring the theory that witch-hunting may have originated in the attempt to eliminate pagan practices.

While earlier episodes often reinforce the stereotype of the witch, "Rednecks and Broomsticks" problematizes it. For example, when Bart sees Lisa viewing a website with a pentagram on it, he is excited to learn that she is coming "over to the dark side." However, he then proclaims that she is too young to be a witch—that certain steps must be followed: college anorexia, failed marriages, career disappointments, a failed pottery shop, and then, once old and alone, a commitment to witchcraft. Bart is integrating two disparate figures here: the early modern witch being elderly and alone and the modern Wiccan, a younger woman often associated with New Age stereotypes. And, yet, even in the midst of questioning this construction, Lisa—often portrayed as the enlightened one—gleefully plays with this traditional configuration. She dons a cape, uses a ruler as a wand, and proclaims Snowball II to be her familiar, much to his horror. To further highlight the ambivalent nature of these conventions, as Ned sees her frolicking around in her room in her "costume," he declares that he always knew that Buddhism was the gateway to witchcraft.[10] Hence, by this point of the episode, *The Simpsons* has challenged many of the conventions surrounding the construction of the witch—a construction that it has reinforced for decades. The episode proposes that she may not be elderly, ugly, or demonic, and, yet, we as a society also cannot seem to move away from these notions.

It is in the very next scene that fear and mob mentality yet again overrule reason. As Lisa is in the midst of being accepted into the coven, in a scene heavily reminiscent of the initiation scene in *The Craft* (1996), the three young witches are arrested. In front of the courthouse, the local television news reporter asks, "Double, double, toil and trouble?" and approaches Patty and Selma. Again, because of the ways in which they resemble the stereotype of the witch, the reporter assumes they are the ones on trial, or at the very least the victims of some hideous spell. However, it is the three younger girls who proclaim themselves to be witches, examples of "women actively [seeking] a social identity as magic-users" (Purkiss 145). Just as Purkiss explains, they are engaging in Wicca as a form of "female agency" (145). Hence, before the commencement of the trial, the three girls cast a spell to make their persecutors blind, and immediately, characters are shown losing their sight, thereby convincing the town of the validity of the accusations. The evidence presented in the trial is unconvincing though, with one of the girls declaring, "We're just kids!" and the judge dismisses the case. However, the townspeople still want justice, and, becoming an angry, torch-carrying mob, again led by Moe, they decide to implement 17th century law: the trial by water. Rosen describes the "water ordeal" as "one in which a suspect was trussed up and thrown into a pond to sink, if innocent or swim if guilty" (19). Note that the contraption is designed to ensure that in either case the accused woman is removed as a problem, either by being found guilty or through death. Luckily, Lisa solves the mystery just in time, proving that the townspeople have been temporarily blinded by the moonshine her father dumped into the reservoir. Although Lisa still savors her time with the Wiccans, in that it is the first time she has ever felt "cool," her mother insists that the only witch in her daughter's life will be "which boy will marry her." It is this juxtaposition that highlights the ambivalence of not only the witch image but the gender expectations for women in modern American culture. While Marge may be merely concerned that her daughter finds a boy to marry, and therefore conform to heteronormative gender roles, Lisa is attempting to assert agency apart from these expectations in conjunction with finding acceptance. As the episode closes to the sounds of Donovan's "Season of the Witch" (1966), with Lisa ice skating alone in pure happiness,[11] it appears, that at least in this episode, feminine roles have not only been challenged but restructured.

"Lady Macbeth" in "Four Great Women and a Manicure" (20.20)

The Simpsons has a long tradition of referencing the plays, and particular lines, of Shakespeare. Sideshow Bob recites Shakespearean lines in almost all of the episodes in which he appears, and episode titles include "Much Apu about Nothing" (7.23) and "Rome-Old and Julie-Eh" (18.15). However, *Macbeth* in particular has been referenced often in the series. This play especially informs the way in which *The Simpsons* constructs the image of the witch, as it is one of, if not the most influential text influencing modern popular culture's understanding of witchcraft.[12] In addition to referencing the play in the episode entitled "Double, Double, Boy in Trouble" (20.3), the Simpson family learns of the *Macbeth* curse from Ian McKellen while visiting England in "The Regina Monologues" (15.4). However, the series' parody of *Macbeth* in "Four Great Women and a Manicure" (20.20) best speaks to this discussion of the witch and the gender implications of its construction.

Marge introduces the tale as "the story of a great woman held back by a not so great husband." The parody takes the form of metatheater, in that the themes and plot of *Macbeth* are mirrored in the characters' production of the play. Marge, as a Lady Macbeth type, is the washer woman for the theater troupe, and the audience is introduced to her with the great line "Out, out, damn spot" as she is washing a costume. Homer has been assigned a small role in the play, as one of the trees and as an understudy to Sideshow Mel who has been given the role of Macbeth. However, Marge has greater ambitions for both herself and her husband, and she devises a plan to have

Homer murder Mel. Yet once Homer is given the part of Macbeth, theater reviewers still offer more praise for the other actors—first, importantly, being Dr. Hibbert as Banquo. Marge insists that he kill every other actor in turn, so that he—and by extension she—can garner praise and respect. Homer at one point wonders if it wouldn't just be easier to take acting lessons, but instead he gives in to her demands. Eventually though, her conscience gets to her, and the ghosts of all those whose murders she has caused come to haunt her, resulting in her death. In terms of an analysis of the witch, a curious moment occurs here. As the reader probably knows, the characters of the Simpson clan all have yellow skin. When Marge sees these phantasms, they emit a bluish hue across the stage, representing their translucency. However, when the frame changes to show Marge on the stage, the blue rays change her normally yellow skin to green—the exact color the series has used to portray every witch in the series' history up to this point. Alone, both onstage and in life, Homer as Macbeth gives the famous "tomorrow and tomorrow" speech, with only his wife's ghost in the audience. Finally proud of him, she insists that he can now play the leads in all of Shakespeare's plays, but as she begins to list them all, Homer shoots himself; he would rather die than have to read more Shakespeare.

While the exploration of the parody of *Macbeth* would be interesting for analysis,[13] it ultimately would not add insight to this particular discussion. However, the juxtaposition between Shakespeare's Lady Macbeth and Marge Simpson will illuminate not only the discussion of gender roles and expectations, but their influence on the construction of the witch. As mentioned above, the Weird Sisters of *Macbeth* greatly influence the popular modern notion of the witch. It is they whose "beards forbid [Banquo] to interpret" whether they are female or male (1.3.46). It is they who hover over a bubbling cauldron, chanting and creating potions (4.1). It is they who discuss *maleficium* such as "killing swine" in response to petty slights (1.3.2). Admittedly, there is much ambiguity concerning the witches. Marjorie Garber in her *Shakespeare After All* asks, "Are they male? Female? Real or imaginary? Benevolent or wicked?" (696). Thus, it has been implied that they are liminal figures. Yet their ambiguity is at least clarified by the fact that they are physical embodiments of witches. In contrast, there is no more liminal figure in *Macbeth* than Lady Macbeth—and the same can be claimed of Marge Simpson in *The Simpsons*.

Many have linked the ambiguity of the witch figures to Lady Macbeth. Garber states, "I think we can say with justice that those unisex witches … are among other things, dream images, metaphors, for Lady Macbeth herself: physically a woman but, as she claims, mentally and spiritually a man" (713). However, the connection between the witches and Lady Macbeth is perhaps most convincingly made in Janet Adelman's "'Born of a Woman': Fantasies of Maternal Power in *Macbeth*." While this essay posits the claim that the ultimate problem in *Macbeth* of masculine vulnerability is solved through the removal of the feminine, it is Adelman's assertion of Lady Macbeth as a witch that is most useful here. She notes that the physical ambiguity of the witches is mirrored psychologically in Lady Macbeth's desire to unsex herself (97). She also connects Lady Macbeth's summoning of spirits to "take my milk for gall" (1.5.47) as analogous to the characteristic familiars feeding off the witch (98). Adelman also notes that while the Weird Sisters are presumed to influence Macbeth's actions, it is actually his wife who has this power both through her words and her threats of emasculation (100–101). Hence, according to Adelman, the witches are merely a metaphor to enhance the audience's perception of Lady Macbeth as the true witch.

Yet equally important about the figure of Lady Macbeth—and this is almost impossible to separate out from her association with the witch—is her liminal status. She can clearly not be claimed as feminine, due to her lack (or disruption) of a maternal instinct, her overt ambition for both her husband and by extension herself, and lack of "milk of human kindness" (1.5.16). Yet she can clearly not be claimed as a man. Instead, she exists in a liminal space in between the two genders, partaking of both and yet being of neither. In the early modern construction of the female, lack of conformity to gender expectations can only render one "other"—which in every respect is how the construction of the witch has also been rendered.

Marge Simpson's identity as a liminal figure both mirrors this idea and complicates it. Henry labels Marge as a "liminal lady," based on Lori Landay's feminist research. He finds that Marge is a metaphor for the contradictory expectations of women in modern American culture; she exemplifies the ambivalence regarding a woman's role in society. As a married mother of three, working in the domestic sphere, Marge adheres to traditional gender role expectations. Yet as someone who came of age during the second wave of feminism, she also challenges those expectations.[14] Henry cites her liberation in contemplating an affair, her ability to excel as a police officer, and her insistence that Homer help out more with household duties. However, he also notes that whenever Marge steps out of the traditional female role, although questions might be raised regarding that role, each episode ends with Marge returning to the domestic sphere, thus reinforcing traditional gender roles. Hence, Henry sees her as "the embodiment of the cultural contradictions of contemporary femininity" (291). On the one hand, American women of the 21st century are encouraged to enter into the public sphere and embody feminist ideals; on the other hand, feminism has become a dirty word, and women are still expected to be in control of the household. The issue of how to balance these two opposing but co-existing ideas of the feminine molds many women in modern culture to be liminal figures themselves, with Marge Simpson embodying the ambivalent notions of just what it means to be "female" in contemporary society.

Therefore, when the viewer witnesses Marge Simpson portraying the figure of Lady Macbeth, a plethora of conflicting but contemporaneous reactions occur. We can count both of these fictional ladies as liminal, but see that they are constrained by ideas of gender from different time periods. However, we can also understand that there is still something deemed "evil" about a woman attempting to control her husband, especially for the sake of ambition. And if Marge (as Lady Macbeth) is also portrayed as a witch, then the impact of gender on the modern construction of the witch is still as essential as it was in the early modern construction.

Conclusion

I would like to end by returning to Lisa's question posed at the beginning of this project: Why is it that when a woman is confident and powerful, they call her a witch? As seen in this discussion, there are many proposed answers to this question in regards to how the witch was constructed for the early modern period. These theories range from socio-economic status to anxieties concerning motherhood and from gender role expectations to notions of identity and agency. What an analysis of the witch in *The Simpsons* has shown is that those very issues still construct the figure of the witch in modern popular culture because much of how the witch is defined is closely related to how we define "woman."

NOTES

1. A version of this essay was originally published in *452°F: Journal of Literary Theory and Comparative Literature*, no. 3, 2010, pp. 115–130. See http://www.452f.com/index.php/sarah-antinora.html.

2. I say "most readers" due to the series' longevity and popularity. As Matthew Henry notes, *The Simpsons* now holds the record as both the longest running animated primetime program and sitcom in American television history (273). Additionally, the McCormick Tribune Foundation reported in 2006 that almost a quarter of Americans can name all five members of the Simpsons' household. While the report finds this fact disturbing, especially in relation to the questions in which the respondents did not fare as well, the report's findings indicate not only the series' popularity but also its importance as a cultural artifact.

3. Note that this slight against the witch, although petty, is deemed important enough to conduct *maleficium*. Sharpe notes that "however trivial the altercation," it could be viewed as the instigation of black magic (62).

4. The name of The Crazy Cat Lady has been revealed to be Eleanor Abernathy. However, this revelation does not occur until "Springfield Up" 18.13 (2007). This is the only episode in which her true name is used.

5. This idea of the feeding of the familiar as indicative of the maternal, especially as discussed in Willis' *Malevolent Nurture,* will be explored more thoroughly in the discussion of "Easy Bake Coven."

6. The age of The Crazy Cat Lady is in dispute. While official sources put out by *The Simpsons'* creators place her age as 78, "Springfield Up" 18.13 indicates that she went to high

school with Homer Simpson. The notion of her craziness is also unsubstantiated, as the "medicine" she takes is revealed to be Reese's Pieces in "Homer and Ned's Hail Mary Pass" (16.8).

7. While it is important to refrain from conflating witch trials and the image of the witch from two different eras and geographical locations, the focus here will be on elements that overlap between American Colonialism and early modern England.

8. "Eye of net, and toe of frog,/Wool of bat, and tongue of dog./.../For a charm of powerful trouble,/Like a hell-broth, boil and bubble" (4.1.14–15,18–19).

9. There is an anachronism here in that Lisa claims that she knows little of Wicca and confuses it with witchcraft. Yet this episode appears after her declaration of dressing as a Wiccan instead of a witch in "Treehouse of Horror XIX."

10. After an exhaustive journey through world religions, Lisa converted to Buddhism in a 2001 episode, "She of Little Faith" (13.6).

11. This scene parodies the final moments of *To Die For* (1995).

12. A case can definitely be made for the influence of *The Wizard of Oz* (1939) as well. However, much of the film's construction of the Wicked Witch is informed by the early modern period. Therefore, much of what can be traced to the film actually originated in the early modern era and *Macbeth*, along with other early modern drama in particular. With the exception of the green skin, perhaps itself influenced by the novelty of color in the film, and the striped socks, the predominant current image of the witch is much more influenced by the times of Shakespeare.

13. This is especially true given the popular parody play *MacHomer* (1995), written by Rick Miller.

14. Henry is clear here in asserting that she came of age during the 1970s. Yet the series is very fluid with its chronology. As the characters do not age, and the series has been on the air for three decades, inconsistencies have arisen regarding age. Did Homer and Marge attend the prom in 1974 as stated in "The Way We Was" (2.12) but not get married until after the age of Nirvana and *Melrose Place* as seen in "That '90s Show" (19.11)?

Works Cited

Adelman, Janet. "'Born of Woman': Fantasies of Maternal Power in *Macbeth*." *Cannibals, Witches, and Divorce: Estranging the Renaissance*, edited by Marjorie Garber and John Hopkins, UP, 1987, pp. 90–121.

"The Burns Cage." *The Simpsons*. Written by Rob LaZebnik, directed by Rob Oliver, 20th Century–Fox, 3 Apr 2016.

The Craft. Written by Andrew Fleming and Peter Filardi, directed by Andrew Fleming, Columbia Pictures, 1996.

Daly, Mary. *Gyn/Ecology*, Women's P, 1979.

Donovan. "Season of the Witch." *Sunshine Superman*, EMI Studios, 1966.

"Double, Double, Boy in Trouble." *The Simpsons: The Complete Twentieth Season*. Written by Bill Odenkirk, directed by Nancy Kruse, 20th Century–Fox, 2008.

"Four Great Women and a Manicure." *The Simpson: The Complete Twentieth Season*. Written by Valentina L. Garza, directed by Raymond S. Persi, 20th Century–Fox, 2009.

Garber, Marjorie. *Shakespeare after All*. Anchor, 2004.

"Gump Roast." *The Simpsons: The Complete Thirteenth Season*. Written by Deb Lacusta and Dan Castellaneta, directed by Mark Kirkland, 20th Century–Fox, 2002.

Henry, Matthew. "'Don't Ask Me, I'm Just a Girl': Feminism, Female Identity, and *The Simpsons*." *The Journal of Popular Culture*, vol. 40, no. 2, 2007, pp. 272–303. *Project Muse*, doi: 10.1111/j.1540–5931.2007.00379.x.

McCormick Tribute Freedom Museum. "Characters from "The Simpsons" More Well Known to Americans than Their First Amendment Freedoms, Survey Finds." *McCormick Freedom Project*, 1 Mar 2006, http://documents.mccormickfoundation.org/news/2006/pr030106.aspx.

Miller, Rick, and William Shakespeare. *MacHomer*. 1995.

"Much Apu About Nothing." *The Simpsons: The Complete Seventh Season*. Written by David S. Cohen, directed by Susie Dietter, 20th Century–Fox, 1996.

Purkiss, Diane. *The Witch in History: Early Modern and Twentieth-century Representations.* Routledge, 1996.

"Rednecks and Broomsticks." *The Simpsons.* Written by Kevin Curran, directed by Bob Anderson and Rob Oliver, 20th Century–Fox, 29 Nov 2009.

"The Regina Monologues." *The Simpsons: The Complete Fifteenth Season.* Written by John Swartzwelder, directed by Mark Kirkland, 20th Century–Fox, 2003.

"Rome-Old and Julie-Eh." *The Simpsons: The Complete Eighteenth Season.* Written by Daniel Chun, directed by Nancy Kruse, 20th Century–Fox, 2007.

Rosen, Barbara, Ed. *Witchcraft in England, 1558–1618.* U of Massachusetts P, 1991.

"Selma's Choice." *The Simpsons: The Complete Fourth Season.* Written by David M. Stern, directed by Carlos Baeza, 20th Century–Fox, 1993.

Shakespeare, William. *Macbeth.* Edited by Nicholas Brooke, Oxford UP, 1990.

Sharpe, James. *Instruments of Darkness: Witchcraft in Early Modern England,* U of Pennsylvania P, 1996.

"She of Little Faith." *The Simpsons: The Complete Thirteenth Season.* Written by Bill Freiberger, directed by Steven Dean Moore, 20th Century–Fox, 2001.

"Springfield Up." *The Simpsons: The Complete Eighteenth Season.* Written by Matt Warburton, directed by Chuck Sheetz, 20th Century–Fox, 2007.

"That '90s Show." *The Simpsons.* Written by Matt Selman, directed by Mark Kirkland, 20th Century–Fox, 27 Jan 2008.

"There's Something about Marrying." *The Simpsons: The Complete Sixteenth Season.* Written by J. Stewart Burns, directed by Nancy Kruse, 20th Century–Fox, 2005.

To Die For. Written by Buck Henry, directed by Gus Van Sant, Columbia Pictures, 1995.

"Treehouse of Horror VIII." *The Simpsons: The Complete Ninth Season.* Written by Mike Scully, David X. Cohen, and Ned Goldreyer, directed by Mark Kirkland, 20th Century–Fox, 1997.

"Treehouse of Horror XVI." *The Simpsons: The Complete Seventeenth Season.* Written by Marc Wilmore, directed by David Silverman, 20th Century–Fox, 2005.

"Treehouse of Horror XIX." *The Simpsons.* Written by Matt Warburton, directed by Bob Anderson, 20th Century–Fox, 2 Nov. 2008.

"The Way We Was." *The Simpsons: The Complete Second Season.* Written by Al Jean, Mike Reiss, and Sam Simon, directed by David Silverman, 20th Century–Fox, 1991.

Wiesner-Hanks, Merry E. *Women and Gender in Early Modern Europe.* 2nd ed., Cambridge UP, 2000.

Willis, Deborah. *Malevolent Nurture.* Cornell UP, 1995.

The Wizard of Oz. Written by Noel Langley, Florence Ryerson, and Edgar Allan Woolf, directed by Victor Fleming, et al., MGM, 1939.

"Owning Your Okayness"

The Simpsons as "Good Enough" Parents

Summer Block

Contemporary mothers and fathers are "helicopter parents" or so the common wisdom tells us. As their name suggests, helicopter parents hover around their children, micromanaging every moment of their lives. The cosseted existence of modern children is often set in opposition to the bad old days of the 1970s and '80s, when kids walked to and from school by themselves, played outside without supervision, watched vast quantities of low-quality television, and ate snacks loaded with every kind of artificial color and flavor.

In this respect, Bart, Lisa, and Maggie seem to enjoy a childhood more like what you would expect to find in 1969 than in 1989, the year of the series' debut. In fact, 1989 marks the beginning of the era of the Helicopter Parent (the phrase itself would be coined the following year, in 1990) (Cline and Fay 23–25). The anarchic (and sometimes appalling) freedom of the Simpson children and the relative laxity of their parents is both a nostalgic nod to a lost era and a suggestion to perfectionist parents that kids can survive and even thrive without constant coddling.

In contrast to over-involved, fretful, and neurotic helicopter parents, Homer and Marge exemplify an old-fashioned style of parenting that may seem lax and even dangerous by contemporary standards. However, they exemplify what pediatrician and psychoanalyst D.W. Winnicott called the "good enough mother," a phrase he coined in 1973 (Winnicott 188). Later, Bruno Betelheim would expand on the idea of the "good enough parent" (and not just the mother) in his 1987 book, *A Good Enough Parent: A Book on Child-Rearing*. Betelheim states that if a child has a mother or father who is generally stable, supportive, and loving, he or she will flourish, even in a less-than-perfect environment. Through their consistent love and devotion, Homer and Marge are "good enough" parents, and a comforting reminder to parents of the helicopter generation that you don't have to be perfect to be a successful parent.

How are Marge and Homer good enough, when they so often fail? To understand how they succeed, we can compare their parenting to the more modern type. A key component of helicopter parenting is trying to make every small moment of a child's day magical, stimulating, educational, or otherwise worthy, leading parents to fear that they've failed if their children suffer any small setback or disappointment, or if they slip and allow their children do something unhealthful or otherwise forbidden, even once. While Homer and Marge do a poor job with the day-to-day "small stuff" of parenting (for example, allowing their children to eat junk food or watch too much television), they prove their devotion to their children in key moments of self-sacrifice, love, and devotion, many times putting their children's needs above their own. This serves as a comforting reassurance to modern parents that you don't have to be perfect every moment to be successful, as long as you get the big things right.

Of course, the examples of bad parenting in *The Simpsons* are legion, from letting their children watch the excessively violent cartoon *Itchy and Scratchy* and play mindless video games like Cat Fight, to serving them unhealthy snack cakes at dinner. The children are almost never supervised, even baby Maggie.

Yet against this backdrop of everyday failures there stand out dozens of examples of good parenting, too. "Lisa the Beauty Queen" (4.4) opens with a school fair at Springfield Elementary, where Lisa sits for an unflattering caricature that causes her to lose confidence in her appearance. The carnival goes better for her father, who wins the raffle's grand prize, a ride on the Duff Blimp. Homer is elated, but after seeing how dejected Lisa feels about her appearance, he sells the coveted blimp ticket to Barney for $250 and uses that money to enter Lisa into a beauty pageant. There is little reason to think Lisa would win a beauty pageant: not only is she not particularly pretty, but she lacks the temperament to win on charm or grace. Not surprisingly, she balks at entering the contest, but after Marge tells her about Homer's sacrifice, she agrees to participate.

The whole family pulls together to help Lisa prepare for the pageant. Even Bart teaches Lisa "the tricks of the trade: taping your swimsuit to your butt, petroleum jelly on your teeth for that frictionless smile, and the ancient art of padding." Supported by her family, Lisa rises to the occasion, and her earnest civic-minded speech and impressive musical performance earn her second place in the competition. When the winner is injured in a freak accident, Lisa is crowned Little Miss Springfield in her stead.

However, she is appalled to learn that one of her new duties as Little Miss Springfield is to serve as a spokesperson for Laramie Cigarettes. Lisa speaks out against the corporation (which is trying to lure young children into smoking), earning the ire of the mayor, the Laramie corporation, and the pageant organizers. This evil cabal looks for a technicality they can use to strip Lisa of her title, and they find it: Homer made a characteristically stupid mistake on the pageant entry form. Lisa is dethroned.

Homer apologizes to Lisa because his error cost her the Little Miss Springfield title, but she reminds him that the whole reason he ever got her involved with the pageant in the first place was so she could improve her self-esteem, and the support of her family, as well as her heroic stance against the Laramie corporation, allowed her to do just that.

In this episode, every member of the family sacrifices to support and help one another, from Homer selling his Duff Blimp ticket to Lisa swallowing her pride and agreeing to be in a pageant in the first place. Even Bart grudgingly admits his sister is "not ugly," a painful admission for a brother.

In "Saturdays of Thunder" (3.9), Homer has to sacrifice something even greater than a ride on a blimp: his own pride. The episode opens with Marge giving Homer a quiz from the National Fatherhood Institute to determine his "fatherhood quotient." Predictably, he fails miserably:

> **Marge:** What are your son's hobbies?
> **Homer:** He's always chewing on that phone cord.
> **Marge:** He hasn't done that since he was two.
> **Homer:** Then he has no hobbies.

Marge suggests Homer see for himself, and so he discovers Bart building a soapbox derby car in their garage. Committed to changing course, Homer signs up for a father-son soapbox derby race. Homer's poorly constructed soapbox racer leaves Bart in last place, and Bart leaps at the chance to race Martin's expertly crafted car instead. Homer is hurt by his son's betrayal and refuses to cheer him on in his final race against Martin. Marge is surprisingly harsh in condemning Homer.

> **Marge:** Don't you have something to say to Bart?
> **Homer:** No. Can't think of a thing.
> **Marge:** I've always said you were a good father. I've always defended you when people put you down… But I guess I was wrong. You are a bad father.
> **Homer:** Leave me alone.

She seems to grudgingly accept that a good father might still not be able to name his son's friends, his heroes, or his hobbies, but refusing to support and encourage him is going too far. Homer recognizes that a good father would support his son and encourage his success, even at the cost of losing face over his own failed racer design. Homer apologizes and wishes

Bart good luck, and Bart goes on to win the race (even if he's not exactly gracious about it).

In the world of *The Simpsons*, kids inhabit their own separate sphere of action. From the time the last school bell rings to when your mother calls you for dinner, your time is largely your own. This might look familiar to an earlier generation of Americans who, like Bart and Lisa, ranged around the suburbs on bikes or holed up in secret forts and tree houses away from parental supervision. This lines up research that suggests that even though there were more stay-at-home mothers in the 1960s than there are today, they actually spent less total time with their kids, leaving them to be entertained by their siblings and friends (and sometimes, by their TVs) (Parker and Wang). Today's helicopter parents are more likely to sit beside their child, overseeing one of his many curated after-school extracurricular activities, and so to them, not being able to name their children's hobbies is simply absurd: they *chose* their children's hobbies. (In fact, when *Stranger Things*, a thriller set in 1980s suburban Indiana, debuted on Netflix in 2016, millennials on social media decried the show as unrealistic less for its depiction of interdimensional monsters and telekinetic children than of kids who spend all day riding bicycles through the woods alone and without helmets.) *The Simpsons* suggests that it's not necessarily a parent's place to micro-manage every facet of their children's lives, but it is their place to offer love and encouragement.

One frequent criticism of helicopter parenting is that it's really all about stroking the parents' ego, whether by earning accolades from other parents on social media platforms or by raising a child successful enough to provide them with "my child is a doctor" bragging rights. This criticism is ungenerous and often unfair—the most common reasons people become overly involved parents are guilt and anxiety, not pride—but it's true that there is often a public element to modern parenting, a sense that parenting choices must be validated through Facebook likes and Instagram comments. While this episode (which aired in 1991) predates social media, its concern with the real business of parenting was as relevant then as now. It's not about the photo-worthy race finish (or the brag-worthy Harvard admission letter), but about treating children with love. By allowing Bart to compete without him and win, Homer is also allowing his son to be independent and to exist as a separate person, not a mere extension of his father's ego, which is perhaps the most important and difficult task in parenting.

In the examples we've given so far, Homer is the "bad parent," but Marge is also far from perfect. Though more involved than her husband in the children's day-to-day affairs, she also projects onto them her many neuroses and anxieties. From letting her fear of flying ruin a family vacation ("Fear of Flying" 6.11) to shouting at her kids for humiliating her at a tony country club

("Scenes from the Class Struggle in Springfield" 7.14), Marge has her flaws. But where Homer is unashamedly crass and boorish, Marge's parenting mistakes often stem from her desperate need to make nice and keep up appearances at all costs.

In "Moaning Lisa" (1.6), when Lisa becomes depressed and listless, Marge gives her the disastrously bad advice, "It doesn't matter how you feel inside, you know. It's what shows up on the surface that counts. Take all your bad feelings and push them down, all the way down, past your knees, until you're almost walking on them. And then you'll fit in, and you'll be invited to parties, and boys will like you … and happiness will follow."

In a dream/flashback, it's revealed that Marge received similar advice when she was a girl, and she's clearly taken it to heart. She's grown accustomed to swallowing her anger and disappointment and now she expects her daughter to do the same. But when Marge watches Lisa smile through schoolyard bullying, she has a dramatic change of heart. Marge says, "Lisa, I apologize to you. I was wrong. I take it all back. Always be yourself. If you want to be sad, honey, be sad. We'll ride it out with you. And when you get finished feeling sad, we'll still be there. From now on, let me do the smiling for both of us."

"And Maggie Makes Three" (6.13) may be the most powerful and affecting of all the many *Simpsons* plots centered on parenting (and arguably parenting—or more broadly, how to live in a family—is one of the show's most salient and perennial themes). In one of the run's most sentimental episodes, we learn that years before, Homer had quit his miserable job at the nuclear power plant and landed his dream job working at a bowling alley. Not only did Homer love working at the bowling alley, but he was good at it (at least as good as he ever is at anything)—he had truly found his passion and calling in life. However, when Marge became unexpectedly pregnant with Maggie, Homer was forced to leave his dream job and return, quite literally groveling, to Mr. Burns, begging for his old job at the power plant. Burns agreed to let Homer return but punished him for his disloyalty by hanging a sign at his desk that read, "Don't forget: you're here forever." After instantly bonding with his baby daughter at birth, Homer realizes that this tremendous and painful sacrifice was worth it. He plasters photos of Maggie all over Burns' sign until it now reads, "Do it for her."

Many episodes revolve around Homer making financial sacrifices for his family. In some ways, this harkens back to the traditional role of patriarch as sole provider. However, it also reminds us that families without large incomes are more often forced into making difficult choices for the sake of their children. While anyone can be a helicopter parent (and indeed, people of all income brackets do just that), helicopter parenting is largely associated with upper middle-class parents who can afford to pay for organic teething biscuits and toddler yoga lessons with relatively little sacrifice. (Of course, these parents have not only the money to buy their children things, but the leisure time to embark on unnecessarily time-consuming tasks like making all their baby food from scratch, tasks that are far more likely to fall by the wayside when a parent is tired, stressed, and overworked with one, two, or even three jobs.)

In "Lisa's Sax" (9.3), we learn that Homer had saved up $200 for a much-needed air conditioner but spent it instead on a saxophone to encourage Lisa's musical talents and support her as a gifted child. This, of course, becomes Lisa's most beloved object and sole creative outlet—and so when Bart destroys the saxophone, Homer dips into the air conditioner fund yet again to buy Lisa a new one.

In the later seasons, *The Simpsons* addresses the issue of helicopter parenting directly. In "Father Knows Worst" (20.14), Homer's taste buds become so super-sensitive he is forced to take his meals in the Springfield Elementary school cafeteria (where the food is bland enough to not inflame his senses). Since he's spending all day at the elementary school, it's no wonder he runs into a helicopter mom, who is also hovering about the elementary school, cosseting her son, Noah. When she mocks Homer's parenting and his children's failures, Homer decides to follow her lead. He takes over Bart's school sculpture assignment, determined to build a challenging Westminster Abbey balsa wood model on his own. At the same time, he pressures Lisa into becoming one of the "popular girls" at her school.

Homer forces Bart out, insisting he can complete the model himself, but predictably, he fails. At the competition, surrounded by what is obviously the work of other helicopter parents, Superintendent Chalmers declares that Bart (really, Homer) is the only one whose flawed model looks like a child actually made it and declares Bart the winner. Bart reveals that it was Homer who made the model. (Meanwhile, Lisa decides she isn't up for the work of being popular and she'd prefer to go back to her bookworm ways.) "I tried to fix the kids' lives," Homer says despondently, "But instead, I led them to rich and rewarding personal decisions of their own."

This 2009 episode sits in interesting contrast to "Saturdays of Thunder," which aired in 1991. In the earlier episode, Homer is hurt when Bart tries to do something on his own but swallows his pride for the good of his son. In "Father Knows Worst," Homer insists on doing his son's work for him, and Bart is the one who rises to the occasion, admitting the truth rather than accepting an award under false pretenses. Maybe the Simpsons are teaching their kids some valuable lessons after all.

In the preface to *The Good Enough Parent*, Betelheim says, "In order to raise a child well one ought not to try to be a perfect parent, as much as one should not expect one's child to be, or to become, a perfect individual. Perfection is not within the grasp of ordinary human beings" (Betelheim xi). It's normal and even healthy to be impatient, to get frustrated. "There are few loves which are entirely free of ambivalence," Betelheim says (23). "Not only is our love for our children sometimes tinged with annoyance, discouragement, and disappointment, the same is true for the love our children feel for us." He concludes, "While we are not perfect, we are indeed good enough parents if most of the time we love our children and do our best to do well by them" (Betelheim 344). *The Simpsons* premiered at a time when American parents were beginning to look back on their own childhoods with retroactive alarm at their own parents' permissiveness. In their decades on air, the pressure on parents has only intensified. Now, every day on social media brings a slew of curated Instagram snapshots of perfect parenting moments, braggy posts by over-involved mommy bloggers, and scare stories about the dangers of everything from too much screen time to too little vitamin D. Every moment of a child's life has to be carefully managed, from pregnancy on. In this anxiety-provoking new landscape, *The Simpsons* reminds parents that being "good enough" is best.

Works Cited

"And Maggie Makes Three." *The Simpsons: The Complete Sixth Season.* Written by Jennifer Crittenden, directed by Swinton O. Scott III, 20th Century–Fox, 1995.

Betelheim, Bruno. *The Good Enough Parent: A Book on Child Rearing.* Vintage, 1978.

Cline, Foster W. and Jim Fay. *Parenting with Love and Logic: Teaching Children Responsibility.* Pinon Press, 1990.

"Father Knows Worst." *The Simpsons: The Complete Twentieth Season.* Written by Rob LaZebnik, directed by Matthew Nastuk, 20th Century–Fox, 2009.

"Fear of Flying." *The Simpsons: The Complete Seventh Season.* Written by David Sacks, directed by Mark Kirkland, 20th Century–Fox, 1994.

"Lisa the Beauty Queen." *The Simpsons: The Complete Fourth Season.* Written by Jeff Martin, directed by Mark Kirkland, 20th Century–Fox, 1992.

"Lisa's Sax." *The Simpsons: The Complete Ninth Season.* Written by Dominic Polcino, directed by Al Jean, 20th Century–Fox, 1997.

"Moaning Lisa." *The Simpsons: The Complete First Season.* Written by Al Jean and Mike Reiss, directed by Wes Archer, 20th Century–Fox, 1990.

Parker, Kim and Wendy Wang. "Modern Parenthood: Roles of Moms and Dads Converge as They Balance Work and Family." Pew Research Center, 14 March 2013, http://www.pewsocialtrends.org/2013/03/14/modern-parenthood-roles-of-moms-and-dads-converge-as-they-balance-work-and-family/5/#chapter-4-how-mothers-and-fathers-spend-their-time.

"Saturdays of Thunder." *The Simpsons: The Complete Third Season.* Written by Kevin Levine and David Isaacs, directed by Jim Reardon, 20th Century–Fox, 1991.

"Scenes from the Class Struggle in Springfield." *The Simpsons: The Complete Seventh Season.* Written by Jennifer Crittenden, directed by Susie Dietter, 20th Century–Fox, 1996.

Winnicott, D.W. *The Child, the Family, and the Outside World.* Perseus Publishing, 1973.

Be Sharp

The Simpsons *and Music*

Durrell Bowman

Introduction

The Simpsons includes a large amount of music. Over the course of twenty-nine seasons and more than six hundred episodes (1989–2018), composer Alf Clausen (from 1990 to 2017), music editor Chris Ledesma, various writers, and the rest of the show's creative team have used music in numerous ways. The six main categories of music on *The Simpsons* are:

1. about 375 instances of original songs
2. more than 11,000 background instrumental music "cues" (segments)
3. several dozen end title and opening title variations of Danny Elfman's main theme
4. an average of at least two references per episode to existing music
5. at least sixty text references to existing pieces of music, such as within episode titles
6. approximately 170 musicians as special guests

Many episodes include examples from all, or most, of those categories. In terms of genres and styles, the show's music includes rock, rock 'n' roll, film and TV music, country, R&B, soul, instrumental pop, disco, and rap. It also includes classical music, jazz, the blues, spirituals, folk, musical theatre, and Tin Pan Alley pop. In addition, it includes electronic Euro-pop, reggae, Asian pop, and other types of world music. *The Simpsons* provides a very rich site for exploring the music-related contexts of its creators, characters, and audience.

The show's music updates the way music functioned culturally in the classic short cartoons of the 1940s, '50s, and early '60s. People numbering in the tens of millions (but perhaps especially adolescents, teenagers, and college students) first heard certain pop song standards, jazz, opera, and/or instrumental art music when such cartoons were first screened in cinemas and, even more so, when they appeared on television in the 1970s and '80s. In the 1990s and 2000s, a similar number of people heard certain music for the first time on *The Simpsons*.

Even an individual episode can reference, re-work, and make fun of music and other cultural forms from a variety of sources. The show can thus be said to be "intertextual"—as in "between" or "across" texts. In addition, the show derives from and enables the encountering of relevant songs and music in other cartoons, TV shows, and movies; in music lessons and courses; and on radio and the internet. Regardless of an individual viewer's starting point, the show's music feeds back into an ongoing, interpretive community of knowledge, understanding, and attitudes concerning genre, style, songs, artists, and references. Indeed, the possibility since the late 1990s of immediately downloading or streaming songs on the internet has vastly increased the possibility of many *Simpsons'* fans further listening to certain songs, genres, and artists after first encountering them on the show.

"Homer's Barbershop Quartet"

One might reasonably wonder why and how "Homer's Barbershop Quartet" (5.1) would use a pleasantly-melodic, old-fashioned genre of vocal music that emerged in the early 20th century. The "why" is that writer Jeff Martin had recently heard a live barbershop group. The episode thus uses an off-the-wall musical style somewhat more extensively than is typical for the show, although the show also based "Colonel Homer" (3.20) around country music and has also created extended parodies of musical theatre and other genres. "Homer's Barbershop Quartet," though, makes numerous references to the Beatles as well. Martin was a Beatles fan before he heard the live barbershop group, but he then combined them. The episode, however, also includes many references to additional types of music and thus provides an excellent place to explore the show's creative ability to sustain a music-themed episode.

We usually think of barbershop music as a white form, but it began among African Americans around the turn of the 20th century. By the time mainly whites were performing it, as of the 1940s, the resultant music was already considered to be part of a revival. The genre usually features four unaccompanied voices (most often male), clear structures, tonal harmonies, romantic lyrics, an earnest and heartfelt approach, a vertical/chordal texture, and the melody placed in the second-highest voice. One of the most frequently-heard barbershop quartets is the Dapper Dans, who perform live at Disneyland.

The Dapper Dans partly inspired the episode and were brought in to help increase the authenticity of the episode's barbershop singing, especially by supporting the harmonies around a lead vocal sung by Homer Simpson or Barney Gumble (who are both voiced by Dan Castellaneta) or, early in the episode, by Chief Wiggum (Hank Azaria).

Within the episode's first of several extended flashbacks, the original, amateur, recreational version of the barbershop group (Wiggum, Principal Skinner, Apu, and Homer) sing "Hello! Ma Baby" for Barney and Moe at Moe's Tavern. "Hello! Ma Baby" is best-known from its use in a jazz/swing-accompanied solo tenor version sung by "Michigan J. Frog" in Chuck Jones' 1955 Looney Tunes (Warner Bros.) cartoon called "One Froggy Evening." During the quartet's performance, Barney (not yet discovered as Wiggum's replacement) acts like a swooning groupie, throwing panties, roses, and keys to the group and coyly waving a handkerchief. As the episode switches back to the present, Bart claims (in "grizzled, 1890s prospector" style) that barbershop "ain't been popular since ought six, dag nabit." In fact, "ought six" (1906) is remarkably consistent with the period of the initial, ragtime-era fad for barbershop performances of Tin Pan Alley songs around the turn of the 20th century, and Joseph E. Howard and Ida Emerson's song "Hello! Ma Baby" (a barbershop "standard" related to the early telephone era) was published in 1899. The next flashback has the vocal group singing another barbershop standard, Les Applegate's 1924 song "Goodbye, My Coney Island Baby," at such venues as the local seniors' home, the local prison (temporarily placating the convicts), the local church, and Moe's Tavern.

At the church, Reverend Lovejoy opportunistically includes the group's performance of this song within a service to make his congregation happy, and they respond (as expected) by contributing heartily to the collection plate. Just before the performance at the church, we hear a plagal (IV–I, "Amen") cadence on the pipe organ, which resembles the end of a traditional, 19th-century church hymn. In fact, the highly-tonal harmonies of barbershop music closely resemble the harmonies of such hymns. The Simpsons' pious neighbor, Ned Flanders, points out to Lovejoy that the romantic, secular song is not a hymn, but the minister easily dismisses him. (Convenience store owner Apu also amplifies the non-church nature of the song by sneaking in the line: "Shop *Kwik-E-Mart* and save!") On the song's final cadence, the group ends its performance with visual jazz hands, although the setting has just segued back to Moe's Tavern. Entertainment manager Nigel (a smarmy Brit) begins to represent the group, and shortly thereafter, Barney replaces Wiggum and debuts with the group singing the lead of "Sweet Adeline" (1903, lyrics by Richard H.

Gerard, music by Harry Armstrong). Moe suspects that Nigel must have paid women to scream for the group, but the enthusiasm is posited as genuine. The locally-ascendant group then selects its name, rejecting Nigel's suggestion of "Handsome Homer Simpson Plus Three" and going with Skinner's recommendation of "something that's witty at first, but that seems less funny each time you hear it": Apu's perfectly-apt suggestion of the "Be Sharps."

At the beginning of the episode's Act II, we are back in the present (1993) as the Simpsons leave the Springfield Swap Meet at which Lisa and Bart have encountered an LP by the Be Sharps. On their drive home, they experience a flat tire, and Homer continues with the group's story of attempting find a more topical hit than the 1899–1924 barbershop songs that the group had so far been performing. One of Homer's attempts (after dozens of similar failures) is based lyrically on the fact that Geraldo Rivera's overly-hyped 1986 opening of Al Capone's vault resulted in no stunning discoveries (such as drugs or corpses). Marge arrives with a "Baby on Board" car sign and Homer, at the family's piano, begins to compose/sing: "Baby on board, something something Burt Ward." (Ward played Robin in the campy 1960s *Batman* TV series.) The group then records the resultant song, with Skinner accompanying on banjo, but with piano, drums, and string bass also later added. The inclusion of such instruments significantly deflects from the authenticity of this song as barbershop music, but the episode's writers presumably wished to make the point that pop success often requires such compromises.

Nigel assures the Be Sharps that "Baby on Board" will be their "first number one," and this highly unlikely outcome does indeed happen. The song becomes a radio hit, and its gentle nature causes sea captain McAllister to end his battle with a giant squid. Then, at the 1986 centenary of the Statue of Liberty, the Be Sharps reprise "Goodbye, My Coney Island Baby." The group also sings "Baby on Board," which also suits the circumstances of the statue, which arrived in the U.S. in 1885 on board a French frigate. (Homer's dedication of the song to a "200-ton woman" frightens a dignitary, who jumps into the harbor.) Despite the Be Sharps' success in 1986, however, the group's career quickly wanes, with unsuccessful songs about such topics as Surgeon General C. Everett Koop and *The A-Team*'s Mr. T.

The Beatles

At the Springfield Swap Meet in the episode's opening scene, Marge unsuccessfully attempts to sell not only wishbone necklaces, but also some of her various artworks. These include a painting of Beatles's drummer Ringo Starr that is similar (but not identical) to her childhood one featured in "Brush with Greatness" (1991). Among Comic Book Guy's LP record offerings, Lisa spots a copy of *Meet the Be Sharps*. The album cover parodies the title and the cover of *Meet the Beatles!* (Capitol, 1964). Lisa and Bart, however, have never heard of the Be Sharps.

Later, Nigel's directive to fire Chief Wiggum from the group is modeled on the Beatles having fired their original drummer Pete Best (in favor of Ringo Starr) just after their first professional recording sessions in the summer of 1962. After Barney replaces Wiggum, we notice that Moe has changed the name on his establishment's outdoor sign from "Moe's Tavern" to "Moe's Cavern," thus referencing Liverpool's "The Cavern," a venue at which the early Beatles frequently performed as a kind of "house band" (still with Pete Best) in 1961–62.

Another Beatles' reference appears as Nigel convinces married group member Homer to keep his marriage to Marge ("bouffant Betty") a secret, so that female groupies (such as in Sweden) will want to have sex with him. This relates to the historical account of attempts having been made in the mid–1960s to keep the marriages of several of the Beatles relatively hidden. Later, the Be Sharps emerge from a private jet to encounter screaming fans at New York City's John F. Kennedy Airport. They also answer questions with an approximation of American-reporter-duping, dry, British wit at a news conference. The scenario comes almost verbatim out of the Beatles' arrival in the U.S. in early 1964.

At a party after the Be Sharps win a Grammy award, former Beatle George Harrison introduces himself to Homer, but Homer's resultant enthusiasm results not from meeting a celebrity more famous even than himself, but from ascertaining the source of the brownie Harrison is enjoying.

In Act III, now back at home in 1993, Homer takes out a box of Be Sharps' merchandise, Lisa expresses surprise at the group's short-lived fame, and Bart asks: "What did you do, screw up like the Beatles and say you were bigger than Jesus?" Homer replies that they claimed that all the time and that the Be Sharps' second album was named after John Lennon's 1966 interview quip. The cover of *Bigger Than Jesus* is based visually on the cover of the Beatles' *Abbey Road* (1969).

In a related matter within the resumed flashback, Barney starts hanging out with his new Japanese conceptual-artist girlfriend—a parody of Yoko Ono—and himself thus approximates an overweight version of late-Beatles' or 1970s era John Lennon.

Barney explains to the rest of the Be Sharps that he wants to take barbershop music to "strange, new places," and he plays for them his new recorded collaboration with "Yoko," featuring her repeated recitation of the phrase "Number 8" in alternation with Barney's characteristic belching. The collaboration thus somewhat parodies the experimental Beatles' "music concrète" song "Revolution No. 9" from 1968's *The White Album* (a.k.a., *The Beatles*).

Toward the end of the episode and back in the present, Homer picks up his copy of *Meet the Be Sharps*. Although the album's front cover parodies *Meet the Beatles!*, its back cover—"featuring" Homer's butt crack—parodies the back cover of the Beatles' *Sgt Pepper's Lonely Hearts Club Band* (1967). Homer then contacts his old band mates for a reunion.

On a downtown Springfield rooftop, the Be Sharps reprise their several-year-old hit "Baby on Board," during which George Harrison pulls up in a limo, making a brief second appearance to exclaim: "It's been done!" He means by this the Beatles' 1969 performance of "Get Back" and other songs on the London rooftop of Apple Records, which similarly took place several years after the group had given up concert touring in August of 1966. In a further parallel, Apu refers to the Be Sharps' reunion "last year, on that stupid Dame Edna special," which thus suggests a media-related event somewhat akin to the Beatles' post-touring, one-off live performance of "All You Need is Love" for the world's first global TV broadcast in June of 1967.

The outfits worn on the rooftop by Homer, Barney, Skinner, and Apu are modeled after the contrasting outfits that were worn in 1969 by Ringo, John, Paul, and George, respectively. This retains Barney as John, and it also subtly connects Apu (who is of Indian/Hindu heritage) with George, the Beatle who was the most associated with Indian music and culture. Additionally, Chief Wiggum approves a long-deferred revenge for having been kicked out of the group by sanctioning his officers' use of tear gas to end the Be Sharps' performance.

In the last phrase of the song, additional instruments (i.e., a clarinet and muted trumpets and other brass instruments), which are not present in the scene or, in fact, in the ending of the original recording, merge with the "live" performance and give it something of the flavor of Dixieland jazz. As the first of the end credits roll during the applause at the end of "Baby on Board," Homer replicates John Lennon's somewhat cheeky words: "I'd like to thank you on behalf of the group, and I hope we passed the audition." Lennon's quip was also inserted, along with applause, at the very end of what is otherwise a studio recording of "Get Back" at the very end the band's last-released album, 1970's *Let It Be*. In the reference on *The Simpsons*, Homer's comment makes the Springfield audience laugh, but oblivious Barney then says: "I don't get it," which provides an ironic comment about cultural literacy. Numerous additional *Simpsons'* episodes reference the Beatles, but the total makes up only about two percent of the show's music.

Other Music

Alf Clausen's jazz-band instrumentation at the end of the final version of "Baby on Board" and the show's usual use of a version of Danny Elfman's theme for the end credits are joined in the episode by additional non-barbershop/non–Beatles music references. During the episode's opening titles' sequence, Bart's chalkboard detention involves writing "I Will Never Win an Emmy." However, by the fall of 1993 (the beginning of the show's fifth season), *The Simpsons* had already won four such awards, and it later won dozens more, including two for music in 1996–97. Meanwhile, shortly after this Emmy reference, the episode's continuing use of Danny Elfman's 1989 opening titles' theme (which was nominated for a 1990 Emmy for Outstanding Title Theme) incorporates one of Lisa's many, vaguely jazzy saxophone solos as she disrupts and exits Mr. Largo's music classroom.

As is often the case on the show, this episode's opening scene (the beginning of Act I) begins with one of Alf Clausen's relatively light, brief, and conventionally-orchestrated (brass, winds, strings, and tuned percussion) version of Elfman's main tune. This episode spends much of its time in extended flashbacks, so each act begins with a theme reference to "reset" the proceedings not only back to *The Simpsons*, but also back to the episode's present of 1993 (the Simpson family as we usually encounter it). Later, a slower strings-and-winds cut time reference to the theme begins Act II, as the family heads back home after an outing. However, the theme reference at the beginning of Act III (with the family back at home) features a twangy banjo-like style, which is consistent with Principal Skinner's use of that instrument to accompany the Be Sharps.

At the beginning of the episode, we arrive at the Springfield Swap Meet, and the initial booth offerings include a military collector who has Principal Skinner's Vietnam-era prisoner mask, the number of which, 24601, references Jean Valjean's prisoner designation in the 1980 musical *Les Misérables*. Then, Homer encounters an old lady (Mrs. Feesh, the church organist) who is selling for 5¢ each such priceless items as a Stradivarius violin (early 18th century), which Homer dismisses as "junk." Even Comic Book Guy is selling not comic books at all, but old music LPs. These records include Krusty the Clown's *S' Wonderful—S'Marvelous—S' Krusty*, which is a title parody of George and Ira Gershwin's 1927 song "'S Wonderful" (originally used in the musical *Funny Face*). The LPs also include an album by "Melvin and the Squirrels," which the proprietor describes to Bart and Lisa as having been a part of the "rodent invasion of the early '60s," which is a parody of the children's music pop group Alvin and the Chipmunks.

Comic Book Guy explains this rodent context further by playing an example from the "scratchy LP" that parodies the type of tape manipulations "David Seville" (Ross Bagdasarian, Sr.) used to produce the high, chipmunk voices of Alvin and the others. The excerpt comprises a version of "Yankee Doodle" that ends with "Rice-A-Roni" instead of "macaroni." Shortly afterwards, Homer suggests (in one of his remarkable leaps of logic) that in 1985 rock 'n' roll had become stagnant and "Achy Breaky Heart" was still seven years away. The episode doesn't mention this connection (although it certainly may have inspired writer Jeff Martin), but the Alvin and the Chipmunks' highly-successful country-themed album *Chipmunks in Low Places* (1992, comprising original songs and cover versions) includes a version of "Achy Breaky Heart." Around the same time, "Weird Al" Yankovic, who later appeared as himself in *The Simpsons* episode "Three Gays of the Condo" (14.17) and "That '90s Show" (19.11), released the parody song "Achy Breaky Song" (1993). In it, he recounts what he considers to be more pleasant alternatives to hearing Cyrus' hit song, including the Village People and Yoko Ono.

As is the case in most of the more than 600 *Simpsons'* episodes, Alf Clausen's post-production instrumental music cues also add to the musical fullness of this episode. For example, as Homer begins to recount his earlier rise and fall as an unlikely pop star between the summer of 1985 and 1988, gentle, string- and piano-based music sneaks onto the soundtrack to accompany the overly-heightened nostalgia for such cultural "achievements" as Joe Piscopo leaving *Saturday Night Live* to "conquer Hollywood," PEOPLExpress introducing "a generation of hicks to plane travel," and Homer singing in a barbershop quartet. Appropriately, this initial instance of non-theme-related underscoring prepares the episode's first flashback. Orchestral cues also occur in later scenes (usually within flashbacks), for Homer taking wide-eyed puppy Chief Wiggum for a car ride to abandon him (after he is fired from the group), for Homer complaining about the lousy auditions for finding Wiggum's replacement, for Homer later losing faith in his career as a celebrity, for Marge attempting to compensate for Homer's frequent absences, and for Homer deciding to reunite the Be Sharps. For the latter, Clausen provides a plaintive, instrumental variation of the barbershop song "Goodbye, My Coney Island Baby."

The episode includes numerous additional references to existing music. For example, when Nigel begins to represent the barbershop quartet group, he finds Chief Wiggum "too Village People," a reference to the contrasting character-performers, including a uniformed policeman, of that disco-era pop group of the late 1970s. The dismal audition-prospects for Wiggum's replacement include Grampa Simpson, singing a 1930s swing-era-inspired version of the folk song "Old MacDonald Had a Farm"; Groundskeeper Willie, singing a heavily Scottish version of Petula Clark's 1964 hit "Downtown"; and Grampa's friend Jasper, hilariously singing the repeated words "Theme from *A Summer Place*" to Max Steiner's usually-instrumental theme for that 1959 film. Then, Wiggum shows up in disguise, singing "If I Could Walk with the Animals" from the 1967 film musical *Doctor Doolittle*, which is also later parodied in "Cue Detective" (27.2).

As Homer complains about the lack of audition success while at Moe's

Tavern, the folk song "Tura-Lura-Lura (An Irish Lullaby)" (popularized by Bing Crosby in the 1944 film *Going My Way*) emanates from the men's restroom. Homer's friend Barney is the unexpected singer; he joins the barbershop group as its new fourth member, which results in Wiggum's manufacturing of an anti–Barney protest. Homer becomes sufficiently rich and famous to be able to buy Grampa a pink Cadillac, which parallels Elvis Presley's similar purchase for his mother near the beginning of his success (in 1955). Also, at a cocktail party after an awards ceremony, we hear light, piano-jazz music in the background. The episode takes a number of swipes at one of *The Simpsons'* favorite targets, the Grammy Awards, which Homer suggests are related to "record company low-lifes."

When the Be Sharps are presented with their 1987 Grammy by folk-rock singer-songwriter David Crosby, the semi-fictitious heavy metal band Spinal Tap (1978-, featuring prolific *Simpsons'* voice-actor Harry Shearer as its bass player) and rapper MC Hammer (who emerged in 1987 but by 1993 had largely fallen from fame) are present in the audience. Also, an Aretha Franklin–like soul singer, a bespectacled/pipe-smoking author, and a rival (mustachioed) barbershop quartet are the Be Sharps' competition for the ironic, ludicrously Frankenstein-like category of "Outstanding Soul, Spoken Word, or Barbershop Album of the Year."

The awards ceremony includes a tympani roll for the announcement of the Be Sharps as the winners and then a brief, instrumental work ironically reminiscent of "Hooray for Hollywood." As Homer begins to show signs of losing faith in his career as a celebrity, he gives his award statuette to a hotel bellhop, who is so dismayed that the award is merely a Grammy that he throws it over the side of the balcony into an alleyway, from which even the bum living there pronounces the award "garbage." When Homer phones home from Hollywood, Lisa (now about two years old and able to speak) for some reason suggests that he had beaten the relatively obscure, early-1980s British pop-soul group Dexys Midnight Runners, whose 1985 album had been so universally panned that it caused the breakup of the group in 1986. Homer, however, assures Lisa that "you haven't heard the last of them." Later, as Homer begins to recount the Be Sharps' final fall from glory as exemplifying an "iron law of show business," Bart adds Frank Sinatra to Lisa's suggestion of Bob Hope that this "law" does not necessarily hold for all performers.

Alf Clausen's Original Music, Emmy Awards and Departure from the Show

When hired in 1990 as the composer for *The Simpsons*, Alf Clausen was already a veteran TV music arranger and composer for such 1970s–'80s shows as *Donnie & Marie* and *Moonlighting*. His experience in jazz and pop band arrangements and background orchestral music served him well in his new role in constructing songs, instrumental music, and various other elements of music for *The Simpsons*. His instrumental music generally used either an orchestra or a chamber ensemble, but he also sometimes made use of jazz and electronic instruments, such as saxophones and synthesizers. The annual Treehouse of Horror (Halloween) episodes and similar fantasy sequences allowed him a certain amount of cartoon-like rein. Those episodes include electronic sounds that had become associated in the 1940s and '50s with such things as disturbed psyches and otherness in such psychological thrillers and science-fiction films as *Spellbound*, *The Lost Weekend*, *The Day the Earth Stood Still*, and *Forbidden Planet*.

Clausen received Emmy nominations for the dramatic underscore of nine Treehouse episodes from 1991–2010 and for additional episodes from 1993, 2001, and 2008. He also wrote the music for *The Simpsons'* numerous songs and mini-musicals, including prime-time Emmy song awards for the music of "We Put the Spring in Springfield" (1996) and "You're Checkin' In" (1997), with seven additional nominations for songs from 1994 to 2005.

Alf Clausen's Emmy-winning music for "We Put the Spring in Springfield" from "Bart after Dark" (8.5) evokes rambunctious dance-club music from the Jazz Age of the 1920s. The creators also certainly had in mind the revival of that style and setting in such musical theatre shows as *Chicago* (1975). The song, with lyrics by Ken Keeler, is an example of a foregrounded piece of music suddenly appearing out of nowhere to strengthen the show's narrative and characterizations. Early in the episode, Homer punishes Bart for one of his random acts of minor property damage by making him work at what turns out to be Springfield's burlesque house, the Maison Derrière. The context of the episode is loosely based on the 1978 country-oriented musical comedy, *The Best Little Whorehouse in Texas*, which is best known in its 1982 film version starring Dolly Parton and Burt Reynolds. Although the song mostly features female vocals, as in *Whorehouse*, the style of Clausen's song is 1920s Dixieland jazz, and he has also released an album of instrumental jazz music.

The episode's opening titles' couch-gag parodies the cover of the Beatles' 1967 album *Sgt. Pepper's Lonely Hearts Club Band* and slightly evokes the orchestral ending of its final song, "A Day in the Life." In fact, "Bart after Dark" has thirty-seven instances of music throughout. Those include the theme song, themes and other music for TV shows within the TV show, small things sung by Lisa and Bart, a title variation, whistling, background scoring, Offenbach's can-can stripper music, rim-shots, piano jazz, and an instrumental version of "We Put the Spring in Springfield" for the end titles.

Clausen's other Emmy-winning song, "You're Checkin' In" from "The

City of New York vs. Homer Simpson" (9.1), parodies contemporary Broadway musicals featuring updated socio-cultural commentaries—such as *Rent*. The made-up musical featuring the song is called *Kickin' It: A Musical Journey through the Betty Ford Center*. Ken Keeler's lyrics reference the real and film-role lives of famous actors struggling with drug addictions. The song thus skewers such out-of-control celebrities as Robert Downey, Jr., and Charlie Sheen.

Despite Alf Clausen's Emmy awards, numerous nominations, other awards, and undeniable dedication to *The Simpsons*, his status as the composer for the show was repeatedly in jeopardy from 2007 to 2017. Co-creator James L. Brooks has had a long-standing friendship with German-born Hollywood film composer Hans Zimmer. For example, as a writer/director, Brooks hired Zimmer to score *I'll Do Anything* (1994)—which, interestingly, begins with someone failing to win an Emmy award. He also hired him to score *Spanglish* (2004), *As Good as It Gets* (2007), and *How Do You Know* (2010). Even though Clausen had also worked in film scoring (mainly as an orchestrator), Brooks again chose to hire Zimmer to score *The Simpsons Movie* (2007), including the *Spider-Man* parody "Spider Pig." Five years later, he also hired him to score the *Simpsons* short film: *The Longest Daycare* (2012). Clausen stoically persevered beyond the movie and short film snubs and continued to compose the TV music for *The Simpsons,* until he was fired in 2017 after working on the show for twenty-seven years. Ironically, Clausen had already long proven himself quite capable of writing in Zimmer's style by parodying his plaintive, semi-electronic, partly percussion oriented, Grammy-winning score for *Crimson Tide* (1995) in the *Simpsons* episode "Simpson Tide" (9.19).

Alf Clausen's approach to the music for *The Simpsons* included composing for combinations of orchestral and/or other live instrumentalists. For some of the several dozen music elements per episode, that included an orchestra of up to thirty-five performers. Those musicians were recorded on a sound stage at the studio, with the music timed to synchronize with the relevant scenes from the episode being completed. The composer conducted his own scores, and various additional staff members worked in an adjacent room. The approach was quite expensive, although it allowed Clausen to build a library from which he could sometimes revisit certain musical moments for thematic continuity across related stories and/or emotional content.

Not surprisingly, as of Season 29, the music for *The Simpsons*—apart from Alf Clausen's for "Whistler's Father" (29.3)—has been entrusted to Hans Zimmer. Each episode's score is credited to his external production firm, Bleeding Fingers Music, produced by Zimmer and his colleague Russell Emanuel and executive produced by his business partner Steve

Kofsky. In addition to involving Zimmer in a renewed and substantial way, the Bleeding Fingers approach saves on the cost of recording live musicians and makes more money for Fox TV and James L. Brooks' Gracie Films. Meanwhile, during the 2017–18 season, Alf Clausen began to be listed in end credits of *The Simpsons* as its Composer Emeritus.

Conclusion

The Simpsons uses a wide variety of music, including original songs, instrumental underscoring, and references. "Homer's Barbershop Quartet" (5.1) provides an example of the show maintaining a music-centered theme for an entire episode. It weaves together new and existing barbershop songs, references to the Beatles, and various additional types of music. TV music and jazz veteran Alf Clausen worked as the composer and conductor of *The Simpsons* from 1990 to 2017. He won several music-related Emmy awards for his contributions to the show and was nominated for many additional ones. However, he left the show in 2017 and was listed in subsequent episodes as its "Composer Emeritus."

Music on *The Simpsons* enables numerous ways for us to explore and interpret the contexts of the show's creators, characters, and audience.

Works Cited

"Bart After Dark." *The Simpsons: The Complete Eighth Season.* Written by Richard Appel, directed by Dominic Polcino, 20th Century–Fox, 1996.

"Brush with Greatness." *The Simpsons: The Complete Second Season.* Written by Brian K. Roberts, directed by Jim Reardon, 20th Century–Fox, 1991.

"The City of New York vs. Homer Simpson." *The Simpsons: The Complete Ninth Season.* Written by Ian Maxtone-Graham, directed by Jim Reardon, 20th Century–Fox, 1997.

"Colonel Homer." *The Simpsons: The Complete Third Season.* Written by Matt Groening, directed by Mark Kirkland, 20th Century–Fox, 1992.

"'Cue Detective." *The Simpsons.* Written by Joel H. Cohen, directed by Timothy Bailey, 20th Century–Fox, 4 Oct 2015.

"Homer's Barbershop Quartet." *The Simpsons: The Complete Fifth Season.* Written by Jeff Martin, directed by Mark Kirkland, 20th Century–Fox, 1993.

The Longest Daycare. The Simpsons. Directed by David Silverman. 20th Century–Fox, 2012.

The Simpsons Movie. Directed by David Silverman, performances by Dan Castellaneta, Julie Kavner, Nancy Cartwright, Yeardley Smith, Hank Azaria. 20th Century–Fox, 2007.

"Simpson Tide." *The Simpsons: The Complete Ninth Season.* Written by Joshua Sternin and Jeffrey Ventimilia, directed by Milton Gray, 20th Century–Fox, 1998.

"That '90s Show." *The Simpsons.* Written by Matt Selman, directed by Mark Kirkland, 20th Century–Fox, 27 Jan 2008.

"Three Gays of the Condo." *The Simpsons: The Complete Fourteenth Season.* Written by Matt Warburton, directed by Mark Kirkland, 20th Century–Fox, 2003.

RIP in Springfield

Rhetorics of Death

JENNIFER RICHARDSON BURG

In Springfield, as in the real world, people sometimes die.[1]

It is, after all, far from a utopian community. *The Simpsons* has never endeavored to portray a version of life that would not include death, despite the fact that the characters never age. Together, Homer, Marge, Bart, Lisa and Maggie represent, in the words of series' executive producer James L. Brooks, "the normal American family in all its beauty and all its horror" (qtd. in Kaufman and Yorks). And for humans, the ultimate expression and realization of horror eternally has been, and most likely always will be, death and dying: "The corpse, seen without God and outside of science, is the utmost of abjection" for our species (Kristeva 4).

Throughout the thirty years that *The Simpsons* has been on the air, both imagined characters in the show and actors who portray them have passed on, leaving both Springfieldians and television audiences at home to mourn and manage, while the show goes on. Although "the death of a familiar face is not a common occurrence in Springfield," there are dozens and dozens of canonical, fictional characters like Shary Bobbins, Larry Burns, Rosemary Chalmers, Chip Davis, Sheldon Skinner, and Snowball the cat who fairly regularly expire (Snierson).[2] Death is not something that the show shies away from or tries to circumvent.

There are cases when these figurative deaths happen with intention, and with plenty of prescient conjecture and media hype, as was the case in early 2000 around the expiry of Maude Flanders. On February 2nd of that year, *Animation World Magazine* reported how

> Fox leaked the scoop that a central Simpsons character would be killed off... Rumors circled that the grim reaper would be swinging his scythe at Maude Flanders, wife of

Jesus freak neighbor Ned. In a bold move of honesty *The Simpsons'* executive producer Mike Scully fully admits the show was a shameless attempt at grabbing sweeps ratings. "We're in our 11th season, and we're always looking for new ways to shake up the show a little and do something that might open up new story possibilities" [DeMott].

Newspapers including the *LA Times* and the *Pittsburgh Post-Gazette* recounted the rumors, and the day after Maude's demise aired in America, the BBC News reported that millions of viewers in Americans had "tuned in to find out the identity of the character after it was announced last month that a member of the Springfield community was going to be killed off," noting that the episode ended "weeks of speculation."

More recently, for nearly a year in advance of the Season 26 premiere, "Clown in the Dumps" (26.1) rumors circulated that Krusty the Clown would be the next to go. Although the axed character was actually Krusty's father, Rabbi Hyman Krustofsky, the show's makers again employed the trope of death and its sensationalization to stir interest and potentially boost ratings. As one *Entertainment Weekly* report warned readers:

> If you think the next new episode of *The Simpsons* will be casualty-free, you've made a grave mistake: The anticipated installment that features the death of a familiar face has been slated as the season 26 premiere. Speaking to *EW* last fall, executive producer Al Jean promised viewers "an emotional story" and dropped just a few hints about who will wind up pushing daisies. One, the actor who voiced this character claimed an Emmy for his/her performance in the role, and two, the character has appeared in more than two episodes. [UPDATE: During a Fox panel at the Television Critics Association summer press tour, Jean noted that the soon-to-be-deceased character could return in a flashback or as a ghost.] [Snierson].

This last bit of information is important because when most characters on *The Simpsons* die, they rarely disappear, often continuing to maintain active roles in Springfieldians' lives and plotlines.

Maude Flanders, for instance, has made a number of post-death appearances on the show. "Treehouse of Horror XIII" (14.1) serves as a notable example, as the Simpsons and Ned Flanders hold a séance to summon Maude's ghost, who goes on to narrate the three included horror stories. She returns again in Season 23's "How I Wet Your Mother" (23.16), where she shows up in Homer's dream among a crowd of women who support drunk driving. These character-only deaths, then, come without the permanency and absolute absence that literal death brings, leaving these dramatis personae gone, but clearly not forgotten, or even really departed.

When an actor who portrays a regular character passes away, however, the role which he or she voiced retires along with them. Permanently. The loss of Marcia Wallace in October of 2013 marks the most recent of these occasions, and Phil Hartman serves as another significant example.[3] This is also true of guest stars who made appearances as themselves in the show, like Michael Jackson, Linda McCartney, George Carlin, and Barry White, among many others. As of 2014, "sixty-three voice-actors and actresses—three considered 'regular cast' and the other 60 special guest stars—have been silenced" (Woolhouse). Their Springfieldian selves are buried along with are their extant selves, and while their memories and their legacies might remain intact on the show, they do not reappear. Their figurative ghosts may sometimes linger, but their literal ghosts are laid to rest.

These different approaches to fictional and nonfictional death and dying in Springfield, and the impacts of those losses both on characters and actual audiences for the show, constitute a public and performed rhetorical approach to a subject not often considered in such venues. There seem to be more differences than similarities between dying in cartoon form and dying in reality, the primary one being that the latter is no joking matter. Mary Roach, in the introduction to her best-selling book on human cadavers, explicitly stresses this point. Although *Stiff* is described in reviews as "witty," "drolly funny," "curiously funny," "genuinely funny," and even "'uproariously funny,'" Roach makes clear that "Death, as in dying, is sad and profound. There is nothing funny about losing someone you love, or about being the person about to be lost" (Roach 11). On *The Simpsons*, where very little—if anything—is off-limits for a laugh, real-life death seems to establish a boundary that even this most irreverent of texts is loath to cross.

Control over death is something that humans have sought in vain ever since there were humans. Our mortality is one of the few actual facts of life, and our inability to predict, to stave off, or to reverse the inevitable remains the essence of human existence: if we are born, then we will die. We have directed our resources in every fathomable field of study, and in some unfathomable, toward trying to comprehend, control, and prevent death. Our quests for immortality are countless. Our attempts to resurrect the dead permeate all realms of our real and imagined stories, and appear in our living and our cartoon towns.

As fiction, Springfield establishes a location where death *can* be controlled, by creators, writers, producers, cast, and crew all making deliberate and conscious choices to eliminate a character. And in these cases, death is something that remains available to jest, to mockery, to manipulation, and to manifestation. The deaths that are controlled are those that can be controlled, and it is acceptable to make fun out of those.

Take, for example, Dr. Marvin Monroe, who is assumed to have died during Season 6, but who then humorously reappears almost ten years later. His demise is established in the Season 7 premiere, "Who Shot Mr. Burns? (Part Two)" (7.1), an episode with a plot fully focused on murder and death, when the hospital where Homer may have been taken is named Marvin Monroe Memorial Hospital. The notion that Springfieldians believe Monroe to be dead is validated in the episode "Bye Bye Nerdie" (12.16), which shows a school gymnasium likewise named after the doctor. His death is seemingly verified in "The Simpsons 138th Episode Spectacular" (7.10), where one of the trivia questions used to introduce commercial breaks queried, "Which two popular characters have died in the past year?" Although the answer provided quipped that "if you said Bleeding Gums Murphy and Dr. Marvin Monroe, you're wrong! They were never popular," the image on the screen was indeed the blues musician and the local psychiatrist. Additional confirmation is found in "Alone Again, Natura-Diddley" (11.14), when Monroe's couch shaped tombstone appears. But then strangely, suddenly, and entertainingly, Dr. Monroe reappears, after almost a decade, much to the surprise of Springfieldians and television audiences alike. In "Diatribe of a Mad Housewife" (15.10), Monroe shows up at a publicity event for Marge's book, *The Harpooned Heart*. Seeing him startles Marge, who remarks that she has not seen him "for years"; he replies that he has been "very sick." Dr. Monroe's death, absence, and revival are comical, making for a laugh-worthy gag that amuses both characters and consumers of the show. Here, death is not serious or appalling or final; rather, it is blithe and malleable and funny.

The same can be said about the demise of Anthony "Fat Tony" D'Amico, a long-standing and popular character, who met his end in "Donnie Fatso" (22.9). After learning that Homer has been acting as a rat for the government, the endearing mob boss suffers a heart attack and collapses dead into Homer's arms. Plagued with guilt, Homer visits his grave to apologize to his pal, only to be kidnapped by Fat Tony's cousin, Fit Tony. The two have a conversation about death, wherein Homer asks, "Are you going to kill me now? 'Cause I'm super ready." But Homer is not killed; instead, he is absolved of blame for Fat Tony's death.

Homer is correct in that he has no need to care about or worry about death. As he himself explains at the close of the "Donnie Fatso" episode, "Fit Tony took his cousin's place running the Springfield mob. The pressures got to him, so he started to eat. Soon, he was known as 'Fit Fat Tony,' then just 'Fat Tony' for short." Thus, in a circumstance akin to those of Snowball II and Snowball V, or of Armin Tamzarian and the real Seymour Skinner, it is as if Fat Tony never *really* died. Or better put, while Fat Tony may have died in Springfield, he returns to life on *The Simpsons*, and once again characters and actual audiences alike escape the repercussions of death: the original animated personality is restored, and all is right in the world.

Not so with the demise of Maude Flanders, when the makers of *The Simpsons* deliver an actual death of a fairly prominent character. After her passing, she often reappears in spirit form, and she also sticks around in memory and in plot action in abundant and varied ways. Although the manner in which she meets her end is neither realistic nor somber—she falls to her death from the top of the grandstand at the Springfield Speedway after being knocked over by the ammunition from a t-shirt cannon aimed at a target that Homer painted on his stomach—the repercussions of her death are handled with an approach that is unique and sincere relative to other deaths in Springfield. Indeed, the show's makers have publicly acknowledged this difference in approach to Maude's death. In the February 2000 issue of *TV Guide*, executive producer Mike Scully explains that killing Maude was "'a chance for one of our regular characters to face a challenge and grow in a new direction.... The idea 'came quickly, we all latched on to it, and it just felt right. We didn't want to kill a character for the sake of killing. We wanted it to have consequences for surviving characters to deal with in future episodes'" (qtd. in Gomes).

Throughout the episode, the consequences of Maude's death are certainly writ large, as it directly affects other characters on the show. There is a funeral and a eulogy and condolences and mourning. Her family is shocked and saddened; her husband is left to manage life as a single father, to cope with sudden loneliness, to navigate the dating scene, and to deal with the day-to-day difficulties of losing the woman he loved. These circumstances are hard for Ned to the extent that losing Maude has been identified as one of "three major crises of faith" he has endured, and the only one where "Ned blames himself, and is crushed to be bereft of his beloved 'Popcorn Ball'" (Pinsky 62, 65). And although the fallout from Maude's untimely fall clearly causes cartoon consequences that approach the real world, Maude's death is another that becomes a means to make fun.

In a 2003 *Today* interview with then co-executive producer George Meyer, the interviewer, who admits that his own "fanship of the show goes back to the very beginning," notes his own reaction to Maude's demise:

> It wasn't so much the fact that her sudden death was straight out of the script of a second-rate soap opera. It was that everyone on the show—Homer most of all, of course—was so unconcerned about Flanders' loss ... the episode underscored the way in which any hint of tenderness or realism had been wrung out of the show... [Bonné].

Another commentator describes her death as "dumb, callous, and cartoon-y" before arguing that "relating an unmitigated tragedy like the sudden death of a woman who was beloved by her community, her husband, and her two small children ... requires walking a very fine line that allows you to express the sadness of it all while still keeping the story moving and the jokes coming" (Schaldenbrand). Schaldenbrand points out that Maude's funeral includes a "supposedly maudlin [shot] of Reverend Lovejoy walking over and putting his hand on Ned's shoulder while the now motherless Flanders boys are sitting right next to him. This is straight up sad, and yet the next thing we cut to is a bunch of Lovejoy administered meta jokes about Apu's kids, the Van Houtens getting divorced, and a t-shirt firing squad clad in black bikinis."

Indeed, Mike Scully himself said "the show planned to deal with the serious subject matter in a somewhat responsible manner to avoid upsetting their viewers. 'There was a lot of discussion about making sure we did deal with some of the emotional ramifications of death and not just make it all joke, joke, joke,' he said. 'But at the same time, we're a comedy, they're animated, they're not real'" (qtd. in DeMott).

The tension between death and comedy is prominent in the passing of Frank "Grimey" Grimes, Homer's co-worker and nemesis from "Homer's Enemy" (8.23). Hank Azaria, who voiced the character, recalls him as one of the "most emotional characters they ever wrote, especially as a guest, with the premise of 'What if a real human being encountered Homer Simpson?'" (Kurp). Truly, Grimes does act as if he's come to Springfield from the real world, and his death is delivered as a disaster: he imitates Homer in an attempt to prove that his archrival is inept and unworthy of all the good things that happen to him, and in a fury grabs hold of high-voltage power cables which electrocute him to death. The moment itself is not inherently amusing, but it is written as comedy, as Grimes last words are "What's this? 'Extremely high voltage.' Well, I don't need safety gloves, 'cause I'm Homer Simp—." The next scene is at Grimes' funeral, but that too is turned into a mockery of mortality when Homer nods off and then snorts awake, mumbling at Marge to "change the channel," and causing everyone assembled to erupt in boisterous laughter as Lenny declares, "That's our Homer!" In Springfield, fictional deaths remain a source of humor, even when the real world tries to visit. Entertainment writer Noel Murray agrees that Grimes' funeral is "another example of how everything falls into place around Homer, and how the only way to respond to that reality is either to laugh it off or to get yourself buried."

But when someone real gets buried, that's not comedy—even for *The Simpsons*. When an actual loss of life impacts *The Simpsons* in a way that the show makers cannot control, death loses its potential for hilarity and becomes a matter of reverence and respect: "When a voice-actor passes away for any cartoon, the writers have three options: re-cast with a similar-sounding actor/actress; send the character on a 'long vacation' until a decision can be made; or permanently retire said character(s) out of respect for the deceased. After being on the air for twenty-five years, *The Simpsons* has, unfortunately, seen their fair-share of voice-actors pass on" (Woolhouse). In the most prominent of these instances, characters are not made to die within the series, and their deaths are rarely, if ever, fully acknowledged or processed by the inhabitants of Springfield. The remaining characters on the show are not made to mourn or to memorialize, there are no funerals or burials or last goodbyes. In Springfield, they either remain alive, or are simply gone.

Death in this manner is dealt with by *not* being dealt with in any meaningful way, a luxury not afforded to anyone in real life, though not for a lack of trying. The shocking murder of Phil Hartman in May of 1998 is exemplary of this approach. You may remember him as the voice of Troy McClure in such episodes as "Homer vs. Lisa and the 8th Commandment" (2.13), "Lady Bouvier's Lover" (5.21), and "A Fish Called Selma" (7.19), and as lawyer Lionel Hutz, aka Miguel Sanchez, aka Dr. Nguyen Van Phuoc, in "Bart Gets Hit by a Car" (2.10), "Marge vs. the Monorail" (4.12), and "Homer the Vigilante" (5.11), among others. Following the incident, Matt Groening told *Entertainment Weekly* that Hartman was "a master," and that he took for granted that the comedian "nailed the joke every time" (qtd. in Turner 454). Although episodes recorded prior to Hartman's death were aired as originally planned, following the last of those, his characters were retired, and the final episode in which his voice appears was dedicated to him "in loving memory, to our friend" ("Bart the Mother" 10.3).

Hartman's characters do not return to Springfield, in recollections, as apparitions, or in any significant shape or form. They live on somewhere, and there are rare reminders of this: Lionel Hutz very occasionally appears as a non-speaking background character in crowd scenes, and both he and Troy McClure appear in photographs (Hutz in "Wedding for Disaster" [20.15] and McClure in "Take My Life, Please" [20.10]) and on signs (both characters in "Rome-old and Juli-eh" [18.15]). So the rest of the town carries on as if nothing has happened, in episodes that the show's audiences consume. The latter, however, do not have the indulgence of obliviousness that Springfieldians do. In real life, the suddenness and helplessness and horror and aftermath of murder, the frustration of lost potential, the bittersweet moments of memory, and the lastingness of death are unavoidable.

Marcia Wallace's passing from complications of pneumonia in October 2013 also led *The Simpsons* to retire her character. As the voice of Bart's teacher, Edna Krabappel, a definitive principal and fan-favorite character for twenty-three years and over 100 episodes, Wallace was beloved both in Springfield and by audiences. Upon her passing, the show's makers gave public statements that expressed both their personal grief and their plans for addressing the loss on screen. Executive producer Al Jean stressed that there was no "inten[tion] to have anyone else play Mrs. Krabappel," but that instead "Bart will get a new teacher" (qtd. in King). Elsewhere, Jean noted that Wallace "was beloved by all at *The Simpsons*[,] and we intend to retire her irreplaceable character.... Earlier we had discussed a potential storyline in which a character passed away. This was not Marcia's Edna Krabappel. Marcia's passing is unrelated and again, a terrible loss for all who had the pleasure of knowing her" (qtd. in Barnes and Hayden). As with Phil Hartman, people in the real world had no option except to deal with loving and losing Wallace in a real way; unlike the example of Phil Hartman, characters on the show were also left to grapple with her death, although not in the explicit ways that the Flanders family did upon losing Maude.

The Simpsons and the characters who live in Springfield have acknowledged and marked the passing of Mrs. Krabappel, but no death scene occurred, no details of her death have been revealed, there has been no funeral, and it took years for her to return in spectral or angelic form. That she is deceased is implicitly announced several ways in Season 25. Nine days after Wallace's death, the episode "Four Regrettings and a Funeral" (25.3) opened with "We'll really miss you Mrs. K." shown on the chalkboard during the title sequence along with a clearly saddened Bart. This episode also "closed with a photo of her character, Mrs. Krabappel, with the caption, 'In loving memory of Marcia Wallace'" (Goldblatt). Ten episodes later, the poignant final scene of "The Man Who Grew Too Much" (25.13) shows Ned Flanders wearing a black armband and "daydreaming about Edna. In the dream, Ned dances with Edna and she proceeds to laugh. Ned then awakens and says, 'I sure do miss that laugh.' The touching moment is then abruptly disrupted by Nelson's signature cackle, but he then says, 'I miss her, too'" (Bacardi).

During Season 28, Krabappel is mentioned, seen in a couch gag and in photos, and is finally seen as a ghost, all leading up to the season finale "Dogtown" (28.22), where her headstone is shown in a dream. For the most part, the cherished teacher is simply retired, and she is understood as having expired, although the whys and hows remain unwritten and unknown for both characters and audiences alike.

Overall, the ways in which The Simpsons both scripts and negotiates death and dying, in cartoon and human forms, reflects common human responses to mortality in that they are sometimes comical and sometimes melancholy. At turns complicated, contradictory, and confusing, the ways in which the makers of the show, its characters, and its audiences respond to both the fictive and extant losses of individuals in those intersecting worlds constitutes a rhetorical approach to death that is as distinctive and idiosyncratic as Springfield, and as life and death themselves. And from their own uses of rhetoric, to please and to humor and to create bonds, the people who make The Simpsons make, of course, an argument.

The rhetorical application of death serves to persuade audiences that it's acceptable to laugh at the grim reaper—who does, of course, make regular appearances in Springfield—as long as it's pretend. Because only in the fictional world can we control both life and death, and that control provides comfort and overshadows our most profound human fears—that we are human. In the words of Jeff Greenberg, psychology professor and researcher at the University of Arizona, "part of the human condition is living with a desire to continue to live and an inherent fear of death on the one hand, and, on the other, the knowledge that this desire will inevitably be thwarted and that what is feared will inevitably occur" (qtd. in. Villarica). In reality, death still conquers all. And that, not even Homer, Marge, Bart, Lisa, and Maggie can make amusing.

NOTES

1. Mahalo and aloha to Torrey Jay Kurtzner for providing editorial assistance and well-timed Homerisms throughout the revision process.

2. This discussion acknowledges but does not address the deaths of fictional characters who appear on *The Simpsons*, like Poochie the cartoon dog, Johnny Stabbo from a movie that Marge watches, or characters on non-canonical episodes of the show, including the Treehouse of Horror episodes, who have died.

3. Editors' note: Burg completed this chapter before the death of Russi Taylor on July 26, 2019.

WORKS CITED

"Alone Again, Natura-Diddley." *The Simpsons: The Complete Eleventh Season*. Written by Ian Maxtone-Graham, directed by Jim Reardon, 20th Century–Fox, 2000.

Bacardi, Francesca. "'The Simpsons' Remembers Marcia Wallace in Edna Krabappel's Final Episode." *Variety*, 10 Mar. 2014, variety.com/2014/tv/news/the-simpons-remembers-marcia-wallace-in-edna-krabappels-final-episode-video-1201128874.

Barnes, Mike and Erik Hayden. "'Simpsons' Actress Marcia Wallace Dies." *The Hollywood Reporter*, 26 Oct. 2013, www.hollywoodreporter.com/news/simpsons-actress-marcia-wallace-dies-651092.

"Bart Gets Hit by a Car." *The Simpsons: The Complete Second Season*. Written by John Swartzwelder, directed by Mark Kirkland, 20th Century–Fox, 1991.

"Bart the Mother." *The Simpsons: The Complete Tenth Season*. Written by David X. Cohen, directed by Steven Dean Moore, 20th Century–Fox, 2012.

Bonné, Jon. "'The Simpsons' has lost its cool." Today.com, 27 Oct. 2003, www.today.com/popculture/simpsons-has-lost-its-cool-wbna3341530.

"Bye Bye Nerdie." *The Simpsons: The Complete Twelfth Season*. Written by John Frink and Don Payne, directed by Lauren MacMullan, 20th Century–Fox, 2001.

"Clown in the Dumps." *The Simpsons*. Written by Joel Cohen, directed by Steven Dean Moore, 20th Century–Fox, 28 Sept. 2014. *Amazon Digital Services*, www.amazon.com/gp/video/detail/B00NT74SB8?ref_=atv_dp_season_select.

"Death hits *The Simpsons*." BBC News, 14 Feb. 2000, news.bbc.co.uk/2/hi/entertainment/642376.stm.

DeMott, Rick. "Simpsons' Scandal Set For Sweeps." *Animation World Magazine*, 2 Feb. 2000, www.awn.com/news/simpsons-scandal-set-sweeps.

"Diatribe of a Mad Housewife." *The Simpsons*. Written by Robin J. Stein, directed by Mark Kirkland, 20th Century–Fox, 25 Jan. 2004. *Amazon Digital Services*, www.amazon.com/gp/video/detail/B071ZQZS97?ref_=atv_dp_season_select.

"Dogtown." *The Simpsons*. Written by J. Stewart Burns, directed by Steven Dean Moore, 20th Century–Fox, 21 May 2017. *Amazon Digital Services*, www.amazon.com/gp/video/detail/B01LFT34Y8?ref_=atv_dp_season_select.

"Donnie Fatso." *The Simpsons*. Written by Chris Cluess, directed by Ralph Sosa, 20th Century–Fox, 12 Dec. 2010. *Amazon Digital Services*, www.amazon.com/gp/video/detail/B0044QZSSA?ref_=atv_dp_season_select.

"A Fish Called Selma." *The Simpsons: The Complete Seventh Season*. Written by Jack Barth, directed by Mark Kirkland, 20th Century–Fox, 1996.

"Four Regrettings and a Funeral." *The Simpsons*. Written by Marc Wilmore, directed by Mark Kirkland, 20th Century–Fox, 3 Nov. 2013. *Amazon Digital Services*, www.amazon.com/gp/video/detail/B00FI9KDO6?ref_=atv_dp_season_select.

Goldblatt, Daniel. "*The Simpsons* Pays Tribute to Marcia Wallace." *Variety*, 4 Nov. 2013, variety.com/2013/tv/news/the-simpsons-marcia-wallace-1200794355.

Gomes, Bruce. "Part I—TV Guide References." *The Complete Simpsons Bibliography*. 5 Aug. 2013, snpp.com/guides/bibliography01.html.

"Homer's Enemy." *The Simpsons: The Complete Eighth Season*. Written by John Swartzwelder, directed by Jim Reardon, 20th Century–Fox, 2006.

"Homer the Vigilante." *The Simpsons: The Complete Fifth Season*. Written by John Swartzwelder, directed by Jim Reardon, 20th Century–Fox, 1994.

"Homer vs. Lisa and the 8th Commandment." *The Simpsons: The Complete Second Season*. Written by Steve Pepoon, directed by Rich Moore, 20th Century–Fox, 1991.

"How I Wet Your Mother." *The Simpsons*. Written by Billy Kimball and Ian Maxtone-Graham, directed by Lance Kramer, 20th Century–Fox, 11 Mar. 2012. *Amazon Digital Services*, www.amazon.com/gp/video/detail/B005PK57BM?ref_=atv_dp_season_select.

Kaufman, Joanne and Cindy Yorks. "*Life in Hell*'s Matt Groening Goes Overboard to Make the Simpsons the First Family of TV 'toons." *People Magazine*, 18 Dec. 1989, www.people.com/people/archive/article/0,20116283,00.html.

King, Susan. "Marcia Wallace dies at 70; Emmy Award-winning actress." *Los Angeles Times*, 27 Oct. 2013, articles.latimes.com/2013/oct/27/local/la-me-marcia-wallace-2013 1027.

Kristeva, Julia. *Powers of Horror: An Essay on Abjection*. Columbia UP, 1982.

Kurp, Josh. "Cletus, Frank Grimes, and Comic Book Guy: Hank Azaria on 5 of His Many Many *Simpsons* Voices." *Vulture*, 24 Sept. 2014, www.vulture.com/2014/09/hank-azaria-interview-simpsons-voices-cletus-dr-nick-comic-book-guy-frank-grimes.html.

"Lady Bouvier's Lover." *The Simpsons: The Complete Fifth Season*. Written by Bill Oakley and Josh Weinstein, directed by Wes Archer, 20th Century–Fox, 1994.

"The Man Who Grew Too Much." *The Simpsons*. Written by Jeff Westbrook, directed by Matthew Schofield, 20th Century–Fox, 9 Mar. 2014. *Amazon Digital Services*, www.amazon.com/gp/video/detail/B00FI9KDO6?ref_=atv_dp_season_select.

"Marge vs. the Monorail." *The Simpsons: The Complete Fourth Season*. Written by Conan O'Brien, directed by Rich Moore, 20th Century–Fox, 1993.

Murray, Noel. "*The Simpsons* (Classic): 'Homer's Enemy.'" *The A.V. Club*, 12 Apr. 2015, tv.avclub.com/the-simpsons-classic-homer-s-enemy-1798183411.

Pinsky, Mark I. *The Gospel According to The Simpsons: Bigger and Possibly Even Better!* Westminster John Knox, 2007.

Roach, Mary. *Stiff: The Curious Lives of Human Cadavers*. Norton, 2004.

"Rome-old and Juli-eh." *The Simpsons*. Written by Daniel Chun, directed by Nancy Kruse, 20th Century–Fox, 11 Mar. 2007. *Amazon Digital Services*, www.amazon.com/gp/video/detail/B071ZQZRX5?ref_=atv_dp_season_select.

Schaldenbrand, Charlie. "compare & contrast: deaths." *Dead Homer Society*, 16 Aug. 2012, deadhomersociety.com/tag/round-springfield/page/3/?r=1&l=ri&fst=0.

"The Simpsons 138th Episode Spectacular." *The Simpsons*. Written by Penny Wise (aka Jon Vitti), directed by Pound Foolish (aka David Silverman), 20th Century–Fox, 3 Dec. 1995. *Amazon Digital Services*, www.amazon.com/gp/video/detail/B072Q1TKWW?ref_=atv_dp_season_select.

Snierson, Dan. "*Simpsons*' character will die in season 26 premiere; 'Futurama' crossover to air in November." *Entertainment Weekly*, 20 July 2014, insidetv.ew.com/2014/07/20/simpsons-character-will-die-in-season-26-premiere-futurama-crossover.

Snierson, Dan. "*Simpsons*' producer on mystery death in Springfield: Even the actor doesn't know yet." *Entertainment Weekly*, 11 Oct. 2013, ew.com/article/2013/10/11/simpsons-which-character-dies.

"Take My Life, Please." *The Simpsons: The Complete Twentieth Season*. Written by Don Payne, directed by Steven Dean Moore, 20th Century–Fox, 2009.

"Treehouse of Horror XIII." *The Simpsons: The Complete Fourteenth Season*. Written by Marc

Wilmore, Brian Kelley and Kevin Curran, directed by David Silverman, 20th Century–Fox, 2002.

Turner, Chris. *Planet Simpson: How a Cartoon Masterpiece Defined a Generation.* Da Capo Press, 2005.

Villarica, Hans. "How the Unrelenting Threat of Death Shapes Our Behavior." *The Atlantic,* 4 May 2012, www.theatlantic.com/health/archive/2012/05/how-the-unrelenting-threat-of-death-shapes-our-behavior/256728.

"Wedding for Disaster." *The Simpsons: The Complete Twentieth Season.* Written by Joel H. Cohen, directed by Chuck Sheetz, 20th Century–Fox, 2009.

"Who Shot Mr. Burns? (Part Two)." *The Simpsons: The Complete Seventh Season.* Written by Bill Oakley and Josh Weinstein, directed by Wes Archer, 20th Century–Fox, 1995.

Woolhouse, Adam. "10 Voice-Actor Deaths That Impacted *The Simpsons.*" *WhatCulture.com,* 4 Apr. 2014, whatculture.com/tv/10-voice-actor-deaths-impacted-simpsons.

The Grotesque
and the Beautiful

The Bodies of Springfield

BRENT WALTER CLINE *and*
MATTHEW NELSON HILL

When Marge informs her family of the death of her Aunt Gladys, Bart shivers when he is reminded of what she looked like: his Aunt Patty. When a clergyman provides a eulogy at the funeral, he mistakes Gladys for a man, saying, "That's a woman? Dear Lord! Well, I guess most of what I said can be salvaged" ("Selma's Choice" 4.13). Later, when Selma agrees to take Bart and Lisa to Duff Gardens after Homer is incapacitated due to a seductive, putrid sandwich, Bart says, "To get to Duff Gardens, I'd ride with Satan himself." In other episodes, staying at Patty and Selma's apartment literally makes the Simpson children shake in fear. Almost every man, from Homer to Groundskeeper Willie, has shuddered at their appearance. The sisters are rarely approached for a relationship, be it straight or gay, for other than manipulative (if not homicidal) reasons. It is ultimately no great stretch of the imagination to say that Patty and Selma are two of the most repulsive, grotesque figures in Springfield.

At the end of the "Selma's Choice" episode, however, Selma, still coping with the baby hunger her Aunt Gladys' last will and testament created in her, takes the newly adopted iguana, Jub-Jub, into her arms. Selma begins to sing "Natural Woman" and rock Jub-Jub, who, even despite crude animation, can be seen with a look of total indifference. The moment is hilarious and repulsive. The grotesque nature of Selma makes it nevertheless somehow appropriate that she can sing of her womanly natural-ness to an uncaring iguana. While the scene is visually grotesque, it is nevertheless played for real emotion as well. Despite how bizarre the match, Selma *does* genuinely feel like her maternal instinct has been satisfied by an iguana (though her desire for a man will soon lead her to a husband with a very different relationship with animals).

That Selma's moment with Jub-Jub contains genuine pathos in the midst of a hideous scene is a representative example of what *The Simpsons* consistently does with bodies that could be considered disabled, freakish, or grotesque. There is little to no attempt to create a politically correct, romantic, or sentimental lens through which physical difference is meant to be shown. Instead, the grotesque nature of the bodies of Selma and the rest of Springfield maintain their otherness. Patty's off-key, raspy singing and physical repulsiveness co-exist with her maternal feelings toward the lizard. After three decades, the initial repulsion may have long worn off, but the bodies of *The Simpsons'* major figures and minor figures alike are seemingly designed to alienate the viewer rather than connect.[1] Homer's weight, intelligence, and hygiene are meant to repel. In Springfield, Marge's hair is only periodically referred to as aberrant, but nevertheless originates from the classic gothic film, *Bride of Frankenstein*. Mr. Burns, Chief Wiggum, Groundskeeper Willie, Comic Book Guy, Moe Szyslak, Barney Gumble, Krusty the Clown, Sideshow Bob—it is perhaps easier to name the characters who are not physically grotesque than those who are. Even the town itself is an example of the physically deformed, as Springfield is no stranger to freak natural features (e.g., gorges, volcanoes, deadly peaks) and human-made ones (e.g., acid storms, the nuclear power plant, the escalator to nowhere, and Main Street, which remains "all cracked and broken" ["Marge vs. the Monorail" 4.12]).

By having the grotesque so ubiquitous, Matt Groening and company have created the physically repulsive to operate as the normative. The grotesque body exists, but when it is in a universe defined by constant, assorted iterations of the grotesque, then what it means to have such a body, as well as what it means to respond to such a body, changes. It is not simply that because there are so many physical "freaks" in Springfield that we simply register them all as normal or beautiful. Instead, the constant grotesquerie of Springfield's citizens makes us aware that what is hideous and what is beautiful is subject to perspective.

A body in *The Simpsons* might be grossly overweight or an impossible stretching of proportions, but the number and variety of those oddities also disrupts what bodies are supposed to mean. In Springfield, the freak body need not be representative of the freak person, nor the attractive body representative of the hero. Thanks to the grotesque nature of all of Springfield, a body can be a body.

Defining the Grotesque

Before any serious discussion of the bodies of Springfield can begin, it seems appropriate to give even the most succinct of reviews of the concept of the grotesque. In both visual art and literature, the grotesque can suffer from such an elasticity of definition that seemingly makes it an empty signifier representing other vague terms such as gothic or romantic. Admittedly reductive, perhaps the best starting point is seeing the grotesque as that which "illustrates how the normal is defined in relation to the abnormal" (Edwards and Graulund 8). The word itself comes to us from the Italian word for cave (*grotta*), when in the 15th century late-Roman era, paintings were discovered under Rome and other areas of the country. As described in the seminal work on the literary grotesque, Wolfgang Kayser's *The Grotesque in Art and Literature*, these paintings were originally criticized for their abnormal, ornamental style and lack of realism. After they were uncovered in Renaissance Italy, however, artists such as Raphael incorporated them into their work, creating works that are alternately described as sinister, playful, imaginative, and horrifying (19–21).

Whether it is in the paintings of Hieronymous Bosch or the writings of Edgar Allan Poe, the grotesque involves a kind of disproportion, often creating responses of horror or fear. Perhaps the reader creates depictions of the grotesque, as when you describe the neighborhood dog snarling with gigantic teeth and a terrifying bark. The dog becomes stretched so that if visually depicted its jaws would be grossly oversized, just as Bosch's monstrous, mocking faces contort in his painting of Christ's walk to Golgotha, or Poe's protagonists turn fear into a pathological, obsessive condition causing self-destructive or homicidal acts. At the same time, the disproportionate, abnormal bodies of the grotesque can also produce laughter, most often in the form of parody or caricature. As Edwards and Graulund state, parody and caricature "create a comic, ludicrous or grotesque effect. As a representational mode, caricature often exaggerates a single body part ... exceeding the limits of harmony and transgressing the aesthetic principles of realism" (67). Of course, one shouldn't assume that the grotesque creates *either* sensations of horror or laughter. Often the two are mixed in an uncanny relationship; Kayser writes that "we smile at the deformations but are appalled by the horrible and monstrous elements as such" (31). The "freak shows" of years past are meant to create just this contradiction: we are horrified by these abnormal bodies, but in some way comforted by them because they assure us of our own normalcy through critique and laughter.

While P.T. Barnum and his circus sideshows are long considered the stuff of Victorian deviancy, we nevertheless continually interact with the grotesque through mass media, primarily through film and television. As

Leslie Fiedler writes, the grotesque has "passed inevitably from the platform and the pit to the screen, flesh becoming shadow" (16). The 1920s and '30s witnessed perhaps the zenith of the grotesque in film with Lon Chaney and Boris Karloff as the greatest examples of the twisted form in characters such as Quasimodo, Frankenstein's monster, and the Phantom of the Opera. Matt Groening admits in an interview with Deborah Solomon that Marge's hair comes from the 1935 movie *Bride of Frankenstein* as well as his own mother's 1960s hair—a grotesque combination of the exotic and domestic if ever there was one (Solomon). Of course, if any understanding of the grotesque and its effect in *The Simpsons* can be made, it has to be remembered that the show exists within a specific genre, or perhaps a mixture of genres.[2] To see the grotesque in *The Simpsons* is to first see its cultural predecessors. There is the traditional family sitcom: a husband, wife, and three children who return to solidarity by the end of every episode no matter what grease or sugar schemes have been attempted. There is the streak of absurdist parody, which critics like Megan Mullen see arise from shows known as "magicoms": "Throughout the early-to-mid 1960s, sitcoms such as *Bewitched, The Munsters, The Addams Family, Mister Ed, I Dream of Jeannie,* and *My Mother the Car* began to populate prime time. These magicoms invested otherwise ordinary domestic sitcom characters and settings with magical powers ... magicoms parodied earlier domestic sitcoms by introducing fantasy elements into familiar formulas" (67). And while certainly not exclusive from the aforementioned absurdist parodies, there is *The Flintstones* (and thus indirectly *The Honeymooners*), which was able to create an otherwise impossible level of parody and caricature because it was animated. What Mullen calls *The Flintstones'* ability to turn "the familiar, perhaps already clichéd, conventions of the genre inside out" (65) is taken to a greater extreme in *The Simpsons*.

The desire to make parody and pastiche within an animated sitcom allows the grotesque in *The Simpsons* to flourish. Caricature need not be only in the spoken dialogue but in the very style of every visual cue. As Jonathan Gray writes in *Watching with* The Simpsons, "When *The Simpsons* takes *any* visual trope from live action and turns it into a cartoon, it therefore removes that trope a few steps from us, potentially allowing us to see the trope with fresh eyes, defamiliarized ... even how people move or make facial expressions all become defamiliarized in cartoon form" (66). And while the bodies of Springfield at times have specific targets of satire (the incessant genial laughter of Dr. Hibbert, the literally unflappable hair of steadfast Principal Skinner), our goal here is to instead examine how all the collected grotesque bodies of Springfield, including the town itself, affect both the show as well as the audience's reaction to it. Anyone reading this book is perhaps so familiar with *The Simpsons* that there may exist the need to be "defamiliarized" all over again. We know what Homer looks like, and some of us may know the exact circumference of the Comic Book Guy's stomach (Worst. Abdomen. Ever.). If this is the case, then we may have been in the freak show too long; we may have forgotten the disproportionate, abnormal bodies that constitute Springfield. By making overt what we instinctively know, we can see yet another effect *The Simpsons* has as a visual and literary text. If visiting the freak show influenced how we see ourselves and the world, then so do our visits to a town that may "embiggen" our soul," but nevertheless is "America's crudbucket. At least according to *Newsweek*" ("The Summer of 4 Ft. 2" 7.25).

The Grotesques of Springfield

When Grampa Simpson and Marge's mother, Jacqueline Bouvier, begin to date one another in Season 5, Homer irrationally assumes that he and Marge will now be related and his already-born children will become products of incest: "horrible freaks with pink skin, no overbite, and five fingers on each hand" ("Lady Bouvier's Lover" 5.21). The Simpson children then evolve within Homer's imagination to be what might be considered a more "realistic" drawing. It is a hilarious sight gag, but for our present purposes it is more important as a reminder of how stylized the world of Springfield is. Yellow skin (for Caucasian members of the town), Linus-like hair, and four fingers on every hand permeate Springfield. To discuss the grotesque bodies of Springfield then, it is clear that the entire world is made to be a kind of stylized freak. When attractive bodies come to town, they are nevertheless yellow (if they are "white"), lack a finger, and have a seemingly incurable, congenital lower mandible problem. While this obviously is an important part of the Springfield grotesque, it is important to look beyond what is simply the "style" of drawing characters from *The Simpsons*. It therefore is understood that these grotesque bodies are discolored and anatomically incorrect; what is vital to the current discussion are those bodies that are grotesque within Springfield itself. Not surprisingly then, it's nearly all of them.

It seems only right to begin with the Simpson family themselves, whose bodies all have a varying level of disproportion. Homer is perhaps the most obvious, depicted not only visually but through the discourse of the town as an obese, slavish man, even when he isn't attempting to go on disability for being a morbidly obese, comically slavish man. While he is certainly not the heaviest man in Springfield, the abnormal size of Homer is constantly referred to throughout the series. When he poses for boudoir shots for Marge, the photographer tells him, "Try not to speak; it's making your body ripple" ("They Saved Lisa's Brain" 10.22). His general health is abysmal, needing a triple bypass before the never-to-be-reached age of forty, and he doesn't need radioactive dye for medical tests because his entire body emanates radiation

("Homer's Triple Bypass" 4.11). When he eats a hot dog from Apu after finding out grease can be sold, his heart nearly stops ("Lard of the Dance" 10.1). In a theoretically positive development of his obesity, Homer can smell foods from great distances, saving himself, Bart, and Ned and Todd Flanders from death at sea ("Boy Scoutz 'n' the Hood" 5.8). To even list all the examples of Homer's grotesque body seems like an unnecessary chore, one that's perhaps best finished by quoting a car engineer from Powell Motors, stating the exact opposite of what he means: "Homer Simpson is a brilliant man with lots of well-thought out, practical ideas. He is insuring the financial security of this company for years to come. Oh yes, and his personal hygiene is above reproach" ("O Brother, Where Art Thou?" 2.15).

While not as obvious as Homer, Marge too is an example of a grotesque body in Springfield. So much of her character is based upon the parody of the content housewife and mother, despite whatever goes wrong. Her body reflects this, perhaps most distinctly through her pearls. When Molloy, the cat burglar, removes them from her neck, imprints are left to suggest how inseparable she is from the family heirloom—both those pearls as well as all the ones in her drawer ("Homer the Vigilante" 5.11). Marge is both attractive—not only in Homer's eyes, but in Jacques' (her French bowling instructor), and Mr. Burns', though definitely not any member of the Hell's Satans biker gang—as well as repulsive, most noticeably through her hair.[3] As stated earlier, her hair is a combination of the Bride of Frankenstein and Groening's mother. The town understands the hair's aberrant nature, and while other characters do have blue hair (Wiggum, the entire Van Houten clan), Marge is the only one to receive mockery. Nigel, the manager of the Be-Sharps refers to her as "bouffant Betty" ("Homer's Barbershop Quartet" 5.1), and when in "Homer Alone" (3.15) a hairdresser accidentally gives a woman a style like Marge's, her response is horror, stating, "I can't even put a bag over my head." While the audience may be numbed to the absurd nature of Marge's hair, the show consistently reminds us of it, at times by letting Marge's hair fall into a normal style, or when Marge happens to be arrested, and the hair gets its own mug shot.

Bart, Lisa, and Maggie are all grotesque as well, though arguably no more than the rest of the children in Springfield. While Bart has his own King-Size Homer-esque episode when he gains weight through massive amounts of junk food, he is nevertheless normally pegged as obese, as when Milhouse reports in "Cape Feare" (5.2) that no one on the playground wants to kill him, but the girls are calling him "Fatty fatty fat fat." One of his dreams is to be like a morbidly obese Homer, so that he might one day tell gawking reports that he washes himself "with a rag on a stick" ("King-Size Homer" 7.7). Lisa and Maggie both share the same starfish hairstyle that makes them strangely akin to their mother in its outlandishness. When Lisa attempts to change the haircut because gum has been stuck in her hair, she looks at the new style and says, "I finally look like a real person." While Nelson's laughter quickly leads her to donning a cap to hide her new style, the moment makes clear that while Lisa doesn't actively complain about her hair, its bizarre, grotesque nature is not missed by her or others ("22 Short Films About Springfield" 7.21).

With each Simpson having their own abnormal hair and absurd body characteristics, their grotesqueness is unique while at the same time consistent with the rest of Springfield. The secondary characters of the show are a treasure trove of misfits and freaks, and while they may all be four-fingered and the majority yellow, they each have their own distinct, grotesque characteristics rather than simply being a part of a stylized whole. Grampa Simpson, for instance, has his elderly nature taken to extremes so that he is more than simply old: he is "itchy, got ants in [his] pants, and is discombobulated" ("22 Short Films About Springfield" 7.21). His decrepit nature is consistently made radical. Without his medicine, he imagines being chased by wolves and ends dressing as a woman, to Jasper's delight ("Cape Feare" 5.2). Is he then a parody of the infirmities and behaviors of old age or a grotesque body that contributes to a larger "freak" population of Springfield? In Grampa's words, "a little from column A and a little from column B" ("Mother Simpson" 7.8). In fact, all the elderly mainstays of Springfield—Jasper, Mr. Burns, Mrs. Glick, Eleanor Abernathy, Jacqueline Bouvier, Agnes Skinner—are grotesque in their decrepitude and surliness. Those elderly characters who simply visit or disappear after a single episode, however—Mona Simpson, Molloy the Cat Burglar, and the gold(car)digging Zelda—are arguably normal. Hans Moleman, perhaps the most revolting figure in the entire Springfield universe cannot be included; he is, by his own admission, only thirty-one years old ("Duffless" 4.16).

Extreme weight receives the same treatment as old age in Springfield, with many characters so large they are seemingly incapable of mundane tasks. Comic Book Guy and Chief Wiggum consistently struggle to get up, and sometimes to even breathe. Barney Gumble is grossly overweight to match his grotesque behavior, notwithstanding finding toothpicks behind the toilet sometimes leads you to Grammy-winning barbershop quartets. Many of the children of Springfield are considerably fat, so much so that Krusty is able to have not just Kamp Krusty, but Chief Starving Bear Weight Loss Center too, so families can hide "daddy's chubby little secret" ("Kamp Krusty" 4.1).

It is indeed a long parade of bodies in Springfield which all amount to aberrations, not just to the viewer, but to Springfieldians as well. Patty and Selma regularly make men shudder. Mr. Burns' body is so absurd that he cannot pedal a bike or wrestle a sucker from a baby ("Who Shot Mr. Burns? [Part Two]" 7.1), and must undergo weekly medical procedures "designed to help

Mr. Burns cheat death for another week, including an extensive chiropractic readjustment, eye drops ... pain killers and a vocal chord scraping" ("The Springfield Files" 8.10). Lunch Lady Doris is aberrant in everything from her homely body to her tendency to spill ashes into the food, while her counterpart Groundskeeper Willie has the unexplained physique of a bodybuilder. Ned Flanders, despite his vanilla sweater and glasses, is also grotesque. Other than being selfless to the point that he spends an entire workday tracking down a man he accidentally kept a quarter from, he is also depicted as having enormous genitalia.

The town of Springfield itself reflects the aberrations of the bodies of its citizens, though its history is not nearly as grotesque as those cousin-loving freaks from Shelbyville. Perhaps one of the best definitions of Springfield itself comes from Mikhail Bakhtin, an early 20th century philosopher, when he describes the carnival festivals of Medieval Europe where hierarchies were temporarily forgotten and parodies abound: "It was like an entire system of crooked mirrors, elongating, diminishing, distorting in various directions and to various degrees" (127). Homer is often the eyewitness to the town's physical "crooked mirrors," falling into the Grand Canyon–like gorge more than once, escaping an avalanche on Widow's Peak as well as Mt. Useful ("Mountain of Madness" 8.12), and causing as well as surviving several nuclear scares at the abysmal power plant. The town's first function in the show is to be an everyplace, so that Springfield can contain any location the creators might imagine. Its second function, however, is to be a horrifying place to live with tire fires burning bright, water towers in need of "de-pythoning," and giant magnifying glasses of which the only function is to ignite popsicle stick skyscrapers ("Marge vs the Monorail" 4.12). Even when the town is not horrifying, it is nonsensical, with buildings made into the letter T and museums that proudly hold the world's largest cubic zirconia ("Homer the Vigilante" 5.11). The town and citizens reflect one another in their grotesque nature: volcanoes and power plants threaten the citizens, and Springfieldians' penchant for environmental destruction and riot-first defense mechanisms threaten the town.

What's a Body to Do?

As stated earlier, *The Simpsons'* grotesque sensibilities are rooted both in the TV history it is indebted to as well as its animated ambitions for parody and caricature. To state, however, that the specific targets of that parody contain the entirety of the grotesque's effect is misleading. At the same time, while animation clearly lends itself to the disproportionate stretching of the grotesque, it is myopic to suggest that the grotesque is merely a style where "deviants like 'stuttering Porky Pig, speech-impaired Elmer Fudd, near-sighted Mr. Magoo, and mentally retarded Dopey' are therefore obscured by their very cartoonalness" (Fink 259). The different styles of animated shows, whether they are the simplistic *South Park* or the seasick Squigglevision of *Dr. Katz* or early *Home Movies*, have a larger effect on the audience and the internal ideology of the programs themselves than only reflecting the persistent effect of animation in general.

In regards to *The Simpsons*, there may be several effects of a persistent grotesque sensibility, but here we concentrate on only three. The first of these is that the abnormality of any single body in Springfield loses any powerful stigma since every other body in some way is grotesque as well. This is not the world of *Looney Tunes* where every abnormality is simply understood by the animated world (and perhaps the audience) as normal. Marge's hair is mocked by other people. When Lisa's face becomes nearly cyborgian due to antiquated braces, the school photographer does not see her as just another girl, but as someone that makes him scream, "There is no God!" ("Last Exit to Springfield" 4.17). Homer's obesity and daftness is commented on by everyone from Smithers to Reverend Lovejoy. Since all are grotesque, however, each person can be the reciprocal subject of mockery. This is perhaps best seen in "Brush with Greatness" (2.18). After becoming stuck in a water slide, Homer is determined to lose weight. Meanwhile, Marge has been commissioned to paint a flattering portrait of Mr. Burns. When Mr. Burns shows his wickedness by mocking Homer for being heavy, saying, "You're the fattest thing I've ever seen, and I've been on safari," Marge responds by immortalizing Mr. Burns' grotesque, naked body in a painting for the fine arts museum. Shown naked, frail, and seemingly impossibly skinny, Burns' ability to see Homer as hideous is checked by his own grotesque appearance.

Secondly, because all bodies are knowingly grotesque to each character, the subject of beauty becomes overtly discursive. The coupling of Homer and Marge is not far removed from those members of Barnum's circus shows who might become romantically involved. The moral center of the show is Marge and Homer's loyalty to one another, and this is buoyed by the fact that they find one another attractive. When Mr. Burns mocks Homer in "Brush with Greatness" for being 239 pounds, Marge is nevertheless ecstatically proud. In "Secrets of a Successful Marriage" (5.22), Marge kicks Homer out for divulging secrets of their relationship. Homer builds a crude replica of Marge and affectionately shapes the hair (just before he accidentally murders the replica by knocking her out of the treehouse). Others may mock Marge for dying her hair or wearing it like the Bride of Frankenstein, but Homer (and Mr. Burns and Artie Ziff and Jacques and others) find her beautiful. Beauty in Springfield is, as seen most clearly through Homer and Marge, clearly discursive. This does mean, of course, that ugliness is, too. Therefore, teasing Lisa for having a "big butt" can cause her to develop an eating disorder that is never fully resolved (Waltonen and Du Vernay 227). The grotesque exists, but because these grotesque bodies find certain members of the town beautiful and others ugly, then the beautiful body is an individual invention rather than a category that can be imposed by citizen or viewer alike. Therefore, Nelson can see Lisa as attractive. Lisa can see Nelson as attractive. Milhouse can see Lisa as attractive (but no one will see Milhouse as attractive).

Both of these effects of the persistent grotesque in *The Simpsons* lead to the third result, arguably the most important: because the bodies of Springfield are in discourse with one another's grotesqueness, any meaning of the body as an identity marker becomes disrupted. Homer is fat, bald, and stupid, but Marge sees him as a beautiful, kind man. The fatness, baldness, and stupidity therefore do not categorize him as a bad man, or even as any kind of man. The grotesque body does not determine the identity of the character, certainly not toward any means of inferiority or wickedness. Chief Wiggum is a corrupt police officer, but so too are Lou and Eddie, who don't share Wiggum's obesity. Mr. Burns' body is grotesque, and he aspires to levels of supervillainy, but Sideshow Mel is equally grotesque, but is (for Springfield) one of the most clear-headed, intelligent people in the show. Moe is so grotesque he can only manage a Sears catalog when spending an evening alone and murdered the original Alfalfa, but Ned Flanders is a perplexingly buff, horse-genitaled man, who is the kindest person in the town. The grotesque in Springfield disrupts any kind of attempt, by citizen or viewer, to suggest that the body serves as a metaphor for the whole person.

In Tod Browning's classic film *Freaks*, a traveling circus is home to a group of grotesque persons. A normal-sized trapeze artist marries one of the little people to steal his inheritance. When the "freaks" find out that she despises them and is cheating on the little person with the circus strong man, they physically deform both the trapeze artist and the strong man so that they are "one of them." While *Freaks* is considered a landmark movie for several reasons, for present purposes it's only important to point out that those who mock the grotesque are punished; grotesque persons are vengeful and punitive, seeing their own state as a kind of punishment. As Martin Norden writes, "The revenge scene thus takes on a chilling, contradictory quality ... [Browning] did not show his Obsessive Avengers receiving any form of punishment for their actions" (116). In Springfield, however, grotesque persons receive mockery all the time, but there are no "normals" upon whom vengeance must be taken. All actions by Springfieldians, good or bad, come from physical otherness, making any claim about what a physical body categorically *means* in Springfield, in the words of Martin Prince to a blathering Grampa Simpson, "highly dubious" ("Raging Abe Simpson..." 7.22).

Conclusion

In the episode "King-Size Homer" (7.7), Homer learns that morbid obesity is a disability, and would allow him not only to work from home but also to avoid Mr. Burns' tyrannical five-minute calisthenics. Homer succeeds at gaining weight and, at 315 pounds, is able to work from a home computer. Homer's massive weight gain is played for laughs on multiple levels: the visual gag of Homer choosing his outfit among academic robes, ponchos, and a muumuu; his attempt at dialing a phone; and the mockery he gets from neighborhood kids, including Jimbo, who repeats the rumor that Homer's "ass has its own congressman." The grotesqueness of Homer's weight gain is perhaps best revealed when the ever-enduring Marge admits she is no longer sexually attracted to him. Clearly, Homer's size is played into a kind of freakishness, one that would have fit well with early 20th century roaming circus shows. Even his attitude becomes freakish: when Lisa tells Jimbo to leave her father alone, that he is really a gentle soul, Homer begins screaming at the kids from inside the house and waving his broom at them.[4] Even by the end of the episode, there is no real "inner beauty" to be found in Homer's obesity. The ugly-duckling archetype is wholly rejected, and Homer remains a physical freak. At the same time, it is Homer's physical freakishness that saves the power plant from nuclear disaster caused by his own laziness. While the episode makes no real attempt to present obese Homer as a misunderstood soul, it does turn his grotesque nature into an overwhelming positive: his massive girth plugs the release vent from exploding.

The entire world of *The Simpsons* works to normalize the supposedly freakish without minimalizing physical difference, so that a morbidly obese Homer is never understood as aesthetically pleasing, nor is his weight a distracting mask to an inner goodness; Homer's very desire to become obese is arguably the most disturbing part of his character in the episode. Instead, Homer's obese body simply *is*. And while the rest of the town looks askance at Homer's weight, he is really just a more extreme version of Springfield's own bizarre, grotesque bodies. Their mockery of one another turns into a loop with no real sense of "normal" to rest upon. Nelson may shout "Ha ha!" but there is always a Tall Man to pull down his pants and make him parade through the town ("22 Short Films About Springfield" 7.21). Beauty itself therefore becomes overtly discursive, not only in the show but to the viewer as well. After all, a ("normally") obese Homer and a woman with two feet of blue hair sincerely love one another and find one another attractive, Waylon Smithers finds the decrepit, hunchback body of Mr. Burns alluring, and nearly no one in the town is rejected simply because of their physical appearance.[5] In a world of grotesque bodies, beauty is clearly discursive, as we watch Sideshow Bob find two wives (the second for more than homicidal motives) and Moe Szyslak find a Diane Lane-esque girlfriend (at least for one episode). In the grotesque Springfield then, the viewer's aesthetics of the body is disrupted. We see the town with freakish appearances, but we see them exist amongst others like them. All are laughed at, and all have the ability to laugh. It is not perhaps the kindest way of disrupting ideas of beauty and normalcy, but after thirty years, it has been one of the most cromulent.

NOTES

1. Consider Tobin Siebers' quote about all bodies, not just those we are repulsed by, in his *Disability Aesthetics*: "Whether the effect is beauty and pleasure, ugliness and pain, or sublimity and terror, the emotional impact of one body on another is experienced as an assault on autonomy and a testament to the power of otherness... Of course, when bodies produce feelings of pleasure or pain, they also invite judgments about whether they should be accepted or rejected in the human community" (25).

2. Jason Mittell writes that any single genre of *The Simpsons* only makes sense "by conceptualizing genre as a discursive process of categorization and hierarchization, rather than as a core textual component" (15).

3. Lest we forget from the successful marriage class, Marge has been "gray as a mule" since age seventeen.

4. Mortiz Fink provides a brilliant analysis of disabled bodies in *The Simpsons*, but his reading of the scene in which Homer is laughed at by strangers at the movie theater seems to be a misreading. Rather than us judging harshly those who laugh at Homer, we are encouraged to laugh with them. What pathos there might be for Homer is undercut by not only his dress, but his failed attempt at the noble gesture. Homer tells the gathering crowd, "Shame on all of you. Give me my dignity." He then follows that with, "I just came here to see *Honk If You're Horny* in peace."

5. What then of Patty and Selma, then? Their loneliness is hardly only because of their physical appearance. If anyone is actually outside the bounds of beauty, it is Hans Moleman. To be fair, however, he was shouting "Boo-urns."

WORKS CITED

Bakhtin, Mikhail. *Problems of Dostoevsky's Poetics*. Translated by Caryl Emerson. UP of Minnesota, 1984.

"Boy Scoutz 'n' the Hood." *The Simpsons: The Complete Fifth Season*, written by Dan McGrath, directed by Jeffrey Lynch, 20th Century–Fox, 1994.

"Cape Feare." *The Simpsons: The Complete Fifth Season*, written by Jon Vitti, directed by Rich Moore, 20th Century–Fox, 1994.

"Duffless." *The Simpsons: The Complete Fourth Season*, written by David M. Stern, directed by Jim Reardon, 20th Century–Fox, 1993.

Edwards, Justin D., and Rune Graulund. *Grotesque*. Routledge, 2013.

Fiedler, Leslie. *Freaks: Myths and Images of the Secret Self*. Anchor, 1978.

Fink, Moritz. "People Who Look Like Things: Representations of Disability in *The Simpsons*." *Journal of Literary and Cultural Disability Studies*, vol. 7, issue 3, 3013, pp. 255–70.

Gray, Jonathan. *Watching with* The Simpsons: *Television, Parody, and Intertextuality*. Routledge, 2006.

"Homer the Vigilante." *The Simpsons: The Complete Fifth Season*, written by John Swartzwelder, directed by Jim Reardon, 20th Century–Fox, 1994.

"Homer's Barbershop Quartet." *The Simpsons: The Complete Fifth Season*, written by Jeff Martin, directed by Mark Kirkland, 20th Century–Fox, 1994.

"Homer's Triple Bypass." *The Simpsons: The Complete Fourth Season*, written by Larry Doyle, directed by Mark Ervin, 20th Century–Fox, 1993.

"Kamp Krusty." *The Simpsons: The Complete Fourth Season*, written by David M. Stern, directed by Mark Kirkland, 20th Century–Fox, 1993.

Kayser, Wolfgang. *The Grotesque in Art and Literature.* Translated by Ulrich Weisstein. Peter Smith, 1968.

"King-Size Homer." *The Simpsons: The Complete Seventh Season,* written by Dan Greaney, directed by Jim Reardon, 20th Century–Fox, 1996.

"Lady Bouvier's Lover." *The Simpsons: The Complete Fifth Season,* written by Bill Oakley & Josh Weinstein, directed by Wes Archer, 20th Century–Fox, 1994.

"Lard of the Dance." *The Simpsons: The Complete Tenth Season,* written by Jane O'Brien, directed by Dominic Polcino, 20th Century–Fox, 1998.

"Marge vs. the Monorail." *The Simpsons: The Complete Fourth Season,* written by Conan O'Brien, directed by Rich Moore, 20th Century–Fox, 1993.

Mittell, Jason. "Cartoon Realism: Genre Mixing and the Cultural Life of *The Simpsons.*" *Velvet Light Trap* vol. 47, Spring 2001, pp. 15–30.

"Mother Simpson." *The Simpsons: The Complete Seventh Season,* written by Richard Appel, directed by David Silverman, 20th Century–Fox, 1996.

"Mountain of Madness" *The Simpsons: The Complete Eighth Season,* written by John Swartzwelder, directed by Mark Kirkland, 20th Century–Fox, 1997.

Mullen, Megan. "*The Simpsons* and Hanna-Barbera's Animation Legacy." *Leaving Springfield: The Simpsons and the Possibility of Oppositional Culture.* Editor John Alberti. Wayne State UP, 2004, pp. 63–84.

Norden, Martin F. *The Cinema of Isolation: A History of Physical Disability in the Movies.* Rutgers University Press, 1994.

"O Brother, Where Art Thou?" *The Simpsons: The Complete Second Season,* written by Jeff Martin, directed by W.M. "Bud" Archer, 20th Century–Fox, 1991.

"Raging Abe Simpson and His Grumbling Grandson in 'The Curse of the Flying Hellfish.'" *The Simpsons: The Complete Seventh Season,* written by Jonathan Collier, directed by Jeffrey Lynch, 20th Century–Fox, 1996.

"Selma's Choice." *The Simpsons: The Complete Fourth Season,* written by David M. Stern, directed by Carlos Baeza, 20th Century–Fox, 1993.

Siebers, Tobin. *Disability Aesthetics.* UP of Michigan, 2010.

Solomon, Deborah. "Screen Dreams: Questions for Matt Groening." *The New York Times Magazine,* 22 July 2007. https://www.nytimes.com/2007/07/22/magazine/22wwln-Q4-t.html.

"The Springfield Files." *The Simpsons: The Complete Eighth Season,* written by Reid Harrison, directed by Steven Dean Moore, 20th Century–Fox, 2006.

"The Summer of 4 Ft. 2." *The Simpsons: The Complete Seventh Season,* written by Dan Greaney, directed by Mark Kirkland, 20th Century–Fox, 1996.

"They Saved Lisa's Brain." *The Simpsons: The Complete Tenth Season,* written by Matt Selman, directed by Pete Michels, 20th Century–Fox, 1998.

"22 Short Films About Springfield." *The Simpsons: The Complete Seventh Season,* written by Richard Appel, David S. Cohen, Jonathan Collier, Jennifer Crittenden, Greg Daniels, Brent Forrester, Rachel Pulido, Steve Tompkins, Bill Oakley, Josh Weinstein and Matt Groening, directed by Jim Reardon, 20th Century–Fox, 1996.

Waltonen, Karma, and Denise Du Vernay. *The Simpsons in the Classroom: Embiggening the Learning Experience with the Wisdom of Springfield.* McFarland, 2010.

"Who Shot Mr. Burns? (Part Two)." *The Simpsons: The Complete Seventh Season.* Written by Bill Oakley and Josh Weinstein, directed by Wes Archer, 20th Century–Fox, 1995.

"Will you take us to Mt. Splashmore?"

Commercials and Consumerism

BRIAN N. DUCHANEY

Home. It's a place where we relax, expecting to shutter the chaos of the world, believing that we are in control of our own destiny. Sitting down, remote control in hand, we scroll through channels, hoping to be inspired by the eventual drivel that we're likely to encounter. But for a show like *The Simpsons*, the sitting down and watching television is part of what drives the idea of real life. While we expect television to offer a respite, *The Simpsons* shows us that the outside world is fully imbued in our sense of identity. For all the moments of clarity when we realize that television is harmless entertainment, *The Simpsons* shows us that the world is actually intrusive, insinuating that viewers are susceptible to the influences of a dangerous contagion, a suggestive mirror exposing our society for what it really is—the reason that we ultimately make bad choices. It isn't Duff beer, or the violence of a show like *The Itchy & Scratchy Show*. The danger lies in what may be the most innocuous aspect of television: commercials.

At first glance, *The Simpsons* appears to show the struggles of the family in a town that knows too well the levels of its own dysfunction. Despite the strangulations, wastefulness, schemes, and drunk driving (and that's just Homer), the Simpsons are a well-grounded family in Springfield. They are widely known, respected (even if not always liked), and incredibly lucky. But like many American families, they've fallen victim to their televisions. This is made clear in the opening credits. In the opening sequence, following the couch gag, the production credits appear (created by Matt Groening/developed by James L. Brooks, Matt Groening, and Sam Simon) on the Simpsons' television set. It should be noted that this opening is a carefully planned moment that takes delight in showcasing the dangers of television while iron-ically doing so in the format of what is now a wildly popular television show.

The opening credits of *The Simpsons*, much like the show itself, is a response to the many writers' views on the absurdity of commercialization and our growing reliance on popular culture as a window into the world. However, the commercials that are featured throughout the show are specific devices that are used to share character impulses with the audience. For instance, after telling Bart and Milhouse a story while they toast marshmal-lows in the fireplace, Bart asks Homer, "…why do all of your bedtime stories have ads for the Container Store in them?" Homer says, "Because if I do it enough, maybe they'll start to pay me" ("Little Orphan Millie" 19.6). The simple logic of selling out, even when no one is around to notice it, isn't a symptom of Homer alone but of society at large. In other words, we're apt to associate ourselves with brands—i.e. build a sense of brand loyalty within ourselves—that we recognize in the hopes of receiving something, simply as a reward for being loyal, whether it is through discounts, free merchandise, or just self-gratification. Though the show strives to be well-versed in its satiric take on American culture, it is the sheer awareness of controlled impulse (or reasoned impulse with a purpose) that establishes *The Simpsons* as a barometer of American attitudes and values.

The fictional commercials in *The Simpsons* play an important role in understanding both the social structure and mentality of Springfield resi-dents, and how the Simpson family is shaped by their TV viewing habits. They act as meta-commentary about life in Springfield, but also direct the audience to see the redundancy of discussing society through the medium of television, especially where watching television is becoming more an iso-lated activity. And perhaps because of their loving-yet-dysfunctional rela-tionships, the television world at times stands in for sincerity, acting as a substitution for real intimacy. Ironically, however, television—specifically the commercials—compel the Simpson family to venture into the world. Often this leads to the development of an episode's plot. For example, the episode "Take My Wife, Sleaze" (11.8) opens with the family watching the absurd *Guinness Book of World's Records* show—which seems to acknowledge its own vapidity by showcasing records like a man with "the least amount of faces"—the family is inspired to try a '50s style café. When Wolfguy Jack (a parody of Wolfman Jack) asks, "Do you remember television, Coca Cola, and Dick Clark?" Homer joyfully responds, "I remember television!" Not only does viewing the commercial prompt the next scene, but it sets up the events of the episode, with Marge and Homer winning a motorcycle during a dance competition and Homer starting a motorcycle gang. But notice that it was the commodity of nostalgia that "sold" the family on experience, prompting a vision of reality (the 1950s) to the family.

Nostalgia and a dreamlike reality are a focus for Homer, perhaps because he lives vicariously through the events he watches. While the show has numerous episodes that break continuity and explore either the past or present, Homer's past is frequently punctuated by his reliance on television shows and commercials to pinpoint the time frame. In "Lisa's Sax" (9.3), Homer and Marge sing a version of *All in the Family*'s iconic theme song while referencing *Gentle Ben*. Further, in "Lisa's First Word" (4.10), Bart's lack of understanding a reference in the Mondale/Hart debate leads to Homer's laughing recognition of the iconic Wendy's catchphrase "Where's the beef?" These instances lead to Homer relying on television to interact with others. For example, Homer, as an icebreaker, asks a stranger if he's "seen any good beer commercials lately" ("Moms I'd Like to Forget" 22.10). This concept has been reinforced since the show's beginning. While Homer is passed out on the floor at Moe's watching a boxing match, he awakens to a commercial of a dysfunctional family fighting, repeatedly telling each other to shut up. The commercial for Dr. Marvin Monroe's family therapy clinic, itself a dysfunctional commercial, provides Homer with the promise of righting tensions in the family ("There's No Disgrace Like Home" 1.4).

The large number and wide scope of commercials in the Springfield universe should be seen first as sources of humor. How else can we explain flashbacks of Rainer Wolfcastle in childhood bratwurst advertisements, or Bart's brief stint as "Baby Stink Breath," in which he shills chemical stickers that alter a baby's DNA ("Barting Over" 14.11)? But even the unrealistic commercials exploit our willingness to accept (and often rely upon) products that either are unthinkable—such as Steakie (the soft drink infused with the great taste of Worcestershire sauce) ("Homer Goes to College" 5.3)—or lampooned as unethical, such as the real company Fruitopia, which is described by a baseball announcer as "the iced tea brewed by hippies, but distributed by a heartless, multi-national corporation" ("Lisa's Sax").[1]

Advertising and consumer culture are at the forefront of the episode "Attack of the 50 Foot Eyesores," which appears in "Treehouse of Horror VI" (7.6). Homer's dissatisfaction with the paltry size of his "colossal donut" drives him to take revenge on "false advertising" by stealing the Lard Lad Donut's sign, whereby the Lard Lad himself comes alive to take it back. With the town's other giant advertisements wreaking havoc on Springfield as well, Lisa turns to the Van Brunt & Churchill Advertising Company—the source of the Lard Lad—to find a way to effectively stop them. What we're told is that "advertising is a funny thing. If people stop paying attention to it, it goes away." With the help of Paul Anka telling residents to "just don't look," the town is rid of the carnage-inducing advertisements. The episode ends with a satiric warning from Kent Brockman telling viewers the inherent danger of taking advertising too literally: "Even as I speak the scourge of advertising could be heading to your town. Lock your doors, bar your windows, because the next advertisement you see could destroy your house and eat your family." Here, Homer's literal fixation and trust in advertising becomes the town's downfall.

While giant advertisements wrecking a town is far-fetched, let's face it; we've all been swayed by advertising, whether it be a flashy sports car or by promises of discounts and savings. And while paper advertisements can be effective, they're no match to what can be shown through television. The illusion of reality is stronger. And while there may be the acknowledgment of the lie by the advertiser (i.e., "Professional driver on a closed course" or "Game pieces do not actually talk"), consumers buy into lies because of our need to exhibit our own Homeric impulses. Yet unlike Homer, we acknowledge the lie because, well, there's no escape from advertising. We simply accept it as we do death and taxes. This is where *The Simpsons* exposes the nature of advertising. There seems to be a parallel between content (those commercials that speak directly to the family) and mindless consumerism (those that are passing references to the absurd notion that we can all be bought). Somewhere in between is the truth.

In *The Simpsons*, the role of the audience is deliberately flipped, presenting what Valerie Weilunn Chow suggests to be a dual role for the show's viewers. Citing Mimi White's *Ideological Analysis and Television*, Chow reasons that viewers of *The Simpsons* become part of a "circuit of televisual commodification, [where] the viewer is ultimately like the Simpson family—both the consumer and the consumed" (108). Commercials must then present an opportunity in which Matt Groening and his team of writers invite viewers into the mercantile chain of the commodity-driven Springfield.

In *Planet Simpson: How a Cartoon Masterpiece Defined a Generation*, Chris Turner explains that Springfield is little more than blind consumerism: "Springfield may have a factory or two, and many locals earn their wages, as Homer does, down at the power plant, but Springfield's *raison d'être* is quite clearly consumption of the crassest kind: useless trinkets, celebrity-endorsed junk, synthetic simulacra of old staples" (106). But television in Springfield offers many things to viewers beyond consumer goods. *The Simpsons* is deftly aware that commercials expose desires, be it a reliable plow company or a detergent from a pair of Japanese conglomerates. But as Turner points out:

> The thing is, our own consumer culture pretty much defies sanitization. It mocks itself so effectively it can't be mocked, and it vaults into self-parody too regularly and effectively to really need outside help. In one *Simpsons* episode, a depressed Homer wanders into the Kwik-E-Mart in search of something to lift his spirits. "Got any of that beer that has candy floating in it?" he asks Apu. "You know—Skittle Bräu?" Apu informs him there is no such product, so Homer buys a six-pack and a few packages of Skittles. A few years later, the online retailer Café-press.com could be found hawk-

ing everything from T-shirts and baseball caps to coffee mugs and mouse pads emblazoned with the Skittle Bräu logo. The product itself was too silly even for Springfield's overheated consumer culture, but the commodification of the show in the real world has become so extensive and relentless that Skittle Bräu gave birth to a whole line of saleable merchandise [107].

Skittle Bräu is just one example of how meta-commentary is central to understanding the intent by writers of *The Simpsons* to have audiences reflect on the gross reliance on the power of the purchase. Similar to the reward felt by Homer and his frozen family in "Treehouse of Horror V" (6.6), as he cajoles his family to "sit in the snow with daddy ... [and] bask in television's warm glowing warming glow," commercialism acts as a panacea for the wanton disregard of social accountability or the compulsive need to acquire. And while the Simpsons may often be viewed as dysfunctional or inept from time to time by neighbors and friends alike (The Lovejoys, Dr. & Mrs. Hibbert, George H.W. Bush, and of course stupid Flanders), they are still both popular and respected. Despite their dysfunction, the family still manages to function (well) within the greater social tapestry that is Springfield. Why? The dysfunction of Springfield is partly the problem.

Springfield is mutable; that is, it changes based on the needs dictated by plot and storyline. It has every topographical feature and every opportunity anyone could want access to. It is even the resting place of Walt Whitman. Yet Springfieldians are never satisfied. They follow a mob mentality that affects every facet of their lives, from politics to recreational activities to charity. While residents of the town willingly chip in to help others when needed, such as rebuilding Ned's house following the hurricane ("Hurricane Neddy" 8.8), or quickly recognize a shared appreciation of culture, including opera ("The Homer of Seville" 19.2), they are equally manipulated by a shared sense of impulse. For example, when Lisa finds what appears to be the skeletal remains of an angel found during a Springfield Elementary archaeological dig organized by Principal Skinner, the entire town's faith is tested ("Lisa the Skeptic" 9.8). Homer brings the skeleton home to store so that it will "appreciate in value," storing it with, among other things, his town crier hat, a pair of heads from Itchy & Scratchy Land, a box of Mr. Sparkle, his Grammy Award, and a six-pack of Billy Beer. When people start appearing at 742 Evergreen Terrace to find support from the angel, Homer sets up a crude display in the family garage, charging fifty cents for the opportunity to "see the angel." Lisa riles the town folk when she states that she brought a piece of the skeleton for scientific testing. The fact that the statue was not only fake but part of a publicity stunt for the Heavenly Hills Shopping Mall is overlooked by the town. Their shared faith and belief in the possibility of a confirmed miracle is overshadowed by the promise of "the end of high prices."

Viewed collectively, the citizens of Springfield speak in a unified voice that asserts authority by "having," displayed in the many town meetings chaired by Mayor Quimby. In these meetings, which seem to be called for crises or good fortune, note that any dissent is often loudly shouted down, regardless of whether the idea presented is "good." Hence, Lisa's pragmatism or Marge's wish for discussion is often undermined by the town's need for immediate action and fulfillment. Repeatedly, from the construction of the monorail to the election of Homer as garbage commissioner, we learn that Springfield seems to be a place where every need is met, and is always met, as fast as possible. This would explain the numerous references to what can be called specialty stores, such as the air conditioner store It Blows to the clothing store for larger men The Vast Waistband. Similarly, there are stores that reference "real world" stores to reflect the same world of commodity for the citizens of Springfield, including the Blocko store and Spiffany's.

Yet with so much available, commodity itself causes problems. For instance, we learn that Springfield has three different bowling shops named "Nick's" as a frazzled and overworked Marge attempts to to get Homer's bowling ball fixed ("Homer Alone" 3.15). Also, Lisa gets into trouble downloading music to her MyPod, one of her many Mapple devices ("Mypods and Boomsticks" 20.7). Perhaps the best indicator for Springfield being a place where every need is met is through Homer's lengthy résumé. Prior to founding his security company—Springshield—he tells Marge one evening, "Y'know, I've had a lot of jobs: boxer, mascot, astronaut, imitation Krusty, babyproofer, trucker, hippie, plow driver, food critic, conceptual artist, grease salesman, carny, mayor, grifter, bodyguard for the mayor, country western manager, garbage commissioner, mountain climber, farmer, inventor, Smithers, Poochie, celebrity assistant, power plant worker, fortune cookie writer, beer baron, Kwik-E-Mart clerk, homophobe, and missionary ... but protecting Springfield, that gives me the best feeling of all" ("Poppa's Got a Brand New Badge" 13.22). Despite his "regular" job in sector 7G at Springfield Nuclear Power Plant, Homer explores every opportunity for more, thus showing that having and getting are not necessarily evidence of satisfaction. This latter point is important to understanding the need for betterment and improvement that is so often a focus in *The Simpsons*.

Commercials highlight the problems of the nuclear (no pun intended) family, but they also point to problems of the larger world. For instance, while Homer and friends sit in Super Bowl jail after obtaining counterfeit tickets, Marge and the children, watching the game from home, see an ad for the Catholic Church, which features scantily clad nuns at a gas station *a la* a ZZ Top video (whose music incidentally plays in the background). The subtle, gravelly voiceover simply states: "The Catholic Church. We've made a few ... changes" ("Sunday Cruddy Sunday" 10.12). The intent of such an ad exploits the rampant consumer mentality of Super Bowl viewers (where 30-second spots in 2015 cost in excess of $4 million, up from approximately $1.5 million when the episode originally aired in 1999). But more than that, the commentary exploits the relationship between viewers and our wish for simulated reality. Like the bespectacled driver of the Catholic Church commercial, we all want a bevy of buxom nuns in an assortment of blonde, brunette, and redhead …or something to that effect. What the commercial really shows us is that advertising is, for lack of a better phrase, sexy. It stimulates our desire for something better.

Douglas Rushkoff explores this very problem within *The Simpsons*, citing our desires for free expression and choice as the *modus operandi* of the show's critique on culture: "[W]e call the stuff on television 'programming' for a reason. Television programmers are not programming television sets or evening schedules; they are programming the viewers. Whether they are convincing us to buy a product, vote for a candidate, adopt an ideology, or simply confirm a moral platitude, the underlying reasons for making television is to hold onto our attention and then sell us a bill of goods" (293). Unsurprisingly, Springfield's residents have been urged to do every one of these acts over the course of the many years that *The Simpsons* has been on the air. But in a town like Springfield, where the larger world is rife with citizens who adopt a lemming-like following of impulsiveness and adopt an utterly blind attitude toward rational thought, Springfieldians' frequent riots, penchant for violence, and belief in vigilante justice may expose the effects of what commercial culture has turned society into: a pack of unthinking automatons.

We can see this realized through Homer, who is no stranger to the television airwaves, often embracing the power of TV commercials to promote his own brand of social justice: entrepreneurship. Along with his well-known Mr. Plow commercial, in which he exposes the danger of doing your own snow clearing as ranging from "having your hands cut off" to "the inevitable heart attack," Homer seems relatively comfortable in front of the camera ("Mr. Plow" 4.9). Beginning with a brief appearance as "Steve" in a commercial for the impotency/hair loss drug Viagrogaine ("Barting Over" 14.11), Homer has starred in or produced several commercials for products meant to deliver him rewards directly, products which are meant to capitalize on the impulsive nature of Springfieldians. Following a particularly harsh heat wave, one that causes rolling blackouts that lead to widespread rioting (ironically caused by Mr. Burns cutting power to the local orphanage in an attempt to *save* energy), Homer starts Springshield—his private security company—due to his dissatisfaction with local law enforcement ("Poppa's Got a Brand New Badge" 13.22). Preying on people's fears, his commercial features a Maurice Sendak–style monster attacking an old woman. Likewise, failing to apologize to garbage collectors after calling them "trash-eating stinkbags," Homer runs for sanitation commissioner to avoid apologizing. The buildup of trash is the result of a new holiday created by Costington's: "Love Day" ("Trash of the Titans" 9.22).

Media theorist Marshall McLuhan states that

> Ads seem to work on the very advanced principle that a small pellet or pattern in a noisy, redundant barrage of repetition will gradually assert itself ... advertising aims at the goal of a programmed harmony among all human impulses and aspirations and endeavors ... When all production and all consumption are brought into a pre-established harmony with all desire and all effort, then advertising will have liquidated itself by its own success" [227].

But, of course, this will never be the case. We're always on the lookout for the next new thing. Tom Hanks shows us this in *The Simpsons Movie* when he lends his credibility to the U.S. Government by advertising the New Grand Canyon, which is better than the same "old and boring" one that we've all been going to. East of Shelbyville and South of Capital City, it is "nowhere near where anything is or ever was" (*The Simpsons Movie*). Central to the humor in this is the promise of something that is newer and improved. In the guise of a TV pitchman, Hanks' sardonic celebrity endorsement is an expressive statement against the tenets of modern consumerism: the newer product—no matter how bad or immoral the process taken to deliver us the goods—becomes the favorable choice. This is the premise behind another satirical ad, this time one crafted by Sideshow Bob. In a bid for Mayor of Springfield, Bob runs the following ad: "Mayor Quimby supports revolving-door prisons. Mayor Quimby even released Sideshow Bob—a man twice convicted of attempted murder. Can you trust a man like Mayor Quimby? Vote Sideshow Bob for Mayor" ("Sideshow Bob Roberts" 6.5).

Central to the idea of meta-commentary with *The Simpsons* is the development of entire plotlines stemming from a relatively innocent suggestion made by a television commercial. While some of these commercials drive the episodes in their entirety, others become a catalyst for actions that present what can only be described as life-altering moments for the family. In these episodes, commercials reflect the innocence of the Simpsons, showing them to be easily swayed by and manipulated by the consumer culture that pervades Springfield. For instance, after a family gathering, the Simpsons and the Bouviers sit at the dining room table singing the "Armour Hot Dog" theme. Lisa asks, "Doesn't this family know any songs that aren't commercials?" She eventually storms away when the family, after a brief silence, begins chanting, "I feel like chicken tonight, like chicken tonight," echoing a refrain from the early 1990s familiar to many viewers of the show ("Lady Bouvier's Lover" 5.21).

For all the fun cultural references peppered throughout the satirization of the commercialized culture of American society, such as the passing references to *Star Trek XII—So Very Tired* and the now infamous all-you-can-eat buffet at The Frying Dutchman (where Homer eats the plastic lobster),

The Simpsons' use of advertising embedded within the show cautions against the reactionary impulses that television promotes. In these instances, the commercials themselves are benign, but the attentiveness of the Simpson family to the impulsiveness offered by television advertising creates an awareness for both the characters and the television audience alike, where the show's writers are most able to caution against blind consumption. After the Springfield Isotopes win the championships, and Homer, Lenny, Carl, and Barney wreck Springfield Elementary joyriding through the hallways in Homer's car, an imposed curfew leaves the kids at home watching prime time television. As Bart is about to wreck the TV—following a small segment of a typical 1990s sitcom titled *Don't Go There*, a commercial for *The Bloodening* inspires the children of Springfield to break curfew ("Wild Barts Can't Be Broken" 10.11). This leads to an elaborate dance number by all the town's residents, espousing the value of freedom and rules. The end result is a new curfew for anyone under the age of seventy. Likewise, it is a commercial promoting a local appearance of Truckasaurus that leads Bart to try his hand at freestyle skateboarding and Homer's first realized version of attentive parenting that leads him to (unsuccessfully) attempt to jump over Springfield Gorge ("Bart the Daredevil" 2.8).

Commercials have factored into motivating all of the Simpson family to try to do more or accomplish more. A segment on *The Krusty the Clown Show* titled "Kroon Along with Krusty" propels the family (through a day-long harangue of nagging by Bart and Lisa) to Mt. Splashmore, the local water park. It is here that Homer gets stuck inside a slide, prompting him to search the attic for his old weights, which allows Bart to discover Marge's forgotten paintings of Ringo Starr, leading her to enroll in a course at Springfield Community College, and ultimately prompting her to show the beautiful—if weathered and liver-spotted—truth of a fragile and naked Mr. Burns ("Brush With Greatness" 2.18). In a similar fashion, a commercial for a model rocket—a new and better version with added "yaw control"—leads Homer, Bart, and Milhouse into a friendly (if albeit over the top) competition against Ned, Rod, and Todd Flanders ("She of Little Faith" 13.6). After Nibbles, the hamster test pilot, ejects, the NASA-like rocket built by Homer's former Springfield University roommates runs afoul and destroys the First Church of Springfield. To rebuild, Reverend Lovejoy enlists the help of Mr. Burns and Lindsay Naegle to build revenue through the sale of ad space within the church. Lisa, appalled by the commercial spectacle that the church has become (and perhaps a bit offended by being labeled a "Pouting Thomas" on the Godcam), abandons the church in search of a religion that hasn't lost its soul.

Impulse surrounds the reactionary attitudes for the family; commercials lead Bart to try karate (which he abandons after one lesson) and get a pigeon, Lisa to take ballet lessons at the Chazz Busby Ballet Academy, and Marge to visit a spa by the name of Rancho Relaxo. Commercials lead Homer to follow Krusty Burger's Ribwich across the country like a Deadhead, while movie trailers prompt him to rebel against advertising in the Cineplex, forcing a legion of teenaged ushers armed with "movie size" Kit-Kats to "advance" on him. The resulting chase leads him to the city square and straight into a statue of Drederick Tatum that is being dedicated by the mayor and carrying forth the storyline that is the episode "Jaws Wired Shut" (13.9). Commercials also lead to Lisa's discovery that Funzo is nothing more than a figure developed by corporate researchers (again, the episode features Lindsay Naegle) after the privatization of Springfield Elementary. Researchers from Kid First Industries use the children to research the commercial appetites of the kids to produce the next Christmas sensation ("Grift of the Magi" 11.9). Another episode features the entire family suffering seizures in Japan following a commercial for a Japanese cartoon called *Battle Seizure Robots* ("Thirty Minutes Over Tokyo" 10.23).

But for all the impulsive tendencies, it is the practiced restraint against consumerism that leads to some of the show's most poignant moments against impulsiveness. Instead of getting the air conditioner he wants, Homer sacrifices his sense of comfort in exchange for Lisa's saxophone ("Lisa's Sax" 9.3) not once, but twice: first in the past when it was originally bought (as "a way to encourage a gifted child") and again after Bart damages the instrument trying to shut up Lisa's practicing. The final gag shows Marge holding Maggie contentedly watching TV, as Homer wipes his brow. This is the set up to the Fruitopia gag, the same corporation that writers depict as unscrupulous money-grubbers exploiting the average worker.

It is the familiar refrain of *Monday Night Football* with a new lyrical spin promoting a soccer match—"Open wide for some soccer!"—that prompts the Simpson family to attend a "local" contest between Mexico and Portugal, all to see who will be the greatest on Earth. And as poor as the event sounds, it is touted as having all the elements that ensure satisfaction: "fast kickin', low scorin', and ties? You bet!" ("The Cartridge Family" 9.5). After being lured to the game by autographs, the citizens of Springfield rush to leave the low scoring game. As a riot ensues, Homer is provoked into buying a gun to protect the family from violence. But what the episode "The Cartridge Family" exploits isn't our desire for firearms or the challenges of interpreting the Second Amendment; it is Homer's abject necessity to have the appearance of immediate safety by having his consumerist desires met immediately:

> **Homer:** "I don't have to be careful. I have a gun."
> **Salesman:** "Well, you'll probably want the accessory kit: holster; bandolier; silencer; loudener; speed cocker…
> **Homer:** "…ooh, I like the sound of that…"
> **Salesman:** "And this is for shooting down police helicopters."

Homer: "Oh, I don't need anything like that … yet. Just gimme my gun."
Salesman: "Sorry, but the law requires a five-day waiting period. We've got to run a background check."
Homer: "Five days? But I'm mad now!"

In what may be the quintessential moment in the Simpsons' interaction with commercials, Keith Olbermann makes a cameo as he tries to talk Marge out of not watching commercials, calling her a "content burglar" when she attempts to fast forward shows via the family's new TiVo. Upon installing the device, Homer states, "Now we can watch shows and skip the commercials!" ("Funeral for a Fiend" 19.8). In an array of Easter eggs for the audience, Homer skips the following: Duff Beer in space; a literacy commercial; a commercial for Funzo; Homer's private security firm; Wes Doobner's World Famous Family Rib Hut, a "Yes on 87" Union Carbide commercial; Frogs in Favor of Wetlands Destruction; finally stopping on Wes Doobner's again, prompting the family to go to the restaurant's grand opening. This is a ruse to entrap the family by Sideshow Bob (the name is an anagram for "Sideshow Bob's World Famous Family Style Return"), prompting Bob to gloat that he will kill the family because they watched a television commercial. Homer responds with "Ooh, next time a television commercial comes on, I'm going to shut my eyes, cover my ears, and scream as loud as I can." Try as he may, and as we may from home, we're aware of the futility of blocking out the very reason shows like *The Simpsons* get made. Of course, this is where the show cuts to commercial.

NOTE

1. Fruitopia was created by the Coca Cola company in 1994.

WORKS CITED

"Bart the Daredevil." *The Simpsons: The Complete Second Season*. Written by Jay Kogen and Wallace Wolodarsky, directed by Wes Archer, 20th Century–Fox, 2002.
"Barting Over." *The Simpsons: The Complete Fourteenth Season*. Written by Andrew Kreisberg, directed by Matthew Nastuk, 20th Century–Fox, 2011.
"Brush with Greatness." *The Simpsons: The Complete Second Season*. Written by Brian K. Roberts, directed by Jim Reardon, 20th Century–Fox, 2002.
"The Cartridge Family." *The Simpsons: The Complete Ninth Season*. Written by John Swartzwelder, directed by Pete Michels, 20th Century–Fox, 2006.
Chow, Valerie Weilunn. "Homer Erectus: Homer Simpson as Everyman … and Every Woman." *Leaving Springfield*: The Simpsons *and the Possibility of Oppositional Culture*. Ed. John Alberti. Wayne State University Press, 2004, pp. 107–137.
"Funeral for a Fiend." *The Simpsons*. Written by Michael Price, directed by Rob Oliver, 20th Century–Fox, 25 November 2007.
"Grift of the Magi." *The Simpsons: The Complete Eleventh Season*. Written by Tom Martin, directed by Matthew Nastuk, 20th Century–Fox, 2008.
"Homer Alone." *The Simpsons: The Complete Third Season*. Written by David M. Stern, directed by Mark Kirkland, 20th Century–Fox, 2003.
"Homer Goes to College." *The Simpsons: The Complete Fifth Season*. Written by Conan O'Brien, directed by Jim Reardon, 20th Century–Fox, 2004.
"The Homer of Seville." *The Simpsons*. Written by Carolyn Omine, directed by Michael Polcino, 20th Century–Fox, 30 September 2007.

"Hurricane Neddy." *The Simpsons: The Complete Eighth Season.* Written by Steve Young, directed by Bob Anderson, 20th Century–Fox, 2006.

"Jaws Wired Shut." *The Simpsons: The Complete Thirteenth Season.* Written by Matt Selman, directed by Nancy Kruse, 20th Century–Fox, 2010.

"Lady Bouvier's Lover." *The Simpsons: The Complete Fifth Season.* Written by Bill Oakley and Josh Weinstein, 20th Century–Fox, 2004.

"Lisa the Skeptic." *The Simpsons: The Complete Ninth Season.* Written by David X. Cohen, directed by Neil Affleck, 20th Century–Fox, 1997.

"Lisa's First Word." *The Simpsons: The Complete Fourth Season.* Written by Jeff Martin, directed by Mark Kirkland, 20th Century–Fox, 2004.

"Lisa's Sax." *The Simpsons: The Complete Ninth Season.* Written by Al Jean, directed by Dominic Polcino, 20th Century–Fox, 2006.

"Little Orphan Millie." *The Simpsons.* Written by Mick Kelly, directed by Lance Kramer, 20th Century–Fox, 11 November 2007.

McLuhan, Marshall. *Understanding Media: The Extensions of Man.* MIT Press, 1994.

"Moms I'd Like to Forget." *The Simpsons.* Written by Brian Kelley, directed by Chris Clements, 20th Century–Fox, 9 January 2011.

"Mr. Plow." *The Simpsons: The Complete Fourth Season.* Written by Jon Vitti, directed by Jim Reardon, 20th Century–Fox, 2004.

"MyPods and Boomsticks." *The Simpsons.* Written by Marc Wilmore, directed by Steven Dean Moore, 20th Century–Fox, 30 November 2008.

"Poppa's Got a Brand New Badge." *The Simpsons: The Complete Thirteenth Season.* Written by Dana Gould, directed by Pete Michels, 20th Century–Fox, 2010.

Rushkoff, Douglas. "Bart Simpson: Prince of Irreverence." *Leaving Springfield: The Simpsons and the Possibility of Oppositional Culture.* Ed. John Alberti. Wayne State University Press, 2004, pp. 292–301.

"She of Little Faith." *The Simpsons: The Complete Thirteenth Season.* Written by Bill Freiberger, directed by Steven Dean Moore, 20th Century–Fox, 2010.

"Sideshow Bob Roberts." *The Simpsons: The Complete Sixth Season.* Written by Bill Oakley and Josh Weinstein, directed by Mark Kirkland, 20th Century–Fox, 2005.

The Simpsons Movie. Directed by David Silverman, performances by Dan Castellaneta, Julie Kavner, Nancy Cartwright, Yeardley Smith, Hank Azaria. 20th Century–Fox, 2007.

"Sunday, Cruddy Sunday." *The Simpsons: The Complete Tenth Season.* Written by Tom Martin, George Meyer, Brian Scully, and Mike Scully, directed by Steven Dean Moore, 20th Century–Fox, 2007.

"Take My Wife, Sleaze." *The Simpsons: The Complete Eleventh Season.* Written by John Swartzwelder, directed by Neil Affleck, 20th Century–Fox, 2008.

"There's No Disgrace Like Home." *The Simpsons: The Complete First Season.* Written by Al Jean and Mike Reiss, directed by Gregg Vanzo, 20th Century–Fox, 2001.

"Thirty Minutes Over Tokyo." *The Simpsons: The Complete Tenth Season.* Written by Donick Cary and Dan Greaney, directed by Jim Reardon. 20th Century–Fox, 1999.

"Trash of the Titans." *The Simpsons: The Complete Ninth Season.* Written by Ian Maxtone-Graham, directed by Jim Reardon, 20th Century–Fox, 2006.

"Treehouse of Horror V." *The Simpsons: The Complete Sixth Season.* Written by Greg Daniels, Dan McGrath, David S. Cohen, and Bob Kushell, directed by Jim Reardon, 20th Century–Fox, 2005.

"Treehouse of Horror VI." *The Simpsons: The Complete Seventh Season.* Written by John Swartzwelder, Steve Tompkins, and David S. Cohen, directed by Bob Anderson and David Mirkin, 20th Century–Fox, 2005.

Turner, Chris. *Planet Simpson: How a Cartoon Masterpiece Defined a Generation.* Da Capo, 2005.

"Wild Barts Can't Be Broken." *The Simpsons: The Complete Tenth Season.* Written by Larry Doyle, directed by Mark Ervin, 20th Century–Fox, 2007.

"I'll repress the rage I'm feeling!"

Food Politics

Timothy L. Glenn

It may seem odd to think that the act of eating is a political act. After all, our bodies are our own, and the choices we make of what to put in them seem to be a private affair. However, the field of food politics studies the connections behind the simple act of eating. Every piece of food produced, sold, and consumed has a history. Barry Estabrook, author of the recent book *Tomatoland*, asks us to consider the tomato as an example. In 2009, he relates, tomatoes were America's second-most popular fruit and generated five billion dollars in sales (x). One-third of fresh tomatoes raised in the United States are grown in Florida, but tomatoes grow poorly in Florida's soil, so the crops are often treated with over one hundred herbicides and pesticides. Many of these chemicals are known to be hazardous to human health, and the effect on tomato field workers includes "eye and respiratory ailments, exposure to known carcinogens, and babies born with horrendous birth defects" (xiii). These workers, mostly poor Latinx itinerant workers, have little health care or legal protection, and some, in fact, have been enslaved. Since the 1990s, Estabrook states, Florida authorities "freed more than one thousand men and women who had been held and forced to work against their will" and suspect the majority of cases went unreported (xv). Men and women were not only enslaved, but sometimes killed: "corpses of murdered farmworkers were not an uncommon sight in the rivers and canals of South Florida" (xv). If this is not enough to ruin the taste of a tomato, the USDA has found residue of thirty-five pesticides still on the fruits by the time they ship to local grocery stores (xiii). By buying tomatoes, do we enable and participate in this treatment of fellow human beings? Does our act of purchase condone slavery and murder? By eating these pesticide-laden fruits, are we also poisoning ourselves? These are troubling, and even paralyzing, questions, but if we are to be engaged, responsible citizens of the global world, these are questions we must ask.

It may initially feel odd to connect the cartoon comedy of *The Simpsons* to the horrors of industrial agribusiness, but the series has always been interested in the ethical problems of consumption. The series has consistently been full of food choices and their consequences. A brief scan yields many examples: Homer and Moe's friendship is tested by the theft of the Flaming Homer's recipe ("Flaming Moe's" 3.10), Homer sells his soul to Devil Flanders for a donut ("Treehouse of Horror IV" 5.5), and Homer neglects his family to chase the Krusty Burger Ribwich across the country ("I'm Spelling as Fast as I Can" 14.12). These issues are assuredly presented as comedy, but *The Simpsons* has always also been a satire, a form intent on "diminishing or derogating a subject by making it ridiculous and evoking toward it attitudes of amusement, contempt, scorn, or indignation" by using "laughter as a weapon" (Abrams 284–285). As Matthew A. Henry notes, the show "is foremost a satire upon the idealized images of family life depicted in the traditional nuclear-family sitcoms of the 1950s and 1960s" that "primarily offered visions of intact nuclear families headed by a genial patriarch, who was portrayed as knowing, correct, and superior to his wife and children" (5). In the case of Homer Simpson, father clearly does not know best, and the satiric impulses of the show are often turned outward from the family toward cultural problems at large.

For example, instead of tomatoes, "Coming to Homerica" (20.21) uses barley to highlight the connections between food production and politics, and serves as a useful introduction to the show's attitudes about food. When neighboring Ogdenville's Norwegian population is impoverished by the failure of the barley market brought on by Krusty Burger's tainted Mother Nature Burger, Ogdenvillians flood into Springfield looking for work. While Ogdenvillians are at first welcomed as day laborers, soon everyone in Springfield is upset that Ogdenvillians are clogging up the hospitals getting hurt doing the jobs no one else will. Even though, as Moe states, "They pay in cash, they keep it clean, and their mythology is rich and enchanting," soon the "Norwads" are blamed for everything from Homer's alcoholism to Maggie's (seemingly) first word being in Norwegian. They are soon banned from Springfield. After Homer's militia is too inept to keep them out, the town builds a wall. But since they aren't skilled enough to build it themselves, the Ogdenvillians help. By the time the wall is finished, everyone is friendly again, and the door the Ogdenvillians built just in case is opened. Everyone in Springfield misses their "kindness," "hard work," and "sweet plain-spoken ways." The ending of "Coming to Homerica" is too rushed to feel particularly poignant, but it does make clear in 2009 what seems appallingly apparent in 2017. By substituting barley for tomatoes and Norwegians for Hispanics, the episode exposes xenophobia—ignorantly and absurdly confused by Homer with "xylophobia," the fear of xylophones—as racism emboldened by specious economic fears.

However, some episodes in the series seem more sharply focused, and "Lisa the Vegetarian" (7.5) and "E-I-E-I-(Annoyed Grunt)" (11.5) more satisfyingly satirize the problematic issues concerning the common foods we eat every day. "Lisa the Vegetarian" investigates food itself by focusing on the beef industry and the impact it has on animal welfare and the moral obligations humans have to other animals. "Annoyed Grunt," on the other hand, investigates the plight of those who produce our food, focusing on modern American farmers and the social and economic pressures they face producing crops for the world. However, unlike Marge's remark that titles this essay, The Simpsons' satirical exploration of food politics does not encourage us to repress our reactions to the consequences of our consumption, but to investigate and act on the unsettling feelings these explorations provoke.

"Lisa the Vegetarian" and Traditional Sitcom Satire

In 1995's "Lisa the Vegetarian," Lisa experiences an ethical crisis. After the Simpson family goes to a petting zoo, Lisa cannot dissociate the lamb from the petting zoo from the lamb chops that appear on her dinner plate that night. Lisa's response is on the one hand emotional, for she envisions the petting-zoo lamb hovering above her food plate pleading for love, but also rational, as she sees the different cuts of meat falling directly off the animals of her imagination. Her realization that there is no real difference between petting-zoo animals and meat animals quickly becomes an investigation of exactly where on an animal cuts of meat originate from. Her last vision is of a hot dog assembled from the leather tongue of an old boot, a pigeon head, a rat tail, and a raccoon foot, foreshadowing the fact that she might feel better remaining ignorant. The closing of the scene suggests that eating meat may lead humans to be just as inhuman as the animals they consume, for Bart and Homer fight over the last lamb chop by chewing and pulling at its opposite ends, like wild dogs fighting over the same scrap of meat. These opening scenes of the episode show the dissonance that Lisa feels as she realizes everything consumed in the home comes from outside the confines of the familiar nuclear family.

While Homer and Marge may be disturbed by Lisa's recent conversion to vegetarianism at home, when she gets to school the next day, the administration is concerned she might create a revolt. When she has a "moral objection" to dissecting a live worm in Miss Hoover's class and requests a vegetarian food option from Lunchlady Doris, their reaction is to push the big red INDE-PENDENT THOUGHT ALARM button. In response, Principal Skinner shows the class a film reel steeped in satiric detail: the title card reads, "The Meat Council Presents: 'Meat and You: Partners in Freedom' Number 3F03 in the 'Resistance is Useless' Series." The film reel shows Troy McClure explaining the beef industry to a young boy. It depicts "a high-density feed lot" and presents a beef processing plant as "Bovine University." As the cows "graduate" and come out as steaks at the end of a conveyor belt, McClure convinces the boy, Jimmy, that anyone who won't eat meat is crazy. When Lisa claims the film reel is "tripe," Principal Skinner distracts the students with actual tripe provided by The Meat Council. Lisa claims that the film is "corporate propaganda," but her classmates repeat the phrases from the film, deciding Lisa is "crazy" and a "grade-A moron." The witless Ralph Wiggum proclaims, "When I grow up, I'm going to Bovine University!" The danger of Lisa's radical thinking is quickly suppressed by the merger of corporate interests and institutionalized education.

To understand how "Meat and You: Partners in Freedom" satirizes the beef industry, one simply has to look at the conditions on modern cattle farms. In their work, *The Way We Eat: Why Our Food Choices Matter*, Peter Singer and Jim Mason illustrate how steak gets to the dinner plate. Raised on crowded high-density feedlots, cattle are given synthetic hormone implants to boost their weight and the farm's profits. The cows, genetically predisposed to eat grass, are fed cheap corn to cut costs. Since the cattle cannot digest corn easily, they are given antibiotics to prevent the ailments that corn diets cause (61). For extra protein, even though this raises concerns for disease transmission between species, the cattle are also fed "slaughterhouse leftovers" and "chicken litter—which includes fecal matter, dead birds, chicken feathers and spilled feed" (62). In addition to the problems their diets may cause, Singer and Mason found typical cattle feedlots could contain five thousand cattle penned together without shade, and that in one case in Nebraska in 2005, summer temperatures in July caused over a thousand cattle deaths in just a few days (63).[1] Once they reach the slaughterhouse, the end of the cattle's lives are often not much more humane. Even though the USDA legally requires that mammals be stunned before they are killed, this process is sporadically effective. Singer and Mason note that when Temple Grandin surveyed slaughterhouse procedures in the 1990s, she found that "only 36 percent of slaughterhouses were able to effectively stun at least 95 percent of animals on the first attempt" (67). They argue any meat eater will "from time to time be eating meat that comes from an animal who died an agonizing death" (68). Even though "Lisa the Vegetarian" only briefly references the feedlot and the slaughterhouse in the filmstrip, the informed viewer knows these realities are the foundation of Lisa's moral objections to eating meat.

The fact that "The Meat Council" sponsors "Meat and You" emphasizes the interconnectedness of business, politics, and food. In *Food Politics*, Marion Nestle outlines how money impacts food choice and food production. She notes that in the 1999–2000 election cycle, the "American Meat Institute PAC [Political Action Committee]" donated $56,500 to federal candidates (103). Unsurprisingly, these contributions often go to the party that supports the fewest regulations, and in same election cycle, "Republican candidates received nearly 64% of the funds from egg and poultry PACs, 78% from livestock producers, and 84% from food processors, which suggests that PAC money preferentially goes to candidates most likely to favor particular corporate interests" (116). On the surface, these contributions may seem benign, but Lisa's claim that "Meat and You" is corporate propaganda is particularly disturbing when one realizes that those who regulate food availability and pass food safety laws are often not doctors, farmers, or scientists, but politicians who may take money from real-life "Meat Councils" like the "American Meat Institute." For example, in 2004, a proposed ban on chicken litter as cattle feed was delayed by the FDA due to lobbying from the chicken industry (Singer and Mason 63), and as late as 2011, Florida had no legal standard for the "maximum allowable amount" of toxic methyl bromide gas allowed to drift off a sprayed tomato field, because the lack of the gas would make growing tomatoes in Florida "financially impossible" (Estabrook 50–53). More recently, Scott Pruitt, then Donald Trump's Environmental Protection Agency appointee, deferred the decision on banning chlorpyrifos—a class of pesticides often routinely used on strawberries, oranges, and apples—until 2022. Under the influence of lobbying from Dow Chemicals and other chemical manufacturers, the E.P.A. refuses to ban the pesticide, even though exposure has been shown to correlate with lower birth rates, "persistent developmental delays" and lower IQ scores in children. Even the E.P.A.'s own scientists have argued for its ban (Rabin). "Lisa the Vegetarian" insinuates that these connections between politics and big business influence Americans at the youngest of ages, as Springfield Elementary is already under the yoke of corporate interests like The Meat Council. While Lisa may see through the propaganda of the film reel, her classmates do not, happily eating both the visual and literal tripe.

Despite its trenchant critiques, "Lisa the Vegetarian" concludes in a traditional sitcom manner. While in a traditional sitcom the father would resolve the situation, here the father is Homer, so the situation is resolved by stand-ins, Apu Nahasapeemapetilon and the McCartneys. When Lisa disrupts Homer's barbeque and storms out of the house, she walks to the Kwik-E-Mart, caves to societal pressure, and eats a hot dog. Apu informs her the dog is actually tofu, which he uses as a replacement because of his religious beliefs, and that customers never notice the difference. Apu then takes Lisa to meet Paul and Linda McCartney, old friends who happen to be in town and who "feel strongly about animal rights." Apu and the McCartneys' advice advocate tolerance. After Lisa realizes Apu is a vegan and does not even choose to eat cheese, something Lisa is not willing to give up, he states, "I learned long ago to tolerate others, rather than forcing my beliefs on them. You know, you can influence people without badgering them always." The satire here is much gentler than the earlier film reel scene. Even though Lisa and Apu disagree, Lisa is not painted as "crazy" or a "grade-A moron." Apu's stance simply illustrates that Lisa can choose to be a vegetarian and still love her meat-eating family, evidenced by her reconciliation with Homer at the end of the episode. The viewer can decide to agree with Lisa and be a vegetarian, to side with Apu and be a vegan, or side with Homer and continue to eat meat. However, at the same time, the episode's critiques are hard for the viewer to shake. By being aware of how beef is produced in America, and continuing to eat it, are consumers as witless to and complicit in the corporate interests of food production as Ralph Wiggum?[2]

"E-I-E-I-(Annoyed Grunt)," Tomacco and the Satire of the Absurd

While the satire of "Lisa the Vegetarian" is ultimately softened by Apu's gentle advice of tolerance at episode's end, "E-I-E-I-(Annoyed Grunt)" (11.5) is more strident in its satire of food politics. Rather than relying on an authority figure like Apu to smooth out the rough edges of real life, the absurd premise and resolution of "Grunt" are more indicative of later *The Simpsons* episodes, typified by Kevin Dettmar's remark that the show runs "against the implicit logic of the sitcom" by working "to explore and exploit the gap between the American Dream and contemporary American reality" (88). "Grunt" turns the focus from the food itself to the food producer, in this case the American farmer who struggles to reach the American Dream.

As "Grunt" opens, the Simpson family goes to the movies to see *The Poke of Zorro*, a film that sets the tone of the episode. The film, a ridiculous mismatch of disparate literary characters, depicts Zorro fighting The Man in the Iron Mask, challenging The Scarlet Pimpernel to a duel, and receiving the English crown from King Arthur. As Bart watches, he states, "It's like a history lesson come to life!" Lisa responds, "No, it's not! It's totally inaccurate!" In the days following, Homer borrows the idea of the duel from the film and uses it to coerce his friends and neighbors into better parking and free beer until he slaps a Southern gentlemen at the Kwik-E-Mart, who accepts his challenge. As the Simpson family speeds through the countryside to escape, they happen upon Homer's childhood farm, somehow still standing even though it burns down in an earlier season. The farm is in severe disrepair, but Homer is intent on making it work, seeing it as the family's "big chance." An enthusiastic Bart states, "I'll dig an outhouse!" A cheerful Lisa exclaims, "I'll weed the floor!" A despondent Marge manages, "I'll repress the rage I'm feeling!" Homer proclaims, "Let the agriculture begin!" The irony here is that the depiction of farm life that follows, in a just world, would be as ridiculous and inaccurate as the plot of *The Poke of Zorro* and could be dismissed as inaccurate fluff. However, even though Homer's struggles as an American farmer may be absurdly presented, they have a harsh reality behind them.

The episode's move to the farm juxtaposes the "inaccurate" histories of *The Poke of Zorro* with the real-world history of American farmers in the twentieth century and illustrates why so many still struggle to meet the American Dream of self-sustainability. Beginning during the Great Depression in the 1930s, American grain farmers were producing more crops than consumers could afford to buy. To prevent American farms from failing, the U.S. government loaned farmers money when crop prices did not meet production costs (Pollan 49). In 1973, after years of changing market conditions, the government did away with the loan program and simply paid farmers directly. Instead of offering farmers a way to survive through low periods in the market, "the new subsidies encouraged farmers to sell their corn at any price, since the government would make up the difference" (52–53). Over time, however, the government lowered the estimated market price, and farmers got less money for the corn they were being encouraged to grow more of— the same corn fed to the cattle in high-density feedlots—in an attempt to dominate global grain markets. In 1996, just a few years before "Grunt" aired, Congress was encouraged by high commodity prices and passed the Freedom to Farm Bill. This bill severely limited subsidies because Congress argued that prices indicated farmers were ready for the free market. Just a few years later, commodity prices had once again dropped so much that Congress again had to support farmers to prevent American farms from failing. By 2002, new legislation was enacted that raised subsidies by eighty percent, at the ten-year cost of $190 billion (Sanger).

"Grunt," first aired in 1999, depicts Homer starting to farm in this exact time frame when American farmers were struggling when their governmental safety net had been taken away. Homer's farm does not instantly turn a profit and initially grows nothing. (It certainly does not help that Homer sows a mixture of tobacco seeds, tomato seeds, gummy bears, and candy corn.) His only recourse is to fertilize with plutonium sent by Lenny from Mr. Burns' power plant. When this extreme measure does not seem to have immediate results, Homer trudges off to hang himself in the barn. The inclusion of plutonium fertilizer surely plays the scene for laughs, but Homer's deliberation of suicide highlights the fact that the suicide rate for farmers in America is double the national average. Farmers have for so long tried to live "up to an old American ideal of rugged independence and individualism," trying to mold themselves into self-sustaining family farmers who grow crops to feed America and the world in a bucolic version of the American Dream (Allen 183–185). In reality, in the last half of the twentieth century, family farms declined at an astonishing rate. In the 1970s alone, the number of American farms declined by half, while the size of individual farms grew exponentially, the result of government authorities encouraging farmers to become more industrial and rely more on agribusiness corporations to produce crops on a mass scale (Allen 114). American farmers have relied more and more on companies like Monsanto and their genetically modified seed to produce enough yield to keep their farms solvent, while much of the profits go to corporations such as Archer Daniels Midland, who act as the corporate middlemen between the farmers who produce the raw grain commodities and food and beverage corporations who want the grain after it has been processed (Pollan 36; Allen 114). Homer's struggle is not only with his own incompetence, but also a battle with the history of unpredictable commodity prices, the corporatization of the profession, and the unreliable and often-contradictory government support farmers had relied on for nearly seventy years. Homer's initial failure reflects the economic hardships of the family farm in the corporate farm era.

Eventually, Homer's hybrid, radioactive crop grows, and his inadvertent creation of tomacco—a highly addictive nicotine-laced tomato—offers the dream of the wildly successful independent farmer. Homer's success, while meteoric, is short-lived. His tomacco sells because it is highly addictive, and Laramie Cigarettes soon comes calling. Eager for the crop because "there's no law against selling kids tomacco," Laramie offers Homer $150 million for the hybrid. Homer, at the behest of Bart and Marge, though to the horror of Lisa—who sensibly thinks selling any kind of tobacco to children is wrong—holds out for $150 billion, but is rebuked. When the family returns to the farm, they find that the neighboring livestock has become addicted to the tomacco and has destroyed all the crops. They manage to save one plant, but the tobacco executives steal it. The executives' helicopter crashes, and the last plant is destroyed. Left with nothing more than they started with, the family returns home, and Homer fights the duel. Homer is shot in one arm, and the episode ends with Homer eating a piece of Marge's mincemeat pie with the other arm. "Grunt," as is indicative of later *The Simpsons* episodes, ends with no clear resolution and no clear moral, but with cartoon violence and Homer's return to gluttony.

It is worth briefly noting here that even though this study has focused on the plight of grain farmers found in the episode, the satire of "Grunt" has three possible targets: the exploitation of grain farmers, the tobacco industry, and the tomato industry. Even though Homer does not actually grow corn in the episode, it is clear that his situation is that of a grain farmer, given the context discussed above. Additionally, all his neighbors in the episode grow corn, and the tomacco plants are clearly depicted as corn stalks with tomato fruits substituted for the ears of corn. On the other hand, the fact that the crop is a mixture of tobacco and tomatoes, along with the introduction of Laramie Cigarettes, evokes the issues raised by tobacco production. However, tobacco farming is inherently a more difficult subject, since tobacco is a crop, but not a food.[3] Ultimately, the episode's tobacco critique seems more focused on the marketing of tobacco products rather than crop itself or the impact of its consumption, something other episodes in the series seem to do much better.[4] Finally, the contemporary, informed viewer, recalling the discussion of tomatoes in the opening of this essay, senses the perhaps unintended allusions to the horrors of tomato farming within the episode.[5]

In the end, "Grunt" satirizes the plight of the American farmer through radical exaggeration and functions as a much darker satire than "Lisa the Vegetarian." Homer can only become a successful farmer through hyperbolic means. His crop only grows because he has doused it with radiation, and it only sells because it is laced with addictive nicotine. The episode seems to argue if the only way Homer can become a successful farmer in the world of *The Simpsons* is through the fantastic, real farmers have little chance in the real world. If "Lisa the Vegetarian" makes viewers ask themselves whether eating beef leads to the inhumane treatment and abuse of cattle, "Grunt" forces them to ask if the consumption of corn—a grain found in nearly every processed food in America—leads to the exploitation of the American farmer. In the earlier episode, the viewer is placated by Apu's advice, but in "Grunt," there is no sitcom-friendly happy ending. Homer's return to Springfield offers no advice and has no moral. The satire of the farm is ruthless, and there is no comfort in the ending. The episode does not rely on the "logic of the sitcom" that everything will turn out fine in the end, and the gap it depicts between the American Dream of the American farmer and the reality of the American farm is more unsettling because of it.

Taken together, these episodes may provoke a rage within the viewer. Like any good satire, they do so with laughter, but their subject matter is ultimately not humorous. The fact that Americans have so little control over how their food is grown, raised, harvested, and sold is deeply troubling. Rather than calling for the viewer to repress their rage like Marge, the series asks the viewer to become informed. Rather than settling for a bullet wound, a piece of mincemeat pie, and a diploma from Bovine University, *The Simpsons* provokes the viewer to become more like Lisa. Through our laughter, we can become educated, conscientious consumers who make food choices not based on their ease or popularity, but on their ethical, economic, and health consequences.

NOTES

1. Water from feedlots, often contaminated with steroids added to cattle diets and found in cattle waste, can also find its way into local rivers and ponds, causing "altered sexual features" in local fish (Singer and Mason 64). Industrial runoff impacting fish has also been the target of *The Simpsons*, as depicted by Marge forcing Mr. Burns to eat the nuclear-mutated Blinky the three-eyed fish in his campaign to be governor in Season 2 ("Two Cars in Every Garage and Three Eyes on Every Fish" 2.4).

2. Interestingly, recent studies have shown that viewing "Lisa the Vegetarian" does have the real possibility of changing children's perceptions of eating meat. A recent study found that showing the episode to 9 to 10-year-old girls from New Jersey found that it did at least temporarily influence their moral reaction to eating meat (Byrd-Bredbenner, Grenci, and Quick 145).

3. The tobacco industry is essentially a "harmful industry," but has also received government subsidies for many years. After the shift on attitudes over smoking in the 1980s, the tobacco industry "coached" farmers to see their subsidies as a kind of "legitimate" "social assistance," even though their crop is non-essential and a known health hazard (Benson 4–5). For these reasons, it is difficult to see tobacco farmers in the same light as beef, tomato, and corn farmers.

4. "Lisa the Beauty Queen" (4.4), where Lisa protests Laramie Cigarette's sponsorship of the "Little Miss Springfield" pageant, has a much more focused critique of big tobacco.

5. It is also worth noting that tomacco can actually be grown through grafting techniques, but is not commercially produced. In 2003, a *The Simpsons* fan did grow a few fruits and met with the producers of the episode, but apparently, they were unaware of the possible existence of tomacco before the making of "E-I-E-I-(Annoyed Grunt)" (Philipkoski).

WORKS CITED

Abrams, M. H. *A Glossary of Literary Terms*. Eighth Edition, 2005.

Allen, Will, with Charles Wilson. *The Good Food Revolution: Growing Healthy Food, People, and Communities*. Gotham, 2012.

Benson, Peter. *Tobacco Capitalism: Growers, Migrant Workers, and the Changing Face of a Global Industry*. Princeton, 2011.

Bryd-Bredbenner, Carol, Alexandra Grenci, and Virginia Quick. "Effect of a Television Programme on Nutrition Cognitions and Intended Behaviors." *Nutrition & Dietetics*, vol. 67, no. 3, 2010, pp. 143–149.

"Coming to Homerica." *The Simpsons: The Complete Twentieth Season*. Written by Brendan Hay, directed by Steven Dean Moore, 20th Century–Fox, 2010.

Dettmar, Kevin J. H. "Counterculture Literacy: Learning Irony with *The Simpsons*." *Leaving Springfield: The Simpsons and the Possibility of Oppositional Culture*, edited by John Alberti, Wayne State, 2004, pp. 85–106.

"E-I-E-I-(Annoyed Grunt)." *The Simpsons: The Complete Eleventh Season*. Written by Ian Maxtone-Graham, directed by Bob Anderson, 20th Century–Fox, 2008.

Estabrook, Barry. *Tomatoland: How Modern Industrial Agriculture Destroyed Our Most Alluring Fruit*. Andrews McMeel Publishing, 2011.

"Flaming Moe's." *The Simpsons: The Complete Third Season*. Written by Robert Cohen, directed by Rich Moore and Alan Smart, 20th Century–Fox, 2012.

Henry, Matthew A. *The Simpsons, Satire and American Culture*. Palgrave, 2012.

"I'm Spelling as Fast as I Can." *The Simpsons: The Complete Fourteenth Season*. Written by Kevin Curran, directed by Nancy Kruse, 20th Century–Fox, 2011.

"Lisa the Beauty Queen." *The Simpsons: The Complete Fourth Season*. Written by Jeff Martin, directed by Mark Kirkland, 20th Century–Fox, 2012.

"Lisa the Vegetarian." *The Simpsons: The Complete Seventh Season*. Written by David S. Cohen, directed by Mark Kirkland, 20th Century–Fox, 2012.

Nestle, Marion. *Food Politics: How the Food Industry Influences Nutrition and Health*. Revised and Expanded Tenth Anniversary Edition, University of California Press, 2013.

Philipkoski, Kristen. "Simpsons Plant Seeds of Invention." *Wired*, Condé Nast Inc., 7 Nov. 2003, www.wired.com/2003/11/simpsons-plant-seeds-of-invention.

Pollan, Michael. *The Omnivore's Dilemma: A Natural History of Four Meals*. Penguin, 2006.

Rabin, Roni Caryn. "A Strong Case Against a Pesticide Does Not Faze E.P.A. Under Trump." *The New York Times*, The New York Times Company, 15 May 2017. www.nytimes.com/2017/05/15/health/pesticides-epa-chlorpyrifos-scott-pruitt.html.

Sanger, David E. "Reversing Course, Bush Signs Bill Raising Farm Subsidies." *The New York Times*, The New York Times Company, 14 May 2002. http://www.nytimes.com/2002/05/14/us/reversing-course-bush-signs-bill-raising-farm-subsidies.html.

Singer, Peter and Jim Mason. *The Way We Eat: Why Our Food Choices Matter*. Rodale, 2006.

"Treehouse of Horror IV." *The Simpsons: The Complete Fifth Season*. Written by Watch Conan O'Brien, The Late Bill Oakley, The Estate of Josh Weinstein, Disfigured Dan McGrath, Greg "It's Alive!" Daniels and Bilious Bill Canterbury, directed by David "Dry Bones" Silverman, 20th Century–Fox, 2012.

"Two Cars in Every Garage and Three Eyes on Every Fish." *The Simpsons: The Complete Second Season*. Written by Sam Simon and John Swartzwelder, directed by Wes Archer, 20th Century–Fox, 2012.

This Is Not a Library!
This Is Not a Kwik-E-Mart!

The Satire of Libraries, Librarians and Reference Desk Air-Hockey Tables

CASEY D. HOEVE

Introduction

Librarians are obsessed with stereotypes. Sometimes even so much so that, according to Gretchen Keer and Andrew Carlos, the fixation has become a stereotype within itself (63). The complexity of the library places the profession in a constant state of transition. Maintaining traditional organization systems while addressing new information trends distorts our image to the outside observer and leaves us vulnerable to mislabeling and stereotypes. Perhaps our greatest fear in recognizing stereotypes is not that we appear invariable but that the public does not fully understand what services we can provide. When we lose our ability to maintain relevancy, we risk the loss of operational funding and weaken the viability of the profession.

Whether the need to investigate library stereotypes is a personal choice or professional obligation for survival, examples offered throughout books, movies, and television are limited and inconsistent in nature. Libraries and librarians often play one-time support characters for specific scenes or purposes, only to disappear as quickly as they surface; such manifestations are exemplified by Mary Bailey's brief fate in *It's a Wonderful Life*. The librarian stereotype is explicitly prevalent, but minimal screen time prevents the opportunity to defend against niche roles perpetuated by the media.

The presence of libraries in *The Simpsons* undoubtedly increases the risk of satirizing the profession. In light of these circumstances, *The Simpsons* has defied the status quo of reducing libraries and librarians to an ephemeral prop. After thirty seasons, the library has played a regular role on the series, with many reoccurring scenes showcasing scads of libraries and librarians in Springfield and beyond. Although these places and characters remain secondary to the significance of the normal cast, the continued references suggest a more than temporary role, and perhaps even an established institution within *The Simpsons'* universe.

Within *The Simpsons*, the concepts of the library as place, attitudes toward the library, and librarian demographics are satirized as general categories. While some instances are grossly fabricated for the purpose of comedic value, a disturbing number of correlations exist between our reality as professionals and our satirical portrayal. Beyond good-natured ribs, *The Simpsons* suggests areas where librarianship should and must change for the better to serve a growing population of diverse library users, interests, and information needs.

The Library as Place

> "We're just as much a part of Springfield as the church, the library, or the crazy house"—"Bart After Dark" (8.5)

Mapping the full spectrum of libraries throughout *The Simpsons* yields a surprising assortment of libraries, surpassing the average representation by the media. The Springfield Public Library is likely the most symbolic example of libraries to the average viewer, but additional libraries are presented that typically fall below the cultural radar. In illustrating the breadth of the profession, *The Simpsons* provides an in-depth portrayal of content and services offered to specialized populations.

Libraries in the series range from their earliest origins to the present day. The library of fictitious ruler Goliath II was hailed as an indicative example of a thriving civilization ("Simpsons Bible Stories" 10.18), representing the first Mesopotamian and Assyrian libraries. In modern Springfield, we find a curious hodgepodge of buildings complementing the citywide library scene. Old Springfield Library, the Springfield Public Library, the Springfield Library, and Springfield Elementary School library constitute significant reoccurring backdrops within the show. Additional libraries presented are not always immediately recognizable to the public. A penitentiary library was featured in The Montgomery Burns State Prison ("The Seven-Beer Snitch" 16.14), and a medical library was used by Dr. Nick Riviera to research techniques for Homer Simpson's triple bypass surgery ("Homer's Triple Bypass" 4.11). For those unfamiliar with college campuses, the Springfield University Library provides an example of academic libraries ("Homer Goes to College" 5.3); other examples are rounded out with the presence of the Bookmobile and the Christian Science Reading Room.

Libraries as a whole are often stereotyped as underfunded organizations, and *The Simpsons* alludes to this problem several times throughout the duration of the series. In one scene, Grandpa Simpson stands outside a crumbling and boarded up (and likely condemned) public library ("Old Money" 2.17). The infestation of bats in the card catalog ("Sideshow Bob Roberts" 6.5) and silverfish in the Old Springfield Library ("НОМЯ" 12.9) highlight shortcomings easily surmountable if adequate funding were available. It is suggested that the Old Springfield Library is so desperate to get rid of book sale items that they are willing to convert any unsold materials into pig feed ("Sweets and Sour Marge" 13.8).

In other instances, the libraries in Springfield appear to be moderately maintained and less hyperbolized as charity cases. The Old Springfield Library is rather impressive, comprised of a red brick exterior and a long reverential stairway with a columned entrance. The Springfield Public library appears much the same as any mid-sized to smaller town library, resonant of a subdued middle-class dignity sustained by humble means.

Despite these contradictory characterizations, most libraries are struggling to provide resources and services under their current budgets. While many libraries produce a steady return on investment (ROI), with Meredith Schwartz et al. demonstrating that the Toledo Public Library produces $2.86 for every dollar invested (12), and Bruce Kingma and Kathleen McClure calculating the Syracuse University Libraries' ROI of $4.49 for every dollar invested (63), inflation frequently outpaces budgets. In 2005, Adrienne Chute and Elaine Kroe determined that the percentage of public library expenditures devoted to collections was thirteen percent (3). This percentage has decreased to 11.77 percent under Deanne Swan et al.'s further investigation in 2010 (9).

Stephen Bosch and Kittie Henderson also found that the Association for Research Libraries had experienced a drop in funding between 2011–2012, with most of the cutbacks coming from pubic university academic libraries. The increased cost of healthcare benefits for employees, as well as continued inflation of databases and periodicals, rising at a steady rate of six percent in both 2012 and 2013, has far outpaced the consumer price index of 1.7 percent (Bosch and Henderson). In reality, *The Simpsons* may be correct in subtly stating what we need to admit: that libraries are financially vulnerable and in need of better sources of sustainable financial support.

Attitude Toward the Library

> "Books are for squares. We're a Multimedia Learning Center
> for children of all ages ... but mostly bums"—"Margical
> History Tour" (15.11)

The public interest in libraries and library use is both increasing and in decline. In separate reports, Adrienne Chute and Kathryn Matthew concluded that public libraries witnessed a tremendous increase in circulation from 1.4 billion (Chute 6) to 2.4 billion checkouts (Matthew 7) per year between 1990 and 2013, with loans to other libraries escalating from 4.6 million in 1990 (Chute 6) to 49.9 million reported by Everett Henderson et al. in 2007 (6). Similarly, Margaret Cahalan et al. noted that academic libraries saw a peak of physical circulation in 1994 at 230.7 million items per year (Cahalan et al, "Academic Libraries 1994" iii), which has since steadied out according to Phan et al. at approximately 138.1 million in 2008 (Phan et al., "Academic Libraries 2008" 2). Academic library loans and borrowing have experienced a steady increase, rising from 8.8 million (Cahalan et al., "Academic Libraries 1994" iii) to 11.2 million loans (Phan et al., "Academic Libraries 2010" 2) between 1994–2010, and 6.3 million (Cahalan et al., "Academic Libraries 1994" iii) to 10.2 million lends to other libraries between the same period (Phan et al., "Academic Libraries 2010" 2). It can be speculated that the decline in circulations may have resulted from more electronic holdings of journals and e-books (the statistics are still lagging behind); however, it is clearly evident that patrons use library services regularly, especially borrowing materials from outside their hometown library collection.

To accommodate our users, librarians not only develop services around our patrons, but we also search for gaps, as suggested by Jeanne Nikolaison, among non-library users, marginalized groups, and those with library anxiety: the fear of belittlement by librarians for the possession of rudimentary research skills, or for being ignorant of library services and building navigation (1). While user groups can demonstrate a startling diversity of needs and identities, The Simpsons presents several themes regarding library user stereotypes, namely that library users derive from populations of the less educated and lower socio-economic strata, as well as the elderly and adolescent, and individuals with less desirable personality traits.

The Simpsons regularly plays upon these attitudes by depicting library users and chronic store browsers as cheap. In the film Ernest Goes Somewhere Cheap, Ernest and Vern visit the public library, resulting in Ernest getting his head stuck in the toilet ("Cape Feare" 5.2). In other instances, the browsing of materials at retail business is also referred to as library-like behavior, insinuating stinginess by the customer. Apu threatens to shoot Bart and Lisa for browsing magazines in the Kwik-E-Mart like a lending library ("Krusty Gets Busted" 1.12), and in a similar occurrence, physically expels Homer for flipping through an issue of *Jet* magazine ("Marge on the Lam" 5.6).

The library is additionally portrayed as a place used by people on a limited income. Reverend Lovejoy needs to check out the *Bible* from the Old Springfield Library for the last nine years, as he cannot afford to buy his own personal copy ("Bart the Mother" 10.3). Lisa Simpson also imagines her future in an impoverished lifestyle, which includes living in a trailer and routinely traveling to the library to "rent" movies ("Lisa the Simpson" 9.17). The library is even presented as a cheaper alternative for fiscally conscious families. Marge believes the family was living above their means and could find free information in the library, rather than spending money on expensive books ("Mobile Homer" 16.13).

In many scenarios, library users are also categorized as hopeless muttonheads. Cletus, the epitome of stereotypical white trash, visits the library to crack a turtle with a Leon Uris novel ("НОМЯ" 12.9). Patrons also mistakenly request Shirley Jackson's "The Lottery," with the fatuous belief it can help improve their chances of winning the state lottery ("Dog of Death" 3.19). And in another thick-witted example, Dr. Nick Riviera, whose educational credentials are highly suspect, is astounded by a library book containing a pregnant woman who had "swallowed a baby" ("Sweets and Sour Marge" 13.8).

Contrary to *The Simpsons'* stereotype, library users appear to be more prevalent among the college educated and those in higher socio-economic brackets. In 2015, John Horrigan completed research on behalf of The Pew Research Center for non-partisan, non-advocacy public opinion, gathering library and information use by Americans. This survey shows greater use of libraries among higher income and educated populations. Individuals with some college or a college education were between ten and sixteen percent more likely to have visited a library in the last twelve months than those with a high school diploma or less than a high school education. Those making less than $30,000 a year were approximately ten percent less likely to have visited a library in the last year when compared to those who earned above $30,000 per year (Horrigan).

Regarding other user stereotypes, *The Simpsons* also suggests that libraries are a place where the less desirable of society congregate, most notably a meeting place for the nerdy, elderly and adolescent, and the creepy and/or lonely. As Edward Fink notes, *The Simpsons* uses incongruity theory, a comedic means to surprise the character (and the audience) with unexpected situations or logical extremes (46–48). Even though the public often ignores or avoids these unwelcome groups, or engages with them on a limited basis, these marginalized groups do, in fact, utilize libraries. The conglomeration of these "social outcasts" in the libraries serve as a stereotype to employ logical extremes, and amplify amusement, as ordinary citizens are forced into uncomfortable and unexpected situations as they interact with the socially, physically, and mentally vulnerable.

Illustrating the more common stereotype, *The Simpsons* often associates the library and users of library services with the nerdy. Homer Simpson believes that libraries and people associated with libraries are strange and lame, poking fun at Marge for suggesting they attend Friends of the Library events ("Realty Bites" 9.9). When Lisa Simpson attempts to create a new and cool persona, she recognizes that the library was part of her old, nerdy self. Instead, she makes friends with the kids who spend their time outside the library, using the façade as a skateboard park rather than going inside to "do stuff" ("Summer of 4 Ft. 2" 7.25).

The Simpsons also has a penchant for depicting most library patrons as either elderly or very young. The usual gang of regulars at the Springfield Public Library is a group of advanced age individuals with gray or balding hairstyles ("Dead Putting Society" 2.6). Marge also mentions that the periodical room is always filled with old people ("Lady Bouvier's Lover" 5.21), and the Springfield Public Library and Springfield Elementary School library consistently show many of their users as being children or young adults (although it is expected that children would use the elementary school library).

However, more than just children, the elderly, and the nerdy use the library. In 2013 alone, Matthew reported there were 1.5 billion visits to the library, averaging out to four million visits each day (Matthew 7). Comparing public library card ownership, Kathryn Zickuhr found no correlation among age and ownership, with sixty-one percent of Americans under age thirty owning a library card, identical to the percentage of card owners over thirty years of age (Zickuhr). Horrigan also determined the percentage of those who visited the library in the past twelve months was fifty-two percent for ages sixteen to twenty-nine and fifty percent for ages thirty to forty-nine (Horrigan). When it comes to the assumption surrounding these particular user groups, *The Simpsons'* stereotype does not appear to hold much water regarding the age of users, or the education and economic status of library patrons.

In quite a few examples, *The Simpsons* highlights the gravitation of creeps toward the library. Homer Simpson mentions that he is "no longer allowed in the big people library downtown, due to some unpleasantness," resulting in his use of the Springfield Elementary School Library instead ("The Wizard of Evergreen Terrace" 10.2). Moe is also banned from the library (while disguised as Dr. Hibbert) in an unspecified incident, implying he had committed inappropriate actions or behavior ("Bart-Mangled Banner" 15.21).

In another episode, Moe also comments that much creepier people are seated next to him in the computer lab of the Springfield Public Library, who happen to be the Crazy Cat Lady, Gil Gunderson, and an unnamed, mentally ill man with a twitchy eye ("Eeny Teeny Maya Moe" 20.16).

In addition to creepiness, the issue of homeless and lonely individuals is also addressed. Lisa Simpson visits the Springfield Public Library, where the librarian comments, "we're now a multimedia center for children of all ages ... but mostly bums" ("Margical History Tour" 15.11). The seating area is filled with unhygienic and possibly mentally ill, homeless types, which disgusts and frightens the visitors.

The Simpsons also casts several library visitors as lonely. Hans Moleman, usually presented as a rather solitary character, thinks he and Marge are hitting it off as friends, when in actuality Marge is talking to herself while conducting research ("It's a Mad, Mad, Mad, Mad Marge" 11.21). Moe Szyslak uses the library computers to meet women through online dating sites ("Eeny Teeny Maya Moe" 20.16), and Lisa Simpson, as an isolated hobbyist, manages to find encouragement through a gardening enthusiast website accessed through the library computer lab ("Stealing First Base" 21.15).

While *The Simpsons* exaggerates to a certain extent, libraries do face concerns regarding homeless and problem patrons. Angie Kelleher reports that many libraries have partnerships with social services to assist the homeless and less fortunate (19). Due to mental illness (and behaviors resulting from) and poor hygiene, some of these individuals may be labeled as creepy or troublesome. Even though most librarians have weird patron anecdotes (sometimes these shared encounters serve as a bonding experience among librarians), Calmer Chattoo concludes the literature is inconsistent in defining what a problem patron is or what constitutes creepy behavior (20). Other than most complaints stemming from the homeless or delinquent activities, which vary by library, the concept of loneliness and libraries is not well understood. The average library probably has its share of creeps, delinquents, and lonesome individuals, but it is an inconclusive stereotype. In all likelihood, the library may not be different than any other publically accessible facility that offers free or low cost activities and services.

The Simpsons, commendably, often presents an alternative view to satirized conceptualization of libraries and librarians. The many instances of satire are often counterbalanced by reverence for the impact and services offered by the library, and the positive recognition of the library as the official destination for life-long learning and information gathering. The library's impact on the life of Lisa Simpson has been immeasurable. She uses the library in a multitude of ways, ranging from learning about football ("Lisa the Greek" 3.14) to ending the estrangement between Krusty the Clown and his father Rabbi Krustofsky ("Like Father, Like Clown" 3.6). The Springfield

Mensa group also laments the reduction of library standards, criticizing the Springfield Public Library for removing the reference desk to "make room for an air hockey table ("They Saved Lisa's Brain" 10.22).

Even the most unlikely characters have been shown using the library with positive results. When Bart Simpson kills a mother bird with a BB gun, he visits the Old Springfield Library to learn how to properly care for the hatchlings ("Bart the Mother" 10.3). He also makes significant inroads to learning during an independent study with Superintendent Chalmers, where they meet in the library to discuss Theodore Roosevelt and manliness ("Bart Stops to Smell the Roosevelts" 23.2). It is one of the few instances in the series where Bart became interested in education and is able to select materials to fuel his enthusiasm. Although seemingly lukewarm at times, *The Simpsons* undoubtedly recognizes the importance of libraries and their contribution to research and learning.

Librarian Demographics

> "There are no books on Eliza Simpson, but I did find this..."—"The Color Yellow" (21.13)

There is a fairly standard image of librarians in the media. From a perspective of age, Katherine Adams states that librarians are typically viewed as old spinsters, "the formidable mistresses of a complex storage retrieval system" (291). The dedication to and edification of the profession is usually implied as a negative or boring life choice, when compared to other ancillary pursuits such as raising a family (Lutz). Further, Jennifer Bartlet argues librarians are often depicted as white and female and rather conservative in dress (2). *The Simpsons* is consistent with other media productions in their conception of physical attributes. The overwhelming majority of librarians in the show are female, with over nineteen appearances by female librarians or library staff, compared to only five male librarians or library staff. Nearly all of the librarians appear to be in their mid-forties and older, many of whom have gray hair or wear glasses.

The Simpsons also exhibits the stereotypical characterization of the non-existent (or minimally existent) epicene male librarian. James Carmichael explains that the library literature describes male librarian stereotypes as lacking social skills and power, or having a lack of ambition for more traditionally masculine occupations (428). Male librarians in *The Simpsons* are mostly overlooked and adumbrative of most of the negative stereotypes attributed to male librarians. Among the low rate of representation, the characters are merely present in the background, completely lacking personality or demonstrably masculine characteristics. Hans Moleman, often depicted as weak-willed and stupid, serves as a librarian in the Springfield Police Station ("Dumbbell Indemnity" 9.16). In another example, a trusting, yet naive male librarian provides Homer with the phone book to Hokkaidō, Japan, and then allows Homer to use the telephone to make a "local call" ("In Marge We Trust" 8.22). The series also exemplifies the man-child male librarian stereotype by staffing the Young Adult section with a red-haired teenaged boy (a position typically reserved for an adult librarian), whom Lisa was enamored with due to his snarky and disagreeable attitude ("Bart's Girlfriend" 6.7).

The American Library Association (ALA), the largest organization uniting most librarians, provides demographics for our professional members. In 2017, ALA documented in a self-reported study that gender distribution among librarians is predominantly female, with a ratio of 81 percent female librarians to 19 percent male librarians. *The Simpsons* is shockingly consistent with ALA data, depicting a strong correlation of approximately nineteen female librarians and library staff (79.17 percent) to five male librarians and library staff (20.83 percent). This data leads us to believe that the stereotype of the female librarian is, by in large, actually correct, and that *The Simpsons* factually represents the statistics in a nearly identical manner.

From a perspective of racial and ethnic identity, *The Simpsons* overwhelmingly portrays librarians as yellow (white); there is only one librarian of darker skin color in the entire series, seen working at the Springfield University Library ("Homer Goes to College" 5.3). Racial and ethnic diversity has been a long-standing issue in librarianship. In 2009–2010, Julia Gonzalez-Smith et al. noted that only 13.9 percent of librarians were non-white, a decrease of 0.5 percent from the previous year (151). In 2017, the ALA showed that ethnicity distributions favored whites as making up 86.7 percent of the library profession, whereas 13.3 percent of librarians came from other ethnicities, with the second highest racial and ethnic identity being Black or African American at 4.3 percent. Looking at the racial distribution in *The Simpsons*, the one non-yellow (non-white) librarian accounts for roughly 4.2 percent of the librarians in the show, which is much lower than the proportion of non-white librarians in the ALA. Regardless, both of these examples clearly display a shortcoming in diversity among librarians and a need for change and increased inclusion in the profession.

The Simpsons is also similar in their portrayal of age demographics on the show. It is very difficult to specifically document age, as no librarian provided this information; however, given the general appearance of the librarians, they look to be overwhelmingly middle-aged and above. A few younger librarians are presented, such as Martha, who assists Lisa with her genealogy project for a class assignment ("The Color Yellow" 21.13). Correlating with this view, 81.8 percent of all librarians in the ALA were age thirty-five years, and older and 54.5 percent were age forty-five years and older (ALA). Presented with the statistics, librarians are conspicuously white, female, and graying.

Personality-wise, a few tidbits in *The Simpsons* illustrate how librarian behavior is perceived. Pauline Wilson comments that a librarian's stereotypical personality consists of orderliness, conformity, passivity, introspection, and anxiousness (9). Bartlet states that librarians are also viewed as distant, unfriendly, and introverted (2). *The Simpsons* depicts librarians in much the same nature. While the personality of younger, hipster librarians have been omitted, the traits of the rational, introverted librarian are offered to the audience. Librarians on the show are rarely confrontational, with only a few extreme examples in the case when Homer is physically removed from the library for eating ("Marge on the Lam" 5.6), or when Lisa is shushed for talking too loudly ("The Color Yellow" 21.13). Otherwise, librarians are frequently depicted as quiet and solemn characters, and in one instance, a robot incapable of understanding love ("Lisa's Wedding" 6.19).

If we examine the true extent of librarian personalities, we find that librarians come from a diverse range of experiences and backgrounds. The varieties of available positions provide opportunities for all types of personalities and skills and offer individuals roles that best match their professional capacities. Juxtaposed with their presentation in *The Simpsons,* consistency is observed in the rationality, respectfulness, and the trusting nature of librarians examined by Jeanine Williamson and John Lounsbury (124). Librarians in the show respond to user questions in a professionally terse and respectful manner, displaying a helpful efficiency to empower library patrons. However, *The Simpsons* fails to address other personality traits that are less understood about librarians. Compared to other professions, librarians are more open-minded, self-reliant, and imaginative (124), which may come as a shock to some users. While employed in underfunded organizations, librarians are constantly finding creative ways to provide patrons with excellent services despite reductions in budgets and staff. We also have an open mind regarding patron needs, as the sheer diversity of people we encounter regularly exposes us to new perspectives and subject matter. The ALA also advocates for equitable access and unbiased service ("Professional Ethics"), leading us to address and interact with content beyond our personal beliefs.

Conclusions

"You made me bleed my own blood"—"Bart the General" (1.5)

The satirizing of libraries and librarians has the potential to negatively impact the profession. While there can be a shred of truth contained within stereotypes, much is exaggerated to promote an agenda, whether to positively or negatively influence an audience. But to what extent has *The Simpsons* perpetuated false stereotypes? And just as importantly, how culpable are librarians in the process of contributing to those faults that are pointed out in jest?

We need to be careful attributing blame, as broad trends are not particularly indicative of individuals, but point out general truths that exist among large groupings of data and observation. Sometimes that truth can hurt, and in other cases, may debunk plenty of cultural hogwash and factoids. As the teacher at Rommelwood Military School discusses, "But the truth can be harsh and disturbing! How can that be considered beautiful?" ("The Secret War of Lisa Simpson" 8.25); the academic analysis of these stereotypes allows us to understand the reality behind these depictions, and the beauty manifests from the opportunity to learn and change our conceptions and improve the profession of librarianship.

Libraries are underfunded. *The Simpsons* and library data point to the veracity of this stereotype. Our return on investment continues to go unrecognized in the public and academic spheres, and libraries are forced to develop exceptional services on a shoestring budget. Despite the misconception presented in *The Simpsons* that libraries are used among the uneducated and low economic populations, libraries are, in fact, used by all groups of people, especially those of more ample fiscal means and higher levels of education. This type of stereotype can be damaging to the public image of librarianship; it reduces the library to something akin of a social service for the indigent and stupid, rather than an affordable place where people of all education and socio-economic levels are welcome to better their knowledge and circumstances.

In addition, the library is not just a meeting ground for people labeled as nerdy, the elderly or adolescent, or the creepy, homeless, and lonely. With more than 1.5 billion visits per year, and an approximately equal percentage of users possessing library cards below thirty years of age, and above age thirty, library users definitively consist of a wide range of personality types and ages. But the library does experience its share of problem patrons. Librarians encounter the homeless and problem patrons (who may be viewed as creepy) at times. However, the poor definition of problem patrons in the professional literature leaves our comparison with *The Simpsons* as inconclusive. One may assume these people do visit the library, but it cannot be concluded if there is any greater concentration of these groups in the library than any other publicly accessible space.

Although *The Simpsons'* satirical exaggeration of user attitudes and groups are slightly askew, there are certain truths evident in the presentation of librarians that actively demonstrate a need for improvement in the diversity of the profession. Overall, the librarian profession is overwhelmingly female, white, and aging. This stereotype is not only prevalent in the series, but it is consistent with the demographics of the ALA. While there is nothing wrong with being white, female, and aging, *The Simpsons* and demographic data demand the examination of the profession and how we can eliminate barriers to make librarianship more inclusive. As our user base continues to expand in diversity, the profession should strive to match our patrons to appropriately meet content and service needs.

While the library literature and *The Simpsons* agree on the fact that librarians are rational, respectful, and trusting, we are surprisingly imaginative, self-reliant, and open-minded. These skills allow us to be flexible and adaptive to the changes in information services. *The Simpsons* does not get every detail correct (which is a realistic expectation of comedy), but it does recognize the importance of libraries and librarians to the citizens of Springfield (and hopefully the viewers). Their reoccurring role on the show is an aberration among traditional media, and allows us to critically analyze our profession to make it better and more representative for all library users without overly stigmatizing or damaging the library profession.

Works Cited

Adams, Katherine C. "Loveless Frump as Hip and Sexy Party Girl: A Reevaluation of the Old-Maid Stereotype." *The Library Quarterly: Information, Community, Policy*, vol. 70, no. 3, 2000, pp. 287–301.

"Bart After Dark." *The Simpsons: The Complete Eighth Season*. Written by Richard Appel, directed by Dominic Polcino, 20th Century–Fox, 2006.

"Bart Stops to Smell the Roosevelts." *The Simpsons: Season 23*. Written by Tim Long, directed by Steven Dean Moore, 20th Century–Fox, 2012.

"Bart The General." *The Simpsons: The Complete First Season, Collector's Edition*. Written by John Swartzwelder, directed by David Silverman, 20th Century–Fox, 2012.

"Bart the Mother." *The Simpsons: The Complete Tenth Season*. Written by David X. Cohen, directed by Steven Dean Moore, 20th Century–Fox, 2012.

Bartlet, Jennifer A. "Coming to Terms with Librarian Stereotypes and Self-Image." *Library Faculty and Staff Publications*, vol. 29, no. 1, 2014, pp. 1–5.

"Bart-Mangled Banner." *The Simpsons: The Fifteenth Season*. Written by John Frink, directed by Steven Dean Moore, 20th Century–Fox, 2012.

"Bart's Girlfriend." *The Simpsons: The Complete Sixth Season*. Written by John Collier, directed by Susie Dietter, 20th Century–Fox, 2012.

Bosch, Stephen, and Kittie Henderson. "The Winds of Change: Periodicals Price Survey 2013." *Library Journal*, 25 April 2013, http://lj.libraryjournal.com/2013/04/publishing/the-winds-of-change-periodicals-price-survey-2013/, Accessed 13 May 2016.

Cahalan, Margaret, et al. *Academic Libraries: 1994*. National Center for Educational Statistics, 1998, NCES 98–275.

Cahalan, Margaret, et al. *Academic Libraries: 1998*. National Center for Educational Statistics, 2001, NCES 2001–341.

"Cape Feare." *The Simpsons: The Complete Fifth Season*. Written by Jon Vitti, directed by Rich Moore, 20th Century–Fox, 2012.

Carmichael, James. "The Male Librarian and the Feminine Image: A Survey of Stereotype, Status, and Gender Perceptions." *Library & Information Science Research*, vol. 14, no. 4, 1992, pp. 411–446.

Chattoo, Calmer D. "The Problem Patron: Is There One in Your Library?" *The Reference Librarian*, vol. 36, no. 75.76, 2002, pp. 11–22.

Chute, Adrienne. *Public Libraries in the U.S. 1990. E.D. Tabs.* National Center for Educational Statistics, 1992, NCES-92–028.

Chute, Adrienne, and Elaine P. Kroe. *Public Libraries in the United States Fiscal Year 2005.* National Center for Educational Statistics, 2007, NCES 2008–301.

"The Color Yellow." *The Simpsons.* Written by Ian Maxtone-Graham and Billy Kimball, directed by Raymond S. Persi, 20th Century–Fox, 2010.

"Dead Putting Society." *The Simpsons: The Complete Second Season.* Written by Jeff Martin, directed by Rich Moore, 20th Century–Fox, 2012.

"Dog of Death." *The Simpsons: The Complete Third Season.* Written by John Swartzwelder, directed by Jim Reardon, 20th Century–Fox, 2012.

"Dumbbell Indemnity." *The Simpsons: The Complete Ninth Season.* Written by Ron Hauge, directed by Dominic Polcino, 20th Century–Fox, 2012.

"Eeny Teeny Maya Moe." *The Simpsons: The Complete Twentieth Season.* Written by John Frink, directed by Nancy Kruse, 20th Century–Fox, 2010.

Fink, Edward. "Writing *The Simpsons*: A Case Study of Comic Theory." *Journal of Film and Video*, vol. 65, no. 1–2, 2013, pp. 43–55.

Gonzalez-Smith, Isabel, et al. "Unpacking Identity: Racial, Ethnic, and Professional Identity and Academic Librarians of Color." *The Librarian Stereotype: Deconstructing Perceptions &Presentations of Information Work*, edited by Nicole Pagowsky and Miriam Rigby, American Library Association, 2014, pp.149–173.

Henderson, Everett, et al. *Public Libraries Survey: Fiscal Year 2007.* Institute of Museum and Library Services, 2009, IMLS-2009-PLS-02.

"Homer Goes to College." *The Simpsons: The Complete Fifth Season.* Written by Conan O'Brien, directed by Jim Reardon, 20th Century–Fox, 2012.

"Homer's Triple Bypass." *The Simpsons: The Complete Fourth Season.* Written by Gary Apple and Michael Carrington, directed by David Silverman, 20th Century–Fox, 2012.

"НОМЯ." *The Simpsons: The Twelfth Season.* Written by Al Jean, directed by Mike B. Anderson, 20th Century–Fox, 2009.

Horrigan, John B. "Libraries at the Crossroads." *Pew Research Center*, 15 September 2015, http://www.pewinternet.org/2015/09/15/who-uses-libraries-and-what-they-do-at-their-libraries/, Accessed 13 May 2016.

"In Marge We Trust." *The Simpsons: The Complete Eighth Season.* Written by Donick Cary, directed by Steven Dean Moore, 20th Century–Fox, 2006.

"It's a Mad, Mad, Mad, Mad Marge." *The Simpsons: The Complete Eleventh Season.* Written by Larry Doyle, directed by Steven Dean Moore, 20th Century–Fox, 2008.

It's a Wonderful Life. Directed by Frank Capra, performances by Jimmy Stewart, Donna Reed, Lionel Barrymore, and Henry Tavers, RKO Radio Pictures, 1946.

Keer, Gretchen, and Andrew Carlos. "The Stereotype Stereotype: Our Obsession with Librarian Representation." *The Librarian Stereotype: Deconstructing Perceptions &Presentations of Information Work*, edited by Nicole Pagowsky and Miriam Rigby, American Library Association, 2014, pp. 63–84.

Kelleher, Angie. "Not Just a Place to Sleep: Homeless Perspectives on Libraries in Central Michigan." *Library Review*, vol. 62, no. 1.5, 2013, pp. 19–33.

Kingma, Bruce, and Kathleen McClure. "Lib-Value: Values, Outcomes, and Return on Investment of Academic Libraries, Phase III: ROI of the Syracuse University Library." *College & Research Libraries*, vol. 76, no. 1, 2015, pp. 63–80.

"Krusty Gets Busted." *The Simpsons: The Complete First Season.* Written by Jay Kogen and Wallace Wolodarsky, directed by Brad Bird, 20th Century–Fox, 2012.

"Lady Bouvier's Lover." *The Simpsons: The Complete Fifth Season.* Written by Bill Oakley and Josh Weinstein, directed by Wes Archer, 20th Century–Fox, 2012.

"Like Father, Like Clown." *The Simpsons: The Complete Third Season.* Written by Jay Kogen and Wallace Wolodarsky, directed by Jeffrey Lynch and Brad Bird, 20th Century–Fox, 2012.

"Lisa the Greek." *The Simpsons: The Complete Third Season.* Written by Jay Kogen and Wallace Wolodarsky, directed by Rich Moore, 20th Century–Fox, 2012.

"Lisa the Simpson." *The Simpsons: The Complete Ninth Season.* Written by Ned Goldreyer, directed by Susie Dietter, 20th Century–Fox, 2012.

"Lisa's Wedding." *The Simpsons: The Complete Sixth Season*. Written by Greg Daniels, directed by Jim Reardon, 20th Century–Fox, 2012.

Lutz, Ann. *From Old Maids to Action Heroes: Librarians and the Meanings of Librarian Stereotypes*. Thesis, University of Maryland, College Park, 2005, UMI, 2005. AAT1426855.

"Marge on the Lam." *The Simpsons: The Complete Fifth Season*. Written by Bill Canterbury, directed by Mark Kirkland, 20th Century–Fox, 2012.

"Margical History Tour." *The Simpsons: The Complete Fifteenth Season*. Written by Brian Kelley, directed by Mike B. Anderson, 20th Century–Fox, 2012.

Matthew, Kathryn K. *Public Libraries in the United States Survey: Fiscal Year 2013*. Institute of Museum and Library Services, 2016.

"Mobile Homer." *The Simpsons: The Complete Sixteenth Season*. Written by Tim Long, directed by Raymond S. Persi, 20th Century–Fox, 2013.

Nikolaison, Jeanne. "The Effect of Library Instruction on Library Anxiety in the Public Library Setting." *Current Studies in Librarianship*, vol. 31, no. 1, 2011, pp. 7–19.

"Old Money." *The Simpsons: The Complete Second Season*. Written by Jay Kogen and Wallace Wolodarsky, directed by David Silverman, 20th Century–Fox, 2012.

Phan, Tai, et al. *Academic Libraries: 2008: First Look*. National Center for Education Statistics, 2009, NCES 2010–348.

Phan, Tai, et al. *Academic Libraries: 2010: First Look*. National Center for Education Statistics, 2012, NCES 2012–365.

"Professional Ethics." *American Library Association*, 22 January 2008, http://www.ala.org/tools/ethics, Accessed 26 April 2016.

"Realty Bites." *The Simpsons: The Complete Ninth Season*. Written by Dan Greaney, directed by Swinton O. Scott III, 20th Century–Fox, 2012.

Schwartz, Meredith, et al. "Toledo Library Studies Return on Investment." *Library Journal*, vol. 137, no. 14, 2012, pp. 12–12.

"The Secret War of Lisa Simpson." *The Simpsons: The Complete Eighth Season*. Written by Richard Appel, directed by Mike B. Anderson, 20th Century–Fox, 2012.

"The Seven-Beer Snitch." *The Simpsons: The Sixteenth Season*. Written by Bill Odenkirk, directed by Matthew Nastuk, 20th Century–Fox, 2013. DVD.

"Sideshow Bob Roberts." *The Simpsons: The Complete Sixth Season*. Written by Bill Oakley and Josh Weinstein, directed by Mark Kirkland, 20th Century–Fox, 2012.

"Simpsons Bible Stories." *The Simpsons: The Complete Tenth Season*. Written by Tim Long, et al., directed by Nancy Kruse, 20th Century–Fox, 2012.

"Stealing First Base." *The Simpsons*. Written by John Frink, directed by Steven Dean Moore, 20th Century–Fox, 2010.

"Summer of 4 Ft. 2." *The Simpsons: The Complete Seventh Season*. Written by Dan Greaney, directed by Mark Kirkland, 20th Century–Fox, 2012.

Swan, Deanne W., et al. *Public Libraries Survey: Fiscal Year 2010*. Institute of Museum and Library Services, 2013, IMLS-2013-PLS-01.

"Sweets and Sour Marge." *The Simpsons: The Complete Thirteenth Season*. Written by Carolyn Omine, directed by Mark Kirkland, 20th Century–Fox, 2010.

"They Saved Lisa's Brain." *The Simpsons: The Complete Tenth Season*. Written by Matt Selman, directed by Pete Michels, 20th Century–Fox, 2012.

"2017 ALA Demographic Study." *American Library Association*, 2017, http://www.ala.org/tools/sites/ala.org.tools/files/content/Draft%20of%20Member%20Demographics%20Survey%2001-11-2017.pdf, Accessed 06 December 2017.

Williamson, Jeanine M., and John Lounsbury. "Distinctive 16 PF Personality Traits of Librarians." *Journal of Library Administration*, vol. 56, 2016, pp. 124–143.

Wilson, Pauline. *Stereotypes and Status: Librarians in the United States*. Greenwood Press, 1982.

"The Wizard of Evergreen Terrace." *The Simpsons: The Complete Tenth Season*. Written by John Swartzwelder, directed by Mark Kirkland, 20th Century–Fox, 2014.

Zickuhr, Kathryn. "Younger Americans and Public Libraries." *Pew Research Center*, 10 September 2014, http://www.pewinternet.org/2014/09/10/younger-americans-and-public-libraries/, Accessed 26 April 2016.

Just a Little Kick in the Bum

The Simpsons *vs. the Nations of the World*

TRAVIS HOLLAND

Did you know that the British have bad teeth? That Australians worship dirt and use corporal punishment? That Japanese cartoons cause seizures, or that Indians work in convenience stores? While we're offending people, did you know that Brazilians speak with strong Spanish accents? That the Irish are violent drunks, and the French not only look like frogs but are also cowards? That Americans will nominate a water cooler for mayor? If you've spent any serious amount of time watching *The Simpsons*, you might know these things because they have all been portrayed in the show.

As a child in rural Australia in the 1990s, my television viewing was dominated by American shows, and *The Simpsons* was a staple part of the diet. Groundskeeper Willie was the only Scot I knew, Apu Nahasapeemapetilon the only Indian. When our favorite family traveled Down Under to face Bart's fraud charge in Season 6, we learned Australians are loutish, prone to violence, indecipherable, criminal, and stupid, or at least that Americans see Australians that way. Are national stereotypes in *The Simpsons*—from British royalism to Irish drunkenness, Italian mobsters to Japanese game shows, American politicians to French winemakers—parodies or something more? Are they fictions or distortions? Are they imagined or remembered? These are important distinctions because of the role that media might play in shaping identity or, at the very least, shaping how we view the world.

There are other reasons to consider how *The Simpsons* views the trappings of nationhood, not the least of which is the real world impact of the show. Think of Willie teaching French at Springfield elementary and welcoming the class with "Bonjourrrrr, you cheese-eating surrender monkeys" ("'Round Springfield" 6.22). This nomenclature became popular among right-wing commentators to describe French opposition to American foreign policy around the 2003 Iraq War. Officials in Brazil and Argentina reacted negatively to portrayals of their countries on the show, while the episode "Thirty Minutes Over Tokyo" (10.23) was banned in Japan for its perceived disrespect of the Japanese emperor. Matt Groening even thought it necessary to apologize to Australian journalist Michael Idato for "Bart vs. Australia" (6.16). When dealing with stereotypes that inherently marginalize or discriminate, a key focus of *The Simpsons* is how the main characters react to those who are marginalized, and to the acts of marginalization themselves. Often, it seems that the regular or main characters are the ones who are really the target of the satire. With a wink and a nod, the makers of the show invite audiences to see how middle America sees the world beyond Springfield.

The political theorist Benedict Anderson says the very concept of nationhood is imagined, and a large part of that imagining comes from shared written and visual texts. As a global media phenomenon, *The Simpsons* is part of the modern imagining process. And whenever we imagine our own nation—whichever it might be—we instantly see other nations existing beyond. These two aspects of national imagining—us and them—are represented in *The Simpsons* in many different ways. Most obviously, those nations outside of America are imagined whenever the Simpson family leaves Springfield on an international trip. But even when they stay in Springfield, we can see this imagining in the characters who are linked with other countries. And Springfield also does a good deal of imagining about the United States itself.

We might call assertions of American symbols of nation a positive imagining, and representations of those other nations portrayed in the show a negative imagining. This is not to assume that all the representations of America are strictly positive, or that images of other countries are necessarily negative, but that the two types of imagining are in opposition to each other. It is a recognition that each assertion of American-ness implies that some values and traits are un–American and that those are the values of other countries and peoples. In the sections that follow, both positive and negative imaginings are discussed. Both of these take place within and outside Springfield and within and outside the United States.

It is neither possible nor desirable to identify what messages the multitude of audiences around the world have taken from *The Simpsons*, not to mention the ways in which particular scenes, jokes, and characters were meant to be understood by the many contributors to each episode. This essay simply explores how *The Simpsons* presents nationality, without any claim about the understandings audiences or individuals might have of these constructions. After all, *The Simpsons* is a comedy, replete with layer after layer of hidden jokes, intertextual references, multiple ironies, parody, satire, and sight gags. As Homer Simpson reminded us in "Mr. Lisa Goes to Washington"

(3.2): "cartoons don't have any deep meaning. They're just stupid drawings that give you a cheap laugh."

Springfield the Brave

Springfield is a microcosm of the USA and, like any good nation, Springfield has everything it needs to be simultaneously self-contained and yet connected to the outside world. Springfieldians have easy access to interstate freeways and railway lines, an international airport, and a harbor. At the same time, they needn't really ever leave town because there are monolithic malls, schools, universities, a casino, and extraordinary natural features like gorges, lakes, rivers, forests, and mountains all within easy drive. Springfield is a small town, but in a big town kind of way. The headquarters of the international television conglomerate, Itchy & Scratchy Publishing, and the chief brewery of Duff Beer are all located in Springfield. News is delivered by a local newsman from Springfield's own Channel 6 studios, as is a variety of local programming, including *The Krusty the Clown Show*.

With all of this in Springfield itself, how do the characters even know they are part of a wider nation, one that is out there beyond the town borders? Michael Billig suggests that one way people are reminded of their nationhood is through the everyday presence of national flags. Counting the appearance of flags in the first ten seasons of *The Simpsons*, to find out just how banal and everyday this key national symbol really was, I located nearly 400 individual appearances of the United States flag, a significant chunk of over 1300 references to the U.S. in total in those 226 episodes. Often, the flag was hanging, limp and unfurled, on school buildings or in classrooms. It is just this kind of background appearance that Billig argues is important in subtly reminding people of their nationhood. This is also part of the national imagining process that Benedict Anderson discusses, and it is as much a part of the scenery for audiences of *The Simpsons* as it is for the characters in the show.

Some episodes of *The Simpsons* focus very specifically on symbols of U.S. nationhood. My favorite examples of these include "Mr. Lisa Goes to Washington" (3.2), "Deep Space Homer" (5.15), "Two Bad Neighbors" (7.3), and "The Secret War of Lisa Simpson" (8.25). It is no accident that two of them feature the most urbane and cynical member of the Simpson family. Lisa is the Simpson most likely to vocalize opposition to forced nationalism and to stand up for people who might be excluded or marginalized and often finds her liberal beliefs at odds with the more conservative institutions of nationhood. Both of these episodes underline a few key ideas about the American nation and Springfield's place within it. The rule of law, justice, military, and political institutions are all prominent. And the Star-Spangled Banner is all over both the military school and Washington, D.C.

In "The Secret War of Lisa Simpson" (8.25), Lisa struggles to reconcile herself to symbols of American nationhood like the military school Rommelwood (ironically named after a German World War II general). Lisa wants to be accepted at Rommelwood, but is rejected by the other students because she is the only female student. It is only at the end of the episode when Bart helps and encourages her, at his own risk, that Lisa is able to fit in. Lisa wanted to study at Rommelwood because of the challenging curriculum, not a desire to join the military or (as in Bart's case) as a punishment. This different motivation between her and the other students comes to stand in for the differences in how characters like Lisa and some American institutions see the world and their places within it.

In "Mr. Lisa Goes to Washington" (3.2), Lisa shows some concern about the nature of Congress and democracy. This episode is replete with American symbolism. Aside from the U.S. flag and national institutions, we see the bald eagle striking a Great Seal–like pose for Lisa in Springfield Forest. This inspires her essay about America's greatness and wins her and the family a trip to Washington. While there, Lisa overhears a Congressman being bribed to allow Springfield Forest to be logged and decides to rewrite her essay, calling it "Cesspool on the Potomac." As Lisa delivers her essay, the instruments of the nation-state swing into action to prevent a little girl from "losing faith in democracy." The Congressman is arrested, and Lisa delights that "the system works."

Two other episodes that focus very strongly on the presentation of the national character are "Deep Space Homer" (5.15) and "Two Bad Neighbors" (7.3), which foreground the Simpson family patriarch, Homer. In "Deep Space Homer," he, like Lisa, becomes disillusioned with a national institution. NASA's televised space launch bores Homer just at the point he turns to TV for comfort after losing out on a worker of the week award to an inanimate carbon rod. After berating NASA scientists by phone, Homer is given the chance to go into space. Inspired by an ill-fated NASA program that really did aim to send everyday people into space, this episode shows the triumph of the everyman as Homer first damages and then saves the shuttle. Like Lisa coming to terms with the nation's democratic and military institutions, Homer emerges from his adventure more at ease with the role NASA plays in U.S. national life. Nonetheless, he is still outshone by an inanimate carbon rod.

"Two Bad Neighbors" (7.3) has a similarly bow-tied ending. Homer instantly takes a dislike to George Bush, Sr., when the former president and his wife move in across the street, upstaging his own grandstanding performance at a rummage sale. After several incidences of feuding, including a spanking, locusts, burnouts on a lawn, glue in a wig, and an actual fistfight, the Bushes move out, and former President Gerald Ford—much more agreeable to Homer—moves in. Despite Springfield having, as Barbara Bush says, "the lowest voter turnout in America," the presence of the Bushes in this episode points to another way the town acts as the nation-in-miniature. *The Simpsons* often makes use of national icons such as presidents. In this episode, in addition to George Bush, reference is made to then President Bill Clinton, former Vice President Dan Quayle, and former President Grover Cleveland (who is said to have spanked Grampa Simpson on two separate occasions). Near the end of the episode, Barbara Bush demands her husband apologize to Homer for the feud, as former USSR President Mikhail Gorbachev looks on. George Bush responds: "But, Bar, we can't show any weakness in front of the Russians." Undoubtedly, the "we" Bush refers to is all of America and not just his own family.

References to symbols of national institutions, flags, and national icons are part of the daily process of imagining nations through media texts. Springfield stands in for the American nation as a whole, so it is only natural that it also shares a commitment to the presence and even preservation of these symbols. Whatever criticism of the nation is implied in any given episode is still delivered in a framework where the national paradigm is firmly in place. The imagining of the nation is constantly reinforced by the daily banal presence of all of these symbols.

The World in Springfield

Since Springfield is a microcosm of the American nation, it too is populated by characters from a range of national and ethnic backgrounds. Alongside the all-American families like the Simpsons, the Wiggums, the Van Houtens, the Muntzs, and the Spucklers, the regular cast includes Indian-born Apu "Nahasapeemapet-whatever" (as Selma Bouvier calls him in "Much Apu About Nothing" 7.23), the Scottish-born Groundskeeper Willie, the Arnold Schwarzenegger–like Rainier Wolfcastle, Italian mobsters, the might-be-Mexican Bumblebee Man, German exchange student Üter, and others. The latter group is characterized by a series of stereotypes that, in one way or another, lead to them be targets of exclusionary behavior and often the butt of jokes. This process of exclusion is sometimes the flipside of the positive assertion of national identity discussed in the previous section. There are also certain characters who come to be seen as their nation of origin writ large.

An episode where Springfield's prejudices are strongly on show is "Much Apu About Nothing" (7.23). In this episode, Springfield Mayor "Diamond" Joe Quimby deflects a fear of bears into a campaign against immigrants and asks the town's residents to prepare to vote on a proposition to kick all "illegal" immigrants out of Springfield. Homer places a sign in the Kwik-E-Mart satirizing American military recruitment posters that says: "We want you … out!" Even the bartender, Moe Szyslak, is forced to take a citizenship test, despite his loud protestations against people he calls "immigants," whom he decries because "they wants all the benefits of living in Springfield, but they ain't even bother to learn themselves the language." Moe's national origins are often deliberately obscured. Dr. Nick Riviera and Groundskeeper Willie are others for whom the borders are closing, though Willie is the only person subsequently deported. But it is Apu who most precariously straddles the border between American and not-American in this episode, struggling to fully reconcile the two sides of his identity.

In an attempt to stay in America in the face of the vote, Apu purchases a forged passport from Italian mobster Fat Tony, who tells Apu he is now from Green Bay and that his parents are named "Herb and Judy Nahasapeemapetilon." Fat Tony suggests to Apu that he needs to "act American," by which he means demonstrations of hyper-patriotism, less courtesy, and laziness. Apu promptly decks out the Kwik-E-Mart in American flags and dons a New York Mets baseball cap and a broad American drawl. Homer seems surprised by the new Apu who serves him, but Apu cannot keep up the charade. He decides to take a citizenship test instead and shows that he is more knowledgeable about America's history than many of the American characters, Homer in particular. The politics in this episode are complex, but the overriding narrative positions Apu and the other "illegal" immigrants as not-quite American. The sub-text is the absurdity of the campaign to denigrate and remove gainfully employed and otherwise contributing individuals from the community just because of their national origins. In the end, the proposition passes overwhelmingly, even though the Simpson family now realizes that immigrants are an important part of the community.

Apu comes to stand in for and represent the Indian nation. Beyond his role as a shopkeeper—which he holds in the show presumably only because of his ethnicity—little is shown of Apu until "Homer the Heretic" (4.3). Before this appearance, he is background filler, characterized only by his enthusiastic service, his chirpy catchphrase ("thank you, come again") and his ability to do things that convenience store shopkeepers are expected to do, like being on the receiving end of armed robbery. This portrayal of Apu has drawn criticism from comedian Hari Kondabolu, among others, in part because he is portrayed by a white voice actor (Hank Azaria). In "Homer the Heretic," Apu reveals that he worships the Hindu god, Ganesh. Later in the same episode, he is shown also to be a volunteer firefighter, who arrives to save Homer as the Simpson home burns. After the fire is out, Reverend Lovejoy tells Homer that God was "working in the hearts of your friends and neighbors when they came to your aid, be they [pointing to Ned Flanders] Christian, [pointing to Krusty the Clown] Jew, or [pointing to Apu] ... miscellaneous." Apu's indignant response is to tell Lovejoy that there are 700 million Hindus in the world, but Lovejoy is unperturbed: "Oh, that's super." The Reverend's condescension is palpable.

Despite this rocky introduction to a well-rounded Apu, from here on in his character is given more time and more detail. In "Homer and Apu" (5.13), he is fired from the Kwik-E-Mart and comes to live with the Simpsons. They grow fond of Apu, and he journeys with Homer to India to ask the mystic, Gandhi-like global head of the Kwik-E-Mart to be reinstated. The parody of Indian people in this episode becomes a little more sustained, with references like the Air India logo promising to "treat you like cattle," simultaneously referencing and skewering Hindu reverence of cattle and a common stereotype that public transport on the Indian subcontinent overflows with people. Apu is further detailed in "The Two Mrs. Nahasapeemapetilons" (9.7), in which he reluctantly agrees to an arranged marriage with Manjula. Despite their reservations, the couple agree they can "always get a divorce," to which Apu says: "God bless America," showing that he has come to terms with his dual nationality. By the end of Season 9, then, the representation of Apu had become more rounded, but he nonetheless is painted as a stand-in for the whole Indian nation.

Like Apu's India, Scotland is experienced primarily through Groundskeeper Willie. Unlike Apu, Willie is *always* represented through vague and often unimaginative stereotypes. When Mr. Burns, Homer, and Professor Frink take a trip to Scotland to capture the Loch Ness Monster in "Monty Can't Buy Me Love" (10.21), who else would accompany them? Willie is there because they are in Scotland, and it gives him a chance to live up to some further Scottish stereotypes. Homer sees a Scottish couple watching the activities by the shore of Loch Ness and says to Willie: "That old couple looks just like you." Willie responds that they are his parents, adding: "They own a tavern hereabouts. They still have the same pool table on which I was conceived, born, and educated." Willie's uncouth behavior suddenly makes a lot more sense—it is because of his upbringing. The implication is that Willie is typical of Scots. But the joke doesn't end there, as Willie then has a brief reunion with his parents.

Ma: So, you're back, son.
Willie: Aye.
Pa: I suppose you'll be leaving soon.
Willie: Aye.
[All shrug and part]

Despite being away from home for many years, this is the extent of his interaction with his parents. The whole passage stereotypes Scots as uncivil.

In two separate episodes, Willie is represented as a pervert—first in "Homer Badman" (6.9) and then in "Thirty Minutes Over Tokyo" (10.23). In "Homer Badman," Willie's practice of videotaping Springfield's residents saves Homer from sexual harassment charges but earns himself the moniker "Rowdy Roddy Peeper," courtesy of a sleazy current affairs program. As Willie shows the Simpson family the tape that will save Homer, he tells them:

> My hobby is secretly videotaping couples in cars. I dinna come forward because in this country, it makes you look like a pervert, but every single Scottish person does it!

Here, the stereotyping is ratcheted up a notch. Rather than leaving it to be gleaned from inference, Willie explicitly states what makes his nation deviant. In this sentence, Scotland is also set up in an oppositional binary with the United States, further strengthening the observation that each nation is defined in opposition—or reflexively—to others. As "Thirty Minutes Over Tokyo" opens, Willie is at Springfield's internet cafe the Java Hut, viewing a website boasting an "up-kilt camera." As the image loads from behind a United Kingdom flag, Willie commentates it for the viewer: "Ew, this lass needs a bit of groundskeeping," he opines, before the kicker: "Ah, that's Willie!" The amateur videographer has become the subject of someone else's video. Willie in his kilt sans underwear is not an unusual occurrence on *The Simpsons*, and the joke is not only made for the audience's benefit: it is also often for the amusement of other characters. In "Bart's Girlfriend" (6.7), Willie forms an unwitting part of Principal Skinner's plan to set up Bart for detention. At a fake "Scotchtoberfest" event, Willie delivers a lecture on Scottish culture: "Now the kilt was only for day-to-day wear. In battle, we donned a full-length ball gown covered in sequins. The idea was to blind your opponent with luxury." As Willie speaks, Bart sneaks up behind him and ties helium-filled balloons to the kilt, lifting it skyward. Willie stands proudly as the crowd reacts with gasps (one woman faints): "Ach! 'Tis no more than what God gave me, you puritan pukes!" Although Willie's kilt is being mocked here, his line about puritanism appears to be clearly aimed at the American audience. As the primary touchstone and the only regular voice of Scotland, Willie has come to represent his nation. Whatever Willie does—be it outbursts of violence or taking great pleasure in using his bare hands to unclog a toilet—he speaks for Scotland.

In addition to recurring characters that seem to stand in for their nation of origin, Springfieldians regularly poke fun at other whole countries whose citizens aren't represented in the regular cast. They do this through the same simplifying and stereotyping behavior applied to Apu, Willie, Üter, and Bumblebee Man. One nation-state that is very clearly the subject of a simplified discourse in *The Simpsons* is the United Kingdom. The term "United Kingdom" is rarely mentioned, and the terms "British" or "Britain" are used less often than individual references to three of the constituent parts of the United Kingdom (that is, England, Scotland, and Northern Ireland, Wales being conspicuously absent). Not only is the official nation-state largely ignored, so too are any possible differences between Northern Ireland and the Republic of Ireland. The appearance of three separate stateless nations in the place of one United Kingdom reinforces the very concept of imagined national communities portrayed through stereotype and simplification. The "Big Book of British Smiles," which contains numerous pictures of disfigured mouths, is one example of this practice ("Last Exit to Springfield" 4.17). Ireland is referenced almost entirely through stereotype, such as when riots break out in Springfield on St Patrick's Day, spurring the police to invoke laws prohibiting alcohol ("Homer vs. the Eighteenth Amendment" 8.18). As drunken louts climb the broadcast tower behind newsreader Kent Brockman, he addresses the audience:

> Ladies and Gentleman, what you're seeing is a total disregard for the things St Patrick's Day stands for. All this drinking, violence, destruction of property. Are these the things we think of when we think of the Irish?

The joke is on the Irish, of course, as Springfield's residents wholeheartedly embrace those things that they think St Patrick's Day stands for. Before the violence, a float in the St Patrick's Day parade celebrates the "Drunken Irish Novelists of Springfield," while Moe has a sign displayed in his bar reading, "Help Wanted: No Irish." The appearance of this sign draws on the historical appearance of similar signs in both the United Kingdom and the United States. For those who have so far missed the joke, a pub adorned with the UK flag is blown up, referencing the Irish Republican Army's campaign against British colonialism. And it isn't limited to just one episode. In "Monty Can't Buy Me Love" (10.21), Mr. Burns announces a plan to capture the Loch Ness Monster, promising something "man has searched for since the dawn of time." Homer innocently asks, "A sober Irishman?" And Burns responds, "Even rarer."

By drawing characters like Willie and Apu as larger-than-life stand-ins for their nation of origin, *The Simpsons* introduces viewers to crude, simplistic stereotypes, even when some of those portrayals are actively rejected by characters in the show. There is an argument that these attempts at portraying outsiders are meant to parody American views of other nationalities, and even present the American characters as dumb and violent. Jonathan Gray's analysis is that the show indulges in "hyper-stereotypes ... to make the *process* of stereotyping the target, rather than the people themselves" (64). An example of this is shown in Homer's turnaround of opinion toward Apu in "Much Apu About Nothing" (7.23). But no matter what some characters think or say, the overwhelming tide still runs against the minority characters. Other nations fare even less well than India and Scotland, being represented solely through what other characters say or see rather than by having their own national representatives. The presence and makeup of other nations is drawn in comparison to assertions of American national character, especially within Springfield.

The Simpsons are going to...

Every now and then, the Simpsons acquire a ticket to visit some far-flung corner of the world. As a family and as individuals, the Simpsons have visited many. Bart went on exchange to France and has couriered human eyes to Hong Kong. Homer has traveled to India with Apu, the South Pacific as a missionary, and Cuba and Scotland with Mr. Burns. The family as a whole has visited, amongst others, Australia, several countries in Africa, Brazil, Canada, China, England, Italy, and Japan. During these trips, the hyper-satirical nature of the show becomes even more apparent, and the presentation of non–American characters becomes more complex than it is when they are safely confined to Springfield. The skewering of Americanism is also more sustained when the Simpsons are outside of America. Partly, this comes about through the obvious points of contrast between what is American and what is not while the Simpsons are traveling.

While in Australia for Bart to apologize for fraud and receive a literal kick in the bum ("Bart vs. Australia" 6.16), both Homer and Bart are boorish and rude and generally live up to a stereotype of the ignorant American abroad. Homer threatens the Australian Prime Minister with "the boot" and Bart unleashes biological destruction in the form of a bullfrog (or a "chaswasser" as the Australian shopkeeper would have called it). The Australia depicted in this episode is drawn in through caricature. We get kangaroos loping around cities, vast distances between houses, giant beers, media characters like Crocodile Dundee, Yahoo Serious, and Mad Max, plus a joke about dingoes eating babies. It's worth remembering that *The Simpsons* draws attention to its own inaccuracies, as shown in the labeling of "Parliament Haus der Austria" with a hand-drawn "al" squeezed in. This is perhaps the most prominent signposting that the inaccuracies are deliberate and what you are seeing is a nation viewed through the eyes of well-educated and urbane writers imagining middle-American prejudice.

Hidden under all this is a sustained reference to another country—Singapore—and the caning meted out to American teenager Michael Fay in 1994. Marge and Homer's moralizing about Bart's proposed punishment mirrors official American sentiment about Fay, though Homer's speech about the results of ending corporal punishment in America (such as old people strutting confidently through dark alleys and nerds being admired for computer skills) suggests the American example isn't entirely adequate either. Speaking of inadequate, the American embassy is poorly protected from a raging Australian mob by a gate "Made with Pride in the USA" that fails to close. "Bart vs. Australia" is a grab bag of national stereotypes, and it takes aim at ideas of Americans at least as much as it does Australians. The episode also sets an example, well followed in future seasons, of how *The Simpsons* would approach international travel.

The difference between the portrayal of Australia and that of many other international destinations in *The Simpsons* is that the non–American stereotypes are nearly all aimed squarely at one nation. By contrast, when the Simpsons visit Brazil (13.15), as Chris Turner says in his book *Planet Simpson*, "Rio is a sort of all-purpose, catch-all Latin American Everyslum" (114). In Season 16, Brazil features in a little more detail as Homer is invited to referee the FIFA World Cup final ("You Don't Have to Live Like a Referee" 25.16). He is bribed by Brazilian gangsters to throw the game Brazil's way in an episode that also foreshadowed global raids and arrests of FIFA officials the following year. The same pattern of a monolithic multi-state bloc standing in for multiple unique countries can be seen in "Missionary: Impossible" (11.15), in which Homer becomes a missionary on a fictional South Pacific island called Microatia, and "Simpson Safari" (12.17) in Africa. Instead of collapsing just one nation into a simplistic discourse, these episodes do it to several nations at once. *The Simpsons'* Rio de Janeiro is crawling with rats, monkeys, and pick-pockets, its Africa little more than a glorified game park with coups every other week, and its South Pacific full of noble savages just waiting on the corrupting influence of American religion and excess. These are the imagined nations positioned alongside, against, and in opposition to Springfield's America.

Despite the inaccuracies, the winking sleight-of-hand with national flags, the casual racism, and the ham-fisted patriotism, international audiences fervently lap up all *The Simpsons* has to offer. Sure, the Rio tourism board threatened to sue over "Blame It On Lisa" (13.15), but the show still attracts a cult-like following outside the U.S. This is because international audiences see *The Simpsons* as more about them (Americans) than us. The laughter comes easily enough because we're really laughing at Homer and Bart, not with them, even when they're laughing at us. *The Simpsons* are co-conspirators for non–Americans, double agents of dissidence, poking fun at the American everyman at least as much as the English royalist or the French winemaker. That makes it easy to swallow the sometimes bitter pill of appalling accents, suggestions of criminality, and other willful and wild national stereotypes.

Bringing it Home(r)

The Simpsons does a great deal of imagining nations and delivers its lessons with both careful and careless satire. Representations of nations are often simultaneously painful and delightful, whether they take place in Springfield or outside it, in the given nation or through the proxy of a nationalized character. Depictions of the American nation are, unsurprisingly, more subtle, nuanced, and common than those of any other. Largely, America is represented inside Springfield itself through use of national symbols such as the flag. Other modes of representing America such as national characters (like presidents) and institutions (NASA) are also prominent. Different methods, more reliant on stereotype and caricature, are used to present other nations and characters, though some, like Apu, come to be more rounded and nuanced than they initially were. Often, imaginings of other nations are presented in opposition to imaginings of America.

Rebellion against the national ideal is something of a theme for The Simpsons. Lisa and Homer both find reasons to rail against overt nationalism and national symbols, whether they are represented by corrupt congressmen or crusading former presidents. This offers an opportunity to rethink what we know about the character of American national life. The criticisms—whether imagined or implied—work in an environment where the national ideal is ever-present and flagged. Similarly, those distinctly not-American characters who reside in Springfield provoke questions in the minds of other Springfieldians and audiences about things like immigration politics and marginalization, but still subside to the hegemonic presence of the national imagining.

Bumbling, self-righteous, and downright rude, the Simpson family abroad seems like a neat negative representation of an American national character. They call out a perceived insularity of Americans but, in doing so, might also point to prejudice among the international audience. The offense caused by particular episodes set outside America seems to be still keenly felt, but it is likely that the main targets of the parody are the Simpson family themselves rather than any of the foreigners. Though Australians might have written volumes of letters to the producers when "Bart vs. Australia" was first aired, it soon became apparent that Americans were really the target and, in any case, that sinister looking koala clinging to the underside of the U.S. Navy helicopter would deliver a nice dose of comeuppance in return for Bart's bullfrog. Compared to the treatment of Americans abroad, any issues foreigners might have with their portrayal on the show are nothing but a "little kick in the bum."

WORKS CITED

Anderson, Benedict. Imagined Communities. Revised. Verso, 1991.
"Bart vs. Australia." The Simpsons: The Complete Sixth Season. Written by Bill Oakley and Josh Weinstein, directed by Wes Archer, 20th Century–Fox, 1995.

"Bart's Girlfriend." *The Simpsons: The Complete Sixth Season*. Written by Jonathan Collier, directed by Susie Dietter, 20th Century–Fox, 1994.

Billig, Michael. *Banal Nationalism*. SAGE Publications, 1995.

"Blame It On Lisa." *The Simpsons: The Complete Thirteenth Season*. Written by Bob Bendetson, directed by Steven Dean Moore, 20th Century–Fox, 2002.

"Deep Space Homer." *The Simpsons: The Complete Fifth Season*. Written by David Mirkin, directed by Carlos Baeza, 20th Century–Fox, 1994.

Gray, Jonathan. *Watching with The Simpsons: Television, Parody, and Intertextuality*. Routledge, 2005.

"Homer and Apu." *The Simpsons: The Complete Fifth Season*. Written by Greg Daniels, directed by Mark Kirkland, 20th Century–Fox, 1994.

"Homer Badman." *The Simpsons: The Complete Sixth Season*. Written by Greg Daniels, directed by Jeffrey Lynch, 20th Century–Fox, 1994.

"Homer the Heretic." *The Simpsons: The Complete Fourth Season*. Written by George Meyer directed by Jim Reardon, 20th Century–Fox, 1992.

"Homer vs. the Eighteenth Amendment." *The Simpsons: The Complete Eighth Season*. Written by John Swartzwelder, directed by Bob Anderson, 20th Century–Fox, 1997.

Idato, Michael. "Matt Groening's Family Values." *The Age*. 18 July 2000, https://www.simpsonsarchive.com/other/interviews/groening00a.html

"Last Exit to Springfield." *The Simpsons: The Complete Fourth Season*. Written by Jay Kogen and Wallace Wolodarsky, directed by Mark Kirkland, 20th Century–Fox, 1993.

"Missionary: Impossible." *The Simpsons: The Complete Eleventh Season*. Written by Ron Hauge, directed by Steven Dean Moore, 20th Century–Fox, 2000.

"Mr. Lisa Goes to Washington." *The Simpsons: The Complete Third Season*. Written by George Meyer, directed by Wes Archer, 20th Century–Fox, 1991.

"Monty Can't Buy Me Love." *The Simpsons: The Complete Tenth Season*. Written by John Swartzwelder, directed by Mark Ervin, 20th Century–Fox, 1999.

"Much Apu About Nothing." *The Simpsons: The Complete Seventh Season*. Written by David S. Cohen, directed by Susie Dietter, 20th Century–Fox, 1996.

"'Round Springfield." *The Simpsons: The Complete Sixth Season*. Written by Mike Reiss and Al Jean, directed by Steven Dean Moore, 20th Century–Fox, 1995.

"The Secret War of Lisa Simpson." *The Simpsons: The Complete Eighth Season*. Written by Rich Appel, directed by Mike B. Anderson, 20th Century–Fox, 1997.

"Simpson Safari." *The Simpsons: The Complete Twelfth Season*. Written by John Swartzwelder, directed by Mark Kirkland, 20th Century–Fox, 2001.

"Thirty Minutes Over Tokyo." *The Simpsons: The Complete Tenth Season*. Written by Donick Cary and Dan Greaney, directed by Jim Reardon, 20th Century–Fox, 1999.

Turner, Chris. *Planet Simpson: How a Cartoon Masterpiece Documented an Era and Defined a Generation*. Random House eBooks, 2012.

"Two Bad Neighbors." *The Simpsons: The Complete Seventh Season*. Written by Ken Keeler, directed by Wes Archer, 20th Century–Fox, 1996.

"The Two Mrs. Nahasapeemapetilons." *The Simpsons: The Complete Ninth Season*. Written by Rich Appel, directed by Steven Dean Moore, 20th Century–Fox, 1997.

"You Don't Have to Live Like A Referee." *The Simpsons*. Written by Michael Price, directed by Mark Kirkland, 20th Century–Fox, 30 Mar. 2014.

"So you're calling God a liar!"

An Unbiased Comparison
of Science and Religion

WM. CURTIS HOLTZEN

> "The answers to life's problems aren't at the bottom of a bottle, they're on TV!"—"There's No Disgrace Like Home" (1.4)

It is not unusual for a television show to repeat itself, especially one with a run as long as *The Simpsons*. But is the only reason a television show repeats itself because it is out of ideas? In November of 1997, "Lisa the Skeptic" (9.8) ran, and less than nine years later, in May of 2006, Fox aired "The Monkey Suit" (17.21). Each show centers on Lisa's championing of science amidst Springfield's zealous embrace of religion. Lisa is skeptical, but Springfield is gullible, believing all sorts of myths and fallacies all too often associated with religion. Lisa may be the only eight-year-old girl to have been put on trial for crimes against religion, twice, no less. Each episode also includes a conversation between mother and daughter about the value of faith in a world of science, and, each time, Marge emerges as the only character willing to consider both science and religion. Finally, in each episode, Lisa emerges, vindicated, and science prevails, but there is an agreement that faith has its own place as well, as long as it does not interfere with science.

So, did the writers simply get lazy and recycle an older episode with some new gags? Possibly. But more likely is that this subject is simply too rich to only mine once. For thirty years, *The Simpsons* has been a funhouse mirror, reflecting, exposing, and exaggerating the sillier and more foolish aspects of modern culture. In these thirty years, the relationship between science and religion, as played out in the media, books, courtrooms, internet, and churches, has provided the writers of *The Simpsons* more than enough material for a dozen

130

episodes, let alone two. While the show has characters who represent various religions, "be they Christian, Jew, or miscellaneous," the American conflict between science and religion is particular to Christianity, the dominant and most vocal religion in the nation. As *The Simpsons* satirizes the way some people war over science and religion, the show advocates the independence of science and religion, but also considers a place for religion and science to dialogue.

Ways of Relating Science and Religion

> "Facts are meaningless. You can use facts to prove anything that's even remotely true!"—"Lisa the Skeptic" (9.8)

There are a few different ways to understand how science and religion might relate to one another. Ian Barbour, in *Religion and Science: Historical and Contemporary Issues,* famously identified these as "Conflict," "Independence," and "Dialogue." These ways of relating science and religion are not limited to scholarship but are found throughout modern culture, but many may be surprised to learn that there is more than one way of relating science and religion (77–105).[1]

The conflict, or warfare, model is popular because it lends itself to extremes and overly simple either/or kinds of arguments. It ignores important subtleties and instead opts for the quick sound bite (Barbour 77). In this model, one gets the image of two gunslingers aiming to shoot down each other because "this town just ain't big enough for the both of us." Americans love a good fight (and all too often a "good war") and so religion and science are pitted against each other in books like *The God Delusion* by biologist Richard Dawkins and *Darwin on Trial* by lawyer Phillip Johnson. The fiercest fighting, however, takes place in social media, blogs, video, and podcasts, where civility and facts are not necessary.

The independence model says that each has a right to do what he/she does, as long as each stays on his/her own side of the street. Science can do what it does as long as it stays in the lab, and religion can do what it does as long as it stays in the church. Advocates of this approach sometimes assert that science and religion simply speak two different languages, with incompatible methods and goals. Galileo may have been advocating independence when he said, "The Bible shows the way to go to heaven, not the way the heavens go." Modern advocates of this approach include theologian Karl Barth and paleontologist Stephen Jay Gould. While this view is not as popular in the media as the conflict model, I suspect it is quite common with the general population.

Dialogue is the United Nations of models (and, depending on your view of the UN, this may or may not be a good thing). The dialogue approach tends to see conflict as destructive and independence as generally unproductive. This approach suggests that both science and religion might have something to offer each other, though what that is can only be worked out in dialogue. Science and religion become conversation partners, even though the conversations are difficult and not always productive. This view requires those in dialogue to speak two languages and understand two cultures, and for those reasons it is found most often among academics and philosophers invested in this exchange of ideas.

Religion's War on Science

"Well, it appears science has failed again, in front of over-whelming religious evidence."—"Lisa the Skeptic" (9.8)

In "Lisa the Skeptic," the producers play with a variety of themes including epistemological justification, consumerism, and apocalypticism, but it is in dealing with the science/religion conflict that they clearly have their most fun. A war of religion against science serves as a foil for Lisa's skepticism and reveals that the residents of Springfield, who are all too much like most Americans, are not just anti-science but anti-intellectual; perhaps that is being redundant.

From the religious perspective, the conflict begins when Lisa, on an archeological dig with her classmates, finds what looks to be the bones of an angel. At first only a large skeleton with arms folded over the chest is unearthed, but, as Lisa sweeps away more soil, we also see two large wing-like sets of bones over each shoulder. Lisa quickly ponders, "What the heck is this thing? It looks like a human skeleton, but these other bones almost look like wings." To this, Ned excitedly asks, "You mean like an angel?!" Lisa responds, "Well, obviously that is impossible..." but is cut off immediately by Moe exclaiming, "Yeah, Lisa's right; it's an angel!" Lisa is right to be skeptical here. Her skepticism fits right in with the accepted methods of scientific discovery, which begin with doubt until the claim can be demonstrated accurate or reliable, in this case, empirically. But Lisa's doubt could have easily have been theological in nature, given that the vast Christian tradition has understood angels to be immortal and incorporeal beings. This means angels cannot die, and, even if they could, there would be no bones left behind. The crowd at the excavation site, however, is quick to believe it's an angel—or perhaps quick to disbelieve anything contrary to their religious beliefs. Lisa, now sure it is no angel, is challenged by Moe, "No? Well if you're so sure what it ain't, how about telling us what it am!" Lisa offers a more natural explanation, suggesting that the wing-like bones may actually be those of a fish that attacked a Neanderthal. Or perhaps the bones of a mutant from the nuclear plant. This theory is squashed when Mr. Burns reveals that their mutants have flippers.[2]

The problem that Ned and Moe seem to have with Lisa's doubt and naturalistic explanation is not that they are far-fetched but that they don't offer supposed proof that angels really exist, like the bones do. The bones really look like an angel, and, more importantly, they confirm what Ned and Moe already believe and cherish—that angels exist. The conflict that religion has with science in this episode is that science undermines religious beliefs, removes the mystery, and replaces it with natural explanations that put questions to bed. This is summed up in Ned's statement, "Science is like a blabbermouth who ruins a movie by telling you how it ends. Well, I say that there are some things we don't wanna know. Important things!" Mystery has always played an important part in religion, Christianity in particular. Most Christians affirm that God is beyond reason, but some have even suggested that in matters of the faith, Christians must be anti-reason. It would be an exaggeration to say that Martin Luther, the Father of the Protestant Reformation, was anti- the science of his day, although he was quite critical of Copernicus.[3] Luther was, however, quite critical of reason when it interfered with a straight reading of the Bible. Luther believed that "reason is the greatest enemy that faith has: it never comes to the aid of spiritual things, but—more frequently than not—struggles against the Divine Word, treating with contempt all that emanates from God" (164). For Ned, reason, or, in this case, science, is not coming to the aid of his faith but is presenting him with struggles. Ned has important things he wants to believe, but blabbermouth science is undermining that belief by providing knowledge, and, if science keeps advancing, there will be nothing left to believe.

In Springfield, the conflict between science and religion escalates to a war, literally. After Lisa's appearance on *Smartline* and Ned's impassioned speech about the importance of ignorance, Agnes, Principal Skinner's mother, stands up and says, "Enough talk! It's smashing time!" An angry mob forms, and a war of words escalates to actual attacks on the scientific establishments of Springfield.[4] The rioting is a logical, although extreme, extension of Ned's plea for ignorance. The idea that if science can be eliminated then what will be left, for the Fundamentalist, is biblical literalism. It is noteworthy that at no time do we see Flanders involved in the rioting. *The Simpsons* depicts Flanders as a very devout and sincere Christian, who takes "love thy neighbor" and "turn the other cheek" as literally as he does other biblical teachings. And even though his beliefs are thoroughly black and white, he is no hypocrite. As Homer once said about Flanders, "this man has turned every cheek on his body. If everyone here were like Ned Flanders, there'd be no need for heaven: we'd already be there" ("Homer Loves Flanders" 5.16). While Flanders may be ideologically at war with science, he would not, and does not, stoop to violence and rioting.

While Ned is not a hypocrite, the same cannot be said for others. After watching Lisa debate Kent Brockman ("Lisa the Skeptic" 9.8), Moe rhetorically asks, "Science? What's science ever done for us? ... T.V. off." And, magically, the television turns off. A few moments later, we see Moe taking a bat to the leg of a woolly mammoth and, in the process, causes one of its tusks to fall and crush him, to which he responds, "I'm paralyzed ... I just hope medical science can cure me." Moe's distrust of, and yet dependence on, science is a dilemma many biblical literalists must face. "Evolution is the basis of biology, biology is the basis of medicine" (Wilgoren), but according to many creationists, medicine and evolution have nothing in common. Michael Egnor, M.D. argues that evolution has only brought shame to medicine, taking it "down the horrific road of eugenics." When asked, "Why would I want my doctor to have studied evolution?" his answer is, "I wouldn't. Evolutionary biology isn't important to modern medicine" (Egnor). The conflict between science and religion is not just philosophical but practical, and perhaps because life and death issues are at stake, this war of words may have some actual casualties.

In both "Lisa the Skeptic" and "The Monkey Suit," the conflict becomes litigious when Lisa is put on trial, defending herself against the accusations of "destroying a religious curiosity" and "for the teaching of non-biblical science." The fact that both episodes include scenes in which the science advocate, Lisa, is put on trial says a lot about the current climate of biblical fundamentalism's war on science. Each episode parodies the Scopes "monkey" trial, which was more of a publicity stunt orchestrated by the ACLU to challenge Tennessee's 1923 Butler Act, which made it illegal to teach any theory that denies "the Story of Divine Creation." Unlike Lisa, Scopes was found guilty and fined $100. The Scopes trial is generally understood to be the first major division in America's continuing gap over evolution and creationism (Numbers 215–223).[5]

"Equal time" has been a key strategy for creationists since the 1970s.[6] The plan has been to argue, through the courts, that alternative scientific theories must be provided. Originally, something called "creation science" was to be that alternative, which would emphasize notable differences from its classroom companion, evolution science. Differences such as sudden creation *ex nihilo*, micro-evolution within a species, distinct ancestry between human and apes, and global flood theory would be highlighted (Giberson 98–99). The case for a "balanced treatment" between creation and evolution science failed in an Arkansas courtroom (and several other states since). It was ruled that creation science was more religion than science. Court cases for equal time have continued in recent years with "alternative scientific theories," omitting references to the Bible, God, or creation, and instead have retooled creationism as "Intelligent Design" theory, or ID. Advocates of ID argue that evolution cannot adequately explain origins of life and biological complexity and so it is necessary, as well as good science, to bring into play an intelligent designer. ID theorists never publicly say this designer is the God of the Bible, but the clear majority of ID proponents are affiliated with conservative Christian movements. Neither of these *Simpsons'* episodes really deals with ID theory, but it is interesting that just a couple years before the airing of "The Monkey Suit" (17.21), another trial was held regarding equal time and the use of an ID textbook. *Of Pandas and People* was ruled to be a creationist text with little real science inside. As Karl Giberson quipped, "*Pandas* was a religious book with the word *religion* crossed out and the word *science* written in" (116).

While creationists have lost in the actual courts, they get a win in Springfield. In "The Monkey Suit" (17.21), after it is decided that Springfield Elementary will give equal time to creationism and evolution, Lisa's class watches the video, *So you are calling God a liar? An Unbiased Comparison of Evolution and Creationism*. As the video begins, an empty stage is shown, and the narrator says, "Let's say hi to two books. One, The Bible, was written by our Lord." At this point, a light shines down from above with angelic music playing and The Holy Bible descends, with light beaming from all around it and a halo, of course. The narrator continues, "The other, *The Origin of Species*, was written by a cowardly drunk named Charles Darwin." Fire then rises from beneath the stage as if hell itself had opened, and *The Origin of Species* rises from the flames all while hard rock music plays on. A close up of the book shows its title begin to run like blood, the book is opened, and Darwin falls drunkenly from its pages. At this point, Lisa stands up in protest, affirming that Darwin was one of the greatest minds of all time, only to have Janey ask, "Then why is he making out with Satan?" We then see Darwin and Satan in a full embrace with lips locked.

The depiction of the two books seems over the top, but while *The Simpsons* does excel at comedic exaggeration, in this case, there was little need. In his book, *The Long War against God*, Henry Morris, widely known as the Father of Modern Creation Science, makes a frontal assault on all things evolution. In the book, Morris depicts Darwin as unoriginal, undereducated in science, and as "a pampered timewaster in college" (152).[7] But that does not really matter because Darwin is not the mind behind evolution. Morris writes, "it is not naïve fundamentalism but essential realism to recognize that Satan … would somehow be very directly involved in this watershed development of 1858–59—when the book was published that would soon banish God from science and enthrone evolutionary uniformtarianism as the dominating premise of the intellectual world" (175). Morris spends dozens of pages tracing the history of evolution, not back to the Greeks, nor to Babylon and the biblical city of Babel (although he does think this is how the "pseudo-science of evolutionary humanism" eventually "permeated every nation"). Morris takes evolution back to the first day of creation. On that day, according to Morris, Satan and the rest of the angels were created. Morris theorizes that Satan's rebellion must have begun with the denial that God was his creator. "But if

God had not created him, then who did? And who made God? What could Lucifer have been thinking? It would seem that the only possible alternate solution (to God being creator) Lucifer could imagine would be *evolution*!" (258). Morris concludes, "this means, finally, that the very first evolutionist was not Charles Darwin or Lucretius or Thales or Nimrod, but Satan himself!" (260). Morris never suggests that Darwin got to first base with Satan. No, it is much worse than that. Darwin was a willing pawn used by Satan in his long war against God. According to Morris and other creationists, the conflict is not between religion and science, the war is between God and Satan, whose first and greatest lie was that evolution, not God, is creator.

When "The Monkey Suit" gets to the courtroom, the case is billed as "Lisa v. God." Science and evolution are rendered heretical, elitist, and liberal. Lisa's ACLU–appointed attorney, Clarisse Drummond, who is, of course, from New York, is met with boos. Prosecuting attorney and "humble country lawyer" Wallace Brady is dressed in all white, and his homespun puns win over the jury. The prosecution's expert witness on "devil-ution" is a "scientist" with a PhD in "Truthology" from Christian Tech. This is not farfetched "Hollywood hooey." Early in the fundamentalist's battle against science, it was uncommon to have a creationist with a doctorate in one of the sciences or from an accredited university. Today, there is creationist Kent Hovind, aka "Dr. Dino," who has a doctorate in "Christian Education" from "Patriot University," an unaccredited correspondence college. Ken Ham, co-founder and president of "Answers in Genesis"[8] and recent debater of Bill Nye "the Science Guy," has only a Bachelor of Applied Science. In recent years, the credentials of some creationists have improved; for example, Kurt Wise, who is Director of Creation Research Center, holds a PhD in geology from Harvard University.

Science's War on Religion

> "God is an impotent nothing from nowhere with less power than the undersecretary of agriculture."—"Lisa the Skeptic" (9.8)

Some of those fighting for science against religion claim the scientific method is threatened by "mystical and authoritarian claims" (Barbour 79). Those who battle *against* religion are not simply saying that religion is wrong but that it is to be conquered, subjected, and put away. Scientists and philosophers who advocate scientism (the belief that only nature is real and that the scientific method is the only valid means of knowledge) take the forefront in the war on religion. While their rhetoric is not nearly as preposterous as the creationists, it is for many no less unkind.

The Simpsons' depiction of the soldiers for science is that they are dismissive of anything that might remotely be religious. In "Lisa the Skeptic," our little hero is immediately unwilling to even consider that these bones might be from an angel. Her skepticism is affirmed and shared by Stephen Jay Gould, who, when Lisa brings him the bone scraping, responds not with inquisitiveness, but immediate dismissal; "Oh yeah, that so-called angel, the whole thing's preposterous, of course." Lisa, seemingly seeking approval, says, "Quite preposterous, but no one will believe me until I can prove what it really is! Can't you do a DNA test or something?" Gould later says the tests were "inconclusive," but, when the bones are shown to be a fake and part of a publicity stunt, Gould reveals he never ran the tests, but why? The commentary by the episode's writers/producers said they originally had him adding, "I had more important things to do," but chose not to include this line because it felt too harsh (Cohen, "Lisa the Skeptic" 9.8). This omitted line and the refusal to do the test actually reflects scientism's attitude that all things religious can be dismissed. Gould's character either believes the tests are beneath him or simply unnecessary. It's interesting to note that had the test been run and the bones shown to be a fake, this could have saved Springfield from riots and the destruction of its prized institutes of science ... but this would have also have led to a ten-minute *Simpsons* episode. And that certainly would have been the "worst. episode. ever."

Those who promote science's war on religion do not merely dismiss and scorn religion, they argue that one must choose between the two. Physicist and astronomer Victor J. Stenger exclaims, "Science has not only made belief in God obsolete. It has made it incoherent" (32). Richard Dawkins has not only denied the usefulness of theology but has denied its very existence as an academic discipline: "The achievements of theologians don't do anything, don't affect anything, don't mean anything. What makes anyone think that 'theology' is a subject at all?" (6). This attitude is played out by Lisa when appearing on *Smartline*. She equates belief in angels with all sorts of mythical creatures, and her conclusion to Kent Brockman is simple, "Look, you can either accept science and face reality, or you can believe in angels and live in a childish dream world." Lisa's either/or approach, which is rampant on each side, leads her into conflict with her mother, who, as we will see below, thinks science and religion need not be at war. When Lisa learns her mother believes in angels, she is confused because Marge is, as she says, "an intelligent person" and only "morons" believe in angels. Lisa eventually walks out of the kitchen, declaring, "I feel sorry for you" because Marge is unwilling to give up her beliefs and faith. These are uncharacteristically Lisa-like scenes. We rarely see Lisa so sarcastic to Marge, belittling her mother's values. Her comments on *Smartline* also betray the Lisa we see in other episodes such as "Lisa the Iconoclast" (7.16). In this episode, Lisa learns the truth about the town's founder Jebediah Springfield, aka Hans Sprungfeld, the pirate who cared nothing about Springfield and even tried to kill George Washington. But when she had the opportunity to tell the town the truth, she decides to keep it to herself because the truth would damage the hope and morale of Springfield. In "Lisa the Skeptic," however, sympathies for others' beliefs is just one of the casualties of war.

There are excellent and well-respected scientists who believe in God and who maintain that science and religion need not be at war.[9] These scholars, however, are dismissed by those on both sides of the science/religion conflict. And while each side says that *belief* in God and science is certainly possible, the god one is left with is hardly worth believing in. Fundamentalists fighting against science claim that evolutionary science makes God a liar, since Genesis would no longer be factually or historically true. Those warring against religion, like Robert Price and Edwin Suominen, portray Christian evolutionists as "offering terms of their own surrender to their foes" (273). They further perpetuate the warfare model in suggesting that Christian evolutionists' only hope is to find some way to shelter God from the fatal blows of science: "Can [Christian evolutionists] at least find a rat hole in the desert for God to hide out, like Saddam Hussein, from the hostile troop of facts gunning for him?" (277). *The Simpsons* does not spare their satire from such attitudes. In "The Monkey Suit," the defense questions Springfield's eminent scientist Professor Frink. Drummond asks, "So does this theory of evolution necessarily mean that there is no god?" Frink responds, "No, of course not," at which point Lisa smiles knowing this will help her case. But Frink continues, "It just says that god is an impotent nothing from nowhere with less power than the undersecretary of agriculture, who has very little power in our system"; to this, Lisa drops her head.

The Simpsons' treatment of the conflict model in relating science and religion is not just a bit of comedic satire. While the show normally does not take sides, on this occasion it seems it has. *The Simpsons* did not create a cartoonish caricature of this model as much as they reveal the actual implications of such an approach, and then appropriately poke fun at it. The literalistic fundamentalists are portrayed as gullible and anti-intellectual. The advocates of materialistic scientism are shown as patronizing and condescending. In each of these episodes, there is a "better" model given, one that allows for everyone to play nice. The argument is understated in one episode but downright preachy in the other.

Independence Model

> "I'm issuing a restraining order. Religion must stay 500 yards
> from Science at all times."—"Lisa the Skeptic" (9.8)

The independence model is a natural response to the warfare generated by the conflict model. This model treats science and religion like unruly children sending each to its own room. There, each one can play as they like, as long as they do not bother the other. This approach is not simply motivated by the avoidance of conflict but because many believe science and religion simply speak different languages, have thoroughly different methods, and are each searching after radically dissimilar kinds of knowledge.

In "The Monkey Suit," the independence model is presented as the solution to the conflict, one that will be better for all involved. After Flanders admits, under oath, that it is possible Homer is related to an ape, the court case is lost (how this leads to the ban on teaching evolution being repealed and Lisa found not guilty for teaching non-biblical science, I'll never know). Dejected, he and his boys start to leave the courtroom, but Lisa stops them, saying, "Mr. Flanders, wait! I want you to know, I respect your beliefs, and I can see how deeply you feel about them. I just don't think religion should be taught in our schools, any more than you'd want scientists teaching at the church." Flanders cheerfully responds, "Well, I wish this world would evolve a few more kids like you, Lisa." Lisa and Ned may disagree on science and religion, but they can agree that the two should never meet. The episode ends with the message that science *and* religion are important and meaningful, but each needs to stay in its own domain, religion in the churches and science in the schools. Here, *The Simpsons* is giving us the moral of the story; there is no reason for these conflicts and courtroom battles if we would each just understand that science and religion rule their own houses. While the solution here is simple, in reality it is thorny, for there are many more places of influence than schools and churches. But we can't expect two episodes of *The Simpsons* to solve all our problems. For that, we would need a full season!

While the message of independence is the clear moral of the story in "The Monkey Suit," it is a bit subtler in "Lisa the Skeptic." This episode ends with the revelation that the angel was a publicity stunt and that the people of Springfield care more about discount rat spray than having their beliefs exploited. When the angel is found upon a hilltop and everyone runs out of the courtroom to see it, Judge Snyder finds Lisa not guilty, but adds this, "As for science vs. religion, I'm issuing a restraining order. Science must stay 500 yards from religion at all times." As if they are a married couple going through a divorce, the judge rules that the two need to stay away from each other. Granted, religion is the stalker who can't quite accept the relationship is over, but the result is the same; the two should go their own way and not interfere with one another.

Another clue to The *Simpsons'* message of independence is that Stephen Jay Gould appears in this episode. Gould is primarily known for his paleontology and theory of "punctuated equilibrium"[10] but is also known for "Non-overlapping magisteria" or NOMA. With NOMA, Gould wanted to establish a "principled resolution of supposed 'conflict' or 'warfare' between science and religion. No such conflict should exist because each subject has a legitimate magisterium, or domain of teaching authority—and these magisteria do not overlap" (274). He argued that both science and religion are equally teachers of their own province. Perhaps this is why Gould's character did not run the tests on the bone scraping, for this would amount to science usurping religion's authority. Or maybe it was a convenient way to keep the episode moving along. While independence is the show's solution, they do give us one other model to ponder.

Dialogue Model

"I think it's good to give both ideas a fair hearing. Maybe they could learn from each other."—"The Monkey Suit" (17.21)

Those who advocate dialogue between science and religion believe that the two share some commonalities and that each might possibly complement the other. The dialogue model does not relegate science and religion to their own rooms but seeks out ways the two can play nicely together, though they are mindful and cautious about any supposed integration of the two. In both "Lisa the Skeptic" and "The Monkey Suit," the dialogue model is suggested by Marge when talking with Lisa at the kitchen table. The model is left undeveloped but is nonetheless put forward. In "Lisa the Skeptic," when Lisa comes into the kitchen, frustrated with the "morons" in the garage, Marge, as in many episodes, is presented as thoughtful, intelligent, and yes, deeply religious. Marge is not the fanatic who riots when her beliefs are challenged, but she has her convictions. Marge believes there is value in taking a "leap of faith now and then," which distinguishes her from folks like Ned Flanders, who seems to be in one long constant leap. Lisa may be a member of Springfield's chapter of Mensa, but Marge is, most often, the true voice of reason on *The Simpsons*, willing to engage with ideas outside her comfort zone.

In "The Monkey Suit," again at the kitchen table, Lisa and Marge talk. Lisa is clearly frustrated that "They're making us learn creation theory in school." And furthermore, "Today we had a test, and every answer was 'God did it.'" Marge responds, expressing her belief in dialogue, "Well, I think it's good to give both ideas a fair hearing. Maybe they could learn from each other." When Lisa exclaims that they are incompatible, Marge offers, "My son's a brat, but he's a special little guy. Your father says he's at work, but there he is jumping on a trampoline." Perhaps here the writers are poking fun at the idea of two seemingly contradictory claims each possibly being true, but Marge is willing to try to see if there is a way to understand science and religion as compatible. Later in the episode, Marge, wanting to see what all the fuss is about, decides to read Darwin's *Origin of Species*. She reads it day and night, in the shower and at the batting cages, and concludes, "Wow, Darwin's argument is incredibly persuasive, and his ship was the Beagle, which reminds me of Snoopy, my favorite Peanut!" But with this conclusion, Marge never abandons her faith nor does she relegate her religion to another domain; she seems to think both can be right, but exactly how is not discussed.[11]

Conclusion

> "Um, can you repeat the part of the stuff where you said all about the ... things?"—"Homer the Smithers" (7.17)

If my assessment is correct, *The Simpsons* brilliantly ridicules the conflict model, ponders the possibilities of dialogue, but preaches the good news of independence. These episodes don't explore the philosophies of these models so much as the psychologies and sociologies of the persons and groups who advance them. In the end, there is no one right way of relating science and religion for sometimes they are in conflict, other times they do operate independently, and still other times there are points of contact that generate dialogue.

It's been over a decade since *The Simpsons* has devoted a show to the science-religion debate, but it may be time for another episode. As a philosopher, I am intrigued by how *The Simpsons* explores our culture, specifically the science-religion question. As a Christian, I am humbled by how *The Simpsons* exposes much of modern Christianity's anti-intellectualism. And as a human, I am delighted by the biting satire, clever gags, and plain old silliness of the show.

Notes

1. Barbour identifies a fourth model he calls "Integration" but, because only three of these models can be found in *The Simpsons,* I will limit my discussion to those noted above.

2. For a discussion concerning why these bones would not be that of an angel, see Jamey Heit (136).

3. Luther dismissed Copernicus' claims because the scriptures clearly teach in Joshua 10:12–14 that the sun stood still.

4. Thankfully, the supposed war between science and religion has only become violent on *The Simpsons,* and to be fair, it seems that Springfield will riot at the drop of a hat. In fact, just three weeks earlier, *The Simpsons* aired "The Cartridge Family," in which a soccer riot overflows into the streets of Springfield, prompting Homer to buy a gun.

5. While the warfare model is most prevalent in America, it is a mistake to assume the conflict is contained to America. Creationism has migrated to Canada, the UK, Australia, New Zealand, South Korea, and beyond.

6. Most recently, those arguing in the courts for equal time have changed their language from terms like "creation science" and have instead argued for "Intelligent Design." Critics, however, have labeled this as "Creationism in Designer Clothes." For more information, see Giberson (111).

7. All of this may be true, but one wonders what the *ad hominem* has to do with the validity of the theory itself.

8. Answers in Genesis (or AIG) is a conservative Christian parachurch organization committed to defending young earth creation as well as other doctrines common among fundamentalists Christians.

9. A full list of such thinkers would take up all the room I have for this essay, but here is a short list of scientists who are also theists: Karl Giberson, Kenneth Miller, Denis Lamoureux, Francis Collins, John Polkinghorne, and Arthur Peacocke.

10. This theory suggests that evolutionary change is not smooth and continuous but has starts and stops with long periods of stasis followed by periods of great change. Some critics referred to his theory as "evolution by jerks" to which Gould famously retorted that gradualism is "evolution by creeps."

11. It is quite telling that at the conclusion of "Lisa the Skeptic" we learn that the townsfolk's ultimate concern was not creationism but capitalism when they run to the mall upon learning everything, including rat spray, is 20 percent off.

Works Cited

Barbour, Ian G. *Religion and Science: Historical and Contemporary Issues.* HarperSanFrancisco, 1997.

Dawkins, Richard. "The Emptiness of Theology." *Free Inquiry*, vol. 18, no. 2, 1998, pp. 6.

Egnor, Michael. "Why would I want my doctor to have studied evolution?" *Evolution News.* 9 March 2007. www.evolutionnews.org/2007/03/why_would_i_want_my_doctor_to003300.html, Accessed 5 May 2016.

Giberson, Karl W. *Saving Darwin: How to Be a Christian and Believe in Evolution.* HarperCollins, 2008.

Gould, Stephen Jay. *Leonardo's Mountain of Clams and the Diet of Worms: Essays on Natural History.* Harmony Books, 1998.

Heit, Jamey. *The Springfield Reformation: The Simpsons, Christianity, and American Culture.* Continuum, 2008.

"Homer Loves Flanders." *The Simpsons: The Complete Fifth Season.* Written by David Richardson, directed by Wes Archer, 20th Century–Fox, 1994.

"Homer the Smithers." *The Simpsons: The Complete Seventh Season.* Written by John Swartzwelder, directed by Steven Dean Moore, 20th Century–Fox, 1996.

"Lisa the Skeptic." *The Simpsons: The Complete Ninth Season.* Written by David X. Cohen, directed by Neil Affleck, 20th Century–Fox, 1997.

Luther, Martin, William Hazlitt, and Alexander Chalmers. *The Table Talk of Martin Luther.* London, G. Bell, 1902.

"The Monkey Suit." *The Simpsons: The Complete Seventeenth Season.* Written by J. Stewart Burns, directed by Raymond S. Persi, 20th Century–Fox, 2006.

Morris, Henry M. *The Long War Against God: The History and Impact of the Creation/Evolution Conflict.* Baker Book House, 1989.

Numbers, Ronald L. "That Creationism is a Uniquely American Phenomenon." *Galileo Goes to Jail and Other Myths About Science and Religion*, edited by Ronald L. Numbers, Harvard University Press, 2009, pp. 215–223.

Price, Robert M. and Edwin A. Suominen. *Evolving Out of Eden: Christian Responses to Evolution.* Tellectual Press, 2013.

Stenger, Victor J. "Yes." *Does Science Make Belief in God Obsolete?* www.templeton.org/belief 30–32. Accessed 31 May 2016.

Wilgoren, Jodi. "Seeing Creation and Evolution in Grand Canyon." *The New York Times.* 6 Oct. 2005. https://www.nytimes.com/2005/10/06/science/sciencespecial2/seeing-creation-and-evolution-in-grand-canyon.html.

"Animation is built on plagiarism"

The Simpsons *and Hitchcock, Parody and Pastiche*

ZACHARY INGLE

Critics of *The Simpsons* have long derided the series for failing to capture the zeitgeist it so ably encapsulated during its first eight to ten years. Yet when it entered its twenty-sixth season in the fall of 2014, *The Simpsons* seemed to respond with a renewed vigor, its cultural relevancy still evident, from the success of FXX's "Every. Simpsons. Ever." marathon that transformed a fledgling network into one of the most watched cable networks during its twelve-day run (Carter B1), to the launch of the *Simpsons World* app, a successful follow-up to *The Simpsons: Tapped Out* game for mobile devices. In a period when newer shows like *Game of Thrones* (2011–2019), *The Walking Dead* (2010–present), and Joss Whedon's creations garner the bulk of scholarly attention, *The Simpsons* continues to draw scholarship partly because, as Jason Mittell contends, "The show fits perfectly into the dual niches of both quality and popularity that appeal to media scholars looking for an object of study acceptable to both academic colleagues and the general populace" (178–179). It is this appeal to both educated and unrefined audiences alike that perhaps led *Time* to declare *The Simpsons* the best TV show of the twentieth century.

Alfred Hitchcock, who directed over fifty films in as many years, has similarly been acclaimed as one of the most influential filmmakers in history. Whenever scholars attempt to make an original contribution to the discourse on Hitchcock, the idea can be overwhelming; there is an abundance of films to examine, but Hitchcock has probably also merited more scholarly articles, biographies, monographs, theses/dissertations, etc. (and in dozens of languages) than any other filmmaker in history. There are frontiers of Hitchcock studies, however, that remain relatively unexplored: the wartime documentaries (*Bon Voyage* and *Aventure Malgache*, both 1944), the role of religion in his films, and his television work come quickly to mind, all deserving further attention. This essay examines how Hitchcock's images and themes are replicated in *The Simpsons*. This intertextuality enlightens a reading of *The Simpsons* and demonstrates how Hitchcock maintains his cultural cache through reappropriation.

Many viewers encounter these allusions in contemporary popular culture before they even know what they are referencing. Of course, an informed viewer, one who understands the allusions, thus attains a greater amount of pleasure, or *jouissance*. As William Irwin and J. R. Lombardo state:

> Why do we find aesthetic pleasure in the allusions others make? Because, as audience members, we enjoy recognizing, understanding, and appreciating allusions in a rather special way. The comprehension of an allusion combines the pleasure we may feel when we recognize something familiar, like a favorite childhood toy, with the pleasure we feel when we know the right answer to the big question on *Jeopardy* or *Who Wants to be a Millionaire?* We derive pleasure from understanding allusions in a way we do not from understanding straightforward statements [85].

The Simpsons has been my favorite show since it debuted thirty years ago. I delighted in it as a preteen, even though I did not yet understand the numerous film references in an episode like "A Streetcar Named Marge" (4.2), in which Marge stars in a musical based on *A Streetcar Named Desire* (1951); homages to *The Great Escape* (1963) and *Citizen Kane* (1941) are also included therein. On that note, only Orson Welles' *Citizen Kane* and Stanley Kubrick's films (particularly *Dr. Strangelove* [1964], *2001: A Space Odyssey* [1968], *A Clockwork Orange* [1971], and *The Shining* [1980]—see the whirlwind of homages in the segment "A Clockwork Yellow" in "Treehouse of Horror XXV" [26.4]) rival Hitchcock for the most film allusions in *The Simpsons*. So why do the writers and animators include these Hitchcock references? As Irwin and Lombardo aptly claim, they offer a greater amount of pleasure for the viewer familiar with his films.

My purpose here is not to merely catalog Hitchcock references on *The Simpsons*; from its first season, *The Simpsons* developed a cult following and a vibrant fan culture, and fans have already documented some of these references on such sites like *The Simpsons Archive* (www.simpsonarchive.org, the central hub for *Simpsons* fandom),[1] as well as wikis devoted to both Hitchcock (The Alfred Hitchcock Wiki) and *The Simpsons*. An outdated Google forum, created by Vic Evans, can also easily be found on the alt.movies.hitchcock group. Fans have created *YouTube* videos such as "Cabecera Simpsons Hitchcock" (created by Jose Sanz Grandos), which runs sixty-nine seconds and includes clips from some of the more notable homages. Rather, this essay investigates the function of these references by examining the role of intertextuality in general in the series, addressing some of the major Hitchcock references, and finally, exploring parody and pastiche.

The Simpsons has long been hailed as definitively postmodern, and academic books and articles have been devoted to *The Simpsons* and postmodern theory,[2] but this statement has become such a given that it may draw the blank stares that Homer, Barney, Carl, and Lenny give Moe as he explains why he overhauled his tavern into a swanky nightclub in "Homer the Moe" (13.3): "It's po-mo! Postmodern! Yeah, all right—weird for the sake of weird." What are the traits that define *The Simpsons* as a prototypical postmodern show? For Jamey Heit, it is that "as a postmodern show, *The Simpsons* relies in part on its viewers to generate meaning" and because of this, "viewers watch the show actively, which necessarily produces a bond between the show and its audience" (12).

This association of *The Simpsons* as one of the first significant examples of postmodern television is largely due to its reliance on intertextuality. Simone Knox's article is more concerned with the "meta" episodes of *The Simpsons* (e.g., "The Simpsons 138th Episode Spectacular" [7.10], "The Itchy & Scratchy & Poochie Show" [8.14], and "The Simpsons Spin-Off Showcase" [8.24] that parody the show itself as well as animated television series) and how the show "addresses itself to postmodern theory" (74), but she also addresses the show's intertextuality that scholars as well as fans have delighted in. Jason Mittell (179–181) questions the show's status as the "postmodernist exemplar," largely due its high degree of reflexivity and intertextuality, correctly noting that animation and television have long contained these two strands, from *Gertie the Dinosaur* (1914) and *Duck Amuck* (1953) to variety shows and *I Love Lucy* (1953–1957). Or, as I&S Studios head Roger Meyers, Jr., states his case in court in "The Day the Violence Died" (7.18):

> Animation is built on plagiarism. If it weren't for someone plagiarizing *The Honeymooners*, we wouldn't have *The Flintstones*. If someone hadn't ripped off Sergeant Bilko, there'd be no Top Cat. Huckleberry Hound, Chief Wiggum, Yogi Bear? Hah! Andy Griffith, Edward G. Robinson, Art Carney. Your honor, you take away our right to steal ideas, where are they gonna come from?

Wherever one stands on how distinctly postmodern these traits of intertextuality and reflexivity are, the depth of intertextuality in *The Simpsons* is inarguable. Julia Kristeva coined the term "intertextuality" for the concept that every text is a "mosaic of quotations" (66). Intertextuality comes in many forms, from allusions to previous texts (literary, cinematic, etc.) and retellings/adaptations, to more outright forms such as parody, pastiche, and even plagiarism. A textbook example of intertextuality, *The Simpsons* is certainly a "mosaic of quotations"; Steven Johnson notes that according to *The Simpsons Archive*, the average episode will include about eight film allusions, whether it is a bit of dialogue, a visual pun, or an entire plotline (e.g., "Cape Feare" [5.2]) (86).

The writers and artists have often catered to cinephilic audiences, from fictional British documentarian Declan Desmond's opening a school assembly with, "When you think of documentaries, you probably think of the Maysles brothers or Barbara Kopple" to blank stares from Springfield Elementary children ("'Scuse Me While I Miss the Sky" [14.16]), or Martin Scorsese quoting French film theorist Andre Bazin in "Angry Dad: The Movie" (22.14) on the complexities of the auteur theory. So it should not be surprising that some of the most lauded American films should be quoted as often as they are.

Jonathan Gray has become one of the most popular media scholars in recent years, particularly for his work in the fields of paratexts and fan studies, but he has also published on parody and satire in television. His first book, *Watching with* The Simpsons: *Television, Parody, and Intertextuality*, a reworking of his doctoral thesis, has become an essential work for all *Simpsons* scholars invested in a more erudite examination of the show. Despite the title, Gray generally has more to say about the show's parody (which I address below) than its intertextuality. Still, Gray attentively maintains that television and its series "have surpassed the novel as hyper-dialogic modes of communication" and are the "current crown domains of intertextuality" (69). Thus, any television series, but especially one that now has 30 seasons and counting, "demands a complex and involved, inescapable intertextuality" (69–70). According to Karma Waltonen and Denise Du Vernay, this intertextuality that the audience connects to is one reason why the show has usually been labeled as a Barthesian "writerly" text rather than a "readerly" text, since it encourages active viewing (285–286). For a show that so often is about watching television (in that the Simpsons are shown watching TV and we in turn often see what they are watching), they are rarely watching the types of films on that "omnidirectional sludge pump" (per Sideshow Bob) that apparently inspires the show's writers (Kubrick, Welles, Hitchcock), but rather fictitious films like *Star Trek XII: So Very Tired*, *The Blunch Black of Blotre Blame*, and *Hail to the Chimp*, along with innocuous television shows like *Police Cops*, *MTC: Monkey Trauma Center*, and *The Krusty the Clown Show*.

This intertextuality not only entertains viewers who are able to grasp the references, but also serves a pedagogical function, enlightening viewers on the major artistic highlights in mass culture, such as the works of Hitchcock, Kubrick, Welles, and, lest we forget, George Lucas. This case was proficiently made by Steven Johnson's bestselling *Everything Bad Is Good for You: How Today's Popular Culture Is Actually Making Us Smarter*, in which he specifically references *The Simpsons* as a show much more complex that its sitcom inspirations. In his discussion of *The Simpsons* and its contemporaries (*Seinfeld* [1989–1998], *Arrested Development* [2003–2019]) vis-à-vis earlier sitcoms

(*Mary Tyler Moore* [1970–1977], *All in the Family* [1971–1979]), Johnson deliberates, "The most telling way to measure these shows' complexity is to consider how much external information the viewer must draw upon to 'get' the jokes in their entirety" (84). But it is not only critics who took up this aspect; it is the expressed intention of the show's creators. As Matt Groening puts it, "That's one of the great things about *The Simpsons*—if you have read a few books, you'll get more of the jokes" (qtd. in Irwin and Lombardo 92). In a somewhat elitist fashion, David Mirkin, showrunner for the fifth and sixth seasons, adds, "We're really writing a show that has some of the most esoteric references on television. I mean really, really, really, strange, odd, short little moments that very few people get and understand. We're writing it for adults and intelligent adults at that" (qtd. in Irwin and Lombardo 81).[3] And it is this trait that ensures the success of *The Simpsons*—appreciated by young children for its scatological humor and the childish antics of Bart and Homer, while Mirkin's "intelligent adults" revel in its literacy.

Likewise, the raving derelict screaming, "Alfred Hitchcock stole every idea I ever had," in "The Day the Violence Died" (7.18) further alludes to this pedagogical purpose, namely that some viewers may come to Hitchcock in a "backwards" manner, seeing the frequent allusions to *North by Northwest* (1959) before they see the actual film. Intertextuality has become increasingly common in our postmodern televisual landscape, reflected in the way we come to some artworks and popular culture artifacts through this backwards lens. I am here reminded of a friend who claimed the "Rosebud" mystery in *Citizen Kane* had already been solved for him before seeing the film because of a brief reference in the children's animated show *Animaniacs* (1993–1998).

When it comes to Hitchcock references on *The Simpsons*, some allusions are subtler, primarily thrown in for interpretive communities deeply familiar with the filmmaker. "Principal Charming" (2.14) features a staircase sequence that recalls the one in *Vertigo* (1958). This *Vertigo* sequence was referenced again in "Homer Loves Flanders" (5.16) in a dream sequence that evokes both Hitchcock's film and the Charles Whitman clock tower shooting at the University of Texas in 1966. There are also throwaway gags, like the photo of Hitchcock with Krusty the Clown in the Brad Bird-directed "Like Father, Like Clown" (3.6), or the title for fake Troy McClure films, *P is for Psycho* (in "Marge in Chains" [4.21]) or *Dial M for Murderousness* ("Mr. Plow" [4.9]). Chris Turner delineates two types of referential humor in *The Simpsons*: the incidental gag and the extended parody (64–65). Obviously, examples such as these fit into the former category. Still, despite being incidental, they are certainly intentional.

Considering it is the film Hitchcock is most remembered for today, it is not surprising that *Psycho* (1960) has merited so many references on *The Simpsons*. The episode "Cape Feare" (5.2) (my personal favorite) parodies the two film versions of *Cape Fear* (1962/1991), but Sideshow Bob is also shown staying at the Bates Motel, with a stuffed owl and other birds of prey on the wall, a strikingly similar *mise-en-scène* to that of the scene in *Psycho*, in which Norman and Marion talk over sandwiches. The Bates home has also appeared more than a few times in the series run, most notably in "Homer Loves Flanders" (5.16,) "Brother from the Same Planet" (4.14), "Bart the Fink" (7.15), and "Realty Bites" (9.9).

Psycho's peephole scene is radiantly captured in "Marge in Chains" (4.21). With a remarkable attention to detail, Maude Flanders adjusts the sailboat painting (a typical innocuous painting in the *Simpsons* universe), just as Norman moves *Susanna and the Elders*. The keen observer will also detect the owl in the hallway. In the final scene of "Black Widower" (3.21), Sideshow Bob turns a chair in which he expects to find the corpse of the murdered Selma, Bart's aunt. He instead discovers Bart, as Selma enters the room. In a nice touch, Sideshow Bob's hand also bumps into the light, and the swinging light replicates the famous flare from the scene, the first of its kind in a Hollywood film, according to some scholars.

One of the most creative and brilliantly conceived of all the Hitchcock references occurs in "Itchy & Scratchy & Marge" (2.9). In this episode, Marge becomes concerned that baby Maggie has been replicating the violent actions she has seen on *Itchy & Scratchy*, the ultra-violent *mise-en-abyme* cartoon popular within the *Simpsons* universe. *Psycho*'s famous shower scene is followed frame by frame as Maggie attacks Homer with a mallet, with Bernard Herrmann's strings score. The scene is reprised just a minute later, as the Simpson family watches another episode of *Itchy & Scratchy*; this time, Maggie comes after the bandaged Homer with a pencil. The cue reappears later in the episode, now a running gag, as Maggie, now influenced by a tamer *Itchy & Scratchy*, instead benevolently offers Homer a glass of lemonade. Herrmann's score cue in all three highlight the reference. Because of its immediate recognizability, the show has inserted the *Psycho* shower scene cue numerous times, including "Treehouse of Horror III" (4.5) and "The Springfield Files" (8.10).

North by Northwest has also served as fodder for Hitchcockian references. In "Fear of Flying" (6.11), Marge attempts to conquer her aviophobia by consulting a therapist. Marge divulges horrific scenes from her childhood involving planes, as a flashback reveals a young Marge with her mother in a cornfield, being chased by a crop duster. Certainly one of the most famous scenes in Hitchcock's oeuvre, the image of the crop duster chasing after characters in the field is repeated in both "I'm with Cupid" (10.14) and "Bart-Mangled Banner" (15.21). A later, though less iconic, moment in the same scene had been used in an earlier episode, "Homer vs. Lisa and the Eighth Commandment" (2.13), in which Homer runs out to stop a truck, in a vein similar to that of Cary Grant's Roger Thornhill (repeated in "Homer Simpson in: 'Kidney Trouble'" [10.8]). The brief scene is copied frame by frame (except that Homer looks straight ahead the whole time and does not glance to the side like Thornhill does at one point). Note the license plate on the truck: "1NBNW," one of the many minute details that multiple viewings rewards. On the DVD commentary, the showrunners and writers observe in amusement that only one minute into the episode they had referenced both Hitchcock and Cecil B. DeMille (the beginning spoofs *The Ten Commandments*) and joke that a *Citizen Kane* reference would probably be coming. (Not this time, guys, but *Jaws* [1975], *Wall Street* [1987], *Die Hard* [1988], *Stardust Memories* [1980], and *Broadcast News* [1987] would all be mentioned explicitly by episode's end.)

At times, it may be difficult to discern if the show's writers are riffing from Hitchcock or from the numerous films that had already borrowed from him. In other words, how many degrees of influence (confluence?) are there between Hitchcock and the creative talent behind *The Simpsons*? One key example occurs in "Three Men and a Comic Book" (2.21), an episode that acts predominantly as an extended parody of *The Treasure of the Sierra Madre* (1948). The ending evokes Hitchcock's *Saboteur* (1942), however, as Bart, from his treehouse, hangs on to Milhouse as his pajama top starts to rip. This device has been plagiarized in other films, but the DVD commentary exposes Hitchcock as their direct referent.

The aforementioned episode, "A Streetcar Named Marge" (4.2), contains a lovely homage to *The Birds* (1963). Homer, Bart, and Lisa are picking up Maggie from her daycare, the Ayn Rand School for Tots. They walk through the mass of babies sucking on pacifiers, much like the finale of *The Birds*. And just in case the audience does not catch this quotation, we then see Hitchcock himself walking two dogs, precisely his cameo from *The Birds*. As Turner points out, "So there you have it: in a minor subplot about Maggie's adventures in daycare, we're given a wicked parody of Ayn Rand's philosophy and hilarious, note-perfect homages to Steve McQueen and Hitchcock" (65). But these allusions are not random, as Carl Matheson emphasizes: "The allusion to *The Birds* communicates the threat of the hive-mind posed by many small beings working as one" (112).

The Birds has merited numerous other references in the long run of *The Simpsons*, possibly because it remains a film that many viewers are aware of, even if they have not actually seen it. In "Homer vs. Dignity" (12.5), the diabolical Mr. Burns, costumed as Santa for the Thanksgiving Day Parade, throws fish guts on the parade attendees, causing a flock of seagulls to attack the crowd. In a scene from the "Night of the Dolphin" segment of "Treehouse of Horror XI" (12.1), dolphins have taken to dry land and demand that the citizens of Springfield live in the ocean. As the citizens exit town hall, the dolphins are perched on jungle gym bars, telephone lines, and rooftops, similar to the eponymous threat of *The Birds*, also recalling its use in "A Streetcar Named Marge." "Itchy & Scratchy Land" (6.4) includes yet another reference, when the Simpsons encounter evil robots at Itchy & Scratchy Land. Marge pines, "I knew we should have gone to that bird sanctuary." Cut to the bird sanctuary, where multi-colored birds are attacking their visitors. Minor character Hans Moleman is even attacked by birds while in a phone booth, à la the fate of poor Melanie from the film. Bird attacks occur in other episodes (e.g., "Bart the Mother" [10.3]), but are less intentional references (or "accidental associations," per Irwin and Lombardo [82–84]), and *The Birds* remains such a cultural phenomenon that many viewers will nevertheless recall Hitchcock's work.

"Bart of Darkness" (6.1) contains one of the more memorable examples of an extended parody of Hitchcock. While the title recalls Joseph Conrad's *Heart of Darkness*, most of the episode faithfully follows *Rear Window* (1954). Bart breaks his leg and is holed up in his bedroom. Lisa gives Bart a telescope to help relieve his boredom, but Bart finds viewing outer space boring and spying on neighbors only slightly more exciting. Scanning through windows, Bart examines people's mundane lives in the late evening, even finding a Jimmy Stewart look-a-like (Mirkin, from the commentary: "When we rip something off, we make sure you know what we are ripping off"). Bart thinks he sees Ned Flanders kill his wife. Still immobilized, he recruits Lisa to investigate in one of the better murder mystery plotlines in the show's history. (As it turns out, Ned had just killed and buried a ficus plant.) But the most brilliant *Rear Window* homage in the episode may be Lisa Simpson lying down on Bart's bed in the exact pose as Grace Kelly's Lisa Fremont, an obscure reference, which may induce a moment of cinephilic pleasure as robust as when Homer cuts up the program in "A Streetcar Named Marge" just as Jedediah Leland (Joseph Cotten) does in *Citizen Kane*.

Cinephiles will particularly enjoy Homer's line in "The Devil Wears Nada" (21.5). In this episode, Homer works briefly as an assistant for his friend Carl, even traveling with him to Paris, but soon misses his family and comes back to Springfield. Feeling abandoned, Carl threatens to fire Homer, to which the latter retorts: "Oh, I don't think so. You know that woman you've been playing 'hide the baguette' with? She's French first lady, Carla Bruni. You fire me, and I'll call Nicolas Sarkozy, and he'll be all over you like Truffaut on Hitchcock." While visual and aural allusions to *The Birds* and *Psycho* would (presumably) be familiar to the majority of the audience, a reference to Francois Truffaut's book of interviews with Hitchcock (1966) requires a greater awareness of film history than most viewers would have obtained.

Besides "A Streetcar Named Marge," Hitchcock's cameo appears in a handful of episodes. His first appearance may have been in "Like Father, Like

Clown" (3.6), in a brief shot of Krusty the Clown and Hitchcock sitting side by side in director's chairs, presumably recalling halcyon days when Krusty was an equal with the Master of Suspense. Hitchcock appears again in "Bart's Friend Falls in Love" (3.23) in television news anchor Kent Brockman's report on obesity, where he mentions Hitchcock as a "jolly fat man" along with Dom DeLuise and Santa Claus. In "Treehouse of Horror III" the *Alfred Hitchcock Presents* (1955–1962) silhouette appears, with Homer mimicking Hitch's trademark "Good evvvveeeening." In "Love Is a Many-Splintered Thing" (24.12), Homer and Bart are watching *Love, Indubitably*, a spoof of *Love Actually* (2003) and other British comedies. The *mise-en-abyme* climaxes with several British clichés, eventually ending in Hitchcock emerging from *Doctor Who's* TARDIS and breakdancing. The Master of Suspense appears again in the Guillermo del Toro-directed opening credits sequence to "Treehouse of Horror XXIV" (25.2), as Hitchcock throws birdseed on Mrs. Krabappel, who is then attacked by birds. Eagle-eyed viewers will also notice his famous self-portrait sketch, used for *Alfred Hitchcock Presents*, painted on a wall by Hans Moleman.

Fans on sites like *The Simpsons Archive* have even compiled the less obvious Hitchcock references, such as this one from "Mom and Pop Art" (10.19): "when Homer is driving in his car, trying to get rid of the BBQ, the shots and music are similar to the famous scene where Janet Leigh is driving in the rain" or that *North by Northwest's* famous ending saturated with sexual innuendo—the train in the tunnel—appears in "Grandpa vs. Sexual Inadequacy" (6.10).

Irwin and Lombardo propose that the "recurrent allusions in *The Simpsons* to Hitchcock films such as *The Birds, Rear Window, North by Northwest,* and *Vertigo* forge a bond between audience members (who recognized them) and the writers of the show" (86). As I hinted at earlier, the references may be rather obvious (*Psycho, The Birds*) or obscure (Truffaut's idolization of Hitchcock), but as Irwin and Lombardo claim, "The writers recognize that not everyone will catch all the allusions, and so they craft them in such a way that the allusions enhance our enjoyment if they are caught, but do not detract from the satisfaction of the show if they are missed. The finely blended texture of the allusions in *The Simpsons* allows both the old and young, sophisticated and naïve, educated and ignorant, to enjoy the same show" (88). This is arguably true for the allusions, but what about when the Hitchcock references go more for a more extended parody or pastiche? Are viewers still able to enjoy an episode like "Bart of Darkness," for instance, sans an awareness of *Rear Window*?

Parody permeates the series, and I will now turn to its more extensive use, found in "Treehouse of Horror XX" (21.4). "Parody" is defined in *A Handbook to Literature* as "a composition imitating another, usually serious, piece…. When a subject matter of the original composition is parodied, however, it may prove to be a valuable indirect criticism or it may even imply a flattering tribute to the original writer" (Harmon and Holman 376). Examples from history can be enumerated, from Jonathan Swift's *Gulliver's Travels* to the film *Airplane!* (1980), and it is a term and concept that most viewers are likely to be familiar with, unlike its closely-related cousin, pastiche.

"Pastiche" has traditionally been a far more slippery term. *A Handbook to Literature* first describes it as the French word for parody or literary imitation, but also notes that the "term is also applied to literary patchworks formed by piercing together extracts from various works by one or several authors" (Harmon and Holman 377). Pastiche has been most closely linked with Frederic Jameson, who, in his frequently cited "Postmodernism, or the Cultural Logic of Late Capitalism," states that "parody eclipses pastiche" and that

> in this situation, parody finds itself without a vocation; it has lived, and that strange new thing pastiche slowly comes to take its place. Pastiche is, like parody, the imitation of a peculiar mask, speech in a dead language: but it is a neutral practice of such mimicry, without any of parody's ulterior motives, amputated of the satiric impulse, devoid of laughter and of any conviction that alongside the abnormal tongue you have momentarily borrowed, some healthy linguistic normality still exists. Pastiche is thus *blank parody*, a statue with blind eyeballs: it is to parody what that other interesting and historically original modern thing, the practice of a kind of blank irony… [65, emphasis mine].

As an example of the two, consider two extended riffs on *Star Wars*: Mel Brooks' *Spaceballs* (1987) and *Family Guy's* three episodes based on the original *Star Wars* trilogy ("Blue Harvest" [6.1], "Something, Something, Something Dark Side" [8.20], and "It's a Trap" [9.18]). While *Spaceballs* is perhaps most memorably linked with *Star Wars*, it really parodies the science-fiction genre in general, including such films as *Alien* (1979) and *Star Trek*. *Family Guy's* "parodies" are too reverent toward its source material, mimicking it often shot by shot and line by line. This fits with Jameson's notion of pastiche as "blank parodies," lacking that critical edge.

The demarcation between parody and pastiche has often been blurred, making it difficult to discern when each is being used on *The Simpsons*. Even Gray initially conflates the two terms, using the aforementioned scene of Maggie at the day care in "A Streetcar Named Marge" as an example of "postmodern pastiche" and "significant parody, argument, and intertextual commentary" (5). With its uncritical eye, pastiche generally has a more negative connotation than parody, even though filmmakers like Quentin Tarantino are still able to make original works of art whilst indulging in pastiche. Some see parody as mocking and pastiche as celebratory (think Tarantino), but how can the viewer discern authorial intent?

Gray is a little clearer elsewhere as to the differences between these concepts: "Parody is often confused with satire or with pastiche, but neither of these forms shares parody's interest in a genre's form and conventions. Parody can be satiric, but pure satire bypasses concerns of form and aims straight at content, whereas pastiche alludes to form and/or content, but with no critical comment on either" (47). He believes parody can also have a didactic function, "teaching media literacy in the very site where generic artifice must be challenged, and thus where viewers will have use for media literacy" (12). Gray adds, "Parody is a teacher, but its method is Socratic, encouraging the audience to make the final and decisive link between criticism and target, rather than merely proselytizing on genre" (47). More specifically, Gray examines the parodic attacks in the series of advertising, consumerism, the news, and sitcoms, but neglects the role of parody in instances such as those discussed below.

As evident in the Hitchcock references cataloged above, almost all the references have been for the five Hitchcock films most people have seen.[4] Yet "Treehouse of Horror XX," much more recent than most of the other episodes mentioned, may contain the most extended homage to Hitchcock in the entire series, even referencing other films than the five most popular. Aired to coincide around Halloween, the "Treehouse of Horror" episodes have aired every season since the second, and according to Johnson, "have historically been the most baroque in their cinematic allusions" (86). They provide the writers with more freedom with their characters, to the extent that minor characters (and sometimes even members of the Simpson family) may die without consequence, due to these stand-alone episodes being unfettered to continuity. Films and television episodes (especially classic *Twilight Zone* [1959–1964] episodes) seem to be parodied at an even faster clip in these episodes.

The segment "Dial 'M' for Murder, or Press '#' to Return to Main Menu" makes explicit allusions to *Vertigo*, *North by Northwest*, *Psycho*, *The Birds*, *Spellbound* (1945), and *Alfred Hitchcock Presents*, but *Strangers on a Train* (1951) merits the most extended string of references. It was the first black-and-white segment since the *King Kong* (1933) parody "King Homer" ("Treehouse of Horror III"), and we can assume that this stylistic choice was made to mimic the monochromatic palettes of some of its referents, namely *Strangers on a Train*, *Spellbound*, *Psycho*, and the *Alfred Hitchcock Presents* television series. Of course, there is also the segment's titular namesake (*Dial M for Murder* [1954]), which *Simpsons'* writers have frequently referred to, as evident in the aforementioned Troy McClure films (*P is for Psycho*, *Dial M for Murderousness*) as well as an actual *Simpsons* episode "Dial 'N' for Nerder" (19.14) and even two other "Treehouse of Horror" segments, "Dial 'Z' for Zombies" ("Treehouse of Horror III" 4.5) and "Dial 'D' for Diddily" ("Treehouse of Horror XXII" 23.3). (Other episode titles explicitly referring to a

Hitchcock film include "The Boy Who Knew Too Much" [5.20], "The Dad Who Knew Too Little" [14.8], "Dangers on a Train" [24.22], and "The Man Who Grew Too Much" [25.13], none of which allude to Hitchcock outside of their titles.)

"Dial 'M' for Murder, or Press '#' to Return to Main Menu" begins with Lisa in trouble with Miss Hoover, even landing in detention, alongside Bart. Just as Bruno (Robert Walker) and Guy (Farley Granger) "agree" to kill the person they most want to dispose of (Guy to kill Bruno's father, Bruno to murder Guy's wife), Bart and Lisa agree to get revenge on each other's teacher, but Bart misunderstands "ding dong ditch" and kills Miss Hoover. Besides visual allusions and settings from the films mentioned above, the segment also includes music from *Psycho* and *North by Northwest*. Even the dolly zoom (aka trombone shot) from *Vertigo* appears. To further hammer home the point, the segment ends with Hitchcock's silhouette.

Of course, this episode aired after the comments on the show's parody made by scholars like Mittell and Gray. One wonders whether they would categorize it as parody or pastiche. While it has some of the "patchwork" qualities associated with pastiche, it does not merely mimic Hitchcock's work, as *Family Guy*, for the most part, impersonates the *Star Wars* saga. Rather, this segment borrows from several Hitchcock films, parodying the Hitchcock "genre" in several humorous and enlightening ways. In terms of its critique, I argue that this segment does offer something to say, just as with the best parodists, even if it be subtle. At the very least, the segment points to the poignancy and cultural cache of Hitchcock, even in 2009, when it originally aired. Furthermore, it comments on the themes and preoccupations of Hitchcock, while this stylized segment, one of the most beautiful of the "Treehouse of Horror" series, points to the possibilities of prime-time animation.

On the DVD commentaries for *The Simpsons*, Groening, showrunners, writers, directors, and voice talent reveal their motivations (or sometimes, lack thereof) for these types of allusions. The following conversation occurs during the commentary for "Principal Charming" (2.14):

> [Showrunner] Mike Reiss: It's only now occurring to me we put [you through] a lot of trouble to do our *Vertigo* stairway … for nothing. I mean, it's a nice shot, and again I guess it's a *Simpsons* trick; if we can throw in a movie allusion, we'll do it.
> [Showrunner] Al Jean: We did a lot more of that earlier. There was a lot of movie referencing.
> Reiss: It's got nothing to do with anything.

Such an offhanded dismissal should not discourage viewers, as the commentaries can also reveal an indebtedness to the Master of Suspense. In the commentary for "Bart of Darkness," the commentators discuss the characters of *Rear Window*, the brilliance of the use of color in the film, the "Herrmannesque" score appropriated for their episode, and even such trivialities as the pianist/songwriter in *Rear Window*, Ross Bagdasarian, who later became better known as David Seville of Alvin and the Chipmunks fame. Clearly, these are not haphazard references. I also argue that the movie references are still just as frequent and intentional than in the earlier seasons, perhaps best exemplified by two of the most extended homages for cinephiles from Season 25: the aforementioned opening credits of "Treehouse of Horror XXIV"; and the extended homage to Hayao Miyazaki in "Married to the Blob" (25.10), which also includes many of the magical creatures from his films. They only steal—er, plagiarize—er, borrow from those filmmakers who most have influenced their own storytelling: Kubrick, Welles, and definitely, Hitchcock. It is the level of complexity, this layer of intertextuality, that has made *The Simpsons* so rewarding for viewers for 30 years.

Critics may decry *The Simpsons* as declining in quality in recent years or for being a pale imitation of its early "Golden Age" self, but the series remains just as innovative and transgressive. For instance, its couch gags have become increasingly ambitious since Season 22, employing animators and artists such as Banksy ("MoneyBart" [22.3]), *Ren & Stimpy* (1991–1996) creator John Kricfalusi ("Bart Stops to Smell the Roosevelts" [23.2]), French animator Sylvain Chomet ("Diggs" [25.12]), and the aforementioned del Toro, not to mention the numerous couch gags animated by Bill Plympton, all of which stretch the limits of network television animation. The ratings may still show a small fraction of viewers it once had, but *The Simpsons* continues as a rich text for scholars, Hitchcock fans, and general cinephiles to explore.

NOTES

1. *The Simpsons Archive*, www.simpsonsarchive.com, was born out of the original alt.tv.simpsons site.

2. Academic work on *The Simpsons* dates to the early 1990s, with many scholars noting the postmodern nature of the show. One good summation of the show's basis in the postmodern theory of Jean-Francois Lyotard, Jean Baudrillard, and Frederic Jameson can be found in Björnsson (indexed on *The Simpsons Archive* under the section "Academic Papers" [www.simpsonsarchive.com/other/papers/bf.paper.pdf]).

3. For more on how *The Simpsons* can more literally serve a didactic function with their film references, see Waltonen and Du Vernay, pp. 192–197.

4. I.e., *Psycho, Rear Window, Vertigo, North by Northwest,* and *The Birds*. These five films have merited the most votes of Hitchcock's films on the Internet Movie Database (www.imdb.com).

WORKS CITED

Abrahams, Jim, David Zucker, and Jerry Zucker, directors. *Airplane!* Paramount, 1980.
Alberti, John, editor. *Leaving Springfield: The Simpsons and the Possibility of Oppositional Culture.* Wayne State UP, 2004.
The Alfred Hitchcock Wiki, the.hitchcock.zone/wiki/Main_Page. Accessed 18 Jan. 2018.
Allen, Woody, director. *Stardust Memories.* United Artists, 1980.
"Angry Dad: The Movie." *The Simpsons.* Written by John Frink, directed by Matthew Nastuk, 20th Century–Fox, 20 Feb. 2011.

Arnaz, Desi, executive producer. *I Love Lucy*. Desilu Productions, 1957.

"Bart of Darkness." *The Simpsons: The Complete Sixth Season*. Written by Dan McGrath, directed by Jim Reardon, 20th Century–Fox, 2005.

"Bart Stops to Smell the Roosevelts." *The Simpsons*. Written by Tim Long, directed by Steven Dean Moore, 20th Century–Fox, 2 Oct. 2011.

"Bart the Fink." *The Simpsons: The Complete Seventh Season*. Written by John Swartzwelder, directed by Jim Reardon, 20th Century–Fox, 2005.

"Bart the Mother." *The Simpsons: The Complete Tenth Season*. Written by David X. Cohen, directed by Steven Dean Moore, 20th Century–Fox, 2007.

"Bart-Mangled Banner." *The Simpsons: The Fifteenth Season*. Written by John Frink, directed by Steven Dean Moore, 20th Century–Fox, 2005.

"Bart's Friend Falls in Love." *The Simpsons: The Complete Third Season*. Written by Jay Kogen and Wallace Wolodarsky, directed by Jim Reardon, 20th Century–Fox, 2003.

Benioff, David and D. B. Weiss, creators. *Game of Thrones*. Television 360, 2018.

Björnsson, Björn Erlingur Flóki Björnsson. *Postmodernism and The Simpsons: Intertextuality, Hyperreality, and the Critique of Metanarratives*. B.A. Thesis, University of Iceland, 2006.

"Black Widower." *The Simpsons: The Complete Third Season*. Written by Jon Vitti, directed by David Silverman, 20th Century–Fox, 2003.

"Blue Harvest." *Laugh It Up Fuzzball: Family Guy Trilogy*. Written by Alec Sulkin, directed by Dominic Polcino, 20th Century–Fox, 2010.

"The Boy Who Knew Too Much." *The Simpsons: The Complete Fifth Season*. Written by John Swartzwelder, directed by Jeffrey Lynch, 20th Century–Fox, 2004.

Brooks, James L., director. *Broadcast News*. 20th Century–Fox, 1987.

Brooks, Mel, director. *Spaceballs*. MGM, 1987.

"Brother from the Same Planet." *The Simpsons: The Complete Fourth Season*. Written by Jon Vitti, directed by Jeffrey Lynch, 20th Century–Fox, 2004.

"Cape Feare." *The Simpsons: The Complete Fifth Season*, written by Jon Vitti, directed by Rich Moore, 20th Century–Fox, 2004.

Carter, Bill. "Homer's Family Album Lifts Ratings for Fledging FXX Network." *New York Times*, 3 Sep. 2014, p. B1.

Conrad, Joseph. *Heart of Darkness*. Oxford, 1902.

Cooper, Merian C. and Ernest B. Schoedsack, directors. *King Kong*. Radio Pictures, 1933.

Curtis, Richard, director. *Love Actually*. Universal, 2003.

"The Dad Who Knew Too Little." *The Simpsons: The Fourteenth Season*. Written by Matt Selman, directed by Mark Kirkland, 20th Century–Fox, 2011.

"Dangers on a Train." *The Simpsons*. Written by Michael Price, directed by Steven Dean Moore. 20th Century–Fox, 19 May 2013.

Darabont, Frank, developer. *The Walking Dead*. Idiot Box Productions, 2018.

David, Larry and Jerry Seinfeld, creators. *Seinfeld*. Columbia Tristar, 1998.

"The Day the Violence Died." *The Simpsons: The Complete Seventh Season*. Written by John Swartzwelder, directed by Wes Archer, 20th Century–Fox, 2005.

DeMille, Cecil B., director. *The Ten Commandments*. Paramount, 1956.

"The Devil Wears Nada." *The Simpsons*. Written by Tim Long, directed by Nancy Kruse. 20th Century–Fox, 15 Nov. 2009.

"Diggs." *The Simpsons*. Written by Dan Greaney and Allen Glazier, directed by Michael Polcino. 20th Century–Fox, 9 Mar. 2014.

Evans, Vic. "Hitchcock References in *The Simpsons*." *Google*. 11 Mar. 2005. groups.google. com/forum/#!topic/alt.movies.hitchcock/rMPr7pNWJug. Accessed 16 Jan. 2018.

"Fear of Flying." *The Simpsons: The Complete Sixth Season*. Written by David Sacks, directed by Mark Kirkland, 20th Century–Fox, 2005.

Granados, Jose Sanz. "Cabecera Simpsons Hitchcock." *YouTube*. 13 May 2008. www.youtube. com/watch?v=FLr8LgzSh6o 11/04/2014. Accessed 18 Jan. 2018.

"Grandpa vs. Sexual Inadequacy." *The Simpsons: The Complete Sixth Season*. Written by Bill Oakley and Josh Weinstein, directed by Wes Archer, 20th Century–Fox, 2005.

Gray, Jonathan. *Watching with* The Simpsons: *Television, Parody, and Intertextuality*. Routledge, 2006.

Harmon, William, and C. Hugh Holman. *A Handbook to Literature.* 7th ed., Prentice Hall, 1996.

Heit, Jamey. *The Springfield Reformation: The Simpsons, Christianity, and American Culture.* Bloomsbury, 2008.

Hitchcock, Alfred, creator. *Alfred Hitchcock Presents.* Revue Studios and Universal, 1962.

Hitchcock, Alfred, director. *Aventure Malgache.* British Ministry of Information, 1944.

_____. *The Birds.* Universal, 1963.

_____. *Bon Voyage.* British Ministry of Information, 1944.

_____. *Dial M for Murder.* Warner Bros., 1954.

_____. *North by Northwest.* MGM, 1959.

_____. *Psycho.* Paramount, 1960.

_____. *Rear Window.* Paramount, 1954.

_____. *Saboteur.* Universal, 1942.

_____. *Spellbound.* United Artists, 1945.

_____. *Strangers on a Train.* Warner Bros., 1951.

_____. *Vertigo.* Paramount, 1958.

"Homer Loves Flanders." *The Simpsons: The Complete Fifth Season.* Written by David Richardson, directed by Wes Archer, 20th Century–Fox, 2004.

"Homer Simpson in 'Kidney Trouble.'" *The Simpsons: The Complete Tenth Season.* Written by John Swartzwelder, directed by Mike B. Anderson, 20th Century–Fox, 2007.

"Homer the Moe." *The Simpsons: The Thirteenth Season.* Written by Dana Gould, directed by Jen Kamerman, 20th Century–Fox, 2010.

"Homer vs. Dignity." *The Simpsons: The Twelfth Season.* Written by Rob LaZebnik, directed by Neil Affleck, 20th Century–Fox, 2009.

"Homer vs. Lisa and the 8th Commandment." *The Simpsons: The Complete Second Season.* Written by Steve Pepoon, directed by Rich Moore, 20th Century–Fox, 2002.

Huston, John, director. *The Treasure of the Sierra Madre.* Warner Bros., 1948.

"I'm with Cupid." *The Simpsons: The Complete Tenth Season.* Written by Dan Greaney, directed by Bob Anderson, 20th Century–Fox, 2007.

"Itchy & Scratchy & Marge." *The Simpsons: The Complete Second Season.* Written by John Swartzwelder, directed by Jim Reardon, 20th Century–Fox, 2002.

"The Itchy & Scratchy & Poochie Show." *The Simpsons: The Complete Eighth Season.* Written by David S. Cohen, directed by Steven Dean Moore, 20th Century–Fox, 2006.

"Itchy & Scratchy Land." *The Simpsons: The Complete Sixth Season.* Written by John Swartzwelder, directed by Wes Archer, 20th Century–Fox, 2005.

Irwin, William, and J. R. Lombardo. "*The Simpsons* and Allusion: 'Worst Essay Ever.'" *The Simpsons and Philosophy: The D'oh! of Homer,* edited by William Irwin, Mark T. Conrad, and Aeon J. Skoble, Open Court, 2001.

"It's a Trap." *Laugh It Up Fuzzball: Family Guy Trilogy.* Written by Cherry Chevapravatdumrong and David A. Goodman, directed by Peter Shin, 20th Century–Fox, 2010.

Jameson, Frederic. "Postmodernism, or the Cultural Logic of Late Capitalism." *New Left Review,* vol. 146, 1984, pp. 53–92.

Johnson, Steven. *Everything Bad Is Good for You: How Today's Popular Culture Is Actually Making Us Smarter.* Riverhead, 2005.

Jones, Chuck, director. *Duck Amuck.* Warner Bros., 1953.

Kazan, Elia, director. *A Streetcar Named Desire.* Warner Bros., 1951.

Knox, Simone. "Reading the Ungraspable Double-Codedness of *The Simpsons.*" *Journal of Popular Film and Television,* vol. 34, no. 2, 2006, pp. 72–81.

Kricfalusi, John and Bob Camp, creators. *The Ren & Stimpy Show.* Spümcø and Nickelodeon Animation Studios, 1995.

Kristeva, Julia. *Desire in Language: A Semiotic Approach to Literature and Art.* Columbia UP, 1980.

Kubrick, Stanley, director. *A Clockwork Orange.* Warner Bros., 1971.

_____. *Dr. Strangelove or: How I Learned to Stop Worrying and Love the Bomb.* Columbia, 1964.

_____. *The Shining.* Warner Bros., 1980.

_____. *2001: A Space Odyssey*. MGM, 1968.

"Like Father, Like Clown." *The Simpsons: The Complete Third Season*. Written by Jay Kogen and Wallace Wolodarsky, directed by Jeffrey Lynch and Brad Bird, 20th Century–Fox, 2003.

"Love Is a Many-Splintered Thing." *The Simpsons*. Written by Tim Long, directed by Michael Polcino. 20th Century–Fox, 10 Feb. 2013.

Lucas, George, director. *Star Wars Episode IV: A New Hope*. 20th Century–Fox, 1977.

"The Man Who Grew Too Much." *The Simpsons*. Written by Jeff Westbrook, directed by Matthew Schofield. 20th Century–Fox, 9 Mar. 2014.

"Marge in Chains." *The Simpsons: The Complete Fourth Season*. Written by Bill Oakley and Josh Weinstein, directed by Jim Reardon, 20th Century–Fox, 2004.

"Married to the Blob." *The Simpsons*. Written by Tim Long, directed by Chris Clements. 20th Century–Fox, 12 Jan. 2014.

Matheson, Carl. "*The Simpsons*, Hyper-Irony, and the Meaning of Life." *The Simpsons and Philosophy: The D'oh! of Homer*, edited by William Irwin, Mark T. Conrad, and Aeon J. Skoble, Open Court, 2001, pp. 108–125.

McCay, Winsor. *Gertie the Dinosaur*. Box Office Attractions Company, 1914.

McTiernan, John, director. *Die Hard*. 20th Century–Fox, 1988.

"Mr. Plow." *The Simpsons: The Complete Fourth Season*. Written by Jon Vitti, directed by Jim Reardon, 20th Century–Fox, 2004.

Mittell, Jason. *Genre and Television: From Cop Shows to Cartoons in America Culture*. Routledge, 2004.

"Mom and Pop Art." *The Simpsons: The Complete Tenth Season*. Written by Al Jean, directed by Steven Dean Moore, 20th Century–Fox, 2007.

"MoneyBart." *The Simpsons*. Written by Tim Long, directed by Nancy Kruse. 20th Century–Fox, 10 Oct. 2010.

Newman, Sydney, C. E. Webber, and Donald Wilson, creators. *Doctor Who*. BBC, 2018.

"Principal Charming." *The Simpsons: The Complete Second Season*. Written by David M. Stern, directed by Mark Kirkland, 20th Century–Fox, 2002.

"Realty Bites." *The Simpsons: The Complete Ninth Season*. Written by Dan Greaney, directed by Swinton O. Scott III, 20th Century–Fox, 2006.

Roddenberry, Gene, creator. *Star Trek*. Desilu Productions and Paramount, 1969.

Ruegger, Tom, creator. *Animaniacs*. Amblin Entertainment and Warner Bros., 1998.

Scorsese, Martin, director. *Cape Fear*. Universal, 1991.

Scott, Ridley, director. *Alien*. 20th Century–Fox, 1979.

"'Scuse Me While I Miss the Sky." *The Simpsons: The Fourteenth Season*. Written by Dan Greaney and Allen Grazier, directed by Steven Dean Moore, 20th Century–Fox, 2011.

Serling, Rod, creator. *The Twilight Zone*. Cayuga Productions and CBS, 1964.

"The Simpsons 138th Episode Spectacular." *The Simpsons: The Complete Seventh Season*. Written by Jon Vitti, directed by David Silverman, 20th Century–Fox, 2005.

"The Simpsons Spin-Off Showcase." *The Simpsons: The Complete Eighth Season*. Written by David S. Cohen, Dan Greaney, and Steve Tompkins, directed by Neil Affleck, 20th Century–Fox, 2006.

Simpsons Wiki, simpsons.wikia.com/wiki/Simpsons_Wiki. Accessed 18 Jan. 2018.

"Something, Something, Something Dark Side." *Laugh It Up Fuzzball: Family Guy Trilogy*. Written by Kirker Butler, directed by Dominic Polcino, 20th Century–Fox, 2010.

Spielberg, Steven, director. *Jaws*. Universal, 1975.

"The Springfield Files." *The Simpsons: The Complete Eighth Season*. Written by Reid Harrison, directed by Steven Dean Moore, 20th Century–Fox, 2006.

Stone, Oliver, director. *Wall Street*. 20th Century–Fox, 1987.

"A Streetcar Named Marge." *The Simpsons: The Complete Fourth Season*. Written by Jeff Martin, directed by Rich Moore, 20th Century–Fox, 2004.

Sturges, John, director. *The Great Escape*. United Artists, 1963.

Swift, Jonathan. *Gulliver's Travels*. Oxford, 1726.

Thompson, J. Lee, director. *Cape Fear*. Universal, 1962.

"Three Men and a Comic Book." *The Simpsons: The Complete Second Season*. Written by Jeff Martin, directed by Wes Archer, 20th Century–Fox, 2002.

Time Staff. "The Best of the Century." *Time*, 31 Dec. 1999, pp. 73–82.
"Treehouse of Horror III." *The Simpsons: The Complete Fourth Season*. Written by Al Jean, et al., directed by Carlo Baeza, 20th Century–Fox, 2004.
"Treehouse of Horror XI." *The Simpsons: The Twelfth Season*. Written by Rob LaZebnik, et al., directed by Matthew Nastuk, 20th Century–Fox, 2010.
"Treehouse of Horror XX." *The Simpsons*. Written by Daniel Chun, directed by Mike B. Anderson and Matthew Schofield. 20th Century–Fox, 18 Oct. 2009.
"Treehouse of Horror XXII." *The Simpsons*. Written by Carolyn Omine, directed by Matthew Faughnan. 20th Century–Fox, 11. Oct. 2011.
"Treehouse of Horror XXIV." *The Simpsons*. Written by Jeff Westbrook, directed by Rob Oliver and Guillermo del Toro (opening sequence). 20th Century–Fox, 6 Oct. 2013.
"Treehouse of Horror XXV." *The Simpsons*. Written by Stephanie Gillis, directed by Matthew Faughnan. 20th Century–Fox, 19 Oct. 2014.
Truffaut, Francois, with Helen G. Scott. *Hitchcock*. Rev. ed., Touchstone, 1983.
Turner, Chris. *Planet Simpson: How a Cartoon Masterpiece Defined a Generation*. Da Capo, 2004.
Waltonen, Karma, and Denise Du Vernay. *The Simpsons in the Classroom: Embiggening the Learning Experience with the Wisdom of Springfield*. McFarland, 2010.
Welles, Orson, director. *Citizen Kane*. RKO, 1941.

Is Yellow the New Green?*

The Banal Environmentalism
of The Simpsons

DAVID KRANTZ

The Couch Gag (aka, the Introduction)

As the clouds part, revealing *The Simpsons* nameplate in the sky of the show's second-ever full episode,[1] and the now-iconic Danny Elfman–composed theme music begins, the nuclear power plant, towering over Springfield, is the first structure to come into view. Its sign is disarmingly friendly: "Welcome to Springfield Nuclear Power Plant." It gives way to a mountain of abandoned tires—engulfed in flames in later episodes—and finally to Bartholomew (Bart) JoJo Simpson's classroom and his very first chalkboard gag, writing over and over again, "I will not waste chalk." Cut to his father, Homer Jay Simpson, mishandling a uranium rod at the power plant and soon thereafter discarding it onto the street ("Bart the Genius" 1.2) on his way to his house on Evergreen Terrace, a street ostensibly named for the trees that were displaced by single-family-home development.

In the next episode, viewers see through a class field trip more of the industrial wasteland that is Springfield. Bart's school bus drives by the town's toxic-waste dump, where frothing liquids spew openly from pipes to pools like a water park, the town tire yard, the prison, and finally the object of the field trip, an inside look at the nuclear power plant, where students march past a guard drinking soda and watching Krusty the Clown on television. Waylon Smithers, Jr., presents Bart's class the animated educational film, "Nuclear Energy: Our Misunderstood Friend," complete with Smiling Joe

*"Is Yellow the New Green?" Copyright 2017-2018 David Krantz, who is supported by an IGERT-SUN fellowship funded by the National Science Foundation (Award 1144616).

Fission, talking rods of uranium 235, and grouchy nuclear waste that Smiling Joe literally sweeps under the carpet, "where no one will find it for a million years." After the film, the students tour the plant and see where the plant's radioactive water rejoins nature—the frolicking grounds of Blinky, the three-eyed orange fish ("Two Cars in Every Garage and Three Eyes on Every Fish" 2.4) (and precursor to four-eyed fish ["Brawl in the Family" 13.7], six-eyed fish ["Homer's Odyssey" 1.3], and a half-dozen other three-eyed mutated animals, including three-eyed lobster ["Homer's Paternity Coot" 17.10], and, most commonly, the three-eyed crow seen in the title scene of later episodes).

The dangers of nuclear energy, wasteful consumption, pollution—from the very beginning of *The Simpsons*, the show has had plenty to say about the environment and our often-destructive role in it. But to what extent is yellow (the hue of most characters in *The Simpsons*) the new green? And if so, does it matter?

The impact of the environmental nature of *The Simpsons* may best be described as the effect of a non-economic form of nudge theory—a way that small inputs can influence individual decision making.[2] In this case, everyone exposed to environmental episodes of *The Simpsons* may not be making more environmentally minded decisions, but the exposure may help push them toward doing so. *The Simpsons* then becomes one of many factors that nudge us toward (or against) environmentally friendly decisions. Think of it as incremental attitude change—or a cultural nudge.

The inclusion of environmental themes in television episodes is an example of what I consider "banal environmentalism"[3]—the use of environmental representations in everyday humdrum life to help shape the public's environmental ethos. The term is derived from "banal nationalism," as coined by Michael Billig, who found nationalism in everyday acts such as using coins emblazoned with "In God We Trust" and using U.S. flag–imprinted postage stamps. To Billig, the unconscious ingestion of patriotism by citizens was partly how the state invented and reinvented itself daily. Banal environmentalism, therefore, describes how seemingly innocuous activities, such as watching television, unconsciously inform our understanding of the environment.[4] In so doing, banal environmentalism helps normalize environmentally oriented social values and actions.[5]

As the longest-running sitcom in American-television history—and arguably one of the most well-known hallmarks of modern American culture—*The Simpsons* may be among the most influential television shows ever. And its tenure has featured many environmentally oriented episodes that are excellent examples of banal environmentalism. For the past three decades, millions of people have tuned in to watch *The Simpsons* weekly, and many millions more have watched the show through DVDs, network syndication, and online streaming. And *The Simpsons* has generated an estimated $13 billion in revenue for its owners, 20th Century–Fox[6] (Klara; Statistic Brain Research Institute)—not just through its 600-plus episodes and its feature film and its rides at Universal Studios in California and Florida but through its 10,000–branded products sold around the world (Klara). But no one has previously analyzed the content of all the episodes of *The Simpsons*, nor has anyone compared that to the content of all the episodes of *The Simpsons'* peers.

To discover just how green *The Simpsons* series is, I conducted a qualitative-content analysis of 76 television shows, consisting of nearly 14,000 television episodes—perhaps the largest such content analysis ever undertaken on television.[7] In comparison to its peers, *The Simpsons* stands out as among the most environmentally minded sitcoms on television—and it has covered environmental issues in decade after decade of production.

The Springfield Shopper (aka, the Literature Review)

The environmental aspects of *The Simpsons* have not gone unnoticed,[8] but they largely have been unstudied. Those researchers who have examined *The Simpsons* from an environmental perspective mainly have focused on *The Simpsons Movie* (Chagan; Küchler, 229–240; Murray and Heumann 229–240; Pike 57–75; Seymour, 207–209; Starosielski) and the show's criticism of nuclear energy[9] (Broderick 244–272). However, four studies have been conducted that are similar to this one—although this one, as described in both the introduction as well as the next section, is more extensive.

In 2002, Anne Marie Todd analyzed the environmental content of 80 percent of the episodes in the first ten seasons of *The Simpsons*. She finds that *The Simpsons* focused on three environmental issues above others: nuclear energy, animal welfare, and society's relationship with nature. "*The Simpsons* functions as a form of environmental activism and thus reveals popular culture's effectiveness as a medium for ecological commentary," Todd concludes. "The show increases public awareness of environmental issues, and educates the audience while entertaining them" (Todd 78).

In 2005, Andrew Wood and Todd documented how geographic place and transportation are ongoing themes throughout *The Simpsons*. Springfield, they wrote, is an "omnitopia," a town representing everywhere but actually existing nowhere—while simultaneously tied to its own local environment, albeit often negatively (Todd and Wood).

"The commodification of place throughout *The Simpsons* illustrates the effects of capitalism on the cultural geography of Springfield," they wrote. "Icons of progress such as the recycling plant are unmasked as slurry factories that empty the fields, forests, and oceans of nutrients, transforming the earth's resources into an omnitopian sludge that melds the different colors of biodiversity and rich textures of ecological tapestries. As Anytown, USA, Springfield illustrates how contemporary cities perceive a zero-sum relationship between environmental sustainability and unfettered economic growth" (Todd and Wood).

Tim Delaney dedicated a chapter of his 2008 book on *The Simpsons* to the environmental nightmares—what he calls *enviromares*—portrayed in the show: air pollution (including global warming) and nuclear pollution (or the potential danger of it). Delaney also finds that episodes of *The Simpsons* included potential solutions, such as electric vehicles ("Beyond Blunderdome" 11.1), recycling ("The Old Man and the Lisa" 8.21), forest conservation ("Lisa the Tree Hugger" 21.4), and climate intervention/geoengineering in the stratosphere (Delaney 218–244).

The third similar study was conducted in 2011 by the journalist Sara Peach, who downloaded transcripts for *The Simpsons'* first thirteen seasons and the summaries for seasons thereafter and searched them for the terms "climate change," "global warming," and "greenhouse effect."[10] Peach finds that one of Bart's two sisters, precocious eight-year-old Lisa Marie Simpson, is often the voice of environmental reason, particularly on climate change. "In their indifference to Lisa's warnings," Peach writes, "Springfield residents mirror the attitudes of many Americans."[11] In the 475 episodes that she examined, Peach finds that climate change, global warming, and/or the greenhouse effect were mentioned in fewer than ten—and that "references to the issue are brief, often consisting of scenes of only a few seconds" (Peach).

Like Peach, I also have found that *The Simpsons* primarily has not taken on climate change as an issue—and even when it has, the take has been somewhat ambivalent,[12] perhaps reflecting Americans' views on how best to act on climate change. But Peach's study was lacking context. Although *The Simpsons* may have directly addressed climate change sparingly, climate change is but one of many environmental issues, and I have found that *The Simpsons* addressed climate change[13,14] as well as other environmental issues at far greater rates than its peers.

As I was writing a revision of this chapter, David Feltmate published an article in which he charged that the humor of *The Simpsons* "critically engaged and undermined ecological issues," that the show did not properly express the urgency of environmental issues or provide their solutions, and that previous studies "oversold the ecological awareness" of *The Simpsons* (Feltmate). But Feltmate's study was very limited: He only examined *The Simpsons Movie* and two television episodes of *The Simpsons*. In his analysis, Feltmate argued that the viewers' takeaway comes from the perspective of Charles Montgomery Burns, the curmudgeonly laissez-faire capitalist and owner of the nuclear power plant. However, I think that Mr. Burns represents the show's example of how not to behave, and that the episodes' takeaways are instead best expressed by Lisa's pro-environmental morality.

Feltmate also criticized *The Simpsons* as a cog in the capitalist, consumerist machine responsible for so much of the world's environmental degradation and destruction (Feltmate). However Feltmate failed to recognize that even if the show's status as a profit-making venture makes it part of the problem, it does not preclude the show from also being part of the solution. Given the scope of environmental issues, so much—perhaps everything—is to varying degrees both part of the problem and part of the solution. In my research, I have sought to quantify to what degree *The Simpsons*, particularly in relation to its peer sitcoms, may be part of the solution. *The Simpsons* can be capitalist and green, and because we live in a capitalist society, success combatting a range of wicked environmental problems such as climate change likely requires the imbuing of environmental values into capitalism.

Lastly, Feltmate, essentially echoed Marshall McLuhan's "the medium is the message"[15] (McLuhan, 23-35), claiming that *The Simpsons* cannot be pro-environmental because of the sheer volume of carbon emissions, toxic chemicals, and unfair labor practices embedded in the televisions, phones, tablets and computers used to deliver the show to viewers. "Ecological awareness," Feltmate wrote about ecologically minded media writ large, "is brought to us by the very tools of ecological devastation" (Feltmate). While I think it is important to recognize and work to reduce the environmental and social ills that arise as a result of the production and consumption of some of society's favorite technologies—and I have written about the merits of restraints on capitalism and consumption, like Feltmate, through the lens of religion (Krantz)—the perfect is the enemy of good (to use the common paraphrase of the Italian proverb misattributed to Voltaire, "the best is the enemy of the good" [Ratcliffe, 389]). In other words, *The Simpsons* and its medium are not perfect (gasp!) but perfection may not be achievable, and as such one should not dismiss the show for its lack of perfection. I think that it is important to evaluate it not just as a producer of but also as a product of our culture, shaped by our society's inescapable consumptionist milieu. And today even the most utopian of environmental movements and the most ardent of environmental figures, save the few true hermits, are ensconced in our shared capitalist resource-intensive society. The key to modern environmentalism then becomes finding how we can best care for our shared Earth and its inhabitants within the restraints of our system while we hammer at those restraints, stretching their walls and helping to shift societal norms in the process. Each one of these boundary-stretching attempts, depending in part upon their degree of overtness, may be good examples of banal environmentalism at work. Among sitcoms on television—in what may be our most popular cultural producer and product—my research finds that *The Simpsons* is among the best at promoting environmental values.

Prof. Frink and Chocolate Microscopes (aka, the Methodology)

The environmental mindedness of *The Simpsons* was evident to me after watching it for years. But I sought to determine exactly how green *The Simpsons* is and how that compares to its television peers. First, I developed a list of *The Simpsons'* peers by reviewing the shows aired by 116 American television networks[16] and selecting for shows that met the following criteria:

- First-run broadcast for seven or more seasons with one or more of those seasons overlapping with at least one of *The Simpsons'* first twenty-seven seasons,[17] through July 2016;
- Aired in English;
- And an American-produced scripted sitcom.

Boundaries were necessary to make the study feasible. To not compare *The Simpsons* with other types of television shows—such as dramas, documentaries, talk shows, or the news—I only compared *The Simpsons* to other sitcoms. I chose shows that were contemporaneous to *The Simpsons* by selecting for those that aired at the same time, but not necessarily the same timeslot, as *The Simpsons*. However, I included all of a peer show's episodes even if some (or many) preceded *The Simpsons'* first airdate. I focused on first-run shows and ignored syndication to keep the peer group from *The Simpsons'* era. While no American sitcom has lasted as long as *The Simpsons*, I filtered for series that aired for at least seven seasons to compare long-running sitcoms to each other. Lastly, all of the shows needed to be American-produced English-language scripted sitcoms to properly compare shows that emerged from the same culture. So NBC's *The Office* qualified while BBC's *The Office* did not (both because it was not American and because it only aired for two seasons). Shows that were hybrids—such as sitcom dramas (*dramedies*) like *Nurse Jackie* and *Weeds*—were counted as sitcoms for purposes of this study. Shows such as *Bob's Burgers* whose seventh seasons occurred after July 2016 were excluded, as were all episodes of all shows airing after July 2016.

Including *The Simpsons*, I found 76 shows[18,19] that met the above criteria. Combined, those shows account for 13,960 episodes,[20] with 596, or about 4.3 percent, of those represented by *The Simpsons*.

The next step was the content analysis. I eschewed throw-away one liners and other offhand references to the environment (which may skew a strict manifest-content analysis) and instead focused on determining whether or not an environmental issue was a major theme of an episode, filtering by the following environmental subcategories, which were developed through the analysis:

- Agriculture, eco-minded food and vegetarianism/veganism[21,22];
- Animal welfare;
- Camping, hiking, and wilderness;
- Energy;
- Generic environmentalism and climate change;
- Pollution;
- Transportation;
- And waste (including recycling and composting).

Each episode was coded as to whether or not it was environmentally themed, and if it was environmentally themed then whether the episode's orientation cast the environment in a positive or negative light. And each episode was coded into only one subcategory, so an episode that addressed more than one subcategory was coded as the subcategory that served as a slightly larger theme than the other(s).[23]

To compare among major themes of episodes, I analyzed their content by reading publicly available episode summaries (such as those found on IMDb, Simpsons Wiki, *TV Guide,* and Wikipedia). (This could be called "distilled-content analysis," since the content analysis was largely of summaries consisting of episodes' major themes distilled into one or more paragraphs.) When summaries were not available, and/or unclear as to whether or not an environmental issue constituted a major theme of the episode, and/or the orientation of the theme as positive or negative, I read episode scripts. And when scripts were not available, I watched the episodes themselves.

For purposes of this study, I only examined television shows[24] and not related films, although it is worth noting that the environmental theme of *The Simpsons Movie*—in which Springfield is nearly destroyed as a result of water pollution (Silverman)—is indicative of the overall eco-consciousness of *The Simpsons* as a television show.[25]

Everything's Coming Up Milhouse! (aka, the Findings)

The results varied among three groups: whether the show dealt with the environment at all, in a positive light, or in a negative light. In this section, I mainly will discuss percentages in the first two groups and only sparsely results from the third. Among its peers and in the timeframe studied as defined above, *The Simpsons* is the third-most pro-environmental sitcom on American television, with 13 percent of its shows portraying environmental issues in a favorable light. *Futurama* ranks first at 16 percent, and *Parks and Recreation* ranks second at 15 percent.[26]

It is unclear why *Futurama* is more pro-environmental than *The Simpsons*. One might suspect that the writers of *Futurama* are more pro-environmental than those of *The Simpsons*.[27] But many of the shows' writers have worked for both shows, and both shows even share the same creator, Matt Groening.[28] The difference then may be each show's time setting, with *The Simpsons* set in the present and *Futurama* set in the future (naturally). There may be something about setting shows in the future that makes them more amenable to environmental commentary.[29,30] But I digress, as that is a topic for future research.

Parks and Recreation, though, has a notable advantage over *The Simpsons*: its overarching theme is about parks.[31] Indeed, 84 percent of *Parks and Recreation*'s pro-environmental episodes featured building and/or protecting parks.

After *The Simpsons*, there is a dramatic drop off in pro-environmental episodes: *Adventure Time* places fourth at 5 percent; two shows tie at 4 percent; four shows tie at 3 percent; seven shows tie at 2 percent; 14 shows tie at 1 percent; and 45 shows tie at 0 percent.[32] *Futurama*, *Parks and Recreation*, and *The Simpsons* certainly stand out as consistently addressing environmental issues in a positive light.

Other shows that one might expect to feature pro-environmental themes actually do not. For example, Vermont–set *Newhart* as well as San Francisco–set sitcoms *Full House* and *Monk* do not have a single episode where a major theme portrayed the environment positively.[33] One of the main characters in *How I Met Your Mother* dreams of being an environmental attorney, and yet only two of its 208 episodes—or about 1 percent—address the environment in a favorable light as one of its themes. And *The Big Bang Theory*—a show that is about the life of scientists—does not include a single episode that features the environment as a theme.

To better understand just how pro-environmental *The Simpsons* is compared to its peers, consider the following: of the 596 episodes of *The Simpsons* included in this study, 77, or 13 percent, include a pro-environmental theme. Of the 13,364 episodes of the 75 other peer sitcoms included in this study, only 152, or about 1 percent, include a pro-environmental theme. Less than half of all the shows contain at least a single episode with an environmental theme in a positive light.

Of course, every time that *The Simpsons* includes an environmental theme is not always in a pro-environmental light. For example, as fun to watch as the Conan O'Brien–scribed episode "Marge vs. the Monorail" is—particularly with its Phil Hartman–voiced "The Monorail Song" inspired by *The Music Man* and also in the tradition of the 1880 Italian song, "Funiculì, Funiculà," by Luigi Denza and Peppino Turco, celebrating the first funicular cable car on Mount Vesuvius—the portrayal of public transit as dangerous and investment in it as foolhardy[34] ("Marge vs. the Monorail" 4.12) makes the episode among the 23 episodes of *The Simpsons* that feature an environmental issue in a negative light.

Overall, regardless of how the environment is portrayed (including both pro- and anti-environmental episodes), *The Simpsons* features an environmental theme 17 percent of the time, the third most of any show in the study. *Parks and Recreation* and *Futurama* (both at 18 percent) tie for first. At 16 percent, *Weeds* is in fourth place. (Many episodes of *Weeds* feature gardening, but engagement in the activity in the show often leads to negative, and sometimes deadly, outcomes.) *Adventure Time* (13 percent) finishes fifth, followed by *The Mentalist*, *SpongeBob SquarePants* (7 percent), *Family Guy*, and *Regular Show* (6 percent). Twenty-three shows are tied at between 2 and 5 percent, another twenty shows are tied at 1 percent, and two are tied at 0 percent—with 22[35] of those shows without a single episode that includes the environment as a theme at all. Essentially 30 percent of the total shows exclude the environment as a theme. As a basis of comparison, 33 percent of all the shows contain at least one episode with Atlantic City, N.J., as a theme and 14 percent of all the shows contain at least one episode with actor Adam West. With the exception of a few shows such as *The Simpsons*, environmental issues have been largely absent from long-running American sitcoms.

Because of its sheer number of seasons and episodes, *The Simpsons* leads all shows studied in numbers of pro-environmental episodes (77), anti-environmental episodes (23), and overall environmentally themed episodes (100).

While it is common for people to consider *The Simpsons* to be past its golden age,[36] the show's 77 pro-environmental episodes are evenly distributed over the 27 years examined in this study. (Twenty-eight of the pro-environmental episodes are found in the show's first nine years; 25 in Seasons 10 through 18; and 24 in Seasons 19 through 27.)

There also is an even distribution in authorship. The 77 pro-environmental episodes were written by 45 different people, all of whom wrote no more than five pro-environmental episodes, with the exception of one writer: the prolific John Swartzwelder, who wrote fourteen of the pro-environmental episodes on his own and co-wrote one with Sam Simon. Little is known about the famously reclusive Swartzwelder, who in his fifteen seasons at *The Simpsons* penned 59 episodes, more than any other writer (Donovan), but he has been described by his coworker, the director Mark Kirkland, as, ironically, a "self-declared anti-environmentalist" (Groening, et al.). And longtime *Simpsons'* writer David S. Cohen (future pen name David X. Cohen) said that he heard Swartzwelder make disparaging (and patently false) remarks about the environment, such as saying that there is more rainforest today than there had been one hundred years prior (Groening, et al.).

Despite having potentially anti-environmental views, Swartzwelder wrote some of *The Simpsons'* most iconic pro-environmental episodes, including "The Old Man and the Lisa" (8.21) (in which Mr. Burns and Lisa team up in the recycling business), "Bart Gets an Elephant" (5.17) (in which Homer relents on giving away Bart's pet elephant named Stampy to an ivory dealer), and, with Sam Simon, "Two Cars in Every Garage and Three Eyes on Every Fish" (2.4) (in which Blinky the three-eyed fish plays a role in both spurring and then spoiling Mr. Burns' gubernatorial bid).

While the pro-environmental episodes of *The Simpsons* run the gamut on issues, some environmental sub-themes are more commonly addressed than others. Of the 77 pro-environmental episodes, there is a concentration in three subcategories: animal welfare (25 episodes, or about a third of all shows), energy (sixteen, or about a fifth) and camping, hiking, and wilderness (fifteen, or also about a fifth). These three subcategories represent about three quarters of all of *The Simpsons'* pro-environmental episodes. And they also generally reflect the three environmental themes that Todd found in her 2002 analysis of the first ten seasons of *The Simpsons*.

Bonfire of the Manatees (aka, the Discussion)

In *The Simpsons'* first twenty-seven seasons, the family (largely at Lisa's instigation) works diligently to save bees ("The Burns and the Bees" 20.8), buffalo ("Simpsons Tall Tales" 12.21), bulls ("Million-Dollar Abie" 17.16), butterfly pupae ("Dial 'N' for Nerder" 19.14), chickens ("The Marge-Ian Chronicles" 27.16), chimpanzees ("Simpson Safari" 12.17), greyhounds ("Two Dozen and One Greyhounds" 6.20), falcons ("Diggs" 25.12), lizards ("Bart the Mother" 10.3), manatees ("Bonfire of the Manatees" 17.1), raccoons ("Smoke on the Daughter" 19.15), snakes ("Whacking Day" 4.20), a single ant ("American History X-Cellent" 21.17), a badger ("A Tale of Two Springfields" 12.2), a bald eagle ("The Musk Who Fell to Earth" 26.12), a bear ("The Fat and the Furriest" 15.5), a canary ("C.E. D'oh" 14.1), a cow ("Apocalypse Cow" 19.17), a dolphin ("Treehouse of Horror XI" 12.1), a duckling ("The Good, the Sad, and the Drugly" 20.17), an elephant ("Bart Gets an Elephant" 5.17), a goat ("Lisa the Veterinarian" 27.15), a goldfish ("Lisa the Veterinarian" 27.15), a horse ("Saddlesore Galactica" 11.13), a lobster ("Lisa Gets an 'A'" 10.7), a St. Bernard ("Lisa the Veterinarian" 27.15), a whale ("The Squirt and the Whale" 21.19), and even alien life forms ("Treehouse of Horror XXII" 23.3). Notably, Lisa is not the only character in the show who protects animals.[37] Rather, it is a family affair, and the effect is that *The Simpsons* clearly stands out as an advocate of animal welfare. And of course, not every scene involving animals is about saving them or treating them well. For example, after Mr. Burns moves his power plant to Bangalore, India, Homer—in command of the plant in a way reminiscent of Marlon Brando's Col. Walter Kurtz in *Apocalypse Now*—orders a monkey to fight an elephant ("Kiss Kiss, Bang Bangalore" 17.17). But more often than not, *The Simpsons*, more than any other long-running American sitcom, is about working to save animals.

Lisa also promotes a vegetarian diet, crystalized perhaps most famously in the episode in which Lisa eats vegetarian food with Paul and Linda McCartney and Apu Nahasapeemapetilon on the roof of Apu's Kwik-E-Mart[38] ("Lisa the Vegetarian" 7.5), as well as in a flash-forward episode to her future academic life on a university campus—where trees have been replaced by holographic projections, placed in memory of actual trees, and Blinky the three-eyed fish outside the Springfield Nuclear Power Plant has been replaced by six-eyed fish, fish that look like severed cow heads, and fish that look and sound like Prof. John Frink, Jr. ("Lisa's Wedding" 6.19).

> "Can we get vegetarian meals at your parents' house?" Lisa asks her boyfriend, Hugh Parkfield.
> "Yes, we can Lisa."
> "That is good, because eating animals is wrong."
> "So very wrong."
> "When will the world learn?"
> "I don't know. I just don't know" ["Lisa's Wedding"].

Despite Lisa, sometimes *The Simpsons* portrays vegetarianism negatively, such as when Krusty Burger starts serving the all-vegetarian Mother Nature Burgers that lead to Springfield–wide food poisoning and the invasion of Scandinavian migrant workers from Ogdenville ("Coming to Homerica" 20.21). And when Lisa's vegetarianism causes an iron deficiency, leading her to eat insects that give her nightmares and, upon release, decimate a corn maze ("Penny-Wiseguys" 24.5). There is even an entire episode that glorifies the grilling and eating of meat ("'Cue Detective" 27.2). And when Homer poses as a bull and ends up in a slaughterhouse—where he narrowly escapes his own slaughter—his preference for eating meat remains only slightly tempered[39] ("Apocalypse Cow" 19.17), likely reflective of how many Americans respond to the thought of eating meat after learning more about how the sausage is made. In so doing, *The Simpsons* speaks to the pervasiveness of meat-eating in American society regardless of anything we learn about it.

The second major environmental subcategory I found is energy. Homer is the character most closely associated with energy, and given that he works at a nuclear power plant—and that the writers placed him there specifically so that they could critique nuclear energy (Turner 66)—it is not surprising that the show has spent so much airtime on nuclear energy. But because so much has been written about *The Simpsons* and nuclear energy,[40] I instead will discuss other energy issues addressed by *The Simpsons*.

If anything, it is surprising how much *The Simpsons* critiques conventional fossil fuels. One example is when oil is discovered beneath Springfield Elementary and the town consequently becomes an example of the resource curse, in which the presence of economically valuable natural resources leads to worse outcomes for residents of the area. At first, great optimism reigns. The expected revenues are tapped to buy a crystal mop bucket for Groundskeeper Willie (formerly known as Dr. William MacDougal) and to hire famed Latin-jazz musician Tito Puente as a music teacher. "Today Springfield Elementary embarks on a new era, an era of unbridled spending, where petrodollars will fuel our wildest educational fantasies," Principal Walter Seymour Skinner declares at "Oil Appreciation Day" ("Who Shot Mr. Burns? [Part One]" 6.25).

Instead, the discovery of oil leads to the destruction of Bart's treehouse, the hospitalization and temporary crippling of his dog, the slashing of the school's budget, the shuttering of Moe's Tavern, the spreading of noxious fumes through Springfield, and the collapse of the Springfield Retirement Castle. The oil also fuels the greed of the nuclear (and now oil) baron Mr. Burns, who feels empowered to challenge a source of competing energy—the sun—by blotting it out in the sky. In so doing, Mr. Burns presages the actions of conventional fossil-fuel companies who today seek policies to block renewable energies such as solar power (Environment America Research and Policy Center and Frontier Group; Marston; Wieners and Hasemyer). Like fossil-fuel companies today, Mr. Burns reaches mixed success in stopping renewables. He does blot out the sun—leading Springfield residents to be dependent upon buying energy from him for lighting both day and night[41]—but he is subsequently shot, collapsing onto the town sundial.

The resource curse reprises with natural gas twenty seasons later, when *The Simpsons* takes on hydraulic fracturing, AKA hydrofracking or fracking. Natural-gas deposits are discovered beneath Springfield, and Mr. Burns appoints Homer as his "chief energy innovation marketing director" in a conversation that could mirror that between someone in the fracking industry and a confused member of the general public:

"All you've got to do is sell fracking to your friends and neighbors," Mr. Burns instructs Homer.

"Woo hoo?" Homer asks. "I don't know, fracking is one of those scary Lisa words."

"Bah! Fracking produces enough clean natural gas to make America independent of sheiks, caliphs, and Scandinavians. Not to mention, it doesn't create any of that awful worker-mutating nuclear waste."

A glowing nuclear worker with four eyes and four ears interrupts to remind Homer to set his fantasy-football lineup.

"Maybe fracking isn't so bad," Homer says.

"Then say yes to this raise, this promotion and this flannel shirt that says, 'I'm not screwing you over!'" Mr. Burns replies[42] ["Opposites A-Frack" 26.5].

The Simpsons also values renewable energy. For example, Springfield is host to an Alternative Energy Derby—a green equivalent of the soapbox Derby, featuring kid-made hydrogen-, wind-, and solar-powered derby cars[43] ("Paths of Glory" 27.8).

And Homer, bothered by his high electric bills, buys a windmill at an alternative-energy expo (which Mr. Burns pickets as "unfair to earth poisoners") and takes the family off grid[44] ("The Squirt and the Whale" 21.19).

That is not to say that all episodes are kind to renewable energy, though. Springfield also hosts a solar-powered (and thereby underpowered and ineffectual) electric chair ("Lisa the Tree Hugger" 12.4).

While Lisa is associated with animal welfare and Homer with energy, Lisa, Homer and Bart—the three characters around whom I have found that *The Simpsons'* plots, particularly those with pro-environmental themes, revolve most—are all featured in episodes that promote nature positively. (With Lisa still featured in more than the others, of course.)

For example, when Lisa joins Dirt First (in perhaps the only sitcom episode to ever address or parody the radical environmental group Earth First[45]), she camps out in the branches of Springfield's oldest redwood tree, using the tactic made famous by Julia "Butterfly" Hill and other tree sitters to attempt saving the tree from the chainsaw ("Lisa the Tree Hugger").

When visiting Arizona, Homer enjoys the splendor of the Grand Canyon despite having a dozen stinging scorpions on his back. "Wow, I never thought there'd be something I'd want to stare at longer than that car wreck on the way here," Homer remarks. "This has got to be the most beautiful thing we ever stole from the Indians" ("Fland Canyon" 27.19).

And even Bart enjoys horseback riding with Superintendent Gary Chalmers around Springfield National Forest ("Bart Stops to Smell the Roosevelts" 23.2).

On the rare occasions when *The Simpsons'* peer sitcoms address nature and wilderness, it was almost always portrayed as a scary place where bad things happened—such as getting lost and being chased by bears. And while *The Simpsons* has had a bit of that fearmongering around nature and wilderness, more often than not the characters in *The Simpsons* have approached nature and wilderness as a place of beauty and awe and worthy of conservation.

Maybe You Can Win Friends with Salad (aka, the Conclusion)

The Simpsons also has had much commentary on protection of nature and the environment writ large—and the role of right-wing politicians in removing legal protections for nature. For example, at a meeting of the Springfield Republicans, Mr. Burns seeks ideas for new legislation (or, as he puts it, "What act of unmitigated evil shall the Republican Party undertake this week?") ("Brawl in the Family" 13.7).

"What about this dang environment?" Rich Texan asks. "Back in Texas we got rid of it and made everyone a lot happier."

"Excellent!" Burns replies, tenting only his pointer fingers. "We shall destroy the environment by scrapping every antipollution law" (Cohen and Nastuk "Brawl in the Family").

Recycling becomes a felony. Smokey the Bear is replaced by Choppy the Lumberjack. Springfield's wetlands are drained. Spotted-owl habitat protections are removed, allowing for Nelson to give noogies to a spotted owl. Steel mills, smoke factories, and even daycare centers belch jet-black smoke into the air. Acid rain drenches the town, dissolving people's clothes, melting the squirrels and even melting the Simpsons' TV antenna ("Brawl in the Family" 13.7). Aired in 2002, the episode served as an exaggerated warning for plans of the second Bush administration to revoke environmental protections—but the warning is just as potent today, as the Trump administration—the rise of which was famously predicted by *The Simpsons* in 2000[46] ("Bart to the Future" 11.17)—revokes environmental protections at an unprecedented rate (Greshko, et al.; Popvich, et al.). In its decades on the air, *The Simpsons* has been not just relevant but insightful and visionary.

Overall, aside from being the longest-running sitcom in American history, *The Simpsons* also consistently has been the one of the most environmentally oriented sitcoms on American television. There certainly have been anti-environmental episodes of *The Simpsons*, but there have been three-and-a-half times as many pro-environmental as anti-environmental episodes. Although we have entered the era of the internet, television programming remains a powerful force, if not the defining element, of American culture—and because of that, there may be no better example of banal environmentalism at work than *The Simpsons*.

Bat Groening, I. Scream Cohen and Friends (aka, the Acknowledgments)

David Krantz (ORCID 0000–0001–6062–6628) is supported by an IGERT-SUN (Solar Utilization Network) fellowship funded by the National Science Foundation (Award 1144616). He is grateful to Sonja Klinsky for her wise guidance and to Tyler Shores for his inspiration. He also thanks all others who have helped and encouraged his learning over his academic and professional career.

NOTES

1. After three years of running as one-minute-long animated shorts on *The Tracey Ullman Show*, the first-ever episode of *The Simpsons* was a Christmas special and began without the typical opening that the show would use for decades. Instead, it opened with Homer and

Marge Simpson driving through the snow on their way to the annual Christmas pageant at Bart and Lisa's school ("Simpsons Roasting on an Open Fire" 1.1).

2. Although they did not originally develop nudge theory, Richard Thaler and Cass Sunstein popularized it. In their book, *Nudge: Improving Decisions About Health, Wealth, and Happiness*, they focused on intentional choices made to push people to make decisions desired by others (Thaler and Sunstein, pp. 1–320). For example, a grocer may nudge a consumer to buy a product by placing it on a prominent shelf within the store.

3. Two other researchers have espoused the notion of banal environmentalism—and, in a case of multiple discovery (synchronicity or simultaneous invention), they did so at nearly the same time at two different universities in England. In September 2008, Ryan Cunningham completed his master's thesis on banal environmentalism at the London School of Economics (Cunningham). The following month at the University of East Anglia in Norwich, England, Tom Hargreaves completed his doctoral thesis, which focused in part on banal environmentalism (Hargreaves).

4. To what degree does each exposure to banal environmentalism affect one's views on the environment? Research into the effects of exposure to other banal factors—such as violence in video games (Bartholow, et al.; Engelhardt, et al.) and body-image types depicted in media (Agliata and Tantleff-Dunn; Harper and Tiggemann)—show a strong correlation between exposure and changes in subjects' actions and attitudes. Whether exposure to environmentally minded media—such as environmentally minded episodes of *The Simpsons*—is similarly impactful warrants research.

5. Banal environmentalism is notably different from mundane environmentalism (Poloni-Staudinger), which refers to environmental activities of little or no consequence and/or sacrifice. For example, driving an electric car or maintaining a vegetarian diet would not be mundane in that such actions can have substantial impact on an individual scale and also can involve sacrifice, but they could be banal in their everyday execution and/or in the consumption of their representation in the media. However, banal environmentalism and mundane environmentalism are not mutually exclusive. Recycling—what may be the quintessential act of mundane environmentalism, since it typically merely requires placing a waste product in a different bin, usually inches away from the standard trash bin—may be a case of both banal and mundane environmentalism at play. Recycling is mundane in that it has little impact compared to more significant environmental issues, and in that it requires little effort or sacrifice. Recycling also can be banal in its daily, repetitive and relatively unconscious practice and devotion. The mundaneness and banality of recycling shows how far our society has come on environmental issues over the lifetime of *The Simpsons*. At the time of the show's debut in December 1989, recycling arguably was the biggest environmental issue on the public agenda. About a month before *The Simpsons*' first episode, *Murphy Brown* aired its first of what would become four episodes that addressed the environment in a positive light—and it was all about encouraging recycling and why it's important to reduce and separate one's waste (Dukane et al.). Recycling may be mundane because of the emergence of significantly larger environmental problems such as climate change, but the banality of recycling—which has gone from a fringe to a mainstream activity over the last few decades (Environmental Protection Agency "Municipal Solid Waste"; Environmental Protection Agency "Recycling and Composting Trends")—is one of the largest success stories in the environmental movement's history (although ample opportunities for waste-management improvement remain).

6. Formerly part of News Corporation and likely by the time you read this to be part of the Walt Disney Company, as predicted by *The Simpsons* in 1998 ("When You Dish Upon a Star" 10.5).

7. The largest other studies of television content that I could find have involved samples of television shows rather than entire populations or a show's entire run—such as researchers watching a few hours of television daily for a week. The sample was used as a basis for estimating frequency across the entire series. In contrast, I did not sample shows but rather analyzed the content of every episode for 76 television shows.

8. Indeed, in its first twenty-seven seasons, *The Simpsons* has won eight Environmental Media Awards, twice that of any other television show, including *Bill Nye the Science Guy*, *Captain Planet*, and *The Lazy Environmentalist* (Environmental Media Association).

9. And Maria Rosaria Di Nucci at the Free University of Berlin's Environmental Policy Research Centre applied *The Simpsons* to the non-animated world by developing theories on how communities that host nuclear power plants relate to them. She labels those towns that "derive strong economic advantages from the nuclear industry connected with the value chain of the nuclear facilities on their territory" as Springfield communities, named after the town the Simpson family calls home. Further, she describes the effect of communities that are proud of their nuclear facilities, like Springfield is in *The Simpsons*, as Springfield Syndrome (Di Nucci, 119–144; Di Nucci and Brunnengräber). Springfield residents tend to be more proud than embarrassed of their nuclear plant (and even their nuclear-enhanced three-eyed fish; hence the moniker for its pending and ultimately unrealized professional football league team is the Meltdowns (Long and Moore) and its minor-league baseball team is the Isotopes (Levine, et al.), a name borrowed later in the non-animated world by the minor-league baseball team in a city with Springfield Syndrome—Albuquerque, N.M., about sixty miles away as the three-eyed crow flies from Los Alamos National Laboratory, where the first atomic bomb was developed.

10. Silvia Ceausu and Tamara Steger took a similar approach, scanning the transcripts of a single season of *The Simpsons*, *Family Guy*, and *South Park* for environmental topics. Their data was limited in covering only a single season and in being comingled among the three shows. In aggregate in the three shows, they described the top environmental topics as automobiles and fuel consumption, wildlife, Al Gore, and extreme weather (Ceausu and Steger).

11. Just as much as Lisa serves as an eco-hero, she is also an archetype of the marginalized eco-feminist vegetarian dissident killjoy (Grant and MacKenzie-Dale, 307-329; Freeman, 193-212; Todd, 73-76).

12. "Urban poultry farming is a great way to reduce our carbon footprint!" Lisa opines. "Or maybe increase it. I'm not sure" (" The Marge-ian Chronicles" 27.16).

13. Homer: "Global warming: Huh. By pure coincidence, every scientist was right" ("White Christmas Blues" 25.8).

14. It is also possible to address climate change without mentioning the term "climate change," both indirectly (for example, Midwestern no-till farmers [Tabuchi]) as well as through metaphors, parables and allegories (for example, the film *Mother!* [Ryzik])—although that method may not always result in the message being received (Brody).

15. Of course, I cannot reference McLuhan without hearing him say, "You know nothing of my work. You mean my whole fallacy is wrong" (Allen).

16. The 116 networks are A&E, ABC, Adult Swim, AMC, American Heroes Channel, Animal Planet, ASPiRE, Audience, AWE, AXS TV, BabyFirst, BabyTV, BBC America, BET, Boomerang, Bravo, Cartoon Network, CBS, Centric, Chiller, Cinemax, Cloo, CMT, Comedy Central, Cooking Channel, Create, Crime & Investigation Network, Destination America, Discovery Channel, Discovery Family, Discovery Life, Disney Channel, Disney Junior, Disney XD, DIY Network, E!, El Rey Network, Epix, Esquire Network, Flix, Food Network, 20th Century–Fox, Freeform, FX, FXM, FXX, FYI, GSN, Hallmark Channel, Hallmark Movies & Mysteries, HBO, HDNet Movies, HGTV, History, IFC, INSP, Investigation Discovery, Ion, Ion Life, Lifetime, Lifetime Real Women, LMN, Logo TV, MGM HD, Military History, MoviePlex, MTV, MTV Classic, MTV2, MyNetworkTV, NASA TV, Nat Geo Wild, National Geographic Channel, NBC, Nick at Nite, Nick Jr., Nick2, Nickelodeon, NickMusic, Nicktoons, Ovation, OWN, Oxygen, PBS, Pivot, Pop, Qubo, Reelz, Science, Showtime, Smithsonian Channel, Sony Movie Channel, Spike, Sprout, Starz, Starz Encore, SundanceTV, Syfy, TBS, TeenNick, The CW, The Movie Channel, TLC, TNT, Travel Channel, truTV, Turner Classic Movies, TV Land, TV One, Universal HD, Up, USA Network, VH1, Viceland, WE tv, and WGN America.

17. However, I only count seasons as they originally aired. For example, even though *Meet the Browns* was released on DVD as seven seasons, it originally aired as five seasons and was subsequently excluded from this study.

18. In chronological order, the 76 sitcoms are *Cheers, Newhart, Night Court, The Cosby Show, Who's the Boss?, The Golden Girls, Growing Pains, Perfect Strangers, Designing Women, Married ... with Children, Full House, Empty Nest, Roseanne, Murphy Brown, Coach, Seinfeld, Family Matters, The Simpsons, Wings, Rugrats, Home Improvement, Step by Step, Beavis and*

Butt-Head, Mad About You, Saved by the Bell: The New Class, Frasier, Boy Meets World, Friends, The Drew Carey Show, Arliss (AKA *Arli$$*), *Everybody Loves Raymond, Sabrina the Teenage Witch, King of the Hill, Just Shoot Me!, South Park, That '70s Show, Will & Grace, The King of Queens, Family Guy, Futurama, SpongeBob SquarePants, Malcolm in the Middle, Girlfriends, Curb Your Enthusiasm, Aqua Teen Hunger Force, The Fairly OddParents, Scrubs, According to Jim, Monk, Two and a Half Men, Entourage, American Dad!, The Office, It's Always Sunny in Philadelphia, Weeds, How I Met Your Mother, 30 Rock, Squidbillies, Psych, The Game, Rules of Engagement, Tyler Perry's House of Payne, Californication, iCarly, The Big Bang Theory, The Mentalist, Parks and Recreation, Royal Pains, Nurse Jackie, Archer, Modern Family, The Middle, The League, Adventure Time, Regular Show,* and *Childrens Hospital.*

19. Inevitably, in scouring the sitcoms aired by 116 television networks over 27 seasons, it is possible I missed a show that meets the criteria set forth in this research.

20. Double-length episodes count as two episodes, triple-length episodes count as three episodes (and so on). *Adventure Time, Regular Show, SpongeBob SquarePants* and *The Fairly OddParents* episodes are for 11-minute segments, with double-length segments counted here as two episodes. A season's worth of *Regular Show* shorts (each about two minutes in length) count here as one episode.

21. Some may take issue with the inclusion of vegetarianism/veganism as an environmental issue, but given that the greenhouse gases released through meat production and consumption is either the single-largest contributor to climate change (Steinfeld, et al.)—or at the very least a major driver of climate change (Hedenus, et al; Ripple, et al.)—vegetarianism/veganism may be the most environmentally oriented subject of them all.

22. "Don't kid yourself, Jimmy, if a cow ever got the chance, he'd eat you and everyone you care about"—Troy McClure in the educational film "Meat and You: Partners In Freedom"—Number 3F03 in the "Resistance Is Useless Series"—presented by the Meat Council, in "Lisa the Vegetarian" (7.5).

23. The coding is inherently subjective, and as such another person may have coded some of the episodes differently. That said, with a population of nearly 14,000 episodes, the addition or subtraction of an environmentally themed episode here or there would not have made significant shifts in the overall percentages of environmentally themed episodes.

24. Crossover episodes are counted only as an episode of the host show. For example, when the characters of *The Simpsons* guest star in an episode of *Family Guy*, the episode only counts as an episode of *Family Guy* and not as an episode of *The Simpsons*.

25. Indeed, *The Simpsons Movie* may be the only non-documentary film whose main characters include the administrator of the U.S. Environmental Protection Agency and whose plot is driven by the actions of the EPA.

26. Given the name of the show, though, perhaps not quite as many pro-environmental episodes as one might expect.

27. *Futurama's* writers include Kristin Gore, daughter of climate advocate and former Vice President Al Gore—but she was only a writer on the show for two seasons, during which only 17 percent of *Futurama's* pro-environmental episodes were written. Gore herself only wrote one of the show's pro-environmental episodes, and the show's seasons with the most pro-environmental episodes occur before and after her tenure.

28. It remains to be seen if Groening's new sitcom, *Disenchantment*, also will take on environmental issues at a great frequency.

29. Have you ever thought about why the grandfather of future-oriented cartoons, *The Jetsons*, is set in the clouds? Perhaps it is because future society has retreated to the heavens after having made the surface environmentally uninhabitable.

30. During the first 27 seasons of *The Simpsons*, episodes that are set in the future feature a pro-environmental theme at a slightly higher rate (14 percent) than those set in the present, but the population of future-set episodes (seven) is small.

31. That the characters of *Parks and Recreation* work in a parks department does not necessarily mean that episode themes will be about parks, although that was the case. By comparison, *Regular Show* is also about staffers at a park, and its episodes feature the environment in a positive light less than two percent of the time.

32. Due to rounding, four shows with less than 0.5 percent are recorded here as 0 percent. (For example, a show with one pro-environmental episode out of a total of 273 episodes is rounded from 0.37 percent to 0 percent.) Similarly, seven shows that fall between 0.5 percent and 1 percent are rounded up to 1 percent.

33. *Newhart* actually has no environmentally minded episodes at all; *Full House* has only one, which portrayed agriculture in a negative light; and *Monk* has four, although all are in a negative light.

34. Although about twenty years later, *The Simpsons* partially makes up for its disparagement of public transit in "Marge vs. the Monorail" by bringing in "greatest living inventor" Elon Musk to develop the Springfield Hyperloop. Like the monorail before it, the hyperloop also fails, but the reason is fiscal rather than technological. While the monorail salesman, Lyle Lanley, was painted as an opportunistic huckster, Musk the hyperloop salesman was portrayed as a futuristic tech-savvy genius idealist willing to sacrifice profit for fulfillment of mission. "Our purpose is to show the planet how to save itself," Musk says. But three seasons later (and outside the purview of this study) the monorail itself returns, wreaking havoc through the city once again and ultimately costing Mayor Joseph (Joe) Fitzgerald O'Malley Fitzpatrick O'Donnell The Edge Quimby his job ("The Old Blue Mayor Ain't What She Used to Be" 29.6).

35. Two of the twenty-three shows are rounded down to 0 percent. A total of twenty-one shows do not have a single episode with an environmental theme.

36. Perhaps most prominently, Canadian journalist Chris Turner posited that *The Simpsons'* best years were from 1992 to 1997 (3).

37. Although Lisa is a card-carrying member of PETA (People for the Ethical Treatment of Amoebas), The League of Women Vultures, The NAACPorcupines, Kids for Squids, ACLUnicorns, and Clamnesty International ("How Munched Is That Birdie in the Window?" 22.7).

38. Sam Simon, co-creator of *The Simpsons*, was a vegetarian and then a vegan for almost all of his adult life, but he dismissed that he was responsible for Lisa's views on vegetarianism (Nell), and he did not write the famous episode "Lisa the Vegetarian" (7.5).

39. Homer: "The things I saw, makes me want to never eat meat again—just fish, chicken, burgers, veal on Fridays, deer but only in season, and if necessary the sweetest meat of all, human" ("Apocalypse Cow" 19.17).

40. From impotence to genetic mutations to the threat of nuclear fallout, *The Simpsons* demonstrates over and over again the dangers of radiation from nuclear energy.

41. The end of sunlight prompts *The Springfield Shopper* to publish a helpful edition titled, "Your Guide to Perpetual Darkness" ("Who Shot Mr. Burns? [Part One]" 6.25).

42. In the next scene, Homer is at home in the kitchen with Bart, practicing saying over and over again in different ways, "I'm not screwing you over" ("Opposites a-Frack" 26.5).

43. And where tents promote some of the derby's sponsors, "National Petroleum: Greening the Arctic" and "Putt-Putt Power: Mini-Golf Windmill Farms" ("Paths of Glory" 27.8).

44. Lisa: "Dad, you are leading the way in clean energy."
Homer: "Yep, I Al Gore'd it pretty good" ("The Squirt and the Whale" 21.19).

45. *The Simpsons* also may be the only sitcom to ever address or parody the environmental guerilla group Earth Liberation Front—or, as it is known in Springfield, the Earth Liberation Army ("Homerland" 25.1) (not to be confused with the actual but much lesser known Earth Liberation Army in the non-animated world).

46. President Lisa Simpson, taking over from President Donald Trump: "My administration will focus on the three Rs: reading, writing and refilling the ocean" ("Bart to the Future" 11.17).

THE COLLECTED WORKS OF AMELIA VANDERBUCKLE, ET AL. (AKA, WORKS CITED)

Agliata, Daniel, and Stacey Tantleff-Dunn. "The Impact of Media Exposure on Males' Body Image." *Journal of Social and Clinical Psychology*, vol. 23, no. Special Issue: *Body Image and Eating Disorders: Influence of Media Images*, 2004, pp. 7–22.

Alk, Nell. "Exclusive Interview with 'The Simpsons' Co-Creator Sam Simon." *Ecorazzi*, 5 May 2014, http://ecorazzi.com/2014/05/05/exclusive-interview-with-the-simpsons-co-creator-sam-simon/. Accessed 31 Dec. 2017.

Allen, Woody. *Annie Hall*. Motion picture, United Artists, 1977.

"American History X-Cellent." *The Simpsons*. Written by Michael Price, directed by Bob Anderson. 20th Century–Fox, 2010.

"Apocalypse Cow." *The Simpsons*. Written by Jeff Westbrook, directed by Nancy Kruse. 20th Century–Fox, 27 Apr. 2008.

"Bart Gets an Elephant." *The Simpsons: The Complete Fifth Season*. Written by John Swartzwelder, directed by Jim Reardon. 20th Century–Fox, 1994.

"Bart Stops to Smell the Roosevelts." *The Simpsons*. Written by Tim Long, directed by Steven Dean Moore. 20th Century–Fox, 2012.

"Bart the Genius." *The Simpsons: The Complete First Season*. Written by Jon Vitti, directed by David Silverman, 20th Century–Fox, 1990.

"Bart the Mother." *The Simpsons: The Complete Tenth Season*. Written by David X. Cohen, directed by Steven Dean Moore, 20th Century–Fox, 1998.

"Bart to the Future." *The Simpsons: The Complete Eleventh Season*. Written by Dan Greaney, directed by Michael Marcantel. 20th Century–Fox, 2000.

Bartholow, Bruce D., et al. "Chronic Violent Video Game Exposure and Desensitization to Violence: Behavioral and Event-Related Brain Potential Data." *Journal of Experimental Social Psychology*, vol. 42, 2006, pp. 532–539.

"Bart's Comet." *The Simpsons: The Complete Sixth Season*. Written by John Swartzwelder, directed by Bob Anderson, 20th Century–Fox. 1995.

"Beyond Blunderdome." *The Simpsons: The Complete Eleventh Season*. Written by Mike Scully, directed by Steven Dean Moore. 20th Century–Fox, 1999.

Billig, Michael. *Banal Nationalism*. Sage, 1995.

"The Bonfire of the Manatees." *The Simpsons*. Written by Dan Greaney, directed by Mark Kirkland. 20th Century–Fox, 11 Sept 2005.

"Brawl in the Family." *The Simpsons: The Complete Thirteenth Season*. Written by Joel H. Cohen, directed by Matthew Nastuk. 20th Century–Fox, 2002.

Broderick, Mick. "Releasing the Hounds: The Simpsons as Anti-Nuclear Satire." *Leaving Springfield: The Simpsons and the Possibility of Oppositional Culture*, edited by John Alberti, Wayne State University Press, 2004, pp. 244–272.

Brody, Richard. "Darren Aronofsky Says 'Mother!' Is About Climate Change, but He's Wrong." *The New Yorker*, 20 Sept. 2017, https://newyorker.com/culture/richard-brody/darren-aronofsky-says-mother-is-about-climate-change-but-hes-wrong. Accessed 31 Dec. 2017.

"The Burns and the Bees." *The Simpsons*. Written by Stephanie Gillis, directed by Mark Kirkland. 20th Century–Fox, 2008.

"C.E. D'oh." *The Simpsons: The Complete Fourteenth Season*. Written by Dana Gould, directed by Mike B. Anderson. 20th Century–Fox, 2003.

Ceausu, Silvia, and Tamara Steger. "Environmental Issues in the Animated TV Series: *South Park, The Simpsons,* and *The Family Guy*." *Film and Media 2011: The First Annual London Film and Media Conference*, edited by Phillip Drummond, vol. 1, The London Symposium, 2011, pp. 87–97. *The London Film and Media Reader*.

Chagan, Sonal A. "Effects of Dumping Pig Manure into a Lake—*The Simpsons Movie*." *Journal of Interdisciplinary Science Topics*, vol. 5, 2016, pp. 1–3.

"Coming to Homerica." *The Simpsons: The Complete Twentieth Season*. Written by Brendan Hay, directed by Steven Dean Moore, 20th Century–Fox, 2010.

"'Cue Detective." *The Simpsons*. Written by Joel H. Cohen, directed by Timothy Bailey, 20th Century–Fox, 4 Oct 2015.

Cunningham, Ryan. "Banal Environmentalism: Defining and Exploring an Expanded Understanding of Ecological Identity, Awareness, and Action." *Department of Media and Communications*, London School of Economics and Political Science, September 2008, pp. 1–43.

"Dancin' Homer." *The Simpsons: The Complete Second Season*. Written by Ken Levine, directed by Mark Kirkland. 20th Century–Fox, 1990.

Delaney, Tim. *Simpsonology: There's a Little Bit of Springfield in All of Us*. Prometheus Books, 2008.

"Dial 'N' for Nerder." *The Simpsons*. Written by Carolyn Omine and William Wright. 20th Century–Fox, 9 Mar 2008.

"Diggs." *The Simpsons*. Written by Allen Glazier and Dan Greaney, directed by Michael Polcino. 20th Century–Fox, 9 Mar 2014.

Di Nucci, Maria Rosaria. "Nimby or Imby Acceptance, Voluntary and Compensations in Site Search for Final Disposal of Radioactive Waste." *Problem Case Repository: Societal Challenges in Dealing with Nuclear Waste*, edited by Achim Brunnengräber, Nomos, 2016, pp. 119–144.

Di Nucci, Maria Rosaria and Achim Brunnengräber. "In Whose Backyard? The Wicked Problem of Siting Nuclear Waste Repositories." *European Policy Analysis*, vol. 3, no. 2, 2017, pp. 295–323.

Donovan, Ned. "John Swartzwelder Wrote Your Favorite 'Simpsons' Episodes." *The Daily Dot*, 21 Feb. 2014, https://dailydot.com/upstream/simpsons-jon-swartzwelder-reclusive-writer/. Accessed 31 Dec. 2017.

Dukane, Sy (writer) et al. "Whose Garbage is it Anyway?" *Murphy Brown*, Warner Bros. Television, 1989.

Engelhardt, Christopher R., et al. "This Is Your Brain on Violent Video Games: Neural Desensitization to Violence Predicts Increased Aggression Following Violent Video Game Exposure." *Journal of Experimental Social Psychology*, vol. 47, no. 5, 2011, pp. 1033–1036.

Environment America Research and Policy Center and Frontier Group. "Blocking the Sun: Utilities and Fossil Fuel Interests That Are Undermining American Solar Power." 2017, pp. 1–45.

Environmental Media Association. "E.M.A. Awards Past Recipients and Honorees." *Environmental Media Association*, http://green4ema.org/ema-awards/ema-awards-past-recipients-and-honorees/. Accessed 31 Dec. 2017.

Environmental Protection Agency. "Municipal Solid Waste." https://archive.epa.gov/epawaste/nonhaz/municipal/web/html. Accessed 15 Nov. 2018.

Environmental Protection Agency. "Recycling and Composting Trends." https://epa.gov/facts-and-figures-about-materials-waste-and-recycling/national-overview-facts-and-figures-materials#R&Ctrends. Accessed 15 Nov. 2018.

"The Fat and the Furriest." *The Simpsons: The Complete Fifteenth Season*. Written by Joel H. Cohen, directed by Matthew Nastuk. 20th Century–Fox, 2003.

Feltmate, David. "Two Days Before the Day Before an Irritating Truth: The Simpsons and South Park's Environmentalism as a Challenge for Mass Mediating Dark Green Ecological Ethics." *Journal for the Study of Religion, Nature & Culture*, vol. 11, no. 3, 2017, pp. 315–339.

"Fland Canyon." *The Simpsons*. Written by Stewart J. Burns, directed by Michael Polcino, 20th Century–Fox, 24 Apr 2016.

Freeman, Carrie Packwood. "Lisa and Phoebe, Lone Vegetarian Icons: At Odds with Television's Carnonormativity." *How Television Shapes Our Worldview*, edited by Macey, Deborah A., Kathleen M. Ryan and Noah J. Springer, Lexington Books, 2014, pp. 193–212.

"Future-Drama." *The Simpsons: The Complete Sixteenth Season*. Written by Matt Selman, directed by Mike B. Anderson. 20th Century–Fox, 2005.

"The Good, the Sad, and the Drugly." *The Simpsons: The Complete Twentieth Season*. Written by Marc Wilmore, directed by Rob Oliver. 20th Century–Fox, 2009.

Grant, Juawana and Brittni MacKenzie-Dale. "Lisa Simpson and Darlene Conner: Television's Favorite Killjoys." *Critical Perspectives on Veganism*, edited by Castricano, Jodey and Rasmus R. Simonsen, Palgrave Macmillan, 2016, pp. 307–329.

Greshko, Michael, et al. "A Running List of How Trump Is Changing the Environment." *National Geographic*, National Geographic Society, 18 Dec. 2017. https://news.nationalgeographic.com/2017/03/how-trump-is-changing-science-environment/. Accessed 31 Dec. 2017.

Groening, Matt (commentator), et al. "The Old Man and the Lisa." *The Simpsons: The Complete Eighth Season*, 20th Century–Fox, 2006.

Hargreaves, Tom. "Making Pro-Environmental Behaviour Work: An Ethnographic Case Study of Practice, Process and Power in the Workplace." *School of Environmental Sciences*, vol. Doctor of Philosophy, University of East Anglia, October 2008, pp. 1–294.

Harper, Brit and Marika Tiggemann. "The Effect of Thin Ideal Media Images on Women's Self-Objectification, Mood, and Body Image." *Sex Roles*, vol. 58, no. 9–10, 2008, pp. 649–657.

Hedenus, Fredrik, et al. "The Importance of Reduced Meat and Dairy Consumption for Meeting Stringent Climate Change Targets." *Climatic Change*, vol. 124, no. 1–2, 2014, pp. 79–91.

"Homerland." *The Simpsons*. Written by Stephanie Gillis, directed by Bob Anderson. 20th Century–Fox, 29 Sept 2013

"Homer's Odyssey." *The Simpsons: The Complete First Season*. Written by Jay Kogen and Wallace Wolodarsky, directed by Wes Archer. 20th Century–Fox, 1990.

"Homer's Paternity Coot." *The Simpsons: The Complete Seventeenth Season*. Written by Joel H. Cohen, directed by Mike B. Anderson, 20th Century–Fox, 2006.

"How Munched Is That Birdie in the Window?" *The Simpsons*. Written by Kevin Curran, directed by Michael Polcino. 20th Century–Fox, 28 Nov. 2010.

"Kiss Kiss, Bang Bangalore." *The Simpsons: The Complete Seventeenth Season*. Written by Deb Lacusta and Dan Castellaneta, directed by Mark Kirkland. 20th Century–Fox, 2006.

Klara, Robert. "How the Simpsons Won Our Hearts, Made Billions and Stayed on the Air for 27 Years." *Adweek*, 2 May 2016, http://adweek.com/tv-video/how-simpsons-won-our-hearts-made-billions-and-stayed-air-27-years-171104/. Accessed 31 Dec. 2017.

Krantz, David. "Shmita Revolution: The Reclamation and Reinvention of the Sabbatical Year." *Religions*, vol. 7, no. 8, 2016, pp. 1-31.

Küchler, Uwe. "'Am I Getting Through to Anyone?' Foreign Language Education and the Environment." *Explorations and Extrapolations: Applying English and American Studies*, edited by Küchler, Uwe and Anne Schröder, LIT Verlag Münster, 2011, pp. 105-135.

"Lisa Gets an 'A.'" *The Simpsons: The Complete Tenth Season*. Written by Ian Maxtone-Graham, directed by Bob Anderson. 20th Century–Fox, 1998.

"Lisa the Tree Hugger." *The Simpsons: The Complete Twelfth Season*. Written by Matt Selman, directed by Steven Dean Moore. 20th Century–Fox, 2000.

"Lisa the Vegetarian." *The Simpsons: The Complete Seventh Season*. Written by David S. Cohen, directed by Mark Kirkland, 20th Century–Fox, 1995.

"Lisa the Veterinarian." *The Simpsons*. Written by Dan Vebber, directed by Steven Dean Moore. 20th Century–Fox, 6 Mar. 2016.

"Lisa's Wedding." *The Simpsons: The Complete Sixth Season*. Written by Greg Daniels, directed by Jim Reardon, 20th Century–Fox, 2012.

"The Marge-ian Chronicles." *The Simpsons*. Written by Brian Kelly, Brian, directed by Chris Clements. 20th Century–Fox, 13 Mar 2016.

"Marge vs. the Monorail." *The Simpsons: The Complete Fourth Season*. Written by Conan O'Brien, directed by Rich Moore, 20th Century–Fox, 1993.

Marston, Jim. "The Oil and Gas Industry's Assault on Renewable Energy." *Environmental Defense Fund*, 26 April 2013, https://edf.org/blog/2013/04/26/oil-and-gas-industrys-assault-renewable-energy. Accessed 31 Dec. 2017.

McLuhan, Marshall. *Understanding Media: The Extensions of Man*. Signet Books, 1964.

"Million-Dollar Abie." *The Simpsons: The Complete Seventeenth Season*. Written by Tim Long, directed by Steven Dean Moore. 20th Century–Fox, 2006.

Murray, Robin L. and Joseph K. Heumann. *That's All Folks: Ecocritical Readings of American Animated Features*. University of Nebraska Press, 2011.

"The Musk Who Fell to Earth." *The Simpsons*. Written by Neil Campbell, directed by Matthew Nastuk. 20th Century–Fox, 25 July 2015.

"The Old Blue Mayor She Ain't What She Used to Be." *The Simpsons*, 20th Century–Fox, 12 Nov. 2017.

"The Old Man and the Lisa." *The Simpsons: The Complete Eighth Season*. Written by John Swartzwelder, directed by Mark Kirkland, 20th Century–Fox, 2006.

"Opposites a-Frack." *The Simpsons*. Written by Valentina L. Garza, directed by Matthew Nastuk. 20th Century–Fox, 2 Nov 2014.

"Paths of Glory." *The Simpsons*. Written by Michael Ferris, directed by Steven Dean Moore. 20th Century–Fox, 6 Dec 2015.

Peach, Sara. "'The Simpsons' Take on Climate Change." Yale University, 5 Feb. 2011, https://yaleclimateconnections.org/2011/02/the-simpsons-take-on-climate-change/. Accessed 31 Dec. 2017.

"Penny-Wiseguys." *The Simpsons*. Written by Michael Price, directed by Mark Kirkland. 20th Century–Fox, 18 Nov 2012.

Pike, Deidre M. *Enviro-Toons: Green Themes in Animated Cinema and Television*. McFarland, 2012.

Poloni-Staudinger, Lori M. "Are Consensus Democracies More Environmentally Effective?" *Environmental Politics*, vol. 17, no. 3, 2008, pp. 410–430.

Popvich, Nadja, et al. "60 Environmental Rules on the Way out under Trump." *The New York Times*, 5 Oct. 2017, https://nytimes.com/interactive/2017/10/05/climate/trump-environment-rules-reversed.html. Accessed 31 Dec. 2017.

Ratcliffe, Susan, ed. *Concise Oxford Dictionary of Quotations*. Oxford University Press, 2011, p. 389.

Ripple, William J., et al. "Ruminants, Climate Change and Climate Policy." *Nature Climate Change*, vol. 4, no. 2–4, 2014.

Ryzik, Melena. "Making 'Mother!,' the Year's Most Divisive Film." *The New York Times*, 19 Sept. 2017, https://nytimes.com/2017/09/19/movies/jennifer-lawrence-darren-aronofsky-mother-explained.html. Accessed 31 Dec. 2017.

"Saddlesore Galactica." *The Simpsons: The Complete Eleventh Season*. Written by Tim Long, directed by Lance Kramer. 20th Century–Fox, 2000.

Seymour, Nicole. *Bad Environmentalism: Irony and Irreverence in the Ecological Age*. University of Minnesota Press, 2018, pp. 207–209.

The Simpsons Movie. Directed by David Silverman, performances by Dan Castellaneta, Julie Kavner, Nancy Cartwright, Yeardley Smith, Hank Azaria. 20th Century–Fox, 2007.

"Simpson Safari." *The Simpsons: The Complete Twelfth Season*. Written by John Swartzwelder, directed by Mark Kirkland, 20th Century–Fox, 2001.

"Simpsons Roasting on an Open Fire." *The Simpsons: The Complete First Season*. Written by Mimi Pond, directed by David Silverman, 20th Century–Fox, 1989.

"Simpsons Tall Tales." *The Simpsons: The Complete Twelfth Season*. Written by John Frink, et al. 20th Century–Fox, 2001.

"Smoke on the Daughter." *The Simpsons*. Written by Billy Kimball, directed by Lance Kramer. 20th Century–Fox, 30 Mar 2008.

"The Squirt and the Whale." *The Simpsons*. Written by Matt Warburton, directed by Lance Kramer. 20th Century–Fox, 25 Apr. 2010.

Starosielski, Nicole. "'Movements That Are Drawn': A History of Environmental Animation from the Lorax to Ferngully to Avatar." *International Communication Gazette*, vol. 73, no. 1–2, 2011, pp. 145–163.

Statistic Brain Research Institute. "The Simpsons Total Franchise Revenue." *Statistic Brain*, 20 May 2017, https://statisticbrain.com/the-simpsons-total-franchise-revenue/. Accessed 31 Dec. 2017.

Steinfeld, Henning, et al. *Livestock's Long Shadow: Environmental Issues and Options*. Food and Agriculture Organization of the United Nations, 2006.

Tabuchi, Hiroko. "In America's Heartland, Discussing Climate Change without Saying 'Climate Change.'" *The New York Times*, 28 Jan. 2017, https://nytimes.com/2017/01/28/business/energy-environment/navigating-climate-change-in-americas-heartland.html. Accessed 31 Dec. 2017.

"A Tale of Two Springfields." *The Simpsons: The Complete Twelfth Season*. Written by John Swartzwelder, directed by Shaun Cashman. 20th Century–Fox, 2000.

Thaler, Richard H., and Cass R. Sunstein. *Nudge: Improving Decisions About Health, Wealth, and Happiness*. Yale University Press, 2008.

Todd, Anne Marie. "Prime-Time Subversion: The Environmental Rhetoric of *The Simpsons*." *Enviropop: Studies in Environmental Rhetoric and Popular Culture*, edited by Mark Meister and Phyllis M. Japp, Praeger, 2002, pp. 63–80.

"Treehouse of Horror XI." *The Simpsons: The Twelfth Season*. Written by Rob LaZebnik, et al., directed by Matthew Nastuk, 20th Century–Fox, 2010.

"Treehouse of Horror XXII." *The Simpsons*. Written by Carolyn Omine, directed by Matthew Faughnan. 20th Century–Fox, 11 Oct. 2011.

Turner, Chris. *Planet Simpson: How a Cartoon Masterpiece Defined a Generation*. First edition, Da Capo Press, 2004.

"Two Cars in Every Garage and Three Eyes on Every Fish." *The Simpsons: The Complete Second Season*. Written by Sam Simon and John Swartzwelder, directed by Wes Archer, 20th Century–Fox, 1990.

"Two Dozen and One Greyhounds." *The Simpsons: The Complete Sixth Season*. Written by Mike Scully, directed by Bob Anderson. 20th Century–Fox, 1995.

"Whacking Day." *The Simpsons: The Complete Fourth Season*. Written by John Swartzwelder, directed by Jeffrey Lynch. 20th Century–Fox, 1993.

"When You Dish Upon a Star." *The Simpsons: The Complete Tenth Season*. Written by Richard Appel, directed by Pete Michels. 20th Century–Fox, 1998.

"White Christmas Blues." *The Simpsons*. Written by Don Payne, directed by Steven Dean Moore. 20th Century–Fox, 2013.

"Who Shot Mr. Burns? (Part One)." *The Simpsons: The Complete Sixth Season*. Written by Bill Oakley and Josh Weinstein, directed by Jeffrey Lynch, 20th Century–Fox, 1995.

"Who Shot Mr. Burns? (Part Two)." *The Simpsons: The Complete Seventh Season*. Written by Bill Oakley and Josh Weinstein, directed by Wes Archer, 20th Century–Fox, 1995.

Wieners, Brad, and David Hasemyer. "How Fossil Fuel Allies are Tearing Apart Ohio's Embrace of Clean Energy." *Inside Climate News*, 29 Oct. 2017, https://insideclimate-news.org/news/29102017/renewable-energy-ohio-rps-law-fossil-fuel-political-donations-coal. Accessed 31 Dec. 2017.

Wood, Andrew and Anne Marie Todd. "'Are We There Yet?': Searching for Springfield and The Simpsons' Rhetoric of Omnitopia." *Critical Studies in Media Communication*, vol. 22, no. 3, 2005, pp. 207–222.

Fear of a Yellow Planet

The Eight-Fingered, Cartoon Version of Anxiety

Seth Madej

Marge's luscious hair drops to the linoleum in blue wads of manifested stress from the tension of keeping her household up to standards ["Simpson-scalifragilisticexpiala(Annoyed Grunt)cious" 8.13]. Bart stalks the midnight streets of Springfield, unhinged from angst for the fate of his eternal soul ("Bart Sells His Soul" 7.4). Lisa's irrational terror of the cemetery outside her window drives her from her bed night after sleepless night ("The Girl Who Slept Too Little" 17.2). Homer's worry-ridden doubt about whether he's found his true soul mate invokes a sexy-voiced space coyote ("El Viaje Misterioso de Nuestro Jomer" 8.9). Man, the Simpsons are one anxious family.

As they should be. Because the Simpsons are just a yellower version of us, and we are all anxious. The International Consortium in Psychiatric Epidemiology estimates that one in four Americans will at some point in their lives suffer from a recognized anxiety disorder, whether generalized anxiety, a specific phobia, panic attacks, or anxiety-related maladies like PTSD and obsessive-compulsive disorder (Koocher, et al 4). That's over seventy-five million people, not including the millions more who will never even realize that they have a problem with anxiety. For many men, women, and children, the regularity and ubiquity of their anxiety inflates it into an enveloping white noise, a constant background presence so completely permeating their lives that they don't realize it's taken over.

I know because I'm one of those people.

I spent thirty years with undiagnosed obsessive-compulsive disorder, one of the most insidious and debilitating anxiety-related disorders. Hidden anxiety took control of my life, a parasite multiplying and reproducing itself inside my brain, until it eventually exploded into a mental breakdown so frightening that at the time I didn't have the capacity to understand it. After putting my life back together through medication and months of intense therapy, I stepped out from under a suffocating blanket of anxiety like a paroled prisoner who never knew he was jailed.

During the decades I endured my unchecked OCD, my anxieties seemed so personal and individual that I believed other people couldn't understand them, that no one else could know what I was going through. So I suffered them alone. The year after my treatment, in 2011, I decided that I didn't want other people to live with the same mistake, so I wrote about my experience in an online essay called "My OCD" (Madej). Since then, I've been contacted repeatedly by readers all telling me the same thing: they now believe other people *can* understand their anxieties. That someone else *does* know what they're going through. That they don't have to suffer alone.

See, anxiety's most powerful secret, the one it relies on no one figuring out, is that it's universal. No matter how unique and peculiar and ungraspable your anxieties might seem, millions of other people experience them identically. Once an anxiety sufferer understands that other people have faced and managed the same fears, suddenly their anxiety becomes a lot less scary. It loses its power and begins to disappear. In fact, a very effective early treatment for OCD—the one that finally made me able to conquer my own—is reading about the experiences of others who suffered through the same fears and worries. The upper hand you need to defeat anxiety is simply understanding that it's as common and innately human as sadness, or heartburn, or thigh pimples. And the Simpsons prove it.

If Homer, Marge, Bart, and Lisa's anxieties all seem a little familiar to you, it's because they're familiar to everybody.[1] And if we recognize that the Simpsons' anxieties are just eight-fingered versions of ours, we can use those eight fingers to get a grip on the throat of our own anxieties and choke them until their eyes bulge out. Metaphorically.

But before one starts viciously choking something, it's generally prudent to know what one's viciously choking. So what is anxiety, exactly? I could quote a clinical definition, but the clinical definitions tend to be imprecise and contradictory, and I can be imprecise and contradictory on my own. Besides, we're not in a clinic. (If you've been given this essay by a clinic, please put it down and go find another clinic.) We need an understanding of anxiety that describes not only what we experience in everyday life, but also describes something that can be helped by watching cartoon people.

Anxiety resembles worry, but it's not quite worry: when you're caught in gridlock because Arnie Pye's traffic helicopter crashed on the freeway, you might worry that you'll be late for work, but that's not really anxiety ("Homer the Great" 6.12). Anxiety also resembles fear, but it's not quite fear: when, in

"Mountain of Madness" (8.12), Homer speeds toward destruction in a propane-fueled log cabin, he prays for God to "protect this rocket house and all who dwell within this rocket house" out of pure terror, not out of anxiety. And anxiety resembles dread, but it's not quite dread: in "The Secret War of Lisa Simpson" (8.25), Lisa's apprehension at her impending mandatory rope crawl over an acre of old-growth thorn bushes at Rommelwood Military School sure doesn't seem like anxiety to me.

Apprehension at a skill test so unpleasant it's been banned by the state supreme court, worry at traffic making you late, and fear of being smashed to goo on the slopes of Mt. Useful all share an important trait: they're all entirely sensible. That differentiates them from the type of anxiety that we're concerned with. Worry, fear, or dread become truly pernicious, and become what we're discussing when they become irrational.

Irrational anxiety, as important and necessary as it seems at the moment we're feeling it, has no relationship to reality. It's mental nonsense disguised as sagacity. It's what anxiety disorder sufferers fight against, but it's familiar to all human beings: the internal lead nugget of unease that forces an introvert to flee the office Christmas party; the mental anguish that pours out as cold sweat over a nervous flyer as she takes her seat on a plane; the cloud of impending doom that clogs the mind of a news junkie when a frightening story scrolls across the CNN ticker. Irrational anxiety eats away at a healthy life. It's evil and awful, but always pointless and ultimately beatable, and it's what we're here to talk about.

So let's define anxiety as the irrational and unwanted chimera of fear, worry, and dread that overtakes one's brain from a specific stimulus. Those stimuli are seemingly endless, so we'll focus on three of the most common: social anxiety, phobias, and fear of catastrophe.[2]

Social Anxiety

Maybe the most pervasive form of anxiety—certainly the most relatable—is social anxiety. From nervousness before making phone calls to unease at meeting strangers to fear of public speaking, we've all had a moment when we've wanted to run away and hide from others. If there's someone out there who's never had one of those moments, that's the person the rest of us are running away and hiding from.

Though the varieties of social anxiety have different specifics, they all boil down to a fear of rejection: What if I bore the audience? What if the person on the other end of the line doesn't want to talk? What if that stranger laughs at me? And fear of rejection viewed from the butt end is nothing but a desire to be accepted. So let's address that familiar angst: the anxiety that you won't be liked by the people whom you want to like you.

Lisa Simpson might feel like she has nothing in common with her mother, but they both share a keen anxiety of acceptance.[3] Marge experiences it acutely when she meets the country-club women in "Scenes from the Class Struggle in Springfield" (7.14), and Lisa endures a similar anxiety when she meets the cool kids of Little Pwagmattasquarmsettport in "Summer of 4 Ft. 2" (7.25). Marge's troubles begin in the form of a usually unobtainable $2,800 Chanel suit she finds discounted to $90. The sight of her in the dress wins her an invitation to the Springfield Country Club, where the high life and the witty repartee of the town's upper-crust wives enchant her. But the suit that got Marge in the door is the only SCC-worthy outfit she owns, and she worries that if the ladies see her in it over and over they'll sniff her out as low class.[4] She alters her new suit repeatedly, trying to make it unrecognizable for each visit. When the dress meets a violent end in a runaway sewing machine the night before an all-important club party, Marge's anxiety erupts into a full-blown freak-out, causing her to desperately and secretly drop three grand for a new frock. Even wrapped in the tranquilizing dress, Marge's anxiety about being accepted bulldozes her family, as she frets aloud that the other Simpsons' behavior, appearance, and odor will be enough to get her shunned for good. Only when she sees the hurt her anxiety-induced shame causes Homer does Marge reach a tipping point and realize that her ambition to be someone better has turned her into someone worse.

Lisa's strikingly similar story demonstrates the universality of anxiety. Unpopular at home, Lisa uses a summer vacation to a beach town as an opportunity to shed her nerd life and reinvent herself as a cool kid. Clad in the nineties second-grade equivalent of a Chanel suit (sideways ball cap, cut-off jeans, and a tie-dyed shirt), Lisa ingratiates herself with the townie slackers, who take to her immediately. Lisa has new friends, but she also has a new anxiety: she worries that at any moment her bookish true self will slip out, leading to exile. When Bart tries to horn in on Lisa's new troupe, just like her mom, Lisa lets her worry about being accepted turn her against her family, and she humiliates her brother to protect her reputation. Bart, hurt and jealous, shows the beach gang Lisa's school yearbook and the irrefutable documentation of her geekiness therein. A devastated Lisa, furious at her brother, worries that her last and only chance at friendship has been ruined. It hasn't, of course—her new friends return to her, proving the irrationality of her anxiety by explaining to Lisa that her newly revealed nerdiness doesn't change any of the things that make them like her.

Both Marge's and Lisa's stress blooms from the worry that their new social group won't accept them for who they are, and they both exacerbate their anxiety with the same mistake: trying to be someone they're not. Marge's Chanel suit serves as a perfect physical manifestation of the mistake of manipulating one's personality. Afraid that the original version isn't good enough to last, she changes it and changes it, making it less sustainable with every stitch she pulls and resews, before it finally self-destructs, leaving her worse off than when she started.

"Be yourself" sounds like a meaningless platitude, but it's a viable and necessary first step to defeating social anxiety. Being yourself makes you more able to resist anxiety by freeing up mental space. To grasp how, it's helpful to understand how anxiety works in your mind.

Imagine your brain as a room. A room with a party going on, crowded with normal, healthy thoughts like Confidence and Wit and the Square Root of Nine. The normal, healthy thoughts (NHTs) mingle and laugh and toss their heads back alluringly, having a lovely time. Then anxiety shows up. In the form of, oh, let's say Comic Book Guy. Naked. No one invited him. Just the sight of his stubbly doughflesh immediately drives a couple of NHTs to the exit. But the moment they open the door, *another* naked Comic Book Guy rushes in. He rubs up against a sultry NHT in an evening gown, who gags and flees, followed by the NHT who has to give her a ride home. They let in more naked CBGs on their way out. As more and more CBGs flow in, more NHTs vacate, admitting more CBGs each time, until all that's left is a cramped and roiling mob of slippery, musky CBGS, eating hummus with their fingers.

That's how anxiety works in your brain. It scares off or overpowers your normal, rational mental processes, gaining strength as it does so, taking over mental space, and making it harder and harder to think normally.

Now imagine that going on while you're also pretending to be someone you're not. At the party with the NHTs are a bunch of other NHTs who are wearing masks disguising themselves as Taylor Swift and Tom Hiddleston. The masquerading Taylors and Toms fidget and act nervous, making up stories about what's in the back seat of Jeremy Renner's Audi. They creep out the normal NHTs, who start to beat feet, of course letting in some naked CBGs on the way out. With space in the room already taken up by the fakers and CBGs pouring in, NHTs are crowded out of the party extra quickly. In just a fraction of the normal time, your brain has turned into a freak show of babbling fakers and CBGs trying to score with them.

The point here is that trying to modify your personality wastes mental space, breeds anxiety, and makes it harder to function normally. Even just thinking about your behavior pulls your mind away from your normal thought patterns and makes you worry. Wondering if you're saying the right things, fretting about if you're smiling too much or not enough—those cause a little bit of anxiety. That anxiety in turn makes it harder to behave normally, which in turn makes you think about how you're behaving, which in turn causes anxiety. Repeat.

Simply being yourself shuts down that loop. You don't have to think about how you're behaving if you're simply behaving. You don't have to worry about the person you're being if you're just being. Freeing up that mental energy not only reduces anxiety but also allows you to be more present, more attentive to the people around you, and more relaxed. All of which come with the perk of making you more likable.

Not that you can judge how much anyone likes you, nor should you. That's the second mistake Lisa and Marge make: assuming they can read other people's minds. So much of our social anxiety comes from believing we know what others think about us. When Marge finally turns her back on the country club, she does it believing that the wives don't truly want her to be part of her group. After Bart reveals Lisa's past to the cool kids, she's so certain they hate her that she's prepared to abandon Little Pwagmattasquarm-settport without ever seeing them again.   We're all guilty of mindreading,[5] despite one of the few certainties in life being that we can never know what someone else is truly thinking, even if they tell us. Trying to divine what other people feel about us is the definition of futile, but mindreading combined with irrational anxiety is particularly self-destructive. That's because anxiety has the superpower of irrationality. Irrationality can't be reasoned with, won't answer to logic, and will bend every piece of evidence against it to prove its own conclusion. So if the idea causing your irrational anxiety is "Ralph doesn't like me," any anxiety-driven mindreading of Ralph you do will always eventually be warped by the super strength of irrationality back to "Ralph doesn't like me," e.g.: "Ralph said he choo-choo-chooses me? Oh, that's just until he finds someone better." Which will, by the way, cause you more anxiety, which will make you try to read Ralph's mind some more. Repeat.

Simply accepting that you can't know someone else's opinion of you isn't easy, but doing so helps significantly reduce anxiety. Remember that both Marge and Lisa are proven wrong about what their friends think of them. The beach kids manage to express their friendship to Lisa before she rides away believing she's unloved. Marge isn't so lucky—she unwittingly walks away from her own welcome party. Don't walk away from yours.

Phobias

Phobias are the superstars of anxiety—the archetypical images of innate terror parading down the red carpet past the flashbulbs while more mundane anxieties are shuffled in the side door. We all recognize the white-knuckled airline passenger, the vertiginous tourist clinging to the back wall of the observation deck, the hyperventilator frozen in the corner of a crowded elevator, the weeping rugby fullback hiding under the settee to escape a millipede.[6] We're familiar with phobias because of their ubiquity. Every year as many as nine percent of Americans experience a phobia severe enough to require professional help (*Diagnostic* 199), but let's face it: you've likely never met anyone who doesn't have a little irrational fear of something.

The key word is again "irrational," because phobias deservedly form the public face of irrationality. While phobias exist as the vestiges of hardwired evolutionary necessity—it was useful for early humans roaming the wild to be involuntarily afraid of poisonous snakes and spiders—they have no basis in real-world danger. Phobias are not the result of cogent risk analysis. Claustrophobes don't carefully weigh the dangers of being in an enclosed space and opt to panic. Nor do people with a fear of flying study the statistical data regarding airline safety and choose intestine-twisting terror as the wisest course of action. Phobias are pure gut reaction.

All of the above make phobias a perfect window into the power of irrational anxiety for those who otherwise don't suffer from it. In my experience, most phobia sufferers know their fear is irrational and might even think it's silly, but nonetheless they can't escape it when it kicks in. Similarly, someone with severe social anxiety might, in calm moments, know that her worries are imaginary and pointless and want to take control of them, but when it's time to meet a friend for lunch, she still won't be able to bring herself to walk out her front door and will forget that she'd ever even wanted to.

Phobias, silly or not, can be severely debilitating. In the twenty-first century, the inability to fly amputates the limbs of a complete life. Or consider the retail worker friend of mine who discovered cockroaches in the stockroom, triggering a phobia so severe that on certain days she couldn't bring herself to go to the store and nearly lost her job. Or just look at the Simpsons.

Marge, we learn in "Fear of Flying" (6.11), has just that, so severely that she can't be aboard an airplane for more than a few moments without erupting into panic, racing up and down the aisle screaming, "Lemmeofflemmeofflemmeofflemmeoff!" In "The Girl Who Slept Too Little" (17.2), the relocation of the Springfield Cemetery to alongside the Simpson house[7] instills a phobia so deeply into Lisa that she's unable to sleep in her own bed.

We can learn from Marge and Lisa's phobias.[8] Specifically, we can learn from how they choose to deal with their phobias. More specifically, we can learn from how they choose *not* to deal with their phobias. Both Marge and Lisa respond to their anxieties the way we all do at first: they avoid the thing that's making them afraid. Marge vacates the plane; Lisa sleeps in her parents' bed. It's a natural reaction to fear, but for irrational anxiety, it's also the wrong reaction. Avoiding the source of one's irrational anxiety offers short-term comfort, but in the long term, it makes the anxiety worse.

The darkest period of my OCD circled around intrusive thoughts of self-harm. I developed an irrational anxiety that I would cut off my hand with a meat cleaver. I don't mean I worried about accidentally dismembering myself while butchering a rack of baby-backs; I was legitimately afraid I would spontaneously walk into my kitchen, grab the cleaver from the drawer, and thunk off my second-favorite hand. Yes, that's super freaky and weird, but trust me that it's not even in the fiftieth percentile of weirdness when it comes to the irrational anxieties OCD can manufacture.[9] My initial reaction to that anxiety was, naturally, to avoid using the cleaver. The anxiety didn't abate, though, because whenever I reached into the drawer containing the cleaver, it would stare up at me and make me afraid. The fear began to spread to the other knives in the drawer. So I started avoiding the drawer. But the anxiety didn't abate, because that drawer would stare up at me, teasing me with its knives tucked away. I was afraid I'd open it, so I started avoiding the kitchen. But the anxiety didn't abate, because the gaping maw of the kitchen would laugh at me, teasing me with its drawer with its knives tucked away. Since the strange layout of my apartment required walking through the kitchen to move from the bedroom to the living room, I found myself trapped on the couch, frozen in fear for hours at a time.

Thanks to the superpower of irrationality, anxiety strengthens the more you evade its source. Lisa experiences that consequence when her phobia of the graveyard intensifies and expands the more she seeks refuge in her parents' bedroom. Similarly, no one with a phobia of spiders has ever become less afraid of spiders by avoiding spiders. Ask yourself who'll be more frightened when a hairy black eight-legger crawls out of the shower drain: the arachnophobe who's occasionally dealt with a spider on her leg, or the arachnophobe who's spent her life carefully avoiding everything spider-oriented?

In fact, one the most effective treatments for phobias (and for some other anxiety disorders) centers entirely on confronting one's fear. Exposure therapy is so named because it boils down to exposing the anxiety sufferer to the source of their anxiety. Aviophobes are shown footage of airplane crashes. Agoraphobes are made to leave their homes. In my case, I held a knife in my hand. The exposure happens gradually, in periods of times prescribed by (and sometimes supervised by) a therapist. And it causes the patient massive anxiety. Sweaty, nauseating, painful, terrifying anxiety. Until it doesn't. Because as the amount and frequency of the exposure steadily increases, the anxiety steadily decreases in severity, eventually disappearing entirely. Just as a strange new house eventually becomes a comfy home simply by living inside of it, living with the source of your fear erodes its menacing unfamiliarity until it becomes mundane. It turns out that, while you can't reason away irrational anxiety, you can vaporize it like a vampire in sunlight by exposing it to the hard rays of its own banality. After weeks of exposure therapy, the reaction I had when picking up the knife for my final sessions was deep, intense boredom. My mind had dismantled the anxiety it created, so there was no reason to be scared of a crappy dollar-store knife.

The principles of exposure therapy can help you confront your minor phobias. If you're a nervous flyer, fly more often and don't hide behind a sleep mask, ear plugs, and Ambien; if spiders creep you out, spend a few minutes watching the next one you see rather than immediately squishing it; if you get antsy in elevators, take a couple of extra trips to the top floor and back. But true exposure therapy should never be undertaken without the guidance of a professional. Learn from Lisa, and know your limits. She tries to face her fears by charging into the cemetery at night, but it's too much too soon. Her recklessness leads her not only to endanger herself physically but also to suffer a paroxysm of hallucinatory terror and come perilously close to seeing Chief Wiggum's ball sack. It's a teaching moment: to treat any seriously incapacitating phobia, you should get some help from someone more qualified than a frightened little girl.

Fear of Catastrophe

All sentient lifeforms share an instinctual fear of death, but only we humans have expanded that into a dread of apocalyptic doom.[10] From childhood nervousness about floods or tornadoes, to city dwellers looking over their shoulders for sleeper cells jumping into action, to survivalists heading for the hills anticipating civilization's collapse, we all occasionally worry about things going to shit. It's an anxiety I can't leave out, because it's one I have a special closeness with.

I wasted decades of my life to fear of catastrophe. What started as a kid worrying about flash flood warnings bloomed in fourth grade, during the height of the Eighties Cold War, into a terror of nuclear war. Fueled by undiagnosed OCD, that anxiety became a ceasing backdrop to my thoughts: staring at the hills on the horizon, I'd inevitably picture a mushroom cloud blossoming overtop them. As the world changed and the threat of atomic holocaust waned, my paranoia shifted focus in tune with current events. I began to sift every moment of my life through a terrorism-detection filter, which strained out anything that controverted the immediate and inevitable threat of death by terrorism. Events as inconsequential as the ringing of a stranger's cell phone would kick me over the edge of an anxiety attack: it's a call from someone that a sarin attack is underway across town! Only at age thirty-five, when I learned of and controlled my OCD, did my irrational anxieties finally calm down.

But one doesn't need to have OCD to have fear of catastrophe, as the Simpsons prove. Homer in particular seems susceptible to paranoia. A panic at the Smart Tykes kids' fun center persuades him of the inherent precariousness of civilization in "Homer Goes to Prep School" (24.9), sending him down an obsessive road of survivalist preparation that nearly costs him his home and family. Frankly, pretty much anything can nearly cost Homer his home and family. Even just watching an apocalyptic Christian movie in "Thank God It's Doomsday" (16.19). Seeing *Left Below* convinces him that the Rapture is nigh (admittedly with the aid of a series of unfortunate events, including blood rain from a wounded whale attached to a passing helicopter). He redirects his life to calculating and then prophesying the exact moment of the Rapture, dragging naive townsfolk along with him.[11] Springfield, of course, teems with naive townsfolk ready to be dragged along by anyone's ridiculous doomsday prophecy, having learned nothing from their false certainty that the end times were upon them after unearthing a purported angel skeleton on the site of the new mall in "Lisa the Skeptic" (9.8).

Despite Homer's repeatedly predicting cataclysms, he stubbornly rejects any sensible preparation for objectively likely danger. Gale-force winds practically blow the Simpson family to North Haverbrook by the time Homer decides to take cover from the storm in "Hurricane Neddy" (8.8). Even a giant flaming space rock visibly hurtling toward Springfield in "Bart's Comet" (6.14) isn't enough to convince him to take some precautions.

That's because Homer falls victim to the malady that affects so many victims of disaster anxiety: the inability to judge the irrationality of our worries. Which we can't be blamed for, really, because if we could always tell when we're being irrational, we would never be irrational. We do, however, have a simple method we can employ to take a step back from our anxiety, objectively examine our own thoughts, and get our heads together: talk to someone you trust.

Irrationality uses its superpowers to spin the anxieties in our heads out of control and to build them strong and resilient to any reasonable thoughts we can generate ourselves. But releasing them into the world forces them to fight for themselves. Your anxiety might be the fiercest goldfish in the bowl, but how long will it survive in the ocean? I vividly remember, and will never forget, a session with my therapist during the early period of my OCD treatment. I described to him in detail the dreadful worry I was having. I laid out to him the monstrous, invincible anxiety that was tearing me up inside. I exposed my awful internal reality. Then he said, "Well, I have to tell you: that's really off the wall."

A cloud in my brain lifted. Someone in my cranium turned on the lights. I had a moment of freeing clarity. Because *it had never occurred to me that I was being irrational.* My mind was so twisted in on itself that I couldn't judge my own thoughts, but another rational human being could. And I could believe him because I trusted him. In that moment, I began to understand that anxiety doesn't know what it's talking about. It wasn't my brain being prudent and watchful: it was harmful noise that should be turned off. It was the start of my being able to take control of my fears, and it came from simply opening my mouth.

I can say, without exaggeration, that every time I talk about my anxiety, it lessens. Often the easing happens before the person I'm speaking to even responds. Something in the act of verbalizing my worries, maybe in the mental processes required to shape them into coherent sentences to be communicated, causes me to immediately think about them objectively and to catch that first glimpse of their irrationality.[12]

Sadly, talking about one's fears isn't as simple as it sounds. During my worst stretches of OCD, the pain of trying to open my mouth to tell someone my feelings was nearly as bad as the pain of the anxiety. That's common for anxiety sufferers, and the unease at talking about your feelings often comes from shame, embarrassment, or fear—shame of your anxieties, preemptive embarrassment at the imagined reaction of the person you tell, fear that the person will think you're crazy or be driven away. Which is why it's easier to open up about your anxieties to someone you trust. A spouse, parent, sibling, partner, friend, teacher, coach. Tell them what you're feeling, even if it's just one sentence. "I'm worried about ____." That little bit will help. And if your anxiety is just a natural passing distress about bad things beyond our control, that conversation alone might be enough to stamp it out.

But for some people, it won't be. Whether you have a fear of catastrophe, a phobia, social angst, or any of the other seemingly infinite varietals of anxiety, sometimes the worry just won't go away. If that happens—if your persistent anxiety degrades your quality of life and prevents you from doing the things you want to do or being the person you want to be—it's time to get help. Have absolutely zero shame or embarrassment for wanting to improve your mental health. Just as readily as you'd seek treatment for a chronic stomachache, you should seek treatment for chronic mental pain.

Help is easy to find. The world is full of people who want to give it and are trained to do so. One way to start is by simply telling your primary care physician that you need someone to talk to about anxiety. You can also search for a therapist, psychologist, or psychiatrist online through the Anxiety and Depression Association of America (adaa.org) or the International OCD Foundation (iocdf.org).

Irrational anxiety is not a necessary part of life. It's as simple as that. Don't have a cow, man.

NOTES

1. In fact, because TV writers find ideas in their own lives, each of the Simpson family anxieties is almost certainly rooted in the real-life anxiety of a three-dimensional human.

2. Throughout this essay, I'll use words like "fear," "worry," "dread," and "apprehension"

as synonyms for "anxiety." They're not actually equivalent, but I bought a thesaurus at Chevron, and I want to get my money's worth.

3. Not surprising, since a proclivity for anxiety is known to be hereditary. More surprising is that not a single Simpson child inherited Marge's blue hair. Or for that matter, hair that's not just a monstrous extension of their skull.

4. An unusual concern for Marge, seeing as how she's spent her entire life to that point happily content to wear the same green dress every damn day.

5. The Simpson men included. Bart and Homer both wrongly assume that their mothers have stopped loving them in "Marge Be Not Proud" (7.11) and "Mother Simpson" (7.8) respectively.

6. Archetypical!

7. Frequent cemetery relocation being the scourge of countless municipalities throughout America.

8. We can learn less from Homer's: xylophobia, AKA the fear of xylophones, "The music you hear when skeletons are dancing" ("Coming to Homerica" 20.21).

9. Any enthusiast of the bizarre will enjoy the catalog of psychotic-seeming, OCD-induced absurd obsessions in Jeffrey M. Schwartz and Beverly Beyette's book *Brain Lock.*

10. Prove me wrong, porpoises!

11. The fact that he's later proven right can be safely ignored. Just because you have a fear of platypuses and later a platypus happens to escape from the zoo and sneak into your house and stab you in the eye with its venomous spur while you sleep doesn't mean the rest of us should devote our lives to platypus-proofing our homes.

12. "Hurricane Neddy" (8.8) goes on to help prove the surprising therapeutic power of talking about your feelings. Ned Flanders, during a post-hurricane-breakdown stint in Calmwood Mental Hospital, launches into a rant about hating the negligent service at the post office that unwittingly leads him to the sudden freeing realization that he also hates his negligent parents.

Works Cited

"Bart Sells His Soul." *The Simpsons: The Complete Seventh Season.* Written by Greg Daniels, directed by Wes Archer, 20th Century–Fox, 2005.

"Bart's Comet." *The Simpsons: The Complete Sixth Season.* Written by John Swartzwelder, directed by Bob Anderson, 20th Century–Fox, 1995.

"Coming to Homerica." *The Simpsons: The Complete Twentieth Season.* Written by Brendan Hay, directed by Steven Dean Moore, 20th Century–Fox, 2010.

Diagnostic and Statistical Manual of Mental Disorders. 5th ed., American Psychiatric Association, 2013.

"Fear of Flying." *The Simpsons: The Complete Sixth Season.* Written by David Mirkin, directed by Mark Kirkland, 20th Century–Fox, 2005.

"Find a Therapist Directory." *Anxiety and Depression Association of America,* anxietydepressionassoc.site-ym.com/?page=FATMain. Accessed 20 Dec. 2017.

"The Girl Who Slept Too Little." *The Simpsons: The Complete Seventeenth Season.* Written by John Frink, directed by Raymond S. Persi, 20th Century–Fox, 2014.

"Homer Goes to Prep School." *The Simpsons.* Written by Brian Kelley, directed by Mark Kirkland. 20th Century–Fox, 30 Sept. 2005.

"Homer the Great." *The Simpsons: The Complete Sixth Season.* Written by John Swartzwelder, directed by Jim Reardon, 20th Century–Fox, 2005.

"Hurricane Neddy." *The Simpsons: The Complete Eighth Season.* Written by Steve Young, directed by Bob Anderson, 20th Century–Fox, 2006.

International OCD Foundation. "Find Help." *International OCD Foundation,* iocdf.org/find-help. Accessed 20 Dec. 2017.

Koocher, Gerald P., et al. *Psychologists' Desk Reference.* 2nd ed., Oxford University Press, 2005.

Madej, Seth. "My OCD." *Seth Madej: Humourist Laureate,* 18 Oct. 2011, sethmad.com/my-ocd. Accessed 20 Dec. 2017.

"Marge Be Not Proud." *The Simpsons: The Complete Seventh Season*. Written by Mike Scully, directed by Steven Dean Moore, 20th Century–Fox, 2005.

"Mother Simpson." *The Simpsons: The Complete Seventh Season*. Written by Richard Appel, directed by David Silverman, 20th Century–Fox, 2005.

"Mountain of Madness." *The Simpsons: The Complete Eighth Season*. Written by John Swartzwelder, directed by Mark Kirkland, 20th Century–Fox, 2006.

"Scenes from the Class Struggle in Springfield." *The Simpsons: The Complete Seventh Season*. Written by Jennifer Crittenden, directed by Susie Dietter, 20th Century–Fox, 2005.

Schwartz, Jeffrey M., and Beverly Beyette. *Brain Lock*. HarperPerennial, 1996.

"The Secret War of Lisa Simpson." *The Simpsons: The Complete Eighth Season*. Written by Richard Appel, directed by Mike B. Anderson, 20th Century–Fox, 2006.

"Simpsonscalifragilisticexpiala(Annoyed Grunt)cious." *The Simpsons: The Complete Eighth Season*. Written by Al Jean & Mike Reiss, directed by Chuck Sheetz, 20th Century–Fox, 2006.

"Summer of 4 Ft. 2." *The Simpsons: The Complete Seventh Season*. Written by Dan Greaney, directed by Mark Kirkland, 20th Century–Fox, 2005.

"Thank God It's Doomsday." *The Simpsons: The Complete Sixteenth Season*. Written by Don Payne, directed by Michael Marcantel, 20th Century–Fox, 2013.

"El Viaje Misterioso de Nuestro Jomer." *The Simpsons: The Complete Eighth Season*. Written by Ken Keeler, directed by Jim Reardon, 20th Century–Fox, 2006.

In Search of Another Story

Satire and The Simpsons

DUNCAN REYBURN

"A noble spirit embiggens the smallest man."—Jebediah Springfield, supposedly.

Introduction

In this essay, I want to provide a fresh understanding of how satire functions, especially as we find it in the richly satirical texts of *The Simpsons*. To do this, I offer a way of reading *The Simpsons* through the lens of mimetic realism—a perspective developed by literary theorist, philosopher, and anthropologist René Girard (1923–2015). Before I get to the finer details of how I plan to do this, a brief definition of satire should help to pave the way.

Although satire is a category with porous borders, it may broadly be framed as a genre that presents a critical stance, expressed mostly through humor or ridicule, on issues that have some relevance to society and politics. In his book *On the Discourse of Satire*, Paul Simpson (no relation to Homer) explains satirical texts as "utterances which are inextricably bound up with context of situation, with participants in discourse and with frameworks of knowledge" (Simpson 1). As this indicates, satire is only effective insofar as it reflects what is familiar and understandable (Turner 56).

Moreover, as the above definition also alludes, satire has a profound social function. It has the potential, depending on intention and delivery, to both challenge and reinforce the natural order of societies. *The Simpsons* is an excellent example of this. It is a satire that, to borrow from G. K. Chesterton, may come across as being "mad and anarchic" only because it admits the "superiority of certain things over others" (Chesterton 66). Satire is always unabashedly ethical in its posture towards the world; it "presupposes a standard" or law (Chesterton 66). And it is precisely in its ethical posture that the interplay of challenge and affirmation is located.

It is this interplay that is the focus of this essay, which explores how *The Simpsons*, as one of contemporary culture's most important visual texts, tries to navigate the gap that emerges between what *should be* (the ideal, what we want or hope for) and what *is* (affirmation, the real, what we get). *The Simpsons* is always a text in search of another story, which is to say that it is a text that wants to explore other ways of being and other ways of seeing things. It offers us a critique of ideology that we would do well not to overlook.

The "Couch Gag" as an Interpretive Key

The critique of ideology offered by *The Simpsons* is already hinted at by the presence of those famous couch gags, which appear toward the end of the opening credits of each episode. The setup is always the same, with only minor variations in the form of Bart's blackboard gag and Lisa's saxophone solo. Through a series of intercut scenes, we see each member of the Simpson family frantically making their way home to be in time for their favorite TV show, which happens, somewhat narcissistically, to be a show about them. The conclusion of the opening credits is also without variation: there is a shot of the television screen that the Simpsons are watching—a picture of a screen within our own screens.

Then, sandwiched between setup and conclusion is a brief scene of pure fantasy, usually, but not always, involving the living room couch. The fantasy takes on any number of forms, each of which may be endlessly interpreted. Nevertheless, there seems to be a consistency in the symbolic function of these fantasy scenes, which may be understood in terms of two primary subversions.

The first is the subversion of narrative form. The couch gags are nothing if not incongruous when considered within the context provided by the setup and conclusion of the opening credits. While the setup and conclusion stick largely to a kind of realism, the couch gag usually departs quite drastically from the rules of this form. Of course, the incongruity that results is one reason that we find them funny.

The second subversion is found in the interplay between the couch gag and the shot of the television screen that concludes the opening credits; it challenges what we might think of the role of mediation. While we might expect the represented television to present us with a fiction apart from our reality, symbolically speaking the couch gag shows us something else: the very act of watching television casts the "reality" of the Simpson family into question. Perhaps, as is discussed in more detail below, this has something to say to us about the way that our own existences are mediated and even fictionalized by the fictions we consume.

It is possible to make use of these two subversions, as we find them in the opening credits, as a double-hermeneutic key by which we can interpret the way that satire works in *The Simpsons*.

Mimetic Realism: A Brief Synopsis and Application

I have already said that my aim is to examine *The Simpsons* through the lens of mimetic realism; I want to focus on the way that *The Simpsons* highlights the way that desire is culturally mediated for us. Mimetic realism, also called mimetic theory, begins with a very simple premise, namely that desire is always mediated by the other (Girard 4, 83). It is a lie, too easily believed, that the self gives rise to desire, when the truth is that it is desire (modeled by others) that gives rise to the self (Girard 38). We exist not as individuals but as interdividuals. In other words, we are not autonomous beings separate from our worlds, but people always bound up in the positions, policies, and politesse of other interdividuals. The self is, therefore, not an object isolated from others, but a relation or locus of interconnectivity formed by its own mediated desires.

Among other things, mimetic realism challenges so called object-focused theories of desire. In such theories, objects have an innate desirability. If a person wants a particular computer (say, a Mapple[1]) or a particular status (to be, like Lisa, the top student in the class) object-focused theories of desire would say that it is because those things (Mapples and status) are intrinsically desirable. When closely examined, however, such thinking does seem naïve, given that it excludes the obvious place of mediation.

The primal fact of our interrelatedness, and the way that this interrelatedness revolves around shared desires, is the source of both unity (peace) and conflict (rivalry). Peace is possible when we share desires that pull us toward social harmony, like, say, the shared desire of the Simpson family members to visit Itchy & Scratchy Land (the "violentest place on earth") and have "the best vacation ever"—a vacation that they will, nevertheless, "never speak of" again ("Itchy and Scratchy Land" 6.4).

Conflict, on the other hand, arises when we share desires while simultaneously believing that the object of desire is in limited supply or else that said object should be treated in alternate ways. Conflict tends to arise out of misunderstanding or misperceiving desire as an autonomous thing: it is the result of forgetting that friends and enemies both exist as the result of shared desires.

This may seem simplistic at first, but mimetic theory's insights into human relationships, as well as their seesawing between unity to disunity, are as profound as they are multifaceted. In this perspective, only two categories of relating are possible, namely the absence of mimesis (perpetuated by indifference or ignorance), or the presence of mimesis (interdividuality and interrelatedness). In terms of the presence of mimesis, there are three possibilities: the mimesis of the model, the mimesis of the rival, and the mimesis of the obstacle (Oughourlian 118).

While there are too many applications to this simple idea to name here, it suggests a starting point for the analysis of any text: when it comes to better understanding the function of desire in a text, especially in a satirical text, we need to keep a lookout for dyads or doubles; that is, we need to get a sense of the role of mirror images or reflections, no matter how distorted they may seem. *The Simpsons* is a profound example of a text replete with doubles, although not all of them are mimetic doubles.

Harmonious relationships are plentiful: Bart and Milhouse, Smithers and Mr. Burns, Lenny and Carl, Selma and Patty, Homer and Marge, Homer and Apu, and a number of others represent a pervasive harmony, although relationships like these are not without their conflicts. Relationships predominantly built on mimetic rivalry include those between Homer and Flanders, Bart and Nelson, Bart and Jimbo (especially when they share a desire for Bart's babysitter Laura in "New Kid on the Block" 4.8), and a number of others. However, the precise status of such relationships is also permanently under negotiation. Then, finally, relationships where the mimetic double takes the form of an obstacle—a more extreme version of a mimetic rival— are also discernable. Perhaps the most obvious example of this is the relationship between Bart and Sideshow Bob: these two have a shared desire for Bart's life, but Sideshow Bob would like that life to be over, whereas Bart has a rather strong desire to keep that life going. Here, the desire is for the same object (Bart's life) but the use of that desire differs depending on the desiring subject.

More concrete case studies of each of these mimetic relationships are, however, not the primary aim of this essay. Satire is. And it is significant that satire offers itself as a double, that is, as a mimetic double of the reality of the (especially American) socio-political sphere. It sets itself up as a mirror of what is happening in that sphere, while at the same time criticizing it. This means that satire itself can be thought of as a model, rival, or even obstacle, in terms of the way that it mediates desire. *The Simpsons*, I would say, may be understood as an example of the first two; it is both a model (a mediator of desires) and rival (a challenger of those very same mediated desires).

With this in mind, we can see that (a) satire navigates the gap between what should be and what is by questioning the way that we desire. By examining this gap, the success or failure of a satirical text can therefore be better understood. Every satirical text exposes the overt tension that exists between the real and the ideal; that is, between (b) the way we should desire and (c) the way we do desire. It therefore has the potential to suggest (d) a direction or orientation according to which we might desire (See Table 1 below). This direction (d) can be thought of as the resolution, in the mind of the audience, of the tensions or even hypocrisies that exist between (b) and (c).

Table. The Satirical Text as a Mimetic Double of Reality

(a) The satirical text negotiates the tension between	
(b) the way we should desire	(c) and the way we do desire
to suggest a direction (d) according to which we might desire	

It needs to be said, though, that this tension between (b), the way we should desire, and (c), the way we do desire, produces a slightly ambiguous (d), direction of desire. The precise manner in which we might interpret (d) the direction of desire may differ from person to person, depending on how they read the visual text in question. This needs to be kept in mind as we turn to examine the two subversions that are hinted at by the couch gag in *The Simpsons*.

Below, I suggest that each of these subversions, which can be discerned throughout the canon of the world of *The Simpsons*, tends to lean on one of the two types of desire noted above, namely (b), the way we should desire, and (c), the way we do desire. I begin with the latter, as it is found in the way that *The Simpsons* challenges narrative form, before moving to the former, which is evident in the way that *The Simpsons* questions the role of mediation in contemporary (visual) culture.

Subversion 1: Challenging Narrative Form

Above, I noted that the couch gag in *The Simpsons* undermines an expected narrative form by sandwiching a scene of pure fantasy into a fairly predictable world—a world that mirrors the laws and conditions of our present reality. Although this stark contrast between reality and fantasy is not generally present during most of its episodes,[2] the basic idea of subverting narrative form is very evident in the world of *The Simpsons*.

This is clearest in the way that *The Simpsons* works with a floating time-line. A floating timeline is a plot device used to explain or explain away inconsistencies in the way that events and characters exist within a world. In *The Simpsons,* the characters never age. Therefore, a number of inconsistencies are evident in the way that memories function for the characters. One famous example of this is found in the discrepancy between two episodes—"I Married Marge" (3.12) and "That '90s Show" (9.11). In the former, a flashback shows us that Homer and Marge conceived Bart in 1980 after watching *The Empire Strikes Back* at a movie theater. In the latter, Marge and Homer are at an earlier stage in their relationship, before conceiving Bart, and yet this is set in the 1990s. Despite this discrepancy, the age of the characters remains the same in the "present."

For the entire duration of *The Simpsons*, time does not seem to move on, and this means that, by and large, things do not really change. This subverts the typical purpose of narrative, which is to create a narrative arc in which characters grow and circumstances change. Because *The Simpsons* takes place in the perpetual present, the people who create *The Simpsons* have forced themselves into a loop that they must ultimately return to. They thus affirm the present, which equates to a symbolic affirmation of the way things are or the status quo. Of course, there are exceptions. For instance, when Maude Flanders dies, she really does stay dead ("Alone Again, Natura-Diddily" 11.14), and when Apu Nahasapeemapetilon gets married, he remains married afterwards ("The Two Mrs. Nahasapeemapetilons" 9.7).

Nevertheless, in the presence of this floating timeline and because of this insistence upon a perpetual present, things must by and large remain the same in world of *The Simpsons*. This means that, for the most part, it is possible to watch any episode of *The Simpsons* in any order without necessarily feeling any sense of dislocation or confusion.

A good example of how radical change is negated in *The Simpsons* is found in the episode "Lisa the Iconoclast" (7.16). During this episode, Springfield's history is revisited, and we discover that the citizens of Springfield are very proud of their founder, Jebediah Springfield, who is said to have been a noble man. Lisa, however, uncovers some rather damning evidence against Jebediah Springfield through her research. She discovers, for instance, that he did not tame the buffalo that he was said to have tamed, but rather mercilessly killed a buffalo that had already been tamed. Moreover, he was not a noble man, but a ruthless pirate named Hans Sprungfeld.

In the end, though, when Lisa has a chance to reveal the truth about Jebediah Springfield, she decides not to. The people of Springfield like this mythical man, and if she shatters their illusion, she risks destroying an ideal that might be emulated for the good. So in the end, the truth remains hidden because Lisa felt that a beautiful lie was preferable to an ugly reality.

There is something cynical in this conclusion, and indeed there seems to be something cynical in the way that *The Simpsons*, by virtue of its own permanent present-tense narratives, appears to oppose change. This hints at the idea that "ideology's dominant mode of functioning is cynical" (Žižek *Sublime* 25). Perhaps this saccharine cynicism in Lisa is proof enough of this. This cynicism does not function to disarm myth or unmask delusion, but rather functions precisely to cover it up. It is a kind of "enlightened self-consciousness" since "one knows the falsehood very well"—as Lisa does—and "is aware of a particular interest hidden behind an ideological universality, but one still does not renounce it" (Žižek *Sublime* 26).

This cynicism functions in much the same way as irony might function. It knows the truth very well, and yet it still affirms the lie. What Lisa's actions show is that this cynicism, which elects a pleasant fiction over a harsh set of facts, is a self-sustaining and self-congratulating phenomenon. Perhaps problematic systems are sustained by the very cynicisms and satires that they produce.

Cynicism creates a kind of ironic distance. As in satire, we can mock the systems that surround us, but we need to ask whether our mockery might be the very thing that prevents any genuine changes from taking place. The problem is that while knowledge changes, desire does not, and ultimately it is desire that would be the greater source of change. This is something that we find represented in many different *Simpsons'* episodes. Two episodes in which Marge Simpson tries to find another story and thus transcend her circumstances are particularly emblematic of this. In "Scenes from the Class Struggle in Springfield" (7.14), for instance, we find Marge trying to climb the social ladder by creatively using a cheaply bought Chanel suit as a sign of wealth. However, by the end of the episode, everything is back to normal. She has given up her dream of being one of the rich in favor of more humdrum, bourgeois concerns.

In "Marge on the Lam" (5.6), a parody of Ridley Scott's film *Thelma and Louise* (1991), Marge befriends her divorced neighbor, Ruth Powers. Toward the end of the episode, Marge and Ruth are being chased toward a cliff by the police just as Thelma and Louise were. However, whereas Thelma and Louise meet a definitive end when they drive their car off a cliff's edge, Marge and Ruth stop just in time. The same, however, cannot be said for Chief Wiggum, who has Homer in the car with him. Wiggum and Homer do not stop in time and sail over the cliff. Luckily, they land safely on a pile of garbage—a profound symbol of the problems with law enforcement's frequent incompetence if ever there was one.

Countless other examples could be named, but the point remains the same. *The Simpsons* is filled with challenges to narrative form, as various characters search for another story. However, such challenges ultimately still seem to pull toward a cynical acceptance of the way things are. The way we do desire (c) trumps the way we should desire (b) what is remains what is. *The Simpsons* points satirically to a number of the flaws and problems in contemporary Western capitalist culture, but, as is evident in almost every show, clever critique alone seems to not be sufficient for promoting change. A deeper subversion is needed for such a thing.

Subversion 2: Questioning the Role of Mediation in (Visual) Culture

Such a subversion has already been named. In the opening credits, we find the Simpson family sitting in front of a television screen. In the process, or so it seems, the family is converted or transported into a fantasy. What is mediated, then, is not just the content of the screen but the way that the viewers (the Simpsons, us) perceive reality.

The symbolic value of this scene is found in the way it questions the role of mediation in (visual) culture. Typically, we are likely to think of fiction as something that results from and is in some sense parasitic upon reality. But this simple interlude presents an alternate possibility. Perhaps, in the end, there is no real distance between fiction and reality. In fact, it is possible to argue that fiction itself may be what gives reality its sense of structure and order; perhaps fiction makes reality as much as reality makes fiction (Žižek *Tarrying* 88).

As outlandish as this idea may first seem, a second glance reveals its sense. Fiction, like *The Simpsons* shows, provides us with ways to make sense of the world. It turns out that stories are "equipment for living"—they participate in a feedback loop that helps us to navigate reality (McKee 11). In terms of the focus of this essay, what is particularly important is the way that fictions, as mimetic doubles, model desires for us, and it this mediation of desire that *The Simpsons* does particularly well because it is a text rooted in very strong ethical values.

In "Radio Bart" (3.13), we get a particularly profound taste of this. In this episode, Bart makes use of a microphone to transmit sound through an AM radio, which he has thrown down a well. Seeing this mistake as an opportunity to play a prank, Bart cries for help and so ends up convincing first Groundskeeper Willie and then the whole of Springfield that a kid named Timmy O'Toole has fallen down the well. Because the well is too narrow, none of the city's overweight police officers are able to fit inside it to rescue "Timmy." A rope sent down the well does not help either because, as "Timmy" explains, his foot is caught under a rock.

This scenario parodies the story of a real-life toddler Jessica McClure (no relation to Troy), who, in 1987, was trapped in a well for almost sixty hours. She was rescued and treated like a hero. This heroic status is mirrored and thus questioned in "Radio Bart," when at one point, in the wake of Timmy

O'Toole's new celebrity status, Lisa and Homer start to discuss precisely what it is that makes someone a hero.

> **Homer:** That Timmy is a real hero!
> **Lisa:** How do you mean, dad?
> **Homer:** Well, he fell down a well, and … he can't get out.
> **Lisa:** How does that make him a hero?
> **Homer (not sure how to respond):** Well, that's more than you did!

In this episode, then, we have a clear example of a fiction, created by Bart, having a real impact on the way that the people of Springfield experience their city and even discuss issues. But of course, this is a fiction we are watching. And while watching this, we are confronted with the way that fictions have structured our own reality—the way, for instance, that sentiment might be conjured by a telling news story (like the story of Jessica McClure), or the way that truth might get subsumed into the machinations of consumerist opportunists (as the fate of "Timmy O'Toole" does). It is here, in this second subversion, that satire has its real power. It is a fictional text that tests the way that we, its audience, experience the world. It feeds our own mass-mediated mimetic desires back at us and asks us to wake up.

This is particularly evident in this same story. Soon, Bart comes to the horrible realization that at some point he will be found out because he has forgotten that he used his new label maker to print his name on the side of the radio that is now stuck at the bottom of the well. While trying to retrieve the radio, officers Lou and Eddie unintentionally untie the rope that he is climbing down. Bart soon explains to Lou and Eddie that it was all a prank and admits that Timmy does not exist. This news gets out, and the city's people, furious for having been deceived, simply refuse to rescue Bart.

This is a powerful commentary on the way that fiction shapes our reality. "Radio Bart" shows us how today the fictions that we embrace can often become more important to us than truly problematic realities. Whereas the people of Springfield would rescue a certain "Timmy O'Toole" because he conforms to their own (flimsy) idea of a hero, they will not save Bart, who is real, albeit it very flawed.

When, finally, Bart cries out in despair, Homer refuses to let his boy suffer any longer. He decides to dig a tunnel and rescue Bart himself. This powerful display of desire (a copy of Bart's desire to live a full life) triggers a powerful mimetic reaction. Groundskeeper Willie is the first to join Homer, and they are then soon followed by the musician Sting and a number of Springfield residents.

Thus, the ultimate subversion of mediation is found in a new way of mediating desires. This is one of the things that *The Simpsons* does best. Despite showing us all the ways that its characters return to a problematic status quo and thus fail to find another story, it powerfully resonates with those core values that return us to our own humanity. In particular, *The Simpsons* tries to consistently model the ways that love might overcome a multitude of private and public errors. This is not a sentimental love, mind you, but a fierce love that remains committed (like Homer to Bart) even in the face of relational tensions (like the tension that exists between Homer and Bart). It is a love that sees the mimetic rivalry that threatens every relationship and yet elects to seek what is good even for the rival other.

It is debatable whether this challenge to our mediated desires will ultimately be enough to effect a change in us, especially with regard to dislodging us from the pedestal of cynical reason that we might more comfortably observe the world from. Nevertheless, the challenge is there, in plain sight. *The Simpsons* remains a satirical text in search of another story, and as such, it is a text that calls into question our story as we perceive and live it. In addition to being many other things, it is certainly a much needed critique of ideology, which navigates the difficult tension between what is and what could be, what we do desire and what we should desire, and poses a simple question to its audience: is this the way you want things to be? Moreover, it asks us whether, in the end, we will land up on the side of cynical reason, or on the side of questioning the role of mediation. Even while the former is certainly part of its horizon of vision, I hope that it is not too much to suggest that *The Simpsons* seems to be on the side of the latter.

NOTES

1. This first appeared in "MyPods and Boomsticks" (20.7).
2. Exceptions found predominantly in *Treehouse of Horror* episodes.

WORKS CITED

"Alone Again, Natura-Diddily." *The Simpsons: The Complete Eleventh Season.* Written by Ian Maxtone-Graham, directed by Jim Reardon, 20th Century–Fox, 2000.

Chesterton, G. K. *Orthodoxy.* Moody, 2009.

Girard, René. *Deceit, Desire and the Novel: Self and Other in Literary Structure.* Trans. Yvonne Freccero. Johns Hopkins, 1965.

"I Married Marge." *The Simpsons: The Complete Third Season.* Written by Jeff Martin, directed by Jeffrey Lynch, 20th Century–Fox, 1991.

"Itchy and Scratchy Land." *The Simpsons: The Complete Sixth Season.* Written by John Swartzwelder, directed by Wes Archer, 20th Century–Fox, 1994.

"Lisa the Iconoclast." *The Simpsons: The Complete Seventh Season.* Written by Jonathan Collier, directed by Mike B. Anderson, 20th Century–Fox, 1996.

"Marge on the Lam." *The Simpsons: The Complete Fifth Season.* Written by Bill Canterbury, directed by Mark Kirkland, 20th Century–Fox, 1993.

McKee, Robert. *Story.* Reagan, 1997.

"New Kid on the Block." *The Simpsons: The Complete Fourth Season.* Written by Conan O'Brien, directed by Wes Archer, 20th Century–Fox, 1992.

"MyPods and Boomsticks." *The Simpsons.* Written by Marc Wilmore, directed by Steven Dean Moore, 20th Century–Fox, 30 November 2008.

Ott, Brian L. *The Small Screen: How Television Equips Us to Live in the Information Age.* Blackwell, 2007.

Oughourlian, J-M. *The Genesis of Desire.* Trans. Eugene Webb. Michigan State University, 2010.

"Radio Bart." *The Simpsons: The Complete Third Season.* Written by Jon Vitti, directed by Carlos Baeza, 20th Century–Fox, 1992.

Simpson, Paul. *On the Discourse of Satire: Towards a Stylistic Model of Satirical Humour.* John Benjamins, 2003.

"That '90s Show." *The Simpsons.* Written by Matt Selman, directed by Mark Kirkland, 20th Century–Fox, 27 January 2008.

"The Two Mrs. Nahasapeemapetilons." *The Simpsons: The Complete Ninth Season.* Written by Richard Appel, directed by Steven Dean Moore, 20th Century–Fox, 1997.

Turner, Chris. *Planet Simpson.* Ebury, 2004.

Žižek, Slavoj. *The Sublime Object of Ideology.* Verso, 2008.

_____. *Tarrying with the Negative.* Duke University, 1993.

"It's not selling out; it's co-branding!"

Watching and Consuming
The Simpsons *in a Digital Age*

TYLER SHORES

Introduction

More than perhaps any other television show in history, *The Simpsons* has always had a distinctive awareness of its place within popular culture, as well as a self-awareness of its (sometimes) complex relationship to its fans. To be clear, there are *Simpsons* fans, and there are *Simpsons Fans*. Recently, when a new Guinness World Record for longest continuous television viewing (86 hours and 37 minutes!) was set, it seemed only fitting that it involved 86 hours and 37 consecutive minutes of *Simpsons* episodes.[1]

There's something *different* about the kind of relationship that *Simpsons* fans have had with a show whose existence now spans parts of four different decades. The show has also led to a fan culture that has undergone a very significant shift in the ways in which its media consumption habits have evolved, thanks to the preponderance of digital and online content and ever-increasing ubiquity of screens and entertainment media in everyday life. This essay will talk about that shift from a television medium to divergent forms of digital media, and how we can now think of *The Simpsons* both as a show and yet something more than just a show—and also just how such shifts enable to us to consume, talk about, and appreciate *The Simpsons* in very different ways.

The Simpsons *in the 21st Century: "It's not selling out; it's co-branding. Co-branding!"*

To best appreciate just how far *The Simpsons* and *Simpsons* fans have come, let's work our way backwards. On May 15, 2016, during the last three minutes of "Simprovised" (27.21), *The Simpsons* made animation history by performing the first ever live animation broadcast. With the help of motion capture technology, Dan Castellaneta was able to respond to live phone calls from fans and viewers (screened ahead of time through *The Simpsons* Twitter feed). The segment garnered a great deal of popular attention—either praised for a novel use of technology or panned as another gimmicky grab for ratings—depending on whom you might have asked. Most critics did at the very least credit the longest-running animated show and longest-running sitcom with bringing new experimentation to a genre of television that it helped to redefine decades earlier.

The most recent seasons of *The Simpsons* have seen a number of interesting experiments—including crossovers such as "The Simpsons Guy" (a forty-five-minute crossover that was technically a *Family Guy* episode for the debut of that show's thirteenth season), as well as a long-awaited *Futurama* crossover ("Simpsorama" [26.6]) in the twenty-sixth season. Some of the abovementioned efforts have been better received than others. One of the best of these outside-the-box efforts was the "Brick Like Me" episode (25.20). The visually engaging episode parallels several elements from the 2014 *LEGO Movie*, including a side helping of existential dread from Homer in brick form and a classic Homer and Lisa father-daughter plot. Homer has created a fantasy LEGO world ("Little Springfield"), where nothing changes, "everything fits together, and no one ever gets hurt." It actually sounds kind of nice when you first think about it. Then, as the realization slowly dawns on him:

> I've created a perfect world with no PG-13 movies to take you away from me. 'Cause in a toy town, everything stays shiny and wonderful, just the way I want it. You'll always be my little girl. Maggie will always be my giant baby. Bart will never move out of the house. I'll work for Mr. Burns forever. Marge and I will never grow old together and live like fat cats on Social Security. Good Lord, I'll never experience the ultimate reward for a life well lived—the gentle slumber of death. Marge, I made a terrible mistake! The fact that kids grow up is what makes time with them special. I think I need to go back.

Embedded within this thinly-veiled *LEGO Movie* takeoff is a sort of open question about the nature of *The Simpsons* itself. Fans have often talked nostalgically about the "Golden Age of *The Simpsons*,"[2] but much like Homer's fictional Simpsons LEGO universe within *The Simpsons'* own animated universe, nostalgia is a poor substitute for reality. It is a nice fantasy to desire everything to stay exactly the same as we fondly remember (or more likely, misremember) it being—perhaps some kind of perennial 1992 or 1993, a tumultuous time for our nation: when the clear beverage craze gave us all a reason to live. The information superhighway showed the average person what some nerd thinks about *Star Trek*. The domestication of the dog continued unabated, and we can't wait for the next classic episode to take its place alongside "Homer the Heretic" (4.3) or "Last Exit to Springfield" (4.17). Perhaps in this way, we have a version of Homer's version of Friedrich Nietzsche's eternal recurrence.

If "Brick Like Me" addresses the topic of world-building, the way in which *The Simpsons* has managed to build up an entire universe populated with so many distinctive characters and its own internal logic has undoubtedly contributed to the show's continued longevity. The lines between that Simpsons reality and our own started to grow fuzzier still in 2013, with the opening of a replica Springfield in the Universal Studios theme park in Florida, along with some fairly convincing recreations of Krusty Burger, Moe's, and the Kwik-E-Mart. Fans can now literally consume *The Simpsons* in the form of Krusty Burgers, Flaming Moe's, and giant pink Lard Lad Donuts.

This world building has found new forms in more recent years still. In *The Simpsons: Tapped Out*, the franchise took advantage of the freemium/mobile gaming platform trend to become one of the most successful mobile games of all time. At the onset, nobody quite knew what to expect—especially not the company behind the game, Electronic Arts—when demand for the brand-new iOS game was so sudden and overwhelming as to crash the company's servers, resulting in the game being briefly pulled from the market.[3] As of early 2018, the game featured over 460 characters and functions as a sort of extended universe of *The Simpsons* animated universe.[4] In a notable departure, *Tapped Out* debuted a character never before seen in *The Simpsons* television show: Chester Dupree, the nephew of Dr. Julius Hibbert (Lussier). The game's plot is simple enough in its presentation through introductory cut scenes: Homer is playing a freemium *Happy Little Elves* game on his MyPad tablet and inadvertently causes a plant meltdown. This time, the whole town of Springfield is blown up, with the reconstruction left up to the game player through a city-building gameplay that also includes storylines, quests, and numerous new episode tie-ins to build and recreate the player's own Springfield, however they choose, with the use of irradiated donuts as a form of in-game currency.

Recently, *The Simpsons* has taken the world-building one step further, with the 2016 launch of *Every. Simpsons. Ever.*, also known as *Simpsons World* app/website/service, which, in addition to functioning as a digital home for every *Simpsons* episode, also touts on-demand *Simpsons* content in clip form—making it the *Simpsons* database only dreamed of by fans in previous years and decades. *Simpsons World* sits somewhere between television (as of this writing it can only be accessed with an active contract with a television cable provider in the U.S.), streaming, and web content (with big changes certainly to come with the recent Fox/Disney merger)—which very much represents a symbolic shift in the nature of the show and offers us an opportunity to reflect upon how much the nature of *The Simpsons* has changed over the decades.

"Television! Teacher, mother, secret lover": *Watching and Consuming* The Simpsons

Times have changed. Back in 1987 and 1988, *The Simpsons* only existed in one-minute shorts as part of *The Tracey Ullman Show*. After the airing of "Simpsons Roasting on an Open Fire" (1.1) on December 17, 1989, new episodes aired alternately on the then-fledgling Fox Broadcast network on Sunday or Thursday evenings, before settling for good at the Sunday night 8 p.m. Eastern time slot. For a generation of fans, *The Simpsons* existed solely in these broadcast times, and then with reruns. Using the most advanced forms of media technology at the time (the videocassette recorder), *Simpsons* viewers could watch, rewind, and re-watch *Simpsons* episodes outside of that specific temporal window. In 2001, the Complete First Season made its way to DVD, the vanguard of offerings that ushered in the Digital Age of entertainment as we know it.

Fast forward to the recent syndication rights deal for the groin-grabbingly record-setting total of $750 million, in which executives talked about the importance of securing "the non-linear rights for the show" (Walker). In an age of Netflix, Hulu, and Amazon Prime, streaming and continuously available on-demand show content is the new normal and represents a seismic shift away from the television broadcast as our primary form of consumption.[5] In the digital age, *The Simpsons* as a television show can now just as equally be thought of as online content, content that has become disaggregated into bits, clips, and memes. Is *The Simpsons* still a television show? Certainly, but it also exists as something much beyond that. According to Jonathan Gray, the literary notion of the paratext is helpful in thinking about what exactly *The Simpsons* is. The paratext is a concept popularized by literary theorist Gérard Genette: think of the text as the words that contain the narrative or story of a book, and think of the paratext as the surrounding material of the physical book as object—such as the book cover, table of contents, footnotes, and those other elements that make up the work as a whole. In this way, it's possible for a large segment of the population to know *The Simpsons* or be fans of *The Simpsons*, without ever having watched the show—these kinds of encounters can come from T-shirts, video games, advertisements, or any of the many, many incarnations of *Simpsons* merchandise found all over the world (Gray *Show* 12–16). Fans or non-fans can now engage with or discover *The Simpsons* in ways that simply did not exist thirty years ago.

Of course, we also need reminding that technology and shifts to new mediums are not always a one-way street. Take for example the recent news that the long-demanded return of *The Simpsons* DVD sets—which had previously halted at Season 18—are scheduled to continue. Perhaps old viewing habits die hard. Perhaps there are different affordances from one type of media format to another that point to the fact that we don't quite live in a post-app *Simpsons* world just yet. *Simpsons* showrunner Al Jean had remarked on the return of the DVD sets: "I think the fans deserve it…. I see people wanting something to hold, they don't want everything to be digitized. It's a human quality" (qtd. in Schneider). Does it sound odd that DVDs are infused with a seemingly nostalgic human quality? Only time will tell what the future of *Simpsons* consumption will look like.

Simpsons' *Fandom, Online: "We got to spread this stuff around. Let's put it on the Internet!"*

Chris Turner, in his book *Planet Simpson*, chronicles the very beginnings of *Simpsons* online culture. We know that the creation of the alt.tv.simpsons message board in March 1990 was the first prominent hub of online *Simpsons* discussion. If it can be said that on or about March 1990, the nature of *Simpsons* talk changed thanks to the Internet, we can pinpoint the arrival of the Internet to *The Simpsons* in 1993 ("Homer Goes to College" [5.3]), when stereotypical college nerds, Gary and Doug, are tying up the Simpsons' home phone line with their dial-up modem: "some guys at MIT are sending us reasons why Captain Picard is better than Captain Kirk."

The Simpsons in a sense evolved along with the media forms—first television, VHS, DVD, Blu-ray and then the Internet—that it was disseminated through. As Al Jean notes: "[W]e really put so much data in the show. We debuted when pretty much everyone had a VCR, so we'd put in freeze-frame jokes, we'd write sign jokes, there'd be things you couldn't even watch and get—you'd have to go back to get them" (qtd. in Fox). During the episode "Homer Badman" (6.9), the tabloid news parody *Rock Bottom* has one of those definitive freeze-frame jokes that fully showed the writers' awareness of *Simpsons* viewers' habits with an almost-too quick for the human eye scroll which included hidden gems such as: "If you are reading this, you have no life" along with "The people writing this have no life." The message was clear—the obsessive attention to detail became an integral part for both the making and reception of *The Simpsons*, unlike any television show before it.

This new mode of interacting with a television show was a prime example of what media scholar Henry Jenkins termed the fan as an "active audience" member. The density and Easter egg nature of the show's humor certainly promoted habits of active viewing and reviewing of episodes in a way unique from any other sitcom of its time. In the essay, "*The Simpsons* and Allusion: Worst Essay Ever," William Irwin and J.R. Lombardo describe how the deft use of cultural allusion becomes an effective means of promoting not just the watching of episodes but also the careful watching and careful re-watching: "We also like allusions because of their game-like (ludic) quality. There is something playful in making an allusion, and we are, in a sense, being invited to play in considering an allusion" (85).

David Mirkin, former showrunner for *The Simpsons*, explains that the density of the show was a key to this dynamic: "It was always the goal to make the show more dense than anything on television and to reward people for paying attention. It was really perfect to grow as the computer and online culture grew, which celebrates minutiae" (qtd. in Fox). *The Simpsons* not only celebrated but thrived in it, as the episodes have been and continue to be written to as intricate, multilayered texts that were watched and repeatedly re-watched. Not only did this mean that fans talked about the show, but even the nature of talk about the show was changing—*Simpsons* talk wasn't the accustomed kinds of sitcom discussion which were plot driven around "what will happen next?" The very nonlinear nature of the show was one of the defining qualities that would ensure the show's appeal. Missing a season, or two, or ten didn't have that large of an effect on a viewer. The relative non-continuity of the show was something that the show embraced early on. In "Homer Loves Flanders" (5.16), Bart is confused by Homer and Flanders remaining friends, a whopping nineteen minutes into the episode:

> **Bart:** "I don't get it, Lise. You said everything would be back to normal."
> **Lisa:** "Don't worry, Bart. It seems like every week something odd happens to the Simpsons. My advice is to ride it out, make the occasional smart-alec quip, and by next week, we'll be back to where we started from, ready for another wacky adventure."
> **Bart:** "Ay, caramba!"
> **Lisa:** "That's the spirit."

For Henry Jenkins, fandom was a "knowledge culture" that was based on collective intelligence through the labor and emotional investment of the many—and the advent of home computers becoming a mainstream household device rather than just a geek culture curiosity signified "an epistemological turning point in the development of collective intelligence" (Jenkins

141). From those early days of electronic mailing lists came Google searches that allowed us to rely less on our imperfect human memories for those obscure quotes, along with entire websites devoted to *The Simpsons*. Noteworthy amongst those was *The Simpsons Archive*, an online repository that includes detailed episode transcripts, articles, and guides, which became a particularly valuable resource for the study of all things *Simpsons*. The early and mid–2000s was also the age of the Fox copyright crusades, with threatening cease-and-desist letters sent for what today seem the like the most benign of uses, as John Orvted noted in his oral history of the show: "the more interesting aside here is that Fox is obviously monitoring for the most minute infringements. They are literally scanning discussion forums on the web, to see if a fan is posting an unlicensed image of Bart with his or her comment on an episode" (547).

The digital shift means that we can think about *The Simpsons* in ways that we could not have before. As one example, there is the project from Ben Schmidt that relies upon the closed captioning throughout the show's long duration to turn over 600 episodes' worth of spoken words into essentially one long, giant text[6]: this database (which functions a lot like Google's nGram viewer) can chart the specific mention of a word over the course of an episode, as well as interesting trends for how characters or words have recurred over the show's long history:

> subtitles are plotted by time, they allow you to understand the shows as they move forward, minute by minute as well as season by season. So they allow you to compare the over-time appearances of, say, Mrs. Krabappel with those of, say, Mayor Quimby.... They allow you to treat *The Simpsons* as, effectively, a single book. A single, enormous, unapologetically four-fingered book [Garber].

For an entire generation and a half, *Simpsons* episodes have become the background music to their childhood, adolescence, and adulthood. *Simpsons* quotations have become a cultural shorthand, a sort of shared cultural literacy. In fact, we may now think and talk about *The Simpsons* as isolated moments and gags more than we do as discrete episodes or seasons. The Frinkiac screenshot search database has in many ways become emblematic of how we think of the show in the digital age. With nearly 3,000,000 images (through the first seventeen seasons, and *The Simpsons Movie*), Frinkiac.com is *The Simpsons* in a bite-sized, quote, meme, and GIF form—making it that much easier to find a *Simpsons* quote and image for every aspect of human experience.

The evolution of *The Simpsons* from the medium of television to an online context is a microcosm of the recent history of media in the digital age, an age characterized by disaggregated content where shows have evolved from a broadcast culture to an always-on culture, where *The Simpsons* exists almost anywhere and everywhere, even on our MyPads and MyPhones.

Simpsons' *Love and Hate: "This is all your fault! Ohh, I can't stay mad at you."*

> **Comic Book Guy:** "Last night's *Itchy & Scratchy* was, without a doubt, the worst episode ever. Rest assured that I was on the Internet within minutes, registering my disgust throughout the world."
>
> **Bart:** "Hey, I know it wasn't great, but what right do you have to complain?"
>
> **Comic Book Guy:** "As a loyal viewer, I feel they owe me."
>
> **Bart:** "What? They're giving you thousands of hours of entertainment for free. What could they possibly owe you? If anything, you owe them."
>
> **Comic Book Guy:** "Worst. Episode. Ever." ["The Itchy & Scratchy & Poochie Show"].

If *The Simpsons* did encourage a unique relationship with its fans and openly displayed an awareness of that ardent fan base's obsession, there was a certain give and take that characterized the early years of that dynamic. Did that give-and-take relationship start to get a little more mean-spirited at times? Perhaps. Chris Turner points out how the episode "The Itchy & Scratchy & Poochie Show" (8.14) represented a growing schism between *Simpsons* fans and *Simpsons* writers. The writers poked fun of what they may have felt was incessant nitpicking of online fans and critics, and writers fired back with their own parody of *Simpsons* nerds:

> **Doug:** "In episode 2F09 when Itchy plays Scratchy's skeleton like a xylophone, he strikes the same rib twice in succession, yet he produces two clearly different tones. I mean, what are we to believe, that this is some sort of a magic xylophone or something? Boy, I really hope somebody got fired for that blunder."

It's not as if either position was entirely wrong or indefensible; as Irwin and Lombardo note, "The viewer has the right to be creative in his viewing" (84). *Simpsons* writers, such as Bill Oakley, would point out that the truth was likely somewhere in between: "Many of their critiques are correct. That was the thing. You had to be able to sort out the valid criticism from the insane blather."[7]

And there was more to this relationship than just nitpicking for the sake of nitpicking. The line between love and hate is a fine one indeed, if it even is a line, as Jonathan Gray has observed in his studies of fandom and antifandom: "Behind dislike, after all, there are always expectations—of what a text should be like, of what is a waste" ("New Audiences" 73). A recent example illustrates Gray's antifandom perfectly: Sol Harris, a British resident and *Simpsons* (anti) fan claimed to have watched every episode of *The Simpsons* for eight hours a day, over the course of months and devised his own personal scale that charted the show's decline.[8] In some ways, perhaps the longevity of the show became a type of failure in the eyes of some fans by comparing it to some previous version of itself (we'll return to this last point later).

But the arc of the fan and show relationship has appeared to swing in a different direction in recent years. Following the $750 million megadeal for syndication rights, the new FXX network made headlines with a *Simpsons* marathon for the ages: over the course of 12 days in late 2014, all (then) 552 episodes, aired consecutively from beginning to end. The Every. *Simpsons.* Ever. marathon did a few of things: it brought *The Simpsons* back into the public eye in a way not seen in years; articles about binge-watching the marathon and guides on how to navigate a dozen days of *Simpsons* may have brought back some *Simpsons* fans who had left the show for years, and new fans were attracted by the novelty of this outdated mode of presentation, the television marathon (itself seemingly a product of a past era).

But binge-worthy marathons have not been the only means of bringing *Simpsons* awareness back to longtime fans. The 2013 death of Marcia Wallace, the longtime voice of Mrs. Krabappel, provoked a genuinely heartfelt response from *Simpsons* fans everywhere. First appearing in "Bart the Genius"[9] (1.2) way back in the second episode of *The Simpsons*, Mrs. Krabappel would evolve into one of the more sympathetic characters in *The Simpsons* universe over twenty-five years. And it would have been easy enough for the writers to have Mrs. Krabappel play the part of a one-gag heavy-smoking, solitary-drinking, unlucky in love middle-aged school teacher stereotype. But what endeared the character in the hearts of fans was a decidedly more human side. In "Bart Gets an F" (2.1), Bart must pass a history test and studies—even on an Act of God snow day—only to get a fifty-nine, still failing by a single point. When we talk about the "Golden Age of *The Simpsons*," we usually aren't just talking about the quality of the jokes. Our favorite *Simpsons* moments had an under-girding of genuine heart that was rarely, if ever, seen in an animated sitcom:

> **Bart:** "I tried. I really tried. ... This is as good as I could get! And I still failed! Oh, who am I kidding? I really am a failure. [sobs] Oh, now I know how George Washington felt when he surrendered Fort Necessity to the French in 1754!"

In our first glimpse of a more complex character, Edna takes pity on Bart and awards him an extra point through showing applied learning and letting him pass (even if he does end up staying in fourth grade indefinitely). In an animated universe that always famously eschewed continuity, the development of Edna Krabappel was a welcome change. *The Simpsons* at its best was and is that balance between emotional valence, cultural satire, and cartoony humor that continues to distinguish the best episodes from the rest.

Conclusion, On the Legacy of The Simpsons

In an era when jokes about fake news feel like statements of facts, *The Simpsons* has been eerily prescient, too. Remember that time ("The Computer

Wore Menace Shoes" [12.6]) when Homer created a gossip news website? Fake news sounded funnier when Homer was talking about it in 2000: "Real news is *great*, son, but I'm getting a thousand hits an hour with Grade A bull plop." Real-life *Simpsons* prediction fulfillments have recently become a thing, for better or sometimes definitely for worse,[10] which seems to belie that great Homer Simpson meta quote: "Oh, Marge, cartoons don't have any deep meaning. They're just stupid drawings that give you a cheap laugh" ("Mr. Lisa Goes to Washington" [3.2]).

There was an interesting, cleverly self-reflexive moment in the 2014 Treehouse of Horror XXV episode (26.4). In the third vignette—a parody of *The Others*—the past, Tracey Ullman–era versions of the Simpsons haunt and attempt to destroy the present-day Simpsons. Present Marge tries to reason with the late 1980s era spooks (who somehow died): "Noble spirits, your time has passed."[11] As the show's way of poking fun of their own awareness of being compared to episodes that were in the past by their sometimes-but-not-always loving fan base, the past comes back to haunt the present Simpsons. Perhaps those behind the show feel like the sometimes-dead-but-also-sometimes-kind-of-not Marvin Monroe speaks for them when saying that he is "in some horrible limbo." Skipping past some of the spoilers, Lisa wonders in a very knowing comment: "If there can be two incarnations of the Simpsons, why couldn't some evil marketing entity produce millions of others?" At this point, we are treated to some cameo introductions to *South Park*-, *Adventure Time*-, *Archer*-, *LEGO*-, and several other Simpsons versions in their respective animation styles. So there is an answer, of sorts. *The Simpsons* can never really end while it continues to exist as a 600-episode long text, as memes, video games, popular culture references, books—just in the same way many enduring works never really can be said to end. That's what the future of *The Simpsons* means. More *Simpsons*!

We noted earlier the kind of love/hate relationship that is perhaps somewhat inevitable with thirty years of *Simpsons* fans and *Simpsons* episodes. It's a not unlike a marriage that's been running for thirty years, when Present Homer (shamefully) is trying to choose between the affections of ghost Ullman Marge and Present Marge:

> **Present Marge:** "There's one reason you should choose me: because I know everything you've done, and yet I still want to be with you."
> **Present Homer:** "You're right, Marge—I could never leave you, not even for you. If there was a dot or a squiggle different, that would be too much."

We as longtime viewers have taken the ups and downs and still want to be with the show, when it comes right down to it. One of the lasting legacies of *The Simpsons'* long run has been a skepticism to media and authority in all forms, and that lesson extends to maintain a healthy, critical skepticism to the show itself.

In the live segment of "Simprovised," Homer/Dan Castellaneta opens by saying: "This is the last episode of *The Simpsons*. It's been a great run ... just kidding. *The Simpsons* will never end." Yes, and no—but mostly no. On the one hand, it feels like it's been the beginning of the end for *The Simpsons* for at least the past dozen years—and the show has continued in spite of the doomsayers. On the other hand, what has contributed towards the longevity of *The Simpsons* is that viewers can miss episodes or seasons and tune right back in with a sense of comfortable familiarity, which is a rarity in current television shows. But *The Simpsons* doesn't appear to have anything that resembles an end. Matt Groening has said in many interviews over the years that *"The Simpsons* is a show that rewards you for paying attention."[12] As long as people are paying attention to the show, whether in reruns, or want to read about *The Simpsons* through books such as this, or even ask the question of whether *The Simpsons* is still relevant, we have our answer.

NOTES

1. To learn more about how this was even humanly possible, see *Guinness World Records*.
2. Like all great halcyon eras, the approximate duration and span varies greatly depending upon the commentator. The "Golden Era" may start anywhere from Seasons 3–4, peaking around Seasons 5–6, or sometimes as late as Season 9. For a good example of such debates, see Topel.
3. For more on *Tapped Out* Gate, see Amini.
4. The number comes courtesy of the constantly updated *The Simpsons: Tapped Out Wiki*, available at: http://simpsonstappedout.wikia.com/wiki/Category:Characters.
5. For a much more detailed discussion on streaming vs. broadcast, see the concluding chapter of Amanda Lotz's *The Television Will Be Revolutionized, Second Edition*.
6. Available at: http://benschmidt.org/Simpsons/.
7. In fact, the history of *Simpsons* online fandom is in many ways a history of online fandom in general. See Siegel.
8. The chart itself has been posted on Twitter.com and covers Seasons 1 through 28 and is definitely worth a look; also of note is that it "pinpoints season six as the best season ever" (see Kelly).
9. Fun obscure *Simpsons* trivia: Marcia Wallace also voiced Ms. Mellon, the gifted school teacher in the same episode; her only other character.
10. For some fun and also weirdly eerie examples of how real life imitates *The Simpsons*, see McCluskey.
11. For those wondering, the Ullman-era *Simpsons* made a split-second appearance where they appear to be fairly dead in the Season 24 episode, "Adventures in Baby-Getting."
12. The original 2000 version of the Matt Groening interview no longer appears to be online but can be found at the invaluable *Simpsons Archive*, at: https://www.simpsonsarchive.com/other/articles/britishstages.html.

WORKS CITED

Amini, Tina. "EA Pulls Simpsons Game from iTunes Due to Overwhelming Popularity." *Kotaku*, 5 March 2012, https://kotaku.com/5890588/ea-pulls-simpsons-game-from-itunes-due-to-overwhelming-popularity.
"And Maggie Makes Three." *The Simpsons: The Complete Sixth Season*. Written by Jennifer Crittenden, directed by Swinton O. Scott III, 20th Century–Fox, 2005.

"Bart Gets an F." *The Simpsons: The Complete Second Season*. Written by David M. Stern, directed by David Silverman, 20th Century–Fox, 2002.

"Bart the Genius." *The Simpsons: The Complete First Season*. Written by Jon Vitti, directed by David Silverman, 20th Century–Fox, 1990.

"Brick Like Me." *The Simpsons*. Written by Brian Kelley, directed by Matthew Nastuk, 20th Century–Fox, 2014.

"The Computer Wore Menace Shoes." *The Simpsons: The Complete Twelfth Season*. Written by John Swartzwelder, directed by Mark Kirkland, 20th Century–Fox, 2009.

Everything Simpsons. FX Networks, http://www.simpsonsworld.com/. 6 June 2018.

Fox, Jesse D. "3 Simpsons Showrunners Reflect on New Fans and the 'Classic Era' Myth." *Vulture*. 23 September 2014, http://www.vulture.com/2014/09/simpsons-showrunners-on-the-classic-era-myth.html.

Garber, Megan. "Behold, a Database That Tracks More Than 500 Episodes of *The Simpsons*." *The Atlantic*, 8 September 2014, https://www.theatlantic.com/technology/archive/2014/09/behold-a-database-that-tracks-all-25-seasons-of-the-simpsons/379590/.

Gray, Jonathan. "Antifandom and the Moral Text: Television Without Pity and Textual Dislike." *American Behavioral Scientist*, vol. 48, no. 7, 2005, pp. 840–858.

_____. "New Audiences, New Textualities: Anti-Fans and Non-Fans." *International Journal of Cultural Studies*, vol. 6, no. 1, 2003, pp. 64–81.

_____. *Show Sold Separately: Promos, Spoilers, and Other Media Paratexts*. NYU Press, 2010.

Guinness World Records. "Simpsons fans set longest marathon watching television record ahead of show's 500th episode." *Guinness World Records*, 16 February 2012, http://www.guinnessworldrecords.com/news/2012/2/simpsons-fans-set-longest-marathon-watching-television-record-ahead-of-shows-500th-episode.

Hills, Matthew. *Fan Cultures*. Psychology Press, 2002.

"Homer Badman." *The Simpsons: The Complete Sixth Season*. Written by Greg Daniels, directed by Jeffrey Lynch, 20th Century–Fox, 2005.

"Homer Goes to College." *The Simpsons: The Complete Fifth Season*. Written by Conan O'Brien, directed by Jim Reardon, 20th Century–Fox, 2004.

"Homer Loves Flanders." *The Simpsons: The Complete Fifth Season*. Written by David Richardson, directed by Wes Archer, 20th Century–Fox, 2004.

"Homer the Heretic." *The Simpsons: The Complete Fourth Season*. Written by George Meyer, directed by Jim Reardon, 20th Century–Fox, 2004.

Irwin, William, and J. R. Lombardo. "The Simpsons and Allusion: 'Worst Essay Ever.'" *The Simpsons and Philosophy: The D'oh! of Homer*, edited by William Irwin, Mark T. Conrad, and Aeon J. Skoble, Open Court, 2001, pp. 81–92.

"The Itchy & Scratchy & Poochie Show." *The Simpsons: The Complete Eighth Season*. Written by David X. Cohen, directed by Steven Dean Moore, 20th Century–Fox, 2006.

Jenkins, Henry. *Fans, Bloggers, and Gamers: Exploring Participatory Culture*. NYU Press, 2006.

Kehrer, Paul, Sean Schulte, and Allie Young. *Frinkiac*, https://frinkiac.com.

Kelly, Aoife. "Someone spent 4 months watching all 28 seasons of *The Simpsons* to make chart outlining show's decline." *The Independent*, 21 October 2017, http://www.independent.ie/entertainment/television/tv-news/someone-spent-4-months-watching-all-28-seasons-of-the-simpsons-to-make-chart-outlining-shows-decline-35946213.html.

"Last Exit to Springfield." *The Simpsons: The Complete Fourth Season*. Written by Jay Kogen & Wallace Wolodarsky, directed by Mark Kirkland, 20th Century–Fox, 2004.

The LEGO Movie. Directed by Phil Lord and Christopher Miller, performances by Will Arnett, Chris Pratt, Will Ferrell, Elizabeth Banks. Warner Brothers Pictures, 2014.

Lotz, Amanda D. *The Television Will be Revolutionized*. NYU Press, 2014.

Lussier, Germain. "'The Simpsons Debuts New Character in Mobile 'Tapped Out' Game Rather Than TV Show." *Slashfilm*, 29 May 2014, http://www.slashfilm.com/new-simpsons-character-tapped-out/.

McCluskey, Megan. "All *The Simpsons* Predictions That Came True." *Time*, 9 March 2017, http://time.com/4667462/simpsons-predictions-donald-trump-lady-gaga/.

"Mr. Lisa Goes to Washington." *The Simpsons: The Complete Third Season*. Written by George Meyer, directed by Wesley Archer, 20th Century–Fox, 2003.

O'Callaghan, John. "*The Simpsons* Takes British Stages by Storm." *The Simpsons Archive*, 16 August 2000, https://www.simpsonsarchive.com/other/articles/britishstages.html.

Ortved, John. *The Simpsons: An Uncensored, Unauthorized History*. iBooks eBook version. Ebury Publishing, 2009.

Schmidt, Ben. *bookworm: simpsons*, http://benschmidt.org/Simpsons/.

Schneider, Michael. "'The Simpsons' Will Return to DVD After A Three-Year Hiatus, After Fans Demand It." *Indiewire*, 22 July 2017, http://www.indiewire.com/2017/07/the-simpsons-dvd-panel-comic-con-1201858712/.

Siegel, Alan. "Best Message Board Ever." *Slate*, 26 September 2013, http://www.slate.com/articles/arts/culturebox/2013/09/the_history_of_simpsons_message_board_alt_tv_simpsons.html.

"Simprovised." *The Simpsons*. Written by John Frink, directed by Matthew Nastuk, 20th Century–Fox, 2016.

The Simpsons: Tapped Out. iOS. Electronic Arts, 2012.

"The Simpsons Guy." *Family Guy*. Written by Patrick Meighan, directed by Peter Shin, 20th Century–Fox, 2014.

The Simpsons Movie. Directed by David Silverman, performances by Dan Castellaneta, Julie Kavner, Nancy Cartwright, Yeardley Smith, Hank Azaria. 20th Century–Fox, 2007.

"Simpsons Roasting on an Open Fire." *The Simpsons: The Complete First Season*. Written by Mimi Pond, directed by David Silverman, 20th Century–Fox, 1989.

"Simpsorama." *The Simpsons*. Written by J. Stewart Burns, directed by Bob Anderson, 20th Century–Fox, 2014.

Topel, Fred. "The 5 Eras of the Simpsons From Golden Age to Postmodern and Beyond." *ThoughtCo*, 5 May 2018, https://www.thoughtco.com/eras-of-the-simpsons-3963144.

"Treehouse of Horror XXV." *The Simpsons*. Written by Stephanie Gillis, directed by Matthew Faughnan, Mike B. Anderson, 20th Century–Fox, 2014.

Turner, Chris. *Planet Simpson: How a Cartoon Masterpiece Documented an Era and Defined a Generation*. iBooks eBook version. Ebury Press, 2012.

Walker, Alissa. "Simpsons World Preview: Nearly 300 Hours of Springfield in Your Pocket." *Gizmodo*, 14 September 2014, https://gizmodo.com/simpsons-world-preview-nearly-300-hours-of-springfield-1639727131.

Aristotle in Springfield

On Friendship

ZACHARY TAVLIN

> Friendship, then, consists more in loving; and people who love their friends are praised; hence, it would seem, loving is the virtue of friends. And so friends whose love accords with the worth of their friends are enduring friends and have an enduring friendship.—Aristotle, *Nicomachean Ethics*, 1159a35

> Remember when we used to kiss like that, Carl ... with our respective girlfriends?—Lenny Leonard, "Marge and Homer Turn a Couple Play" (17.22)

The Simpsons has been appropriately lauded by fans and critics for, among many things, developing a memorable cast of recurring minor characters. This essay focuses on two in particular: Lenny Leonard and Carl Carlson, looking closely at the philosophical implications of their friendship (which is probably the closest thing in the show to a representation of what Aristotle called a "perfect friendship"). Through a reading of Books VIII and IX of Aristotle's *Nicomachean Ethics*, I argue that, despite their occasional (or even semi-regular) lapses in virtue, Lenny and Carl's relationship provides a model for true other-directed friendship in a society that incessantly pushes against its possibility. This becomes even more apparent in comparison with Bart and Milhouse's pre-adolescent friendship, which is mired in an appropriately childish asymmetry of adulation. I draw this contrast out with reference to the competing values of the pairs' "work" relationships. Whether in Bart and Milhouse's impromptu factory project or in their co-management of the comic book store, they assume boss-laborer roles that Lenny and Carl avoid.

This exploration includes a reading of a few relevant episodes, including "Half-Decent Proposal" (13.10) and "The Saga of Carl" (24.21), but will generally proceed as a survey. I discuss the way Lenny and Carl engage in the typical "bromance" buddy genre, foregrounded by their class condition, racial identities, unfulfilled love lives, and engagement with typical male hobbies and social expectations. Rarely seen apart, they also flirt with the homosexual status that underlies the paradoxically masculine, hetero-normative perspective that's coded into popular television and entertainment genres. However, the strength of their relationship is in their occasional transcendence of mainstream masculinity. With Aristotle, we can see Lenny and Carl break with the disordered forms of self-love that keep friendships in the domain of a primordial narcissism. I also argue that, comparing their attitudes toward one another in sequences where they are either together or apart in the narrative, the symmetry in which they view the other as a part of their lives provides a beacon for true friendship in a town, Springfield, where role models of any sort are hard to find. To the extent that their relationship might be *one* possible future for Bart and Milhouse, it is likely not the worst of them.[1]

Aristotelian Friendship: An Introduction

The *Nicomachean Ethics* is not primarily about friendship. Insofar as it is a study about of the practical possibility of human happiness and flourishing (*eudaimonia*), friendship (*philia*) is examined in Books VIII and IX to delineate its conceptual relationship with virtue (which in turn has already been examined in its originary relation to happiness). Ultimately, friendships of virtue are the most satisfying, and Aristotle works through the various permutations of friendship, both ordered and disordered, as a way of developing a taxonomy that recognizes the proximity or distance of each category from true ethical virtue. The three types of friendship correspond to "the three objects of love" (1156a7)[2]: utility, pleasure, or goodness.

These three object-qualities have the power to bind people together in friendship—in the two main forms of imperfect friendship, individuals find others useful for some end or as the bearer of pleasure for oneself. In both of these cases, one is fond of one's friend "not insofar as the beloved is who he is, but insofar as he is useful or pleasant" (1156a16). As such, these types of relationships are easily dissolved "when the friends do not remain similar [to what they were]; for if someone is no longer pleasant or useful, the other stops loving him" (1156a20). Utility and pleasure are so context-specific that the relationship based primarily on either cannot transcend context shifts on the part of each individual over time. Aristotle claims that friendships of utility "arise especially among older people, since at that age they pursue the advantageous, not the pleasant" (1156a24), while friendships of pleasure arise more often in the young, whose "lives are guided by their feelings, and they pursue above all what is pleasant for themselves *and what is at hand*" (1156a33, emphasis mine).

Behind these classifications is the assumption that friendship is an *activity*, and the more the activity is a shared one, the closer the friendship comes to perfection. What characterizes friendships of utility and pleasure are their asymmetrical natures: since in both cases the individuals involved desire the company of the other for reasons that reflect back on themselves, each agent is not treated as an end in himself or herself. Ideal friendships have precisely the opposite character, where "complete friendship is the friendship of good people similar in virtue; for they wish goods in the same way to each other insofar as they are good, and they are good in their own right" (1156b7). True friendships can be perfect or imperfect depending upon the symmetry of the virtuous characters of each person—large gaps in the moral development of the friends, even if they both legitimately desire the good for the other, can prevent a friendship from attaining perfection. In part, when one friend lacks the magnitude of the other's ethical virtue, the ability of both to share in their activities together is (relatively) limited.

As I examine the respective relationships between Lenny and Carl and Bart and Milhouse in *The Simpsons,* I will continue to develop a reading of Aristotle's theory of friendship in detail, particularly as it pertains to these representations of friendship in the series (two of many, of course, but two particularly enlightening ones). These cases demonstrate, quite helpfully, differences in homosocial symmetry between two men/boys, as well as differences that correspond with the age profiles Aristotle generally draws. In addition to merely demonstrating key differences in Aristotle's "types" of friendship, these characters provide practical maps toward the possibility of virtue in friendship, toward true friendship, as well as depictions of the deadlocks that prevent it. They also repeatedly contest the gendered ideologies of friendship commonly reinforced in popular culture. At the heart of this investigation, though, is an attempt to locate what Aristotle calls "goodwill" (*eunoia*) in these characters, a reciprocal and reciprocated desire for the good in the other (for if two individuals "[are to be friends], they must have goodwill to each other" (1156a4)). What I hope will be evident as well is that this kind of friendship *produces* humor in the other and in oneself, and provides much of what is so memorable in the wonderful personages of Lenny and Carl.

The Problem of Lenny and Carl

Lenny and Carl are seen together more often than they are seen apart. In fact, of the two, Lenny makes far more appearances on his own, though he is often depicted as listless and directionless without his friend at his side. When Lisa and her Mensa group change the traffic light patterns in town ("They Saved Lisa's Brain" 10.22), a solitary Lenny, driving through a light, remarks to no one in particular, "I'm making record time! If only I had some place to be." One might reasonably wonder whether this "place," in true Aristotelian fashion, is the company of his best friend. To the extent that, upon first glance, Lenny and Carl approximate (and parody) male buddy genre stereotypes, they also satisfy a few key Aristotelian conditions of true friendship, including the necessity of living and communing together in proximity (which reflects the idea that "you cannot live with many people and distribute yourself among them ... it is good not to seek as many friends as possible, and good to have no more than enough for living together" [1171a3]).

The elements of (male) Aristotelian friendship that generate constant proximity and exclusivity are indeed reflected, in contemporary terms, through the prism of the homosocial "bromance" ethos. Through a running in-joke about the possibility of latent homosexuality in their relationship, Lenny and Carl's friendship occupies a liminal space between heteronormative assumptions about masculine characters on television and a form of full-blown gay minstrelsy that depicts homosexual males as inherently humorous perversions. Indeed, it is that ambiguity, not considered as such in Aristotle's account (which represses the question of gender), which charges the mutual appearance of the characters around town. In "Ice Cream of Margie (with the Light Blue Hair)" (18.7), two popsicle-stick sculptures of Lenny and Carl are stuck together:

> **Lenny:** I can't tell where Carl ends and I begin!
> **Carl:** See, it's statements like that that make people think we're gay.

One example of a number of similar double entendres (that in later seasons are often finally acknowledged as such), latent homosexuality is often suggested in visions of Lenny and Carl possessing one body or soul, in forms of irreducible inseparability.

The buddy clichés, however, may often seem to commodify that inseparability. After all, while homosexuality serves as a comment on the extremes of Lenny and Carl's commitment to one another, there is also the (seemingly) obvious racial difference to consider. The pair is the show's most typical manifestation of the racial binary black/white, often foregrounded by Homer, who once "joked," "white guys have names like Lenny, whereas black guys have names like Carl" ("Monty Can't Buy Me Love" 10.21). There is, however, a parallel running joke wherein Homer repeatedly confuses the racial characteristics of his friends, so that he needs, for instance, to scribble a key on his hand. Lenny and Carl's status in the town, insofar as they give off the requisite appearances of the multicultural, homosocial buddy coupling, involves a constant attempt at separation (if even just categorically or conceptually) on the part of other characters, as if the townspeople themselves are threatened by the odd strength of the friendship. This leads to a repetitive attempt to map their relationship in various ways. Characters like Marge and Chief Wiggum have speculated about their romance, and Homer once tells Lisa, "You and science go together like Lenny and Carl," only to add that "the science is Carl" ("Fat Man and Little Boy" 16.5).

The townspeople of Springfield might be seen to stand momentarily, in their various judgments of Lenny and Carl, for the viewer who should be forgiven for her skepticism that a true friendship can exist in the hotbed of selfishness and cynicism that is the (nonetheless beloved) community to which they belong. Aristotle was clear that friendships of virtue will often be seen as threats to those outside of them, at least insofar as "base people"—a not-inappropriate tag for many of Springfield's inhabitants—"cannot be in concord, except to a slight degree, just as they can be friends only to a slight degree; for they seek to overreach in benefits [for themselves], and shirk labors and public services" (1167b10). This type of person "interrogates and obstructs his neighbor": while we could certainly apply this principle to Homer and Flanders, it is also an appropriate way to describe the reduction of Lenny and Carl to stock caricatures of work buddies, the "black guy and the white guy," repressed homosexuals, or the classic local drunks. The fact that this occurs within the diegetic space of the series marks an element of self-reflexivity regarding the difficult, largely contradictory project of devoted friendship in contemporary, cynical space.

It can be argued, however, that Lenny and Carl do not achieve the level of friendship Aristotle prescribes anyway: is it really the case that their relationship is one between "equals" in the sense of devotion, care, concern, and virtue? Perfect friendship attains a sense of aforementioned symmetry; friendship consists in "loving," but that love should be stable and symmetrical, moving freely in both directions. When Lenny reveals that he's lied to Carl "all along" about being married to a beauty queen—which can also, incidentally, be taken either as a sign of repressed homosexual desire or a piece of evidence against it—is it a cute example of friendly adoration and respect or a disturbing sign of mistrust and poor communication ("In Marge We Trust" 8.22)? More significantly, when Homer takes Lenny with him away from Springfield to work on an oilrig, Homer's dissatisfaction with his marriage— due to a misunderstanding involving Marge's high school prom date Artie Ziff—is paralleled by a dejected Lenny, who sympathizes with Homer's inability to keep Marge off his mind. The latter sees her face and hair in the passing cacti and clouds ("Half-Decent Proposal" 13.10). Their bus proceeds to pass "Mount Carlmore," a Rushmore-style bust of Carl's face carved out of the side of a mountain:

Lenny: I carved that one wonderful summer.
Homer: What did Carl think?
Lenny: You know, we've never discussed it.

The episode climaxes with Marge and Carl's rescue of Homer and Lenny from an oil field fire, but Mount Carlmore still stands as an emblem of Lenny's Carl-worship that exceeds any reciprocation. That Lenny builds monuments to Carl for his own purposes (they never discussed it), sees Carl's face in the stars (though Carl sees himself, not Lenny), and even at one point sees a herd of Carls in his vision of heaven, challenges the notion of a mutual other-directed friendship of virtue. On that note, comparing Lenny and Carl to Milhouse and Bart, now, should help to slightly re-draw some of the distinctions already made, and looking at a particular late episode that re-evaluates Carl's character should help to settle certain ambiguities that bewildered viewers earlier in the series' run.

Childish Pranks and Workplace Hijinks

Bart and Milhouse form the most constantly displayed "friendship" throughout the series, occupying far more screen time together than Lenny and Carl. Though they are pulled apart quite often, whether by their parents, by girls, by teachers, or just by themselves, their breaks are always only temporary. The obvious question, of course, is whether their relationship is indeed a friendship it all—it doesn't take a bit of Aristotelian knowledge to recognize the problems with that categorization. Looking closely at the history of their relationship and the respective status of both characters in their line of (mis)-adventures should provide an informative account of how *The Simpsons* treats childhood friendships as such (as this is indeed the central one) as well as in relation to Lenny and Carl, whose friendship may not be as different as I originally posited.

In a flashback to Bart and Milhouse's kindergarten days ("Lisa's Sax" 9.3), the two are shown to have met on the elementary school playground: their friendship is secured when Bart's armpit noises make Milhouse laugh hard enough that milk squirts out of his nose. Indeed, the suggestion here is that Milhouse's reaction is the impetus for Bart's assumption of the class clown role, since soon after their meeting he tells Principal Skinner, for the first time, to "eat [his] shorts." From the beginning, then, Bart and Milhouse's friendship centers on Bart's performance, which forces Milhouse into the audience role; there is a clear active-passive dichotomy at play. This is also, according to Aristotle's categories, an obvious example of a friendship of pleasure (which, as already mentioned, is supposed to inhere primarily in friendships of the young).

When Bart and Milhouse affirm their platonic love for one another, it is almost always in the aftermath of some friendship trauma. These traumas take two general forms: Bart abusing Milhouse's loyalty through pranks or dares, or Milhouse abandoning or tattling on Bart to avoid further trouble for himself. The wealth of both types of examples suggests that while Bart is most often in control of Milhouse, and while their friendship of pleasure is usually directed toward the pleasure of Bart, their relationship results in breakdowns of virtue that run in both directions. The performer-audience relation, perhaps most obvious in the constant play of Milhouse as Bart's sidekick in the latter's role as the Springfield Elementary class clown, occasionally flips. Whether it's Bart getting Milhouse placed as a criminal on America's Most Wanted list ("Lisa's Rival" 6.2) or convincing him to dress up like his dad to give the pair access to adult entertainment ("Hardly Kirk-ing" 24.13), Bart often uses his friend in a utility-relation for his own entertainment—one can certainly find elements of both categories of imperfect friendships here. Milhouse often finds himself in trouble, either with Skinner or with the law, when Bart decides that he's willing to pass his daredevil streak onto his friend.

But even the pushover has his limits. Milhouse has sold Bart out since the beginning of the series, whether to continue playing his new video game *Bonestorm* by telling his mom that Bart was swearing and smoking ("Marge Be Not Proud" 7.11) or to avoid getting in trouble for switching the church hymn to "In A Gadda Da Vida" by tattling on Bart to Reverend Lovejoy ("Bart Sells His Soul" 7.4). Milhouse has literally bought Bart's soul, has fought with his friend over the love of Rainier Wolfcastle's daughter Greta, and has abandoned Bart for new friends after a brief move to Capital City. Those beautiful moments in which two friends, having each chosen an end to live for, find that they can "pursue [it] in [their] friend's company" (1172a3), occur between Bart and Milhouse, just not very often (this is perhaps to say, in plainer terms, that they're rarely on the same page).

Nonetheless, those moments exist, most often in the form of pranks in which Milhouse is *not* the victim (for instance, in "22 Short Films About Springfield" 7.21):

> **Bart:** Milhouse, do you ever think about the people in those cars?
> **Milhouse:** I try not to. It makes it harder to spit on 'em.

Bart and Milhouse's friendship is based on a principle of *imaginative play*, an extension of Aristotle's observation that since the young "are guided by their feelings, [...] they pursue above all what is pleasant for themselves and what is at hand" (1156a33). What is "at hand" is so context-specific that "their friendship shifts with [what they find] pleasant, and the change in such pleasure is quick" (1156a36). These types of fickle pleasures include "erotic passion," so that they often "love and quickly stop, often changing in a single day" (1156b3): for Bart and Milhouse, one observes the occasional antagonisms of the inexperienced with regard to girls who break through the veneer of their female-hatred, including Greta Wolfcastle and Samantha Stankey.

More often, though, it is the opportunities of immense childhood pleasure or pranks that just happen to present themselves to the boys in the course of their play—like the pair's improbable loosening of all the screws that hold Springfield Elementary together ("The Good, the Sad and the Drugly" 20.17)—that illustrate the principle of the "at hand" in Bart and Milhouse's friendship. The status of their commitment to one another depends almost wholly on their momentary individual positions with regard to pleasure, punishment, authority, and popularity. They both inhabit an eternal present, characteristic of childhood, in which the idea of the effects of their choices on long-term friendship simply does not come up. So when, in the course of the aforementioned episode, only Milhouse is caught and suspended from school, and Bart promises to visit him every day only to neglect this promise when he starts going out with a girl named Jenny, Milhouse chooses the take revenge by facilitating Jenny's discovery of Bart's troublemaking past. At the end of the episode, Bart apologizes to and reconciles with Milhouse not through a mature transformation in his understanding of friendship, but with a return to that state of play: they drive a Zamboni over and ice down the (now-rebuilt) school's floors, to the detriment of their classmates.

One element of this play, paradoxically, is work—more aptly, one might call Bart and Milhouse's adventures in the workplace "play-work" (undoubtedly a popular form of childhood entertainment). Despite the imaginative nature of these episodes, though, patterns quickly emerge as to the governing fantasy-structure of their play. In "Homer's Enemy" (8.23) and "Worst Episode Ever" (12.11), Bart and Milhouse take over an abandoned factory and The Android's Dungeon (Comic Book Guy's store), respectively. Their roles in both cases, Bart as boss-supervisor-foreman and Milhouse as employee, replicate the aforementioned active-passive distinction that typically characterizes their friendship.

The boys come to manage the comic book store after Dr. Hibbert orders Comic Book Guy, following a heart attack, to take a break from work. This arrangement, initially, involves Bart as manager and Milhouse as lowly underling—the fact that they manage the store successfully at first suggests that these are their "natural" roles. Milhouse's dissatisfaction becomes apparent when Lisa walks in (as both sister and crush, her presence often leads to awkwardness between the two friends):

> **Lisa:** Milhouse, I'm impressed. The store is so busy; you and Bart are really great businessmen.
> **Milhouse:** Well, I'm really the brains. Bart's just the eye candy.

To impress a skeptical Lisa, Milhouse makes his first executive decision: he orders 2,000 copies of *Biclops*, a comic published by LensCrafters starring a mild-looking, glasses-wearing hero (like Milhouse himself). The disastrous business decision costs the boys their entire budget as well as the smooth functioning of their work relationship:

> **Bart:** Oh, it's my fault for leaving you in charge. Sometimes I forget how young you are.
> **Milhouse:** I'm only three months younger than you!
> **Bart:** Oh, look, you're getting cranky. You haven't had your juice.
> **Milhouse:** Well, my straw broke off in the carton ... that's not the point!

Their argument ends with a freeze-frame in comic book form of Milhouse, depicted as Bart's sidekick, attacking his unimpressed partner.

Eventually the two reconcile (as always) after a chance discovery of Comic Book Guy's illegal video cache leads to a fresh business opportunity: late night viewings of the townspeople's activities recorded on CCTV cameras. After getting busted by the police, Bart and Milhouse walk into the sunset once again:

> **Milhouse:** Well, we may not have the store, but at least we're friends again.
> **Bart:** Yep. And, we haven't been to school in days and days and days.

This moment of closure is another example of the principle of childhood's temporality, an eternal present in which events move circularly, folding back on themselves, instead of linearly. Bart and Milhouse's breakups resolve into reconciliation and inevitably fall apart again in a constant episodic oscillation. But what then about the status of Lenny and Carl's work relationship? How much does it differ from Bart and Milhouse's?

Though we learn in "Homer's Enemy" that Lenny and Carl both have master's degrees in nuclear physics, viewers are rarely privy to any real demonstration of high intelligence from either of them (and they are far more likely grouped with local drunks and rabble-rousers than with the town's Mensa community). Indeed, their work lives at the power plant are reminiscent of the blue-collar, working class ethos of the male buddy genre. Their home lives, depicted occasionally in a few different episodes, span from respectable, middle class arrangements to utter squalor (Lenny has lived in a very well-decorated penthouse-style apartment that shares a wall with a jai-alai court as well as in a run-down hovel). Most importantly though, Lenny and Carl are depicted as equals in their work relationship, except for one episode when, after Mr. Burns loses his money, Lenny is temporarily put in charge of the plant ("a real bear on tardiness," Lenny's short time as boss is described by Smithers as a "reign of terror" ["The Old Man and the Lisa" 8.21]).

These work relationships, following Aristotle's categorization, can only be a subordinate part of any holistic treatment of or judgment upon the strength of a friendship. Nevertheless, they provide helpful test cases for the ways inequality (in some sense a necessary engine for comedy) can creep into these respective representations of friendship. Whereas Lenny and Carl's disputes seem to arise mostly from the occasional, subordinate utility-seeking aspects of their relationship (for instance, as a result of Carl's reportedly horrendous speech at Lenny's wedding), with Bart and Milhouse, conflict arises directly from the hierarchal character of their friendship. In the former case, disputes occur when there is some deviation from the generally stable symmetry of the friendship (exemplified in Lenny and Carl's work relationship, and Lenny's lack of direction without his friend's presence). In the case of the latter, "the better person thinks it is fitting for him to have more, on the ground that more is fittingly allotted to the good person" (1163a26).

In addition to the way this works in Bart and Milhouse's business ventures, one can extend this principle outward and recognize that Bart often sees the friendship as a whole along the lines of a business in which it is wrong "for someone to have an equal share if he is useless" (1163a28) (the "shares" being anything from peer recognition to pleasure itself). Even accepting this distinction, however, it is difficult to argue that Lenny and Carl's friendship, outside of the workplace, is a model of symmetry. One final look at Carl, undoubtedly the more enigmatic of the two, will allow us to come back to the tenability (or untenability) of the proposition that Lenny and Carl represent, at least within the coordinates of friendship in the abstract, a best-case scenario for the future of Bart and Milhouse.

The Saga of Love

Certainly Lenny and Carl's friendship is not nearly as troubled as Bart and Milhouse's, possessing neither the constant ebb and flow of affection nor its unique dialectic of love and abandonment. Nevertheless, one might argue that it is not exactly a good example of full maturity and other-directedness either. I will now turn my attention to a late episode, "The Saga of Carl" (24.21), which stands as the series' partial revision of the long running and much joked-about relationship, before looking back on the comparison and attempting to come to a final Aristotelian "judgment" about the representation of friendship in the show.

"The Saga of Carl" gives us a sense of where things stand between Lenny and Carl thirty years after we first met them (though their story goes back further than that, they haven't actually aged in thirty years, so one might profitably call it even). The initial plot device of the episode centers around Carl's betrayal: when Homer, Moe, Lenny, and Carl win the lottery with their weekly lottery ticket ($200,000 in winnings), Carl cashes the ticket and flees

Springfield while the others are throwing a "raging party" to celebrate. Despite Homer's claim that "the power of friendship is so amazing, [he doesn't] feel at all suspicious of Carl," they ultimately discover that Carl fled with the money to his home country of Iceland and leave to track him down. In Reykjavik, they learn that the Carlson family is much maligned historically in Iceland for acts of cowardice as "watchmen of the coasts," which led to the success of a series of barbarian invasions and resulted in the loss of lava fields, sweaters, and tiny horses. Carl's plan is to use the money to purchase a lost page from the Icelandic saga that, supposedly, will clear his family's name. When confronted, he tells his friends that he chose not to confide in them because they're not his real friends, since friends "share their feelings, their hopes, their dreams; friends know their friends are from Iceland!" According to Carl, though, they are "just guys who sit next to each other at a bar and talk about 'guy stuff.'"

Though this episode's conflict concerns a larger group, Lenny and Carl occupy the center of the drama. Lenny, of course, is the last of the jilted to accept Carl's betrayal, always holding out (a delusional) hope for a misunderstanding, initially believing that "he flew to Quebec to bring [them] back authentic French Canadian sugar-pie": "I can taste it already!" he shouts, "thanks for the sugar-pie, Carl!" While Moe initially decides he never wants to see Carl's face again, Lenny continues to gaze questioningly at a framed picture of his friend, which he packs with him on the trip along with a hat and t-shirts that all sport Carl's face on the front. When they finally confront him, Lenny asks Carl to "tell them the good reason you had for borrowing the money." After Carl finally tells them that he doesn't consider their respective relationships meaningful, Lenny loses his cool and violently attacks him; the revelation is undoubtedly the most significant and most shattering, for him.

After realizing that Carl might, in a sense, be right in his judgment (represented through a memory-montage of the four doing "guy stuff" like drinking at Moe's, attending Isotopes games, and going to see the *Hangover* movies) and after learning that the additional page of the saga will not restore the Carlson family's honor, the guys convince a crowd of Icelanders that Carl and his family deserve forgiveness by telling of Carl's small acts of friendly kindness, like helping Lenny move and leaving beer in Homer's fridge. This leads to the final reconciliation with Carl, who acknowledges that the three are indeed his friends and that they taught him "the true meaning of male friendship": pointing to his heart, he admits that "the stuff that comes from in here, that *is* 'guy stuff.'" Of course, Carl's redemption depends in part upon a certain conception of male friendship that is not, within the confines of the male buddy genre, universalizable across gender lines.

Most relevantly, "The Saga of Carl" is a challenge to the symmetry of

Lenny and Carl's relationship, exposing explicitly what was, to that point in the series, largely implicit: that there *is* a real difference in the way each sees the other. Since that is also clearly true of Bart and Milhouse, what then is the ultimate difference between the two cases? For one, it is probably not the case that Bart and Milhouse *love* one another, and true friendship, for Aristotle, contains as a necessary condition a form of platonic love (if Bart loves anyone, it's Krusty, and if Milhouse loves anyone, it's probably, pathetically, his Puppy Goo-Goo doll).

As far as love is concerned, however, Aristotle writes that "friendship seems to consist more in loving than in being loved" (1159a28), using the example of the mother "who loves the child even if ignorance prevents him from returning to her what is due to a mother" (1159a33). But love, "the virtue of friends," accords "with the worth of [one's] friends" (1159b1). Lenny and Carl are not virtuous people *par excellence*; they are often ignorant and petty, and Carl particularly is often reluctant to demonstrate his affection. But in addition to loving one another and sticking together in almost every conceivable way and function—so that their relationship is often interpreted as homoerotic—they have nothing to give one another but company. They are not wealthy, nor are they particularly knowledgeable or useful to one another. While Bart and Milhouse "[enjoy] each other's vice" (1159b11), Lenny and Carl's attraction to one another does not conform easily to common social roles—they are *too* friendly to be merely male companions of convenience (and thus, as I've suggested, their friendship is somehow threatening or at least confusing to the rest of the townspeople in its weird excess).

Ultimately, *The Simpsons* is a vehicle for humor. Lenny and Carl are not primarily purposed, as characters, for an investigation into Aristotelian friendship. But their relationship is, to be sure, the closest thing to an extended representation of middle-aged male friendship, just as Bart and Milhouse's is the closest thing to an extended example of male childhood bonding. Lenny and Carl may not be the best cipher for an Aristotelian friendship of virtue, but they are likely the closest thing to it in the otherwise twisted, selfish (though wonderfully funny) town of Springfield. They are the cause of wit in the other, which is indeed one of Aristotle's prime virtues. When Lenny publishes his personal newspaper, *The Lenny Saver* ("Fraudcast News" 15.22), its headline reads, "The Truth About Carl: He's Great." Shedding a tear, Lenny says, "It had to be told." That their love for one another transcends most forms of narcissistic self-love found in lesser forms of friendship, like the one Bart and Milhouse have yet to grow out of, and that it is indeed possible for such to occur among seemingly shallow, working-class, heterosexual males: it also had to be told.

Notes

1. Special thanks to Tyler Nash for constantly offering a passionate and well-reasoned defense of Lenny. And additional thanks to Sideshow Mel for just being there.

2. All in-text citations refer to the line numbers of Aristotle's *Nicomachean Ethics* (edition referenced at the end of the chapter).

Works Cited

Aristotle. *Nicomachean Ethics*. Edited by Terence Irwin, Hackett, 1999.
"Bart Sells His Soul." *The Simpsons: The Complete Seventh Season*. Written by Greg Daniels, directed by Wes Archer, 20th Century–Fox, 2010.
"Fat Man and Little Boy." *The Simpsons: The Complete Sixteenth Season*. Written by Joel H. Cohen, directed by Mike B. Anderson, 20th Century–Fox, 2013.
"Fraudcast News." *The Simpsons: The Complete Fifteenth Season*. Written by Don Payne, directed by Bob Anderson, 20th Century–Fox, 2012.
"The Good, the Sad and the Drugly." *The Simpsons: The Complete Twentieth Season*. Written by Marc Wilmore, directed by Rob Oliver, 20th Century–Fox, 2010.
"Half-Decent Proposal." *The Simpsons: The Complete Thirteenth Season*. Written by Tim Long directed by Lauren MacMullan, 20th Century–Fox, 2010.
"Hardly Kirk-ing." *Simpsons World on FXX*, written by Tom Gammill and Max Pross, directed by Matthew Nastuk, FX Networks LLC, 2014.
"Homer and Marge Turn a Couple Play." *Simpsons World on FXX*. Written by Joel H. Cohen, directed by Bob Anderson, FX Networks LLC, 2006.
"Homer's Enemy." *The Simpsons: The Complete Eighth Season*. Written by John Swartzwelder, directed by Jim Reardon, 20th Century–Fox, 2006.
"Ice Cream of Margie (with the Light Blue Hair)." *Simpsons World on FXX*. Written by Carolyn Omine, directed by Matthew Nastuk, FX Networks LLC, 2014.
"In Marge We Trust." *The Simpsons: The Complete Eighth Season*. Written by Donick Cary, directed by Steven Dean Moore, 20th Century–Fox, 2006.
"Lisa's Rival." *The Simpsons: The Complete Sixth Season*. Written by Mike Scully, directed by Mark Kirkland, 20th Century–Fox, 2005.
"Lisa's Sax." *The Simpsons: The Complete Ninth Season*. Written by Al Jean, directed by Dominic Polcino, 20th Century–Fox, 2007.
"Marge Be Not Proud." *The Simpsons: The Complete Seventh Season*. Written by Mike Scully, directed by Steven Dean Moore, 20th Century–Fox, 2006.
"Monty Can't Buy Me Love." *The Simpsons: The Complete Tenth Season*. Written by John Swartzwelder, directed by Mark Ervin, 20th Century–Fox, 2007.
"The Old Man and the Lisa." *The Simpsons: The Complete Eighth Season*. Written by John Swartzwelder, directed by Mark Kirkland, 20th Century–Fox, 2006.
"The Saga of Carl." *Simpsons World on FXX*. Written by Eric Kaplan, directed by Chuck Sheetz, FX Networks LLC, 2014.
"They Saved Lisa's Brain." *The Simpsons: The Complete Tenth Season*, written by Matt Selman, directed by Pete Michels, 20th Century–Fox, 2007.
"22 Short Films About Springfield." *The Simpsons: The Complete Seventh Season*. Written by Richard Appel, et al., directed by Jim Reardon, 20th Century–Fox, 2010.
"Worst Episode Ever." *The Simpsons: The Complete Twelfth Season*. Written by Larry Doyle, directed by Matthew Nastuk, 20th Century–Fox, 2009.

Homer as Homework

The Simpsons
in the College Classroom

LISA WHALEN

When I began teaching at a Minnesota college five years ago, I considered the framed scene from *The Simpsons* hanging near my office an odd—and perhaps inappropriate—image for an academic setting, especially a hallway of faculty offices. I had never seen the show and assumed it was similar to Saturday morning cartoons I'd watched as a child. When my husband, an avid fan, introduced me to his favorite episodes, I realized *The Simpsons* was much more than a typical cartoon, but I didn't see its potential for anything other than entertainment until I taught Jonathan Swift's essay, "A Modest Proposal."

I anticipated that students would struggle with the essay's vocabulary, since they aren't used to reading 18th century British English, but I was surprised by their vehemence at its content. They expressed disgust at Swift's suggestion that Irish families who couldn't afford to feed their children should sell them to British landowners for consumption as a delicacy. They failed to grasp the essay's satiric nature, instead reading it as a genuine proposal for addressing poverty. Explaining how the essay functions as a satire wasn't enough; the circumstances that prompted it were too far removed from students' experience for them to grasp Swift's intent or the essay's brilliance. Fortunately, *The Simpsons* proved an ideal model for bridging that gap and fulfilling what I consider the most important learner outcome for Introduction to Literature: critically analyzing and evaluating texts.

Evaluating a text requires examining how effectively it accomplishes the author's intended purpose. First, however, readers have to identify that purpose. They also have to identify the text's audience, tone, and the context

233

(historical, social, political, economic, religious) in which it was written. Developing these skills is crucial not only to academic success, but also to sustaining a healthy democracy. Informed citizens apply these skills to filter advertising messages, shape personal values, participate in political discussion, and choose which candidates to elect. Swift's essay is ideal for introducing these skills because unlike most of the messages students encounter daily, it is almost incomprehensible until readers become familiar with its historical context. *The Simpsons*, being much closer to students' experience and written in modern American English, serves as a stepping-stone to Swift's essay. "Bart vs. Thanksgiving" (2.7) provides an appealing framework for approaching Swift's essay because both it and the essay highlight absurdities in the dominant culture. While "A Modest Proposal" skewers English landowners for their callous greed, "Bart vs. Thanksgiving" pokes fun at Americans' obsession with freedom, family, food, and football (not necessarily in that order).

When teaching Swift's essay, I purposely assign it without any explanation because I want students to read for comprehension, the first step in evaluating any text. The majority grasp that Swift is concerned about Ireland's poverty and suggesting parents turn their children into livestock; however, few understand why Swift would propose such a dehumanizing solution. I tell them we'll come back to that and ask how many are familiar with *The Simpsons*. Every hand in the room goes up. I explain that the show is a satire and invite students to share what they know about that concept. I record their responses on the whiteboard and combine them with the results of an internet search conducted on the classroom's computer to arrive at a definition: satire is a literary technique used to make fun of the vices of society for the purpose of change (Harman and Holman 491). It includes hyperbole (extreme exaggeration), understatement, irony, ridicule, sarcasm, caricature, euphemism, allusion, and/or parody (Harman and Holman 491). A satire can be classified as indirect, which often takes the form of a "fictional narrative, in which the objects of the satire are characters," or formal, where the speaker uses first person address (Abrams and Harpham 321). In Horatian formal satire, the speaker is an "urbane, witty, and tolerant man of the world, who is moved more often to wry amusement than to indignation ... and who uses a relaxed and informal language to evoke from readers a wry smile at human failings and absurdities—sometimes including his own" (Abrams and Harpham 321). In Juvenalian formal satire, the speaker is biting, bitter, and angry (Nilsen and Nilsen), "a serious moralist who uses a dignified and public style of utterance to decry modes of vice and error which are no less dangerous because they are ridiculous and who undertakes to evoke from readers contempt, moral indignation, or an unillusioned sadness at the aberrations of humanity" (Abrams and Harpham 321). Having arrived at this definition,

I tell students we're going to watch an episode of *The Simpsons*. They reply with a volley of enthusiastic approvals, from "Yes!" to high-fives. I ask them to write down every element of satire they observe in the episode and try to determine whether it is an example of indirect or formal satire. If they decide it is formal satire, I ask them to determine whether it fits Horatian or Juvenalian style.

As I look around the darkened room, students' expressions display gleeful disbelief that I've sanctioned watching a cartoon during class. Some appear hesitant to laugh at first, as if they are convinced learning can't be fun and suspect punishment will follow if they enjoy it. Eventually, however, they relax and chuckle at the episode's funniest moments.

We identify the show's audience as middle- and upper-class American adults. The Simpsons' lifestyle is something people in that socioeconomic class will recognize and relate to. They are also likely to have experienced many iterations of the "typical" American Thanksgiving and arrived at an age where they are now responsible for their own families' holiday traditions (e.g., providing a turkey dinner). Those traditions are the foundation of the episode's humor.

We conclude that the purpose of "Bart vs. Thanksgiving" is to highlight absurdities in how its audience celebrates Thanksgiving. In particular, the episode focuses on family squabbles that mark holiday gatherings as well as the consumerism and anti-intellectualism that pervade both the holiday and American culture as a whole.

The first satiric element we discuss is caricature. The show's opening credits present the Simpsons as a typical middle-class American family: Bart is frequently in trouble at school and spends his spare time careening recklessly through town on his skateboard. Lisa is an overachiever, intelligent and mature beyond her years but also a showoff who gets kicked out of band rehearsal for launching into a solo that drowns out the other players. Maggie doesn't have a voice (literally or figuratively, like many youngest children who have a hard time making themselves heard within their families) and is frequently left unsupervised, which is reflective of parents' tendency to be more laid back and distracted by the time they have their third child. Marge, a homemaker, grocery shops and runs errands. Homer serves as the family's breadwinner. Viewers see why he garners little respect from his coworkers and family, however, when he drops a radioactive rod in his haste to leave work the moment the quitting whistle sounds. He then tosses another rod into the street after finding it lodged in his shirt collar and is nearly run down by Bart on his skateboard, Lisa on her bike, and Marge and Maggie in the car as they all arrive home at the end of the day.

The caricatures are reinforced in the exposition of "Bart vs. Thanksgiving," which depicts a scene eerily familiar to many Americans. Marge preps the turkey, while Homer watches TV. Lisa struggles to create a centerpiece for the dinner table despite Bart's smothering her with a couch cushion as he tries to take away a bottle of glue. He claims the glue is his; Lisa says it belongs to the whole family. Tired of Bart's harassment, Lisa gives him the glue and explains to Homer as if she is the teacher and he the student that Bart's interest in the glue is just "territoriality": he only wants the glue because she's using it. Bart looks at the glue bottle he now holds and declares, "Hey, man, I don't want your stupid glue," thereby proving Lisa's theory. He tosses it on the floor, where Maggie mistakes it for her milk bottle and almost drinks it. Maggie then wanders from the room unnoticed and crawls up a staircase littered with, in what students recognize as hyperbole, the most dangerous items imaginable: a skateboard, a rake, and a series of extension cords linked by exposed connections.

In addition to poking fun at the way family members are more apt than usual to irritate each other on this holiday devoted to family togetherness, Bart and Lisa's fight over the glue also ridicules Americans' short attention spans, a side effect of the consumerism that drives our economy. From clothing to cars and electronics to espresso (or in Bart's case, glue) Americans exhibit a child-like desire to possess what we don't have. We seem to interpret the Constitution's guaranteed pursuit of happiness as equivalent to a hunt for the latest and greatest material possession. Once we have that possession, we succumb to advertising that convinces us we need something better. We tire of the new possession quickly, discard it, and forget about it to pursue the next object we glimpse just around the corner.

Part of that consumerism is the monetization of sports, particularly that most American game, football. "Bart vs. Thanksgiving" points out the inherent irony in placing a game that venerates violence and nets exorbitant profits for wealthy team owners at the center of a holiday intended to promote kindness, gratitude, and generosity. In fact, Homer, like many American males (and some females), pays more attention to the game on TV than he does to the family he has been granted time away from work to appreciate. Worse, his interest is driven by vice rather than love of the game. He roots against his favorite team, the Dallas Cowboys (who are also known as "America's team") because he bet on their opponent to win. Even as he anticipates eating a meal to reenact part of America's origin narrative, he bets against the success of "America's team" in a game known throughout the world as "American football" (to differentiate it from soccer, which the rest of the world calls "football"). The episode takes a final shot at Americans' casual acceptance of football's violence during the only portion of the game we viewers see: a player lies sprawled, unconscious and twitching, on the turf after an excessively damaging tackle. Homer is unfazed by the injury. The color commentator acknowledges that it could result in brain damage and/or paralysis by quipping that "it looks like they'll be feeding [the player] Thanksgiving dinner through a tube" and laughing.

The episode's ridicule of Thanksgiving football continues with its depiction of halftime. An announcer introduces the halftime spectacle as a "salute to the greatest hemisphere on earth … the Western hemisphere." An enormous globe cut in half rises over the field, making it appear as if North, Central, and South America are the only land masses on earth. The spectacle attributes the Western hemisphere's greatness to its status as "the dancingest hemisphere"—not exactly a ringing endorsement. However, the spectacle seems designed to avoid excluding anyone in the viewing audience or including anything that could be considered objectionable, an ironic contrast to the game's grittiness, violence, sexism, and U.S.–centric attitude. It features the "well-groomed young go-getters of 'Hooray for Everything,'" a tagline that refers both to the group's physical appearance as well as its similarity to 1990s boy bands like The Backstreet Boys, 98 Degrees, and O-Town that displayed questionable musical ability but were groomed by record labels for mass appeal and maximum merchandizing opportunities. Homer reinforces this idea by stating that he likes the group because its members have "a great attitude"; he doesn't mention their talent. To increase Hooray for Everything's/O-Town's appeal, producers strip the songs of any content consumers might object to; that way, they can sell more albums and merchandise. Lyrics consist of repeated "doo-dot" and "dancin'," which sounds like an infant's pre-language babble. In fact, the spectacle seems to aim for a level of intellectual sophistication appropriate for infants; its success is apparent from the fact that Maggie is the only one who watches. If viewers had any doubt about how the writers of "Bart vs. Thanksgiving" assess football fans' intellectual capacity, the commentator eliminates it by noting sarcastically that the stands are "ablaze with flashbulbs" despite common knowledge that flash photography doesn't work in large outdoor stadiums.

Another Thanksgiving tradition, the Macy's Thanksgiving Day Parade, is portrayed as sharing many of football's attributes. The parade's commentators admit their narration is not only inane but nonsensical. Instead of images that reflect the holiday's historical origins or family values, parade floats feature pop culture icons and corporate mascots, while balloons pay homage to classic cartoon characters. Here, students recognize that although the episode's fictional nature classifies it as indirect satire, it incorporates elements of Horatian formal satire by poking fun at itself. Bart complains that the characters immortalized as balloons are so old he doesn't recognize them. Homer explains, "If you start building a balloon for every flash in the pan cartoon character, you'll turn the parade into a farce," as a Bart balloon floats across the screen in the background. Their exchange acknowledges the obsession with pop culture and the short attention span that led parade organizers to honor a character who had only been on TV for a single season when this episode originally aired. The exchange also presents an early example of self-referentiality—another element of satire.

Parade float operators, halftime entertainers, and football players aren't the only ones working while families like the Simpsons and members of the wealthy one percent like Mr. Burns spend the holiday relaxing at home. The episode ridicules economic and employment disparities in America by showing guards at the plant eating frozen turkey dinners on microwave trays while they work. One of the guards is even reading *Les Miserables*, a fictional depiction of how economic inequality and deplorable working conditions spurred the French Revolution. Hyperbolic comparison of modern-day America with conditions similar to pre-revolution France continues with a shot of Mr. Burns' mansion. His estate looks down over the town from a hill at the corner of Croseus and Mammon, an allusion to his greed and wealth. Croseus, king of ancient Lydia, is credited with being the first to stamp gold coins and use them as money (The British Museum). The Greeks adapted his system of currency for use in their democracy, which is the model on which American democracy is based. Mammon refers to riches obtained through greedy pursuit and is frequently personified as a false god ("Mammon"). In fact, Jesus declares in the New Testament Gospel of Matthew 6:24, "you cannot serve God and Mammon," something American culture seems to have forgotten.

The episode's last depiction of American economic disparity is Bart's exploration of life on "the wrong side of the tracks." As soon as he crosses the tracks, Springfield transforms from a suburban Utopia to what he refers to as "skid row." Here, hyperbole abounds. Signs advertise "massages" and liquor stores; disreputable figures loiter on every street corner. Desperate for food to quiet his growling stomach, Bart uses a fake ID to sell blood in exchange for money, another comment on what people who are down on their luck must do to feed themselves or their families. He also gets a cookie for his blood but passes out in the gutter before he can eat it. He awakens to find two homeless men asking if he's OK. They lead him to a mission, where all three receive a free meal, no questions asked. A local news reporter parodies the "true meaning of Thanksgiving" stories that air every year during the holiday by describing the scene. In a clear example of irony, however, he uses every available slur (e.g., derelict, freeloader, etc.) to refer to the people eating at the mission. He leaves as quickly as possible after finishing his report and mutters under his breath that doing the story will be worth it if he wins an Emmy. In direct contrast to the holiday's focus, he is motivated by self-interest and taking advantage of those less fortunate than he is to gain rewards and status.

Next, students and I discuss Homer's trip to pick up his father from Springfield Retirement Castle. Homer makes it clear to Marge that he'll wait to leave until halftime—another depiction of how football comes before family. When Homer arrives, the home's residents are receiving last-minute "personalized" holiday greetings, as relayed by staff, from their families. One resident in particular gets a fax and declares proudly, "I knew they wouldn't forget me!" The scene ridicules American families for putting seniors in complexes where they live among strangers and are cared for by low-wage employees, a stark contrast to other cultures, where the elderly hold exalted positions in the community, play active roles in family life, and retire under the care of children and grandchildren with whom they reside until the end of their lives. Should viewers misunderstand the homes' motives in caring for seniors, Homer's dad explains later in the episode that if he's late returning, the staff will declare him legally dead and collect on his life insurance policy.

"Bart vs. Thanksgiving" also uses irony to imply that adults at the end of their lives are treated like children. Springfield Retirement Castle looks like a preschool. Residents sit at round tables in a room decorated with brightly colored turkeys and produce holiday-themed arts and crafts. They have turkey puree for dinner. They are protected from the harsh realities of real life by a sign thanking visitors "for not discussing the outside world." Entrance doors that only swing inward prevent them from leaving without permission or supervision, calling to mind a certain hotel where residents "can check out any time [they] like, but [they] can never leave" (Eagles).

This anti-intellectualism and the consumerist mentality that accompanies it even impact holiday food. Economies of scale have replaced home-grown turkeys with hormone-injected, factory-farmed birds that are slaughtered in mass processing plants, frozen, shipped across country, and sold in big box stores for pennies per pound. The holiday's "home-cooked meal" is now almost as inauthentic as football's halftime show. Marge dons latex gloves and imitates a proctologist by reaching through the base of the turkey to remove its internal organs, which have already been removed, wrapped in plastic, and returned to the body cavity along with cooking instructions and warnings about salmonella.

Canned cranberries are another example of factory food and come with a side of irony when Bart offers to help Marge in the kitchen. His help consists of asking what he can do, where to find the cranberries, where to find the can opener, how to operate the can opener, and, once Marge opens the can, dumping the cranberries into a bowl and leaving the kitchen without hearing Marge's request to put them in the refrigerator. She ends up doing that herself. In the end, Bart's "help" creates more work for his mom.

Marge's mom and sisters also offer help that is less than helpful. Her sisters bring their own food, claiming Marge's turkey is always dry. Later, viewers see all three of them basting the turkey with so much juice it leaves puddles on the kitchen floor, another veiled reference to the dreaded dry turkey that has become a Thanksgiving cliché. Marge's mom is suffering from laryngitis, so she condenses an entire day's worth of criticism into a single comment: "You never do anything right." Homer isn't immune from parental critique either. His dad scolds him for not putting enough kindling in the fireplace and mocks his inability to start a fire. Marge's sisters jump on the bandwagon; never passing up an opportunity to point out Homer's flaws, they tell him, "even a caveman can start a fire." This seems tame, however, in comparison to the trio's childish bickering when the sisters first arrive. Not unlike Lisa and Bart, who open the episode with their fight over the glue, Homer greets Marge's sisters with sarcastic enthusiasm and then mixes up their names, clearly baiting them the way one sibling might bait another. The sisters mutter about Homer's insincerity and imply that he's an unsuitable husband. He imitates them in a mocking, singsong voice, again calling to mind playground disagreements.

Lisa is the only character who understands the real purpose and origins of Thanksgiving. She invites Maggie to contribute to her centerpiece even though she knows Maggie will only scribble on it. After Maggie has, indeed, scribbled on it, Lisa thanks and hugs her, showing the inclusiveness and gratitude intended to be part of the holiday. Unfortunately, her efforts are thwarted at every other turn. When she tries to explain contributions to American history made by the women in her centerpiece, Bart interrupts by presenting the fully-cooked turkey to a chorus of "oohs" and "ahhhs." He claims there isn't enough room for both the centerpiece and the turkey on the table and sends the centerpiece flying into the fireplace, an indication of which values win out on Thanksgiving. Ironically, the centerpiece then ignites the blaze Homer failed to light in the fireplace.

When Lisa's attempts to inject a literary element into the occasion by reading a poem she has written, she's cut off by the family's surprise at seeing the runaway Bart on TV. (He is part of the reporter's story at the mission.) The title of Lisa's poem is "Howl of the Unappreciated," a reference not only to her, but also to the women in her centerpiece. The poem's first line, "I saw the best meals of my generation destroyed by the madness of my brother" is an allusion to Allen Ginsberg's poem "Howl," which begins, "I saw the finest minds of my generation destroyed by madness." No one in the episode notices the allusion. Turkey over history, TV over literature: both choices illustrate the anti-intellectualism lurking in Thanksgiving traditions and therefore in wider American culture.

In the end, the show as a whole parodies every "special holiday episode" of television sitcoms that airs during Thanksgiving week because Bart discovers the true meaning of the holiday despite his efforts to the contrary. He gives the $12 he earned selling blood to the homeless men at the mission. He apologizes for destroying Lisa's centerpiece. Then he joins the rest of family at the kitchen table for turkey sandwiches.

"Bart vs. Thanksgiving" is rich with examples Horatian satire; therefore, my students and I use it as a point of contrast for analyzing Swift's "A Modest Proposal," an example of Juvenalian satire. While *The Simpsons* doesn't hold much back in its examination of flaws and hypocrisy in American culture, its tone is light. "A Modest Proposal," on the other hand, points a finger directly at those responsible for Ireland's woes.

I ask students to look at Swift's essay again and identify words they don't understand. I then divide the class into groups of four and assign each group a handful of those words (e.g., Papists, Popish, the Pretender in Spain, commonwealth, etc.) to research for our next class period.

When students return to class, their definitions provide a foundation for piecing together the historical, social, economic, religious, and biographical context necessary to fully appreciate Swift's satire. We establish that Swift was born in Dublin, Ireland, in 1667. His father's death seven months prior left the family without a breadwinner at a time when many Irish citizens were suffering from the effects of famine and relegated to working their own land as tenant farmers. Wealthy Englishmen purchased Irish land and charged exorbitant rent to live on it, demanding a percentage of all the food raised/grown. As meager as their produce was, they were forced to export what little food they grew.

Swift grew up in similar circumstances. He was frequently ill and was eventually abandoned by his mother, who couldn't afford to care for him. He was fortunate enough, however, to receive a formal education under the patronage of his uncle, with whom he was sent to live. As an adult, he moved to Leicester, England, in pursuit of a graduate degree.

Though Protestant, living in England, and educated like a gentleman, Swift's sympathies lay with the Irish, whom most of Protestant England considered inferior and anachronistic because of their poverty, lack of education, and adherence to Catholicism. In particular, the English looked down upon the Irish for having more children than they could afford to feed. Swift's disdain for England's attitude toward Ireland's dire circumstances prompted his "modest proposal." Distributed as a pamphlet, "A Modest Proposal" employs nearly every element of satire the students and I recognized in "Bart vs. Thanksgiving" but to very different effect. While *The Simpsons* seeks to generate laughs while pointing out societal issues, Swift hoped to shame English landlords into extending mercy to their Irish tenants.

Once students gain some awareness of the proposal's context, I divide the class into small groups again and give each a portion of the essay to re-read. They are to identify every element of satire they can find and explain how that element helps the essay accomplish its purpose.

This time, students recognize the essay's formal language, reasonable tone, false humility, and willingness to assign blame as reflective of Juvenalian formal satire. They point out the irony of using phrases like "humbly propose" and "humbly offer" to put forth a drastic and unreasonable solution. They also see irony in Swifts' emphasis on the benefits of his proposal for all involved, such as new delicacies and increased profits for English landlords, adequate sustenance and income for Irish farmers, less crime spurred by desperation in Ireland, fewer abortions and murdered infants, and a smaller population of Catholics pledging loyalty to the Pope, who represents a challenge to the English monarch's authority. They point out Swift's unnecessary use of statistics and count how many times words like "computer" and "calculate" appear, as if he is explaining an appropriate solution to a mathematical problem. Most significantly, however, they discuss Swift's implication that Englishmen would willingly consider consuming human flesh. This, in particular, struck a nerve with Swift's audience for several reasons. First, the English elite were obsessed with propriety, and cannibalism represented the worst form of barbaric savagery. Second, cannibalism was a grave sin that carried stiff penalties in the afterlife. Lastly, English citizens heard rumors that the Irish had resorted to cannibalism during previous periods of famine (O'Dowd). In a few cases, those rumors were later proven true (O'Dowd). Swift also suggests Americans can offer cannibalism tips based on experience, a condemnation in the form of comparing American settlers' treatment of Native Americans to the English aristocracy's treatment of the Irish. Therefore, while Swift's proposal seems so ridiculous as to be comical now, his audience couldn't as easily dismiss what he described as a realistic possibility. And if it happened, they would be responsible. The more students examine Swift's choice of words and examples, the more they demonstrate their ability to critically evaluate a challenging text. And "Bart vs. Thanksgiving" plays a key role in helping them develop that skill.

Contrary to conventional wisdom, *The Simpsons* is a valuable educational tool. A wide variety of episodes that are now 20+ years old prove relevant for framing debate about current political issues, such as wages, economic disparity, and immigration, as well as discussions about the role literature plays in society. Perhaps most importantly, however, they make learning fun. Now I understand and take pride in the image that adorns our hallway wall.

WORKS CITED

Abrams, M. H., and Geoffrey Galt Harpham. *A Glossary of Literary Terms.* 9th ed., Wadsworth Cengage, 2009.
"Bart vs. Thanksgiving." *The Simpsons: The Complete Second Season.* Written by George Meyer, directed by David Silverman. 1990. 20th Century–Fox, 1990.
The British Museum. "Gold Coin of Croesus." *A History of the World,* 2014, http://www.bbc.co.uk/ahistoryoftheworld/objects/7cEz771FSeOLptGIElaquA. Accessed 24 July 2014.
Eagles. "Hotel California." *Hell Freezes Over,* Geffen, 1994.

Harman, William, and Hugh Holman. *A Handbook to Literature.* 11th ed., Pearson, 2009.
"Mammon." *Merriam-Webster Dictionary,* 2014, http://www.merriam-webster.com/dictionary/mammon.
Nilsen, Don, and Alleen Pace Nilsen. "Satire." *Arizona State University Don and Alleen Nilsen Division of the Humanities Emeritus College,* http://www.public.asu.edu/~dnilsen/. Accessed 3 Dec. 2017.
O'Dowd. Niall. "Cannibalism was Likely Practiced in Irish Famine Says Leading Expert." *Irish Central,* 15 May 2012, http://www.irishcentral.com/news/cannibalism-was-likely-practiced-in-irish-famine-says-leading-expert-151504185–237447661.html.
Swift, Jonathan. "A Modest Proposal," 1729.

What We All Came
Here to See—Sex

KARMA WALTONEN

In a parenthetical aside in his article on *The Simpsons*, Ben McCorkle asks, "Could the fact that the 'good' members of the family all happen to be female reflect some feminist statement on Groening's part?" (98). My college students respond to the question in ways that reflect a divergence in definitions and ideologies. The students find the show "good," but whether they consider feminism "good" determines whether they believe Matt Groening is a feminist. Echoing McCorkle's essentialist question (which assumes feminism is the belief that women are morally superior to men), the students at first often engage in a problematic cognitive dissonance—they believe in equality, but often dismiss feminism (due to both a misunderstanding of the word and to contemporary society's demonization of it). The show's satiric bent is inherently progressive and thus inherently feminist, but to understand the show holistically, one must avoid judging it by the actions of a few characters. *The Simpsons* represents America—the same America our students live in, one that embraces cognitive dissonance. Thus, Marge burns bras in her youth ("The Way We Was" 2.12) yet embraces a traditional homemaker role soon after. Lisa creates a feminist doll ("Lisa vs. Malibu Stacy" 5.14) yet falls victim to body image issues ("Sleeping with the Enemy" 16.3). The women—and men—on the show are complex, illustrating a world in which we know there should be equality—and in which all sexes should battle against the status quo.

In other words, the show represents American culture but also critiques it. This oppositional mode is signaled in a recurring title motif: the "X vs. Y": among them, "Homer vs. The Eighteenth Amendment" (8.18), "Marge vs. Singles, Seniors, Childless Couples and Teens and Gays" (15.8), and "Lisa vs. Malibu Stacy" (5.14). In the latter, Lisa fights against feminist stereotypes, but struggles when language itself becomes a barrier to engagement:

244

Stacy: Let's buy makeup so the boys will like us.
Lisa: Don't you people see anything wrong with what Malibu Stacy says?
Celeste: There's something wrong with what *my* Stacy says.
Stacy: [*in a low voice*] My Spidey sense is tingling—anybody call for a web-slinger?
Lisa: No, Celeste. I mean, the things she says are sexist.
Girls: [*giggle*] Lisa said a dirty word!

The conflation of "sexist" and "sex" is funny here, but "sexist" *is* a dirty word—to some, especially those who are anti-feminist, as it is used to identify a problem that the listener either doesn't see or doesn't see as a problem.

Our society is currently struggling with a new vocabulary. *Feminist* has been made into a bad word by anti-feminists (along with its dysphemism, femi-nazi), leaving feminists with no good word to use unless they want to have a consciousness-raising talk every time they use it. *Sex* and *gender* are conflated constantly; feminist scholars use the term *sex/gender system* to discuss society expectations—that is, the way we expect gender expression to be aligned with biological sex (in other words, since I'm a biological woman, I'm expected to act feminine); *sex* means various acts (which, if you listen to politicians and narrow definers of virginity, we have problems classifying), but it's also a word used in biological distinctions (male/female vs. masculine/feminine gender distinctions); *sexuality* is usually used to mean whether one is gay or straight or bi, but encompasses so much more; even those of us who advocate for equality struggle to find the right terms sometimes. Recently, I asked what my friends and colleagues thought the new "LGBT" acronym was. The answer: QUILTBAG (Queer, Questioning, Intersex, Lesbian, Transgender/Transsexual, Bisexual, Asexual, Gay). Even the most all-inclusive phrases, however, cease to be so in some contexts (my British friends would not use the word "queer"—in their country, this is still just a slur that hasn't been reclaimed). Many of my students use the word "pansexual" (not represented in QUILTBAG)—they want to explode the sex/gender binary rather than just allow for movement along the spectrum. In 1997, the GLAAD award-winning episode "Homer's Phobia" (8.15) explored these linguistic issues. When John, a gay man, calls himself *queer*, Homer objects: "Yeah, and that's another thing! I resent *you* people using that word. That's *our* word for making fun of you! We need it!!" At the end of the episode, Homer's mind about John has changed, as John has saved his life:

Homer: Hey! We owe this guy, and I don't want you calling him a sissy. This guy's a fruit, and a … no, wait, wait, wait: queer, queer, queer! That's what you like to be called, right?
John: Well, that or John.
Lisa: This is about as tolerant as Dad gets, so you should be flattered.

We have about three decades of material to trace the ways this fictional community tackles these issues, from the show's relationship to feminism to sex and sexuality in all their meanings.

Feminism

> I made a modern studio apartment for my Malibu Stacey doll. This is the kitchen; this is where she prints her weekly feminist newsletter—"Lisa the Greek" (3.14)

In our book, *The Simpsons in the Classroom: Embiggening the Learning Experience with the Wisdom of Springfield*, Denise Du Vernay and I briefly discuss feminism on the show (225–7). Like most contemporary feminists, male and female, Denise and I identify with materialist feminism, a feminism predicated not on an ideology of feminine superiority (essentialist) nor one that defines a woman's success via the dominant hegemonic position's terms (liberal). Materialist feminism strives for equality in all forms, regardless of sex/gender/sexuality, race, nationality, religion or lack thereof, etc. Materialist feminism sees power as a matrix. For example, as educated, white, mostly able-bodied, neurotypical, cis-gendered, straight Americans, Denise and I hold more power and privilege than most of the people who've ever lived on this planet. However, we are still subject to institutional/societal sexism, the drawbacks of being non-tenured faculty, the pressure on the middle class, and the bias against atheists (among the many other ways in which we might define ourselves and by which society may define us).[1]

The Simpsons typically explores these and other issues in a left-leaning way, as it critiques racism, sexism, the power of the wealthy over the poor, etc. Matt Groening is, after all, famously anti-establishment. That is not to say that the show is unabashedly liberal, however. In fact, a study by Kenneth Michael White and Mirya Holman found "that *The Simpsons* makes fun of Democrats and Republicans rarely and equally" (103). Politicians of all stripes are ridiculed and the excesses of the left are critiqued—e.g., extremism in political correctness. For example, in "Behind the Laughter" (11.22), Lisa's attorney at a contentious family dinner exclaims, "That is assault" during the argument. She is identified as "Gloria Allred, Shrill Feminist Attorney." (Gloria Allred is a real person—a high profile lawyer, most famous perhaps for representing Nicole Brown Simpson's family against OJ Simpson; Allred coincidentally has a daughter named Lisa.)

Notably, Allred (not playing herself) is critiqued not for being a feminist, but for being a "shrill" feminist—shrill is often code for essentialist.

In my *Simpsons* classes, we start down the rabbit hole of discussing feminism with a deceptively innocent question: Is Marge a feminist?

Once we establish the different types of feminism, the question still needs a lot of unpacking, as Marge, like most people, is inconsistent.

The students often remember her stronger moments first:

- Marge consistently encourages all her children, regardless of sex, to succeed.
- Marge is an activist for women's rights in high school ("The Way We Was" 2.12).
- Marge regrets being told that she couldn't be an astronaut when she was young—her sisters told her she couldn't because she was a girl ("Last Exit to Springfield" 4.17).
- Marge becomes a police officer—a good one—despite the sexism displayed by her police unit and her husband ("The Springfield Connection" 6.23).
- Marge is also a talented "handyman," despite also suffering from people's unfair sex/gender expectations ("Please Homer, Don't Hammer 'Em" 18.3).
- Marge fights sexual harassment at work ("Marge Gets a Job" 4.7).
- Marge doesn't want Bart to be taught to objectify women ("Homer's Night Out" 1.10).
- Marge has her consciousness raised by Professor Stephane August ("That '90s Show" 19.11).

Yet there are many moments that question Marge's feminist resolve, many of which involve Marge's role as a stereotypical housewife, such as when Marge doesn't see what's wrong with the talking Malibu Stacy doll saying sexist things (both Marge and the doll believe we can "forget our troubles with a big bowl of strawberry ice cream" ["Lisa vs. Malibu Stacy" 5.14]).

Marge represents the lives of many married American women—she can choose to stay home and focus on being a homemaker. That it is a *choice* is note-worthy. The mommy wars, which pit homemakers against working mothers, depend upon choice. Moms who *must* stay home because they aren't able to work, because of extremely repressive cultures, disability, or other factors and women who *must* work because they are the sole breadwinner (like me) are ignored in conversations about motherhood. Marge, of course, enters the workforce several times over the series, usually because the family is in such a precarious financial position that she **must**, but she usually chooses to quit. In many episodes, she claims to be fulfilled by this choice, such as when she says homemaking allows her to be creative in "Separate Vocations" (3.18) or when she shows she can express herself, as Homer says, "In the lovely home you keep and the food you serve," serving Blinky the three-eyed fish to Mr. Burns and subsequently ruining his campaign for governor ("Two Cars in Every Garage and Three Eyes on Every Fish" 2.4).

However, in other episodes, Marge feels taken for granted and exhibits stress, as in "Simpsoncalifragilisticexpiala(Annoyed Grunt)cious" (8.13), in which she's "going bald from stress."

Many episodes feature Marge being clearly conflicted and hurt by the tension between old-fashioned middle-class motherhood, which she embodies, and Lisa's dreams, which reject that role. In "Separate Vocations," for example, Lisa becomes depressed and rebellious when she is told that she's destined to be a "mommy" rather than a great jazz musician. Marge grumbles, "It's not that bad" when Lisa says, "I might as well be dead." In "She Used to be My Girl" (16.4), a former Springfieldian, Chloe, returns as a successful reporter. Marge is confronted with what her life could have been like if she made choices parallel to Chloe's (Chloe was dating Barney when Marge was dating Homer). Marge is also threatened when Lisa sees Chloe as a role model. Uncharacteristically, Marge gets drunk and fights with Chloe, forbidding Lisa from attending a women's conference with her. In "Lisa Simpson, This Isn't Your Life" (22.5), Lisa learns that Marge's grades were good until she fell in love with Homer—Lisa vows to be different and wants desperately to go to a private school. Marge is incredibly hurt by Lisa's dismissal of her role but sacrifices her time and energy so Lisa can attend the school. As when Lisa got rid of her pony to save her father in "Lisa's Pony" (3.8), Lisa gives up her dream of a private school out of appreciation for her mother.

Marge also defends parenting in "Marge vs. Singles, Seniors, Childless Couples and Teens and Gays" (15.8), when she feels judged by those without young children in the public sphere. In contrast, when Marge realizes that the "cool" parents who've just moved to town would judge her for bottle feeding Maggie, she fakes being a nursing mother for a while and later admits, "I guess I do feel a little bad about not breast-feeding my kids" ("The Day the Earth Stood Cool" 24.7).

One of the ways in which Marge's feminism is also complex is in her relationship to QUILTBAG rights.[2] Liberal feminism, common during the second wave among middle class women, has often been criticized for neglecting the needs and concerns of women of color, women in poverty, noncisgendered, and non-heterosexual women. Too often, Marge, like many in her generation, has been weak about gay rights. For example, Lisa complains in "Summer of 4 Ft. 2" (7.25) that Gore Vidal has "kissed more boys than I ever will." Marge quickly responds, "*Girls*, Lisa. Boys kiss *girls*." Often, however, Marge is shown as very tolerant of gays. She is in favor of gay marriage, going so far as to argue with her pastor ("There's Something About Marrying" 16.10) and is quick to accept John, who's homosexual, as a friend (and criticizing Homer when he displays bigotry) ("Homer's Phobia" 8.15). While at one point, she didn't really understand the concept of a gay bar ("I heard about a new bar where men dance with men. Doesn't that sound adorable?"

("Brother's Little Helper" 11.2), we see her at Smithers and Moe's new gay bar in "Flaming Moe" (22.11). Significantly, though, her tolerance often does not extend to her family, at first. After arguing for gay marriage, she rejects her sister, Patty, when Patty officially comes out to her and announces her engagement.[3]

In all, however, when Marge veers from a progressive point of view, whether it be her insistence on heteronormativity in her family or the façade about homemaking being perfectly fulfilling, the show is not on her side. We are supposed to laugh when Marge misunderstands gay culture and cringe when she spouts homophobic ideas. Similarly, we are asked to admire everything Marge does for her family (there's a reason she is consistently voted one of the best TV moms), while understanding that what's important is that homemaking be her choice, with Lisa free to choose a different path.

Thus, the show certainly takes a feminist and progressive point of view when it comes to the sex/gender system and to QUILTBAG rights. But what about other uses of the words *sex* and *sexuality*?

Dirty Words

> Hi, I'm Karma Waltonen. You may remember me from the first half of this essay, "and I'll leave you with what we all came here to see: *hard-core nudity!*"—"The 138th Episode Spectacular" (7.10)

In college *Simpsons* classes (and other classes too, of course), students are exposed to and are somewhat prepared to talk about issues of sexism, identity, and sexuality (in relation to object choice/identity). In one class, years ago, students and I generated lots of potential topics for one of our sessions. I had the students vote anonymously for what they wanted. Not surprisingly, they wanted sex (we had already done a unit on sexuality, in terms of object choice/identification).

As we prepared to watch our episodes, I introduced some of the things we might include under this new umbrella of sex and sexuality: desire, fulfillment, morality/societal expectations, frequency, fidelity and infidelity, the inexperienced to experienced spectrum, the sex drive spectrum, and the vanilla to kinky spectrum.[4]

I did not expect all students to be comfortable with every aspect of the topic, and we didn't have all that much time, but I thought it was important to put the ideas out there. After all, just as power is a matrix (I'm white, hetero, American, etc.), sexuality must also be understood as a matrix, as the sex/gender of one's object choice isn't the only aspect of who one is sexually.

We watched a few episodes, "Grampa vs. Sexual Inadequacy" (6.10), "Natural Born Kissers" (9.25), and "The Last Temptation of Homer" (5.9), so we could tackle sexual desire and lack thereof, light kink (i.e. sex in public), and temptation.

This is tricky stuff—discussions of sexuality are more open now, but those discussions are still divisive. Caitlyn Jenner's transformation means that my students know the word *transgender,* but they don't know much— they often confuse transgender individuals with people who simply present as butch or effeminate or with drag queens. Students aren't the only ones who are confused. When I recently wrote an article on asexuality in *Sherlock,* my editor urged me to include more theory. I had to explain that there wasn't much out there (which is why my article was necessary and exciting). Researching academic theories of kink was also fairly fruitless. (I felt that googling would be *too* fruitful, and not with anything edible for this essay.)

Depictions of sexuality on *The Simpsons* started as fairly tame, but sexuality and sexual situations have been a part of the show since the beginning. The very first episode produced, "Some Enchanted Evening"[5] (1.13), features Homer and Marge spending a night at a motel. Marge's nightgown caused problems with the censors, as revealed in the DVD commentary. Marge and Homer in bed happily post-coitus includes Homer saying, "I suppose my work here is done."

Sexuality has both remained a theme, been used for jokes, and has been able to become more overt, such as when Homer is raped by a panda ("Homer vs. Dignity" 12.5).

Transgender

As with many sitcoms from the '90s, trans individuals have not been main featured players, but have been used for comedy (Chandler's father, a trans woman, played by Kathleen Turner, was featured on *Friends* in 2001, to comic effect). In Season 4 (2002) of *The Simpsons,* Homer's reference to his cousin implies that transgender is the result of "warping."

> **Homer:** I've got it all figured out. The baby can have Bart's crib and Bart'll sleep with us until he's twenty-one.
> **Marge:** Won't that warp him?
> **Homer:** My cousin Frank did it.
> **Marge:** You don't have a cousin Frank.
> **Homer:** He became Francine back in '76. Then he joined that cult. I think his name is Mother Shabubu now ["Lisa's First Word" 4.10].

The Simpsons has yet to tackle transgender in a substantial way.

Fidelity

Homer: Now I know I haven't been the best Christian. In fact, when you're up there yak-yak-yaking, I'm usually either sleeping or mentally undressing the female parishioners—"Homer's Triple Bypass" (4.11)

While there's been a marked rise in people coming out as non-monogamous (in various forms of polyamory), monogamy is still the normalized ideal for heterosexual couples, especially in regard to marriage. Of course, biology and social science show us that we as a species are bad at monogamy; it's not surprising, therefore, that *The Simpsons* has always explored temptation. The ninth episode, "Life on the Fast Lane," features Marge being tempted by her bowling coach. Temptation in this case is precipitated by Homer's bad treatment of her: specifically, he gives her a bowling ball with his name on it for her birthday. Marge resists cheating, for the sake of her marriage. The commentary on the DVD says that Groening got irate letters—marriages on TV weren't supposed to have real life problems.

This was only the first of many temptations—for both Marge and Homer. One of my students once asked why, when Marge is suspicious that Homer might be cheating, she fights for him and confronts him, but when Homer is suspicious, he tends merely to feel victimized. For example, in "Life on the Fast Lane" (1.9), Homer finds a gift from Marge's suitor—a bowling glove, with *her name* on it. He merely puts it in her drawer. I asked the student to think through the answer to this difference in behavior. He concluded that it's because Homer knows he doesn't deserve Marge.

The Simpson family isn't the only one who grapples with this issue. Edna was left for her marriage counselor, and Luann found a new beau immediately after separating from Kirk. And we know that nonmonogamy is sometimes embraced by Springfieldians, as Homer and Marge unwittingly ended up at a key party ("500 Keys" 22.21). This kind of sharing is not always welcome, however, as Homer realizes after agreeing to a "Half-Decent Proposal" (13.10).

Predation and Consent

Homer: "That's kind of a gray area"—"Homer Badman" (6.9)

While people can debate many aspects of sex and sexuality, society says consent is required (though not uniform about what consent entails). As *The Simpsons* is a comedy show, Marge and the other characters are not often confronted with sexual assault. However, the show has certainly dealt with the issue. In "Treehouse of Horror XII" (13.1), *Demon Seed*, a film in which a house computer rapes a woman, is parodied. The house computer in the Simpsons' home is called (and voice by) Pierce Brosnan. Although he claims to be "merely a pile of circuits and microchips," Pierce is definitely attracted to Marge, noting her "elegant, swan-like neck." His attempt to kill her husband so he can have her is mirrored in "Treehouse of Horror XX" (21.4), when Moe gets rid of Homer to have his way with Marge. It is notable that many of the times Marge has been in danger have been in Halloween episodes. However, when she does succumb to having sex with other men (or in the case of "Send in the Clones" (Treehouse XIII 14.1), with a clone of Homer), it's consensual.

Thus, Marge is never raped, but several episodes feature sexual harassment. In "Marge Gets a Job" (4.7), Mr. Burns sexually harasses her. Marge calls him on it—saying that she'll "sue the pants off [him]." Unfortunately, Mr. Burns is confident enough in his powers and his lawyers to say, "you don't have to sue me to get my pants off." Marge is also a victim of "busy hands" when she's in high school. Artie Ziff seems like a good match, but pushes her too far, ripping her dress and getting slapped before finally acknowledging her "no" ("The Way We Was" 2.12). In both cases, the audience is clearly meant to be on Marge's side. No means no—men who sexually harass and assault women are vilified.

Surprisingly, Marge's professor, Stephane, is not vilified in the same way, although his relationship with Marge is clearly unethical ("That '90s Show" 19.11). While Stephane is very careful—some would say ridiculously careful—about getting Marge's consent, as a professor, he should know that he's not allowed to have a relationship with a current student. His power over her (via her grade) questions whether consent can ever truly be given. As an extremely liberal person (while watching a football game between the Patriots and the Redskins, he exclaims, "This isn't entertainment; it's genocide"), he should be sensitive to the power dynamics at work.

Homer is accused of sexual harassment in "Homer Badman" (6.9), an episode exploring contemporary media and its sensationalism. Homer is innocent—his lust is actually for a rare gummy candy—but the accusation becomes a teachable moment for the family.

> **Lisa:** I don't understand. What is she saying you did?
>
> **Homer:** Lisa, remember that postcard Grampa sent us from Florida of that alligator biting that woman's bottom? [...] We all thought it was hilarious. But it turns out we were wrong. That alligator was sexually harassing that woman.

The show also makes it clear that women can be guilty of predation. For example, Lindsay Naegle keeps changing jobs because she's "a sexual predator" ("Blame It on Lisa" 13.15). Homer is also victimized when he has a stalker, who wants to get rid of Marge so she can have him ("Homer of Seville" 19.2). A reference to the threat of rape occurs in "22 Short Films About Springfield" (7.21), but the viewer would probably have to know *Pulp Fiction* to get it. Overall, the threat to men follows a pattern of how men are not usually subject to the fear of rape in pop culture, as explained by Catherine Scott in *Thinking Kink: The Collision of BDSM, Feminism and Popular Culture*, except when it "is being played for comedy" (42).

The relationship between consent and alcohol is hazy. "Duffless" (4.16) features an ad showing feminists protesting a sexist advertising company (named after the company in *Bewitched*). The ad becomes self-referential as men spray the women with beer, turning them into bikini-wearing bimbos. One woman's protest sign changes into "Get Me Drunk!"

We are supposed to read this as wrong, but we are not asked to see Marge's inebriation during her first sexual encounter as problematic. Is Marge too drunk to give meaningful consent? *"Maybe it's the Champale talking,* but I think you're pretty sexy" ("I Married Marge" 3.12).

Issues of bestiality and child abuse are also issues of consent, but *The Simpsons* have rarely raised them. Recently, though, Bart noted how strange it was that his parents allowed an adult male mental patient, "Michael Jackson" ("a crazy man"), to stay in his bedroom ("Walking Big and Tall" 26.13).

Kink and Appetite

Marge: Do you want me to…?
Homer: No, don't do that!
Marge: Well, we used to…
Homer: Yeah, but I don't like it ["Natural Born Kissers" 9.25].

There's something to be said for bad writing. Or, rather, I'll say one good thing about a piece of particularly bad writing: *Fifty Shades of Grey* (which began its life as *Twilight* fan fiction) brought kink into the mainstream. I have yet to meet a kinky person who thinks the book actually captures the spirit of kink, but at least the world now has a starting point and some basic vocabulary for talking about it, even if the speakers don't fully understand it.

One of the ways in which humans can identify themselves in terms of sexuality is on the vanilla to kinky spectrum. As with many spectrums, where people place themselves depends on what one considers kinky. That is, some people would consider any non-procreative act kinky, whereas others would consider any evening with fewer than seven adults, a vat of lube, and a replica Italian castrati opera training room as all too tame. (In fact, readers of Freud know that any non-procreative act, including kissing, can be labeled deviant. Freud made the point to stress that all human sexuality includes deviance; however, Freud gets taken out of context quite a lot).

The Simpsons has explored many common forms of kink, especially through our main couple. There are several instances of role-play, for example. In "Selma's Choice" (4.13), Homer and Marge are left alone when Selma takes the children for the day. They watch *The Erotic Adventures of Hercules*, starring Troy McClure. Later, Homer appears in the kitchen in a toga and calling himself "Homercles," carrying her off to the bedroom (before being interrupted). In "Waverly Hills, 9–0–2–1-D'oh" (20.19), Marge and Homer role-play by going to a party with young people and pretending that they don't know each other. This particular game plays out over several scenes, as they enjoy the erotic tension. Not surprisingly, however, their game heads toward their status quo, as their alter egos fall in love and move toward commitment.[6]

Some of Marge's aforementioned tolerance toward alternative lifestyles may come from Homer's kinks, many of which involve hints of heteroflexibility (a term for people who identify as hetero, but who have some curiosity or inclination toward the same sex). My son and I have been keeping a list of Homer's sexual quirks for years, which is reprinted in *The Simpsons in the Classroom*. In brief, Homer sometimes wears women's underwear, admits to being "a little curious" when he thinks Mr. Burns is hitting on him, sketches Lenny and Carl in the nude, and finds Ned sexy while skiing, to name of a few. In "The Night of the Dolphin," Homer shows an appreciation for an anonymous homosexual sex outlet when he lists some of humankind's greatest inventions: "Don't forget—we invented computers, leg warmers, bendy straws, peel-and-eat shrimp, the glory hole…" ("Treehouse of Horror XI" 12.1).

Although she has only been shown as interested in other women in Homer's fantasy life, Marge is not without her quirks. Specifically, Marge has a fetish for having her elbow nibbled, a secret Homer reveals in "Secrets of a Successful Marriage" (5.22). Coincidentally, in "Homer Simpson, This is Your Wife" (17.15), Charles, who falls in love with Marge after being paired with her when Homer signs them up for a wife swap show, describes himself as "a bit of an elbow man."

Marge is also unphased when Homer brings back a bag of items from a shopping trip: "Hi … ummm … let me have some of those porno magazines … large box of condoms … bottle of Old Harper … a couple of those panty shields and some illegal fireworks and one of those disposable enemas. Ehhh … make it two." Instead of being alarmed, Marge just says, "Gee, I don't know what you have planned for tonight, Homer, but count me out" ("Summer of 4 Ft. 2" 7.25).

Marge and Homer's sex life sometimes also consists of mild BDSM. In "The Springfield Connection" (6.23) when Marge arrests Homer and puts him in cuffs, at first he thinks she's playing: "Please, Marge, not here." In "The Island of Dr. Hibbert," when Marge is turned into a cat-woman, Homer is at first turned on by her sharp claws on his back in the shower, finding the pain erotic ("Treehouse of Horror XIII" 14.1). However, mild BDSM is as far as they'll go. When Homer is encouraged to romance Marge in a *50 Shades* way, he makes her a sex dungeon that neither of them actually want. They only keep one of the toys, and Marge is coy, so we're left to imagine what would require sixteen D batteries ("What Animated Women Want" 24.17).

One of the more interesting ways in which Marge's and Homer's sexualities are explored in the show is in relation to desire. Although not often talked about in the same way as object choice sexuality, one's position on the no sex drive (asexual)[7] to high sex drive (sex addict) scale is hugely important, especially when it comes to finding sexual compatibility. Advice columnists, like Dan Savage and "Dear Prudence," constantly offer advice to those in relationships with partners with a very different sex drive level.

"Grampa vs. Sexual Inadequacy" (6.10) features a problem in the Simpsons' marriage: Homer isn't in the mood. After Marge declares that she can't just wait for the issue to resolve on its own, they try a book's advice for revitalizing their sex life. When their "unsatisfying sex life" persists, Grampa makes a tonic. It proves effective and popular; apparently, many Springfield men, including Kirk Van Houten and Dr. Hibbert, need some help.

In "Natural Born Kissers" (9.25), both Homer and Marge have lost the urge, which they discover on their anniversary when attempts to celebrate fall short. Eventually, they discover that sex with "the fear of getting caught is a turn-on." While Homer and Marge are publically shamed when they are caught, the end of the episode shows that they are not planning to give up their newfound kink.

A story episode, "Love, Springfieldian Style" (19.12), takes things a bit further, when Homer (as Clyde) realizes that Marge (as Bonnie) finds violence to be sexy. "Halloween of Horror" (27.4), a canonical episode, shows drunken adults in an array of "sexy" costumes, celebrating adult Halloween, or, in Dan Savage's words, "the straight pride parade," after trick or treating is over.

Some of the vocabulary of BDSM—that which has entered the mainstream—is used on *The Simpsons*. In "Treehouse of Horror XXIII" (24.2), Homer makes a deal with the devil to keep his family together—he will engage in a three-way with the devil and another demon. They establish that the safe word is "cinnamon."[8] While we don't see what happens, almost immediately as the three-way commences, the devil and the demon begin using the word.

The same episode features Moe as a Mayan priest, seduced by Marge in a plot to free Homer from being a blood sacrifice. Moe says he's "into rough stuff" and says something that can either be a signal of his famous unattractiveness, his kinkiness, or both:

> **Marge:** Before we make love, would you mind putting a sack over your head?
> **Moe:** Is there any other way?

A few years earlier, in "Treehouse of Horror XX" (21.4), Moe was much more explicit about his kinks: "My taste for romance is kinda perverse./I can only make love in the back of a hearse./Plus, I gotta be dressed as a Civil War nurse,/And then when I'm finished, I'll go through your purse."

References to more hardcore BDSM (with pop culture's shorthand for it—whips and leather) tend to be visual—a Halloween costume here, a parody of *Pulp Fiction*'s ball gag there. Yet Catherine Scott notes, "There was the moment I laughed out loud as one of my interviewees pointed out that Mr. Burns and Smithers from *The Simpsons* must be the longest running master/slave relationship on television" (6). (In "Flaming Moe" (22.11), Smithers' attraction to Mr. Burns is referred to as participation in a "lemon party," as he must be a "geezer squeezer.")

Scott laments some of the ways in which BDSM appears in popular culture: "What troubles me, and appears to trouble a lot of feminists, about how BDSM is often read in popular culture, is the automatic association of the submissive role with femininity, and the corresponding treatment of male submission as an aberration" (35). The moments in which Homer is heteroflexible often play upon the submissive man humor trope—we are meant to laugh when Homer admits to wearing women's underwear (and expresses fear about the desire—"it's strictly a comfort thing" ["The Springfield Connection" 6.23]), when he lifts his leg in response to a kiss. However, Principal Skinner takes the brunt of emasculation in the series. The most vivid example, besides his admission to being a virgin, is when he attempts to win Edna back from Comic Book Guy while wearing a leather Cat Woman suit ("My Big Fat Geek Wedding" 15.17). Unfortunately, *The Simpsons* perpetuates a problem Scott identifies: "Much of how male submissives are portrayed in popular culture—being made to wear women's clothes or 'sissified,' perform female tasks, or assume the receptive role in sex—implies that in this supposedly liberated, gender-neutral society, there remains a belief that the best way to humiliate a man is to make him act like a woman" (40).

Yet the kinkiest reference on the show is relatively inexplicable, as *The Simpsons* never quite tell us what it is. Since he won't sleep with her, despite their marriage, Selma asks Troy a question:

> **Selma:** Are you gay?
> **Troy:** Gay? I wish! If I were gay there'd be no problem! No, what I have is a romantic abnormality, one so unbelievable that it must be hidden from the public at all cost ["A Fish Called Selma" 7.19].

Still, the episode gives us some clues—Troy's house has a gigantic aquarium, and Troy's bumper sticker says, "Follow me to the Springfield Aquarium." Ultimately, we know just as much as Homer does via rumors:

Homer: Yeah, who'd have thought he'd turn out to be such a weirdo?

Marge: What are you talking about?

Homer: You know, his bizarre personal life. Those weird things they say he does down at the aquarium. Why, I heard…

Marge: Oh, Homer, that's just an urban legend. People don't do that type of thing with fish!

Looking back at the earliest episodes, the censors' problems with Marge's nightie are incredibly quaint, especially now that Marge has been the cover model of a real-life *Playboy* issue. Scott's observation, "Now that previously 'erotic' acts such as oral and anal sex are seen as increasingly mainstream, the pattern of keeping people in a constant state of paranoia that their sex lives are still too 'vanilla' dictates that something—which may well be BDSM—must take their place as the ultimate transgressive act" (50), indicates that the show will continue to push boundaries of propriety.

NOTES

1. I, notably, am a single mother and became one while a teenager. While my son and I have defied the expectations of society, we still bristle at people's assumptions when they learn about our life circumstances. I, for example, am tired of polls asking if "single mothers are still a problem in America." The question makes a *person* a problem, rather than making a *situation* a problem. We might, for example, ask people to weigh in on single parent households, unintended pregnancies, teenage pregnancies, or, if we must talk about people, include dead-beat dads in the question. Furthermore, it is highly unlikely that we will ever ask the same question about single parents, as fathers raising children alone (or even co-parenting) are considered generous, courageous men, worthy of parades, in stark contrast to what Reverend Lovejoy threatens the children with after church one day: "If I withhold the truth, may I go straight to Hell, where I will eat naught but burning hot coals and drink naught but burning hot cola! Where fiery demons will punch me in the back. Where my soul will be chopped into confetti and strewn upon a parade of murders and single mothers" ("Bart Sells His Soul" 7.4). Not much has changed: just one month prior to the first draft of this article, a candidate for President blamed an Oregon school shooting on many things besides guns, including single mothers.

2. Matthew Henry has an excellent chapter in his book, *The Simpsons, Satire, and American Culture*, about depictions of gays in mainstream TV and in *The Simpsons*, specifically.

3. In an earlier episode, Patty was courted by Seymour ("Principal Charming" 2.14). He proposes. She says she loves him, but she can't leave Selma. Viewers must decide now if she really turned him down for that reason, if she actually loved him romantically (or thought she did), etc.

4. "Spectrum" isn't quite the right word, but we don't have a great replacement. For some options, see the conversation between Dan Savage in his sex/relationship column, here: http://www.thestranger.com/blogs/slog/2015/10/07/22975845/savage-love-letter-of-the-day-taking-it-easy-on-sherman-alexies-birthday.

5. This was the first episode produced; however, due to problems with the initial animation, it was redone, becoming the last broadcast episode of the first season.

6. One of the criticisms of *Fifty Shades of Grey* is this move toward vanilla "normalcy"—at the end of that book, Mr. Grey gives up kinky ways, having been "cured" of his kinky desire by true love.

7. As *The Simpsons* hasn't really dealt with asexuality, I won't really talk about it much here; however, I have a detailed article on asexuality in relation to *Sherlock* in *Gender and the Modern Sherlock Holmes* (McFarland 2015).

8. "Cinnamon" is also revealed as a safe word on *Dirk Gently's Holistic Detective Agency*, a show about how there are no coincidences.

Works Cited

"Bart Sells His Soul." *The Simpsons: The Complete Seventh Season*. Written by Greg Daniels, directed by Wes Archer, 20th Century–Fox, 8 October 1995.

"Behind the Laughter." *The Simpsons: The Complete Eleventh Season*. Written by Tim Long, George Meyer, Mike Scully, and Matt Selman, directed by Mark Kirkland, 20th Century–Fox, 21 May 2000.

"Blame It On Lisa." *The Simpsons: The Complete Thirteenth Season*. Written by Bob Bendetson, directed by Steven Dean Moore, 20th Century–Fox, 2002.

"Brother's Little Helper." *The Simpsons: The Complete Eleventh Season*. Written by George Meyer, directed by Mark Kirkland, 20th Century–Fox, 1999.

"The Day the Earth Stood Cool." *The Simpsons*. Written by Matt Selman, directed by Matthew Faughnan, 20th Century–Fox, 9 December 2012.

"Duffless." *The Simpsons: The Complete Fourth Season*. Written by David M. Stern, directed by Jim Reardon, 20th Century–Fox, 1993.

"A Fish Called Selma." *The Simpsons: The Complete Seventh Season*. Written by Jack Barth, directed by Mark Kirkland, 20th Century–Fox, 1996.

"500 Keys." *The Simpsons*. Written by John Frink, directed by Bob Anderson, 20th Century–Fox, 15 May 2011.

"Flaming Moe." *The Simpsons*. Written by Matt Selman, directed by Chuck Sheetz, 20th Century–Fox, 16 January 2011.

"Grandpa vs. Sexual Inadequacy." *The Simpsons: The Complete Sixth Season*. Written by Bill Oakley and Josh Weinstein, directed by Wes Archer, 20th Century–Fox, 1994.

"Half-Decent Proposal." *The Simpsons: The Complete Thirteenth Season*. Written by Tim Long directed by Lauren MacMullan, 20th Century–Fox, 2002.

"Halloween of Horror." *The Simpsons*. Written by Carolyn Omine, directed by Mike B. Anderson, 20th Century–Fox, 18 October 2015.

"Homer Badman." *The Simpsons: The Complete Sixth Season*. Written by Greg Daniels, directed by Jeffrey Lynch, 20th Century–Fox, 1994.

"The Homer of Seville." *The Simpsons*. Written by Carolyn Omine, directed by Michael Polcino, 20th Century–Fox, 30 September 2007.

"Homer Simpson, This is Your Wife." *The Simpsons: The Complete Seventeenth Season*. Written by Ricky Gervais, directed by Matthew Nastuk, 20th Century–Fox, 2006.

"Homer vs. Dignity." *The Simpsons: The Complete Twelfth Season*. Written by Rob LaZebnik, directed by Neil Affleck, 20th Century–Fox, 26 November 2000.

"Homer vs. the Eighteenth Amendment." *The Simpsons: The Complete Eighth Season*. Written by John Swartzwelder, directed by Bob Anderson, 20th Century–Fox, 1997.

"Homer's Night Out." *The Simpsons: The Complete First Season*. Written by Jon Vitti, directed by Rich Moore, 20th Century–Fox, 1990.

"Homer's Phobia." *The Simpsons: The Complete Eighth Season*. Written by Ron Hauge, directed by Mike B. Anderson, 20th Century–Fox, 1997.

"Homer's Triple Bypass." *The Simpsons: The Complete Fourth Season*. Written by Gary Apple and Michael Carrington, directed by David Silverman. 20th Century–Fox, 1992.

"I Married Marge." *The Simpsons: The Complete Third Season*. Written by Jeff Martin, directed by Jeffrey Lynch, 20th Century–Fox, 1991.

"Last Exit to Springfield." *The Simpsons: The Complete Fourth Season*. Written by Jay Kogen and Wallace Wolodarsky, directed by Mark Kirkland, 20th Century–Fox, 1993.

"The Last Temptation of Homer." *The Simpsons: The Complete Fifth Season*. Written by Frank Mula, directed Carlos Baeza, 20th Century–Fox, 1993.

"Life on the Fast Lane." *The Simpsons: The Complete First Season*. Written by John Swartzwelder, directed by David Silverman, 20th Century–Fox, 1990.

"Lisa the Greek." *The Simpsons: The Complete Third Season*. Written by Jay Kogen and Wallace Wolodarsky, directed by Rich Moore, 20th Century–Fox, 21992.

"Lisa Simpson, This Isn't Your Life." *The Simpsons*. Written by Joel H. Cohen, directed by Matthew Nastuk, 20th Century–Fox, 14 November 2010.

"Lisa vs. Malibu Stacy." *The Simpsons: The Complete Fifth Season*. Written by Bill Oakley and Josh Weinstein, directed by Jeff Lynch, 20th Century–Fox, 1994.

"Lisa's First Word." *The Simpsons: The Complete Fourth Season*. Written by Jeff Martin, directed by Mark Kirkland, 20th Century–Fox, 1992.

"Lisa's Pony." *The Simpsons: The Complete Third Season*. Written by Al Jean and Mike Reiss, directed by Carlos Baeza, 20th Century–Fox, 1991.

"Love Springfieldian Style." *The Simpsons*. Written by Don Payne, directed by Raymond S. Persi, 20th Century–Fox, 17 February 2008.

"Marge Gets a Job." *The Simpsons: The Complete Fourth Season*. Written by Bill Oakley and Josh Weinstein, directed by Jeff Lynch, 20th Century–Fox, 1992.

"Marge vs. Singles, Seniors, Childless Couples and Teen, and Gays." *The Simpsons: The Complete Fifteenth Season*. Written by Jon Vitti, directed by Bob Anderson, 20th Century–Fox, 2004.

McCorkle, Ben. "*The Simpsons*: A Mirror of Society." *Workload 57 Rhetoric and Handbook*. Ed. Workload Faculty. Pearson, 2011. pp. 97–99.

"My Big Fat Geek Wedding." *The Simpsons: The Complete Fifteenth Season*. Written by Kevin Curran, directed by Mark Kirkland, 20th Century–Fox, 2004.

"Natural Born Kissers." *The Simpsons: The Complete Ninth Season*. Written by Matt Selman, directed by Klay Hall, 20th Century–Fox, 1998.

"Please Homer, Don't Hammer 'Em." *The Simpsons: The Complete Eighteenth Season*. Written by Matt Warburton, directed by Mike B. Anderson and Ralph Sosa, 20th Century–Fox, 2006.

"Principal Charming." *The Simpsons: The Complete Second Season*. Written by David M. Stern, directed by Mark Kirkland, 20th Century–Fox, 1991.

Savage, Dan. "Happy Heteroween." *The Stranger*. 29 Oct. 2009. https://www.thestranger.com/seattle/happy-heteroween/Content?oid=2594616.

Scott, Catherine. *Thinking Kink: The Collision of BDSM, Feminism and Popular Culture*. McFarland, 2015.

"Secrets of a Successful Marriage." *The Simpsons: The Complete Fifth Season*. Written by Greg Daniels, directed by Carlos Baeza, 20th Century–Fox, 1994.

"Selma's Choice." *The Simpsons: The Complete Third Season*. Written by David M. Stern, directed by Carlos Baeza, 20th Century–Fox, 1993.

"Separate Vocations." *The Simpsons: The Complete Third Season*. Written by George Meyer, directed by Jeffrey Lynch, 20th Century–Fox, 1992.

"She Used to Be My Girl." *The Simpsons: The Complete Sixteenth Season*. Written by Tim Long, directed by Matthew Nastuk, 20th Century–Fox, 2004.

"The Simpsons 138th Episode Spectacular." *The Simpsons: The Complete Seventh Season*. Written by Jon Vitti, directed by David Silverman, 20th Century–Fox, 1995.

"Simpsonscalifragilisticexpiala(Annoyed Grunt)cious." *The Simpsons The Complete Eighth Season*. Written by Al Jean and Mike Reiss, directed by Chuck Sheetz, 20th Century–Fox, 1997.

"Sleeping with the Enemy." *The Simpsons: The Complete Sixteenth Season*. Written by Jon Vitti, directed by Lauren MacMullan. 20th Century–Fox, 2004.

"Some Enchanted Evening." *The Simpsons: The Complete First Season*. Written by Matt Groening and Sam Simon, directed by David Silverman and Kent Butterworth, 20th Century–Fox, 1990.

"The Springfield Connection." *The Simpsons: The Complete Sixth Season*. Written by John Collier, directed by Mark Kirkland, 20th Century–Fox, 1995.

"Summer of 4 Ft. 2." *The Simpsons: The Complete Seventh Season*. Written by Dan Greaney, directed by Mark Kirkland, 20th Century–Fox, 1996.

"That '90s Show." *The Simpsons*. Written by Matt Selman, directed by Mark Kirkland, 20th Century–Fox, 27 January 2008.

"There's Something about Marrying." *The Simpsons: The Complete Sixteenth Season*. Written by J. Stewart Burns, directed by Nancy Kruse, 20th Century–Fox, 2005.

"Treehouse of Horror XI." *The Simpsons: The Complete Twelfth Season*. Written by Rob LaZebnik, et al., directed by Matthew Nastuk, 20th Century–Fox, 2000.

"Treehouse of Horror XII." *The Simpsons: The Complete Thirteenth Season*. Written by Joel H. Cohen, et al, directed by Jim Reardon, 20th Century–Fox, 2001.

"Treehouse of Horror XIII." *The Simpsons: The Complete Fourteenth Season*. Written by Marc Wilmore, Brian Kelley, and Kevin Curran, directed by David Silverman, 20th Century–Fox, 2002.

"Treehouse of Horror XX." *The Simpsons*. Written by Daniel Chun, directed by Mike B. Anderson and Matthew Schofield. 20th Century–Fox, 18 October 2009.

"Treehouse of Horror XXIII." *The Simpsons*. Written by David Mandel and Brian Kelley, directed by Steven Dean Moore, 20th Century–Fox, 7 October 2012.

"22 Short Films About Springfield." *The Simpsons: The Complete Seventh Season*. Written by Richard Appel, et al., directed by Jim Reardon, 20th Century–Fox, 1996.

"Two Cars in Every Garage and Three Eyes on Every Fish." *The Simpsons: The Complete Second Season*. Written by Sam Simon and John Swartzwelder, directed by Wes Archer, 20th Century–Fox, 1990.

"Walking Big & Tall." *The Simpsons*. Written by Michael Price, directed by Chris Clements, 20th Century–Fox 8 February 2015.

"Waverly Hills 9-0-2-1-D'oh." *The Simpsons: The Complete Twentieth Season*. Written by J. Stewart Burns, directed by Michael Polcino, 20th Century–Fox, 2009.

"The Way We Was." *The Simpsons: The Complete Second Season*. Written by Al Jean, Mike Reiss, and Sam Simon, directed by David Silverman, 20th Century–Fox, 1991.

"What Animated Women Want." *The Simpsons*. Written by J. Stewart Burns, directed by Steven Dean Moore, 20th Century–Fox, 14 April 2013.

White, Kenneth Michael, and Mirya Holman. "Partisan Bias in *The Simpsons*?" *Studies in Popular Culture*, vol. 34, no. 1, Fall 2011, pp. 87–107.

About the Contributors

Sarah **Antinora** earned her Ph.D. in English at the University of California, Riverside, completing a dissertation on rhetoric, humor studies, and early modern theater. She has presented at MLA, the CCCC, and SAA, and published an article about laughter and Shakespeare in *Cerae* (2014). She teaches first-year composition, Shakespeare studies, literary analysis, and critical thinking at San Joaquin Delta College.

Summer **Block** has contributed to *Catapult*, *The Awl*, *The Toast*, *The Rumpus*, *McSweeney's*, *The Nervous Breakdown*, and *Electric Lit*. Her work has been included in several anthologies, including *Critically Acclaimed* (Rare Bird Books). She's working on a book about Halloween.

Durrell **Bowman** has a Ph.D. in musicology from UCLA. For about a decade, he developed and taught music history courses at seven institutions all across North America. He has presented numerous conference papers, including several on music in *The Simpsons*, and published the books *Experiencing Peter Gabriel* (2016), *Experiencing Rush* (2014), and the coedited volume *Rush and Philosophy* (2011).

Jennifer Richardson **Burg** lives in Bennington, Vermont with Scott, Josephine, and Alana. She holds a Ph.D. in rhetoric and composition from Washington State University, where she studied with Victor Villanueva. She thinks and talks about composition, communication, and rhetoric at every opportunity, with the goal of promoting intellectual engagement with texts of all kinds. She has failed at every attempt at masonry.

Brent Walter **Cline** is a professor of ecogastronomy at Spring Arbor University in Michigan. Besides watching too many *Simpsons* episodes, he enjoys running the Dressage Waterloo Classic in Grass Lake, Michigan.

Brian N. **Duchaney** is a Ph.D. student at Boston University's Editorial Institute. His memoir about his military service was published by the journal *War, Literature, & the Arts*, and he is the author of *The Spark of Fear* (2015). He teaches at Bridgewater State University and Curry College, both in Massachusetts.

Denise **Du Vernay** taught some combination of courses in composition, humanities, speech communications, literature, *The Simpsons*, and business writing for nearly two decades. Her first book, *The Simpsons in the Classroom: Embiggening the Learning Experience with the Wisdom of Springfield* (McFarland, 2010) was also co-authored with Karma Waltonen. She has also written on *Breaking Bad*, *SpongeBob SquarePants*, *The Handmaid's Tale*, "Weird Al" Yankovic, and many other topics in popular culture. She has been an active member and officer in the Margaret Atwood Society since 2007. Denise works in Advancement for Loyola University Chicago. She lives on the Far North Side with her husband, who is allergic to cats and dogs.

Timothy L. **Glenn** teaches English and the humanities in Southern California. He has written on the works of Thomas King and John Barth. "Homer vs. the Eighteenth Amendment" is his favorite *Simpsons* episode.

Matthew Nelson **Hill** is an associate professor of philosophy at Spring Arbor University in Michigan, writes in the field of evolutionary biology and ethics, and considers Robert Underdunk Terwilliger, Jr., his academic mentor.

Casey D. **Hoeve** is an associate professor and content development librarian at Kansas State University. His research interests include library management of team-based models, *The Simpsons*, popular culture, digital humanities, and collaborative partnerships in the humanities. He is the co-chair of the Libraries, Archives, and Museums subject area for the Popular Culture Association.

Travis **Holland** is a lecturer in communication and digital media and a course director at Charles Sturt University, Australia. Before joining CSU, he lectured and tutored at the University of Wollongong, Australia, in communication and media studies for several years. His writing, teaching, and research includes work on fan studies, politics, digital media, television, and local government.

Wm. Curtis **Holtzen** is a professor of philosophy and theology at Hope International University in Fullerton, California. He is the author of *The God Who Trusts: A Relational Theology of Divine Faith, Hope, and Love* (IVP Academic, 2019), is coeditor of several books, and has published essays on *Peanuts* as well as *Bruce Almighty*. His favorite quotation: "You tried your best and you failed miserably. The lesson is: never try."

Zachary **Ingle** teaches film and television studies at Roanoke College. He has edited four books, including *Robert Rodriguez: Interviews* (2012), *Gender and Genre in Sports Documentaries* (2013), *Identity and Myth in Sport Documentaries* (2013), and *Fan Phenomena: The Big Lebowski* (2014). He has also published articles in journals such as *Post Script*, *Literature-Film Quarterly*, and *Journal of Sport History*.

David **Krantz** is a National Science Foundation IGERT–SUN Fellow at Arizona State University's School of Sustainability, where he researches the intersection of environmentalism with public policy and culture, predominately religion. He has a lifelong interest in both *The Simpsons* and cartooning, and he served as coeditor-in-chief of the now-dormant *John Doe Comics* in New Jersey.

Seth **Madej** spent twenty years as a writer and producer in television and other media. During that time, his work won an Emmy Award and was nominated for a second. In 2017, he left the entertainment industry to pursue a career as a psychotherapist. He lives in Los Angeles.

Duncan **Reyburn** is a senior lecturer at the Department of Visual Arts at the University of Pretoria in South Africa. His research—covering a range of subjects including zombie movies, mimetic theory, humor studies, and philosophical hermeneutics—deals broadly with the relationship between philosophy, theology, and culture. He is the author of *Seeing Things as They Are: G. K. Chesterton and the Drama of Meaning* (2016).

Tyler **Shores** is a Ph.D. student in education at the University of Cambridge. He received his master's degree from the University of Oxford. His research is on reading and digital culture. At the University of California, Berkeley, he created and taught a course on *The Simpsons* and philosophy, which became one of the university's most popular courses.

Zachary **Tavlin** is an adjunct assistant professor of liberal arts at the School of the Art Institute of Chicago. His work has been published in *ESQ, The Wallace Stevens Journal, Transatlantica, Mississippi Quarterly, The Edgar Allan Poe Review, Nathaniel Hawthorne Review, Continental Philosophy Review*, and *The Comparatist*, among other venues.

Karma **Waltonen** is a senior lecturer in the university writing program at UC Davis. She teaches courses on Margaret Atwood, *Doctor Who*, writing and performing stand-up comedy, and *The Simpsons*. Her publications include articles on *Star Trek, Doctor Who*, sex in science fiction/fantasy by women, and *The X-Files*. Her previous books are *The Simpsons in the Classroom* (co-authored with Denise Du Vernay), *Margaret Atwood's Apocalypses*, and *Twenty Writing Assignments in Context* (co-authored with her work wife, Melissa Bender). Her blog is KarmicWisdom, at www.dr-karma.com.

Lisa **Whalen** has a Ph.D. in postsecondary and adult education and teaches writing and literature at North Hennepin Community College in Brooklyn Park, Minnesota. Her essays have been featured in *An Introvert in an Extrovert World, WorkingUSA: The Journal of Labor and Society*, and *MotherShould?* She is a regular contributor to *The Feisty Writer* and The Emily Program blog. She also maintains her blog, *Writing Unbridled*, on her website, https://lisawhalen.wixsite.com/lisawhalen.

Index